The World Fundraiser's Handbook

A Resource Mobilisation Guide
for NGOs and Community Organisations

Michael Norton
In association with Resource Alliance

THIRD EDITION

DIRECTORY OF SOCIAL CHANGE

Published by
Directory of Social Change
24 Stephenson Way
London NW1 2DP
tel. 08450 77 77 07; fax 020 7391 4804
email publications@dsc.org.uk
www.dsc.org.uk
from whom further copies and a full books catalogue are available.

Directory of Social Change Northern Office
Federation House, Hope Street, Liverpool L1 9BW
Policy & Research 0151 708 0136
Directory of Social Change is a Registered Charity no. 800517

First published 1996
Second edition 2003
Third edition 2009

ISBN 978 1 906294 33 5

British Library Cataloguing in Publication Data
A catalogue record for this book is available from the British Library

Cover design by Kate Bass
Text designed by Linda Parker
Typeset by Keystroke
Printed and bound by CPI Antony Rowe

Contents

Foreword

It is now more than ten years since the first edition of this handbook was published. In that time the world of fundraising has changed greatly. Perhaps the most obvious area of change is in the field of technology. The use of email and online payment systems are now pervasive, and the recent growth of social networking websites is further extending the potential for fundraising in the virtual world.

The integration of new media channels with traditional techniques such as direct mail, and the increasing speed and sophistication of databases, gives fundraisers the opportunity to combine channels and media in ways never possible before.

Yet there is still a core set of basic truths about fundraising which any practitioner needs to learn. With the growth of civil society around the world and increasing interest in the potential for local fundraising, more and more people are acquiring this knowledge. Some learn by trial and error, others through attending workshops and courses, which are expanding in number as the demand grows.

The number of associations of fundraisers has grown, with more than 30 countries now having an association of some sort. A global ethical code has been developed and the different associations are starting to map out ways to collaborate so as to strengthen the provision of education and training in fundraising. More and more books and online resources are becoming available to support fundraisers in different parts of the world.

In the sphere of philanthropy we have also seen much change. Big donors like Bill Gates and Warren Buffet are being emulated by other wealthy philanthropists around the world – people like Carlos Slim in Mexico and Victor Pinchuk in Ukraine. In April 2008 the *China Daily* reported that China's top 100 philanthropists had donated $1.8bn over the previous five years. At the other end of the spectrum, websites like Kiva and Global Giving are mobilising gifts from ordinary citizens through connecting the donor directly with the recipients.

Alongside the growth in giving there appears also to be an increasing demand for evidence of impact, for results-focused programmes with demonstrable outcomes. 'Social enterprise' is a concept which has caught the imagination of many of the 'new' philanthropists – a section of the giving public which looks to market-based approaches. They aim to nurture social interventions which can fund themselves through a business approach. This, they believe, is the route to true sustainability.

Wherever you are, this is an exciting time to be in fundraising. Though at the time of writing the global economic outlook is far from sunny, I'm sure we'll look back and see this as just a temporary dip in the overall history of increased giving. Even at times of economic contraction there are many fundraising opportunities. Some would argue that it is in tough times that experience, knowledge and skilful execution really count.

This handbook is designed for both novice and experienced fundraisers. It is a comprehensive guide to all the main sources of income and the techniques associated with these different sources. For the third edition, the book has been extensively updated and many new case studies have been included. Some of these case studies have been taken from the Showcase of Fundraising Innovation and Inspiration (SOFII) – a project of the Resource Alliance. SOFII is a free online library of great fundraising. Visit www.sofii.org for more examples of the techniques described in this book. In fact, why not share your own stories with SOFII?

Simon Collings
CEO, Resource Alliance
May 2009

About the authors

Michael Norton

Michael is the founder of the Directory of Social Change and was its director until 1995. Since then he has created several other highly successful enterprises. In 1995 he founded the Centre for Innovation in Voluntary Action (CIVA) encouraging innovation and new thinking on the role of charities.

Michael has also established Changemakers, challenging young activists to design and manage their own community projects. He is a founder of the Youthbank UK and also a founder and trustee of UnLTD – the foundation for Social Entrepreneurs, which makes awards to over 1,000 individuals in the UK each year who wish to create change in their communities. He also helped set up UnLtd India, and is currently working on parallel initiatives in South Africa and Canada.

Michael is currently promoting and supporting a number of projects including MyBank to promote young people's banking, Otesha UK where young people take out the climate change message and encourage action through bicycle tours and performances, and FoodWorks where young people cook meals for those in need using donated food in donated kitchen space. He also runs literacy and library programmes in India.

The Resource Alliance and Simon Collings

The Resource Alliance's mission is to help voluntary sector leaders worldwide acquire the tools to build the financial sustainability of civil society. It started as the International Fund Raising Group (IFRG) in 1981 and it is now in its third decade of supporting the NGO sector. The role of the organisation has expanded from being an event organiser to developing and running an international programme of information and training for fundraisers worldwide.

The Resource Alliance works predominantly in the global South, responding to the need for a participatory skills transfer and capacity building programme. To date the workshops and events that the Resource Alliance organises have attracted almost 12,000 delegates from more than 100 countries.

Simon Collings, is former CEO of the Resource Alliance and is now CEO of Global Village Energy Partnership. Before working for the Resource Alliance, Simon was Director of Fundraising at Oxfam.

About the contributors

Richard Holloway

Chapter 5 on 'Generating Income through Self-Financing' was written by Richard Holloway. Richard, is presently the director of the Civil Society Programme at the Aga Khan Foundation in Geneva, following a 40-year career in the field of civil society and rural development in Asia, Africa, the Caribbean and the South Pacific. He has been a grass-roots worker, a project manager, an aid administrator, a trainer, and a consultant, and has published books, particularly handbooks, on different aspects of not-for-profit management. In particular, he authored *Towards Financial Self-Reliance*, a guide to resource mobilisation strategies for the non-profit organisations in the South.

Derek Humphries

Chapter 8 on communications was originally written by Derek Humphries and has been updated by Michael Norton. Derek is a director with Think Consulting. He has directed the creative and strategic elements of communications for over 100 not-for-profit organisations – from small local charities to international causes. His work has won many industry awards.

Derek served as Managing Director of Burnett Associates for eight years until 1999. He is a founder member of the UK's Institute of Direct Marketing, has been Vice-Chairman of the UK's fundraising institute (IoF), and also served on the board of the UK's national fundraising convention.

Jason Potts

Section 6.12 on digital fundraising was written by Jason Potts. Jason is director of digital activities with Think Consulting Solutions. He is widely recognised within the global not-for-profit community as an expert on direct-response fundraising and as a pioneer in the development of the e-commerce and e-business market place.

Jason speaks regularly at conferences around the world about the future of digital media for the sector and writes widely on the subject. Jason has worked with many global NGOs on using the medium both to communicate their mission and deliver revenue. This work has meant gaining experience of markets outside Europe, including; North America, Latin America and Asia Pacific. You can find out more at www.thinkcs. org or follows his tweets @Leneva.

Jason would like to acknowledge the contribution to his section by Martin Gill from HomeMade Digital, UK for his technology insights and Spanish market knowledge. Also thanks go to Philip King of Artez Interactive, Canada, for his thoughts on global peer-to-peer digital fundraising and to WSPA for being brave enough to share detailed case studies with the rest of the sector.

Preface

This book was originally published in 1996 to provide a comprehensive overview of fundraising practice and techniques for those whose job it is to raise money for a charity or a development organisation – whether as a volunteer or as a paid fundraiser or as an external fundraising consultant.

A note on terms used in this book

This book is intended for people fundraising for non-profit organisations, and this includes the following:

- **NGOs** (Non-Governmental Organisations). This term may have different meanings in different countries, and in some countries there is a formal procedure for registering an NGO.
- **CSOs** (Civil Society Organisations). This term is increasingly being used by Northern donors to describe a wider range of organisations and activities that can play a role in creating social change.
- **Charities**, which are organisations established for charitable purposes under charity law, which again will differ from country to country. Some of these raise money for particular purposes, such as health care or the welfare of the elderly. Others have their own programmes of work that they are raising money for.
- **Development Organisations**, which seek to promote community development. These are not charities in the real sense of the word, as they seek to empower and enable people to do things for themselves, rather than provide services for those in need – although most are constituted under charity law.
- **Community-Based Organisations** and **People's Organisations**, which operate at the grass-roots level and are often informally constituted, and which often need to mobilise support locally.
- **Campaigning** and **Advocacy Organisations**, which seek to promote change through research, information, campaigns and lobbying. There is now a great deal of emphasis placed on advocacy as part of the development process.
- **Trusts** and **Foundations**, which are grant-making bodies, usually established under charity law with the specific function of making grants for charitable purposes. Many are endowed, but some have to raise money if they are to make grants. The two terms 'trust' and 'foundation' are used interchangeably. 'Trust' is used because many foundations are constituted under trust law.

All these organisations are **Voluntary Organisations** and form the **Voluntary Sector** (sometimes also known as the **Third Sector**). The term 'voluntary' is used because these organisations share a common feature – that they are all managed by a voluntary management board and they operate independently of government. These organisations all need to obtain resources for their work, which they will try to do from a variety of sources.

This book is particularly aimed at the Southern fundraiser, and has been written from that perspective, and is illustrated with examples from many Southern countries. *North* refers to the developed world; *South* to the countries of Asia, Africa and Central and Southern America, where most of the world's poor people live.

There are two major differences between NGOs and voluntary organisations operating in the South as compared with their Northern counterparts:

- The availability in the South of large amounts of aid and development money from foreign sources, including governments, NGOs and charitable foundations.
- There are far fewer opportunities for raising money locally.

Overseas funding has helped a great many voluntary initiatives to get started, to develop their work and even to grow into substantial institutions. International donors have been willing to part with quite large sums of money (at least in terms of purchasing power) and often for relatively long periods of time (in the UK a three-year grant is considered long term!). NGOs have been able to expand their work, obtain grants to meet their capital needs and even create corpus funds (sometimes known as endowments) as a 'nest egg' for their future.

But international help is fickle. This year's concern may not be next year's. In India, the NGOs in some of the Southern States are fearful that donors are becoming more interested in putting their limited resources into the more 'backward' States of Bihar, Madhya Pradesh, Rajasthan, Uttar Pradesh and Orissa. Donors may decide to withdraw from a country for a variety of reasons, including political instability, corruption, and conflict. For example, international funding is harder to get in Kenya than in Uganda, and several important donor agencies have been reviewing their commitment to Zimbabwe. Or donors may transfer their affections completely to other countries, such as Rwanda after the genocide, or for the reconstruction of the constituent countries of the former Yugoslavia, where they feel that there are real and immediate challenges for them. They may decide that countries such as India, which are undergoing relatively rapid economic development and which have even faster growth rates than in the North, are now able to look after themselves. Or they may have seen political change at home, where the 'old idea' of helping the world's poor has become less fashionable, as has happened in the Netherlands, despite the pressure from the 2002 World Summit on Sustainable Development to increase the flow of development aid from the North.

Whatever the reasons, and there may be several, it is not a very satisfactory situation for any organisation to make itself the victim of the whims and practices of foreign donors – who are often in a position to determine whether an organisation continues and to exert a great deal of control over the nature and style of its work. This is where domestic fundraising can begin to play an important role.

Domestic fundraising can:

■ Help your organisation develop its own sources of income, and therefore give you more control in deciding your own agenda and your organisation's future. More income also means that you can do more work, and this will become increasingly important as the role of NGOs in promoting development continues to grow.

■ Develop links between the organisation and the local communities in which the work is being done, for example by developing funding relationships in the local community with individual and corporate donors or mobilising cash support and volunteer time in the local communities where you are doing your work.

■ Create an important support base of people who share your views and are prepared to give money to make things happen. If you are fighting child labour, you will become a much more powerful organisation if you have thousands of local supporters than if you are entirely foreign funded.

■ Encourage those who are actually doing the work to understand the urgency and importance of what they are doing – which they will need to do if they are to communicate their need for support successfully to those with the power and the resources to help them.

■ Create new lines of accountability. If you fundraise locally or generate support within your own community, you are no longer just accountable to large overseas agencies, which are often remote and bureaucratic. You are accountable to every man, woman and child who gives you money for your work. The fact that they live nearby and you can easily communicate with them is also important.

Southern NGOs and voluntary organisations can succeed in fundraising, just as their Northern counterparts are doing. Two examples from India spring to mind:

■ Lok Kalyan Samiti (LKS) is an eye hospital in New Delhi. It now raises all the money it requires from a direct mail fundraising programme involving more than 30,000 active supporters. LKS is now coordinating a network of over 30 eye hospitals in South Asia that are seeking to adopt similar fundraising methods.

■ CRY – Child Relief and You – is an Indian donor agency that successfully raises money from India's middle class and corporate sector, and also runs a substantial greetings card operation that contributes half its annual budget. CRY started with a few concerned individuals deciding to do something and pooling their small donations. It now has tens of thousands of individual and corporate donors all contributing regularly. CRY believes that it is only scratching the surface, and that the alleged 300 million-strong Indian middle class presents a real challenge for fundraisers.

In Africa, and indeed in Central/Eastern Europe and Latin America as well as in Asia, there are similar possibilities for developing local fundraising. Techniques including direct mail, organising fundraising events and involving volunteers are all being used successfully. There are many local companies as well as local branches of multinational companies that are willing to give support in cash or in kind.

As well as raising funds, there is another possibility of gaining an income for NGOs and voluntary associations – making your own money (or generating your own income). Many NGOs have pioneered techniques by which they sell their services (in part or in whole), run an enterprise (either linked to their main activity or not), or in some way generate income that they can use for their main humanitarian activities.

The problem is not so much a lack of opportunity, but rather knowing where to start and finding ways of building your fundraising (or your income-generation scheme) from a small or not-yet-existent base. The important thing is to get started. You will probably not be able to raise a huge amount immediately, but you should be able to build up your fundraising so that you raise more and more with each year that passes. We hope that this book will provide you with the ideas, the techniques and the necessary skills to be successful. We hope that it will not only encourage you to identify the opportunities, but that it will also give you the enthusiasm and the confidence to make a good job of your fundraising and your income generation.

Michael Norton
May 2009

CHAPTER 1

Introduction

1.1 Why fundraising is important

Fundraising is extremely important for your organisation's success. Here are some of the reasons why.

Survival

Every organisation needs enough money to survive. It has to meet its project costs and develop its programmes for the future, pay the wages and salaries of its staff plus all its administrative overheads, keep its buildings and vehicles in a good state of repair, and pay for any new equipment that it needs. The list is endless. And the stark truth is that if the money is not raised, the organisation will not be able to carry out its work. And if the work is not done, all those pressing needs will remain unmet.

The tool you will use to manage your fundraising is your annual budget. This will show the amount of money that you plan to spend. It will also show the amount of money that has already been raised or which has been promised, and what extra support needs to be raised during the year so that you can meet all your planned outgoings.

You will monitor your progress in achieving your targets by keeping a record of money that has been received or promised, and by discussing your management accounts at regular management committee meetings (which you might hold monthly, or perhaps quarterly for smaller organisations). If the income isn't coming in as you have planned, you will need to take some sort of action – put more effort into your fundraising, cut costs, defer planned projects, or agree to subsidise the likely deficit out of your reserves.

Expansion and development

If your organisation is to meet the challenges of the future, you may need to expand the work, improve the quality of service, extend your activities into other areas, carry out research, add campaigning and advocacy to basic service delivery, and continue to innovate. All this requires more money – money that you will need to raise.

You may want to prepare a proper business plan. At the very least you will need a 'sketch budget' for the next few years so you can start to plan for any major developments or expansion that you wish to undertake. This will provide you with a starting point for raising the resources you will need to do this. Remember, fundraising always takes longer than you think. The more you plan ahead, the more likely you are to get the money when you need it.

Reducing dependency

Many organisations have one or perhaps several major donors who provide most of the funds they are spending. This situation can lead to a state of dependency. If one of your large grants is withdrawn, this could create a financial crisis. Not only this, but this dependency can make it difficult for your organisation to determine its own agenda since it will be constantly having to adapt to the priorities of its donor organisations.

Broadening your fundraising base by bringing in other donors and by generating other sources of income can reduce your dependency. But it is up to you to decide whether your organisation is too dependent on any one source, and if this is the case, whether to negotiate some form of long-term funding partnership with your current donors or to develop other sources of income.

Building a constituency

Fundraising is not just about the amount of money you raise; it is also about the numbers of supporters you can attract to your cause. Each supporter is important to you. They can be persuaded to give again and to give even more generously. They might like to volunteer or might be able to persuade friends and contacts to support you. Their numbers are an indication of the level of support that your organisation is attracting, and this can add strength to your lobbying and campaigning work.

You need to think about the sorts of people that you would like to mobilise and who will be attracted to the kind of work you are doing. Is it businesses? Or middle-class people? Or students and activists? Or women? Or retired people with time on their hands? Or doctors? Or lawyers? Or some other special category? And then you will need to think about how best you can reach them and the sort of message they will respond to.

Creating a viable and sustainable organisation

Fundraising is not simply about generating the resources you need to survive from this year to the next, and paying for any planned expansion and development. It is also about helping to create a viable and strong organisation which is able to sustain itself into the future.

There are many ways you can do this. One is to build a substantial and active donor base – getting people to support you who feel involved and important to the organisation, and who will continue to give their support over a long period of time. Other ways include: organising successful fundraising events (which can be repeated and run even more successfully in subsequent years); creating capital within your organisation, such as buildings and equipment (which reduce your need for running costs or can help you generate an income) or an endowment or 'corpus' fund; and developing some sort of income-generating activity within the organisation itself.

Many organisations are addressing long-term needs: for example, through community development that will not yield immediate results, or by looking after disabled or elderly people where you will have a continuing commitment to provide them with care. It is important that you create an organisation that is financially strong and positive about its future, rather than one that is plagued by annual deficits, which is running at or near bankruptcy, and where the financial concerns are beginning to affect the morale of everyone involved. If you think carefully, you should be able to find ways of strengthening your organisation's financial position and developing a sensible fundraising strategy for the future.

1.2 The challenges for fundraisers

Fundraising is never easy. But there are particular challenges for Southern fundraisers:

The development of fundraising

Fundraising in the South is not as well developed as it is in the North. This means that the Southern fundraiser has to help in developing the habit of giving, finding fundraising methods which work well within the local culture, and identifying and mobilising those constituencies of support you would like to tap. In the North, there is plenty of experience, good practice, published case studies, practical training and support services for the fundraiser to draw upon. The South is starting lower down on the learning curve. Which is perhaps where this book comes in!

Growing need

Many poorer countries have underfunded health, welfare and educational programmes, and this particularly affects poor people. In those countries where population growth is outstripping economic advance, poor people will be growing poorer year by year. And even where countries are experiencing rapid economic growth, the rich may be getting richer, but wealth is not trickling down to the marginalised and the dispossessed. Then there are always new needs and new concerns – from the problems of water scarcity to the consequences of rapid urbanisation.

The challenge for NGOs is to develop solutions to people's needs rather than simply provide services that improve the quality of life. They need to create more imaginative and effective approaches to the problems that exist in society, so that they can respond to the growing levels of need without necessarily creating a continuing demand for funding that is just not there. The challenge for fundraisers is to find the funds to make this happen.

Establishing a vibrant local NGO sector

There is a growing recognition that NGOs should be playing a more important role in partnership with government and business as delivery agencies for poverty alleviation and development programmes. If the flow of development funding increases – as was promised at the G8 Summit in 2005 and as part of the arrangements for debt relief – this should lead to a greater availability of international development funds for NGOs.

You will be competing for these funds with country-based branches of the large international development agencies, such as Oxfam. In the long run, your job is to develop the local NGO sector so that it is seen as competent, creative and accountable, and to obtain a growing share of international development assistance for locally run and led NGOs, including your own.

Competition

The fundraising world is extremely competitive. More organisations than ever are thinking about fundraising and beginning to develop independent sources of income for themselves. This means that many of the more obvious sources, such as larger local companies and rich individuals, are receiving increasing numbers of requests for support – and they can't support all of them, however worthwhile each request is.

Then there are the large international networks, such as HelpAge International (welfare of the elderly) and SightSavers (blindness), who may have developed far better-resourced local fundraising than you could ever hope to do. Increasingly you will be competing with international development agencies, such as PLAN or Oxfam, which are starting to develop their local fundraising as well as seeking to access grants locally from large international donors, many of whom now decide their grants in the regions or countries where the money is being spent.

You will also be competing with new organisations, full of energy and enthusiasm. These may be addressing similar needs to those that your organisation is tackling. Each of these 'competitors' will be striving to show that they are 'the best'. Your job then is to persuade donors that your organisation is successful, effective, cost-effective, innovative and lively – in short, that you are the best recipient for the donor's funds.

The difficulty of making money

People are now talking about income generation as a way forward for funding NGO work. However, it is not easy to start and sustain a money-making enterprise. Most NGOs are largely inexperienced in business methods. Many have doubts about the whole idea of making money as part of a sensible financial strategy. If you do decide to go down this path, there will be plenty of good opportunities for NGOs to manufacture and sell products or services that are closely linked to their main work, or to provide their expertise to others on a consultancy basis. A growing body of experience on income generation is being built up. Hopefully this book will encourage you and others to explore the possibilities.

1.3 Who should read this book

The simple answer is that everyone who has any sort of fundraising responsibility needs to understand the fundraising process:

- **Board members** will want to know what to expect of fundraisers, how to employ them, what qualities they should have, and what support they will need to succeed. They will need to understand fundraising sufficiently to agree a fundraising strategy and to explore the options for income generation.
- The **director and other senior managers** may need to play a significant part in the fundraising process. They also need to know when it's time to employ specialist fundraisers or fundraising consultants and how to manage them to achieve the best results.
- **Fundraisers** will of course need a good background guide to the many techniques available to them, and an understanding of which are most likely to be relevant to their organisation.

- **Volunteers** who are raising money for you should read the book so that they can develop ideas for improving their own contribution.
- **Consultants and advisers,** who will often be charging for their services, need to know the fundraising process inside out to ensure that they are giving the best fundraising advice and helping their clients raise real money.
- **Trainers,** who might wish to use some of the material as handouts or checklists for people attending their courses.

This book has been written from as many points of view as possible, taking into account the interests of both large and small organisations, those with some experience of fundraising and those considering the possibility for the first time.

1.4 How this book is structured

The book is divided into eight sections:

- **Introduction** – this section – which sets out why fundraising is important and the challenges for fundraisers.
- **Getting started,** which describes some of the key principles of fundraising (to give you a better understanding of the process) and some of the personal skills required in a fundraiser (so you will know your strengths and weaknesses for the job). It also explores who should do the fundraising, and what is needed to equip a fundraising office.
- **Developing a fundraising strategy,** which describes some of the factors to take into account and suggests ways of developing a strategy for your own organisation. This section also covers testing, evaluation and control, to enable you to be more cost-effective in your fundraising.
- **The sources,** which covers international aid and grants, grants from government sources and programmes, foundation support, company giving and business sponsorship, getting support from individuals, and a range of other sources that you might want to consider. This section will give you an understanding of how money is given away, and will help you identify opportunities for getting support for your own organisation.
- **Making your own money,** which covers the opportunities for developing income-generation schemes to earn money for your organisation, as part of a strategy for creating greater financial independence and reducing reliance on grant aid.
- **Techniques for raising money,** which covers everything from house-to-house collections and direct marketing to organising a fundraising event, getting a legacy, raising money from overseas non-resident communities and running a capital appeal. The full list of topics is given on the contents page.
- **Working with people,** including volunteers, overseas volunteers, celebrities and patrons, board members and donors.
- **Communication skills,** which will help you articulate your fundraising need and communicate this to people with the resources to help you. This section covers writing fundraising proposals and appeal letters, producing leaflets and reports to support your fundraising, using the telephone, marketing and market research, and effective

public relations (which is an essential ingredient of successful fundraising). It also gives advice on how to present your organisation to the public – everything from your name and logo to the way you answer the telephone and the impression people get when they visit your office.

CHAPTER 2

Getting started

This chapter covers some of the key aspects of fundraising. It will help identify the people, the attitudes and the approaches that you will need to get a successful fundraising programme under way.

2.1 Some key principles of fundraising

'Fundraising is a science. But its rules are more like a rainbow than a formula. You need to paint with the most delicate shades of colours and moods. You will surely become a success if you paint with love and friendship.'

Ekaterina Kim, Contacts-I, Moscow

You have to ask

A piece of research commissioned by a major charity asked people who had not yet supported it what was their main reason for not giving. The answer was simple – *they had never been asked.*

So to raise money, you have to ask for it. And there are plenty of opportunities available for doing this. Some fundraisers do not get around to asking those who might wish to give. Others ask, but do so ineffectually. The good fundraiser must ask clearly for exactly what they want, having regard to the donor's ability and willingness to give when deciding what to ask for. They may need to repeat the message in order to emphasise the point. The call to action, the punch line which asks people to give, is the essential part of the message. And you must make it as easy as possible for the donor to respond.

The personal approach

The general rule is that the more personal you can make your approach, the more effective you will be. So:

1. Asking in person at a **face-to-face** meeting is better than . . .
2. Giving **a presentation** at a meeting to a group of people, which is better than . . .
3. **Telephoning** someone to ask for support, which is better than . . .
4. Writing a **personal letter** to someone, which is better than . . .
5. Sending an **email** to someone, which is better than . . .
6. Sending a **circular letter** to lots of people, which is better than . . .
7. **Mass emailing** all the addresses in your address book.

Many fundraisers prefer to work by sending letters asking for support. This is not the most effective way of asking, so you may need to think carefully about how to make your approach more personal. Two other points are worth considering:

A meeting at your project where the prospective donor can see your work and meet some of the beneficiaries is often the most effective method of all. If that can't be managed, you can try to illustrate your work with a short video, or with photographs, or by taking along some of the people you are working with to fundraising meetings.

A request from someone who has given or from someone important (such as a business leader or an expert in the field) can often be more effective than a request from a fundraiser or from the project director. Part of the skill in fundraising is knowing who is the best person to do the asking.

Understanding the donor's viewpoint

When deciding to give, the donor may be motivated by a wide range of feelings and thoughts. It is important for the fundraiser to understand a donor's thought processes when deciding how to ask.

The act of giving includes elements of faith, hope and charity. *Faith* that the fundraiser truly represents the cause and will act as an efficient conduit for the donor's money. *Hope* that the gift, however small, will make some difference. *Charity* because giving is an act of altruism, providing support without the expectation of any material return.

It is also important for the fundraiser to understand that the donor might have some personal reason for wanting to give, and that it is useful to be able to build on that interest. People may want to support a cancer charity, for example, through fear that they might get the disease, or because a family member or close friend has recently died of it. They may feel strongly about an issue – such as the environment – and want to do something about it. In supporting your cause, they are also supporting their cause, doing something that they feel needs doing and which they want to see done.

The return to the donor

People support charity without the expectation of any material return. But they do want something for their money, even if it is intangible. For example:

- **A feeling of having done something worthwhile**, and perhaps of having made a difference to someone else's life.
- **Recognition from other people** and from the public of their generosity – although some people prefer to give anonymously.

Fundraising is a people business

People do not give to organisations. They do not give to abstract concepts. They give to help other people or to do something positive to create a better world. Your job as a fundraiser is to show how you are helping do this. One way of showing this is by using case studies – illustrating your work with actual examples of the people you have been able to help, showing how you have been able to change their lives, showing what you have done to create a better environment and so on. In this way you can demonstrate to donors how their money can make a difference.

Another way is to focus your fundraising on particular aspects of your work: the beekeeping project you are planning to introduce in the school, which will provide skills that pupils will be able to use in their future lives and will at the same time generate income for the school; the community publishing programme you are developing, which fills you with excitement about its potential. Focusing on specific projects rather than the overall work of your organisation makes it far easier to enthuse your donors.

How to turn a goat into an ox

Arume is a widow who lives in the Boreda area of southern Ethiopia. Seven years ago she found herself unable to make ends meet for herself and her three children. When we started work in her village, she decided to apply for a loan under the small animals credit scheme we were targeting at female-headed households. Using the loan, she was able to purchase a goat. This initially provided the family with milk; but subsequently the goat reproduced, and the offspring were sold to generate an additional income for Arume. With this profit, Arume was able to purchase a draught ox, thereby enhancing her capacity to engage in agricultural activity. She is now a proud mother, having met the food and other requirements of her family, with her elder son soon to complete school and go on to college.

Source: This story was provided by Action for Development, Addis Ababa, Ethiopia, and was illustrated with a picture of Arume ploughing with her ox.

Fundraising is selling

Fundraising is a two-stage process. The first stage is showing people that there is an important need which you can help to meet. If they agree that the need is important, and that something should be done; and if they agree that your organisation is doing something significant to address that need; and if you can show them how some extra support could enable you to do even better – then asking for money becomes easy. Fundraising is more about selling an idea that the donor can make a difference than about the actual asking for money. Once people have been sold the idea, you will find that they will want to give. This is why fundraising is more about 'selling' than 'telling'. It is about persuading people to give, and showing reasons why the work is important. Your success depends on your ability to inspire people to do something to help.

Credibility and PR

People prefer to give to organisations and causes that they have heard of. This means that your organisation's credibility and good public relations are both extremely important. Press coverage of your work, trumpeting your successes in the newsletters you send to supporters, and getting endorsements of the quality of your work from experts and prominent figures can all encourage people to recognise the importance of what you are doing. If they are confident you are doing something both worthwhile and successful, they are much more likely to support you. Putting some effort into strengthening your organisation's credibility and getting good publicity for what you are doing is extremely important. You need to recognise this and devote sufficient time and effort to this aspect of your fundraising.

Donors don't know how much to give

One problem is that donors don't know how much they are expected to give. They may not want to give an enormous amount. On the other hand, they may not want to give too little, and so seem mean.

Ways of asking for a specific amount

- **Ask for a specific sum** to cover an item of expenditure: for example, £200 to sponsor an afternoon eye clinic at the hospital.
- **Provide a shopping list** of different items at different prices: for example, if you are equipping a hospital, you can list all the items you will need to purchase and ask a donor to contribute to one or more – the Lok Kalyan Samiti eye hospital suggests donations of Rs100 (£2) per patient for eye care and Rs200 per patient for cataract operations, and asks donors to sponsor one, five or ten patients.
- **Give examples of gifts** already received. This will give people a good idea of how much to give, depending on their level of generosity and on whether they see themselves making a largish or a smaller gift.
- **Break down the total** into the numbers of gifts of different sizes that you will need to achieve if you are to reach your target.

Saying thank you

Saying thank you is extremely important. It recognises and values the donor's generosity. It can also be an act of enlightened self-interest on your part: if you can get your donors to feel more warmly about your organisation, they may consider giving again at some time in the future.

Many organisations only say thank you when they have actually received a donation. Those who say thank you on every appropriate pretext will see the effort of doing this repaid handsomely in donor loyalty and may well be surprised at the level of repeat-giving it will stimulate. Not saying thank you, however small the donation, can generate ill will towards your organisation. Donors complain that many of the organisations they support never even bother to say thank you!

Saying thank you can pay

A former director of a major aid charity made a point of telephoning donors who had given £500 or more at home in the evenings to thank them personally. 'We're thrilled with your support. We're going to put it to good use immediately by using it to help establish a new health clinic for the Turkana. And we'll keep you in touch with progress.' All this makes the donor feel that the organisation is doing a good job

---

and that their money is actually having some impact. A fundraiser from an Asian NGO made a personal visit to thank a donor who had recently given £600. At the end of the visit, the donor made another donation of more than twice as much again.

Long-term involvement and commitment

What you really want are people who will give to you regularly and substantially. All your efforts to find donors and persuade them to give will really only bear fruit if they continue to give over many years and maybe increase their level of giving. And if they are then prepared to ask their friends to help you or to put in long hours as volunteers, then that will be an added bonus.

To achieve this means getting your donors to feel involved with the work of your organisation and committed to its continuing success.

Involvement and commitment

The difference between involvement and commitment is well illustrated by the Bacon and Eggs story. A chicken and a pig were discussing the forthcoming breakfast in which they were both to play a part. The pig said crossly to the chicken, 'It's all very well you being so cheerful. You're just involved. I'm committed!'

You want your donors to be committed. You can try to achieve this by:
- **Saying thank you** immediately and telling them what you plan to do with their money.
- **Reporting back** regularly, showing them what you have been able to achieve with their money.
- **Sharing your ideas** and hopes for the future with them.
- **Encouraging them to visit you** to see your organisation at work, and getting them to meet some of the people that they have been helping.
- Offering them opportunities to **meet the staff and volunteers** who are actually doing the work, and also **prominent personalities** who are associated with you.

Accountability and reporting back

When you take money from somebody, you are responsible for seeing that:
- The money is spent on the purposes for which it was raised. Failure to do this will be a breach of trust.
- The money is well spent and actually achieves something: that is, you have done your very best to make the project as successful as possible.

You may be obliged to report back to the donor as a condition of the grant. But you will want to do this anyway to show them that you have used their money effectively. This is not only polite, it is good fundraising practice – an enthusiastic donor who has seen that their money has made a difference may consider becoming a more committed supporter.

2.2 The skills required in fundraising

There are a number of important skills that you will need if you are to be successful. Once you have understood what skills are required, you can:

- **Assess your strengths,** so that you concentrate on doing those things you are good at.
- **Learn what skills you need to acquire,** and set about obtaining the necessary training or experience.
- **Find ways of compensating for your weaknesses** by mobilising others to help you wherever this is appropriate.

Commitment to the cause

Commitment is one of the most important attributes that a fundraiser can bring to the job. If the cause does not seem important to you, how can you convey to others the urgency of doing something about it? You must really believe in what your organisation is doing. Your enthusiasm and commitment will encourage others to become equally committed through their giving.

The starving baby syndrome

You are watching TV. There is a programme about a refugee camp in Darfur. Men, women and children have arrived there with nothing, absolutely nothing. They have walked for days and are near starvation. A picture flashes up of a starving baby, who seems to be crying out to you, 'Help me. Please help me. Please.' How can you resist giving to the aid charity running the feeding programme at the refugee camp? Then you think about the cause you are working for. 'If only *I* were raising money for starving babies, it would be so much easier,' you are thinking.

But your cause is important too. You have to make it seem as important to yourself and to others as saving starving babies. And interestingly, the fundraiser for the starving baby charity probably believes that it would be much easier to be raising money to save endangered animals from being poached. And the animal fundraiser would much prefer to be raising money for a cancer charity . . .

You have to believe wholeheartedly in what you are doing, and make your cause compelling to others. If you can do this, fundraising will become very much easier.

The ability to ask

Many people feel uncomfortable with the notion of actually having to ask for money – whether the task in hand is to write a four-page appeal letter, make a speech at a meeting of the Rotary Club, telephone a business to ask for an in-kind donation, organise a committee to run a fundraising event, pay a personal visit to seek the support of a major donor, or just persuade someone you meet that your cause is worth supporting. All this requires an ability to ask effectively. If you find this difficult, you are not a natural fundraiser, and you will need to push yourself to do it and to feel comfortable doing it. Remember that you are asking for money to help support an important cause or address an urgent need. You will get better as you start to do it, and may even come to enjoy it.

Persuasiveness

People have choices about what to do with their money. They have competing demands on their spending. They could go out to a restaurant, buy a new item of clothing . . . or make a donation to you. Your job is to persuade them that supporting your organisation is a really worthwhile 'investment' of their hard-earned money. You need to make a really good case and present it in a persuasive way. This requires good communication skills. You need to be able to marshal compelling arguments, write letters which excite interest, talk fluently and interestingly in public or in private about the work your organisation is doing, create a sense of excitement through your enthusiasm, and share your hopes and visions for the future.

Confidence and dealing with rejection

When you are asking for money, you need to radiate confidence. If you are apologetic or hesitant, people are less likely to give to you.

One of the biggest problems is maintaining your confidence in the face of rejection. Since more people are likely to say 'no' to you than to say 'yes' – that's a fact of fundraising life – it is very easy to get downhearted. Many of your approaches will be unsuccessful, simply because of the enormous competition for funds, or just through bad luck. After a couple of rejections, you will really begin to believe that nobody wants to support you. You then start acting as if nobody wants to support you. You become apologetic and you talk as if you expect to be refused. And maybe you even avoid asking – so as not to be rejected yet again. A good fundraiser has to be able to cope with rejection. You have to start each fresh approach as if it were the first and be prepared to learn from experience so that you become better at asking.

Persistence

Most fundraisers give up too soon. People often take 'no' to mean 'no' – rather than as a challenge to try to convert the 'no' into a 'yes'. If you give up immediately, there's no chance at all. If you feel that people really should be interested in supporting you, you will try to find a way of getting them to change their mind, or to find some other thing that they might like to support. You have approached them in the first place because you need support and because you feel that they might be interested in giving it. Don't just give up at the first setback. Use the rejection as an excuse to enter into a discussion with them. Go back to them again at a later date with another approach. You will find that persistence really does pay.

Persistence pays

'Some years ago I produced an environmental colouring book for children for a schools education programme. I thought that this might be sold in bookshops, so I decided to see whether bookshops might be interested in taking copies. I went first to my local bookshop. "Not our sort of book," they said. "No thank you." I had a similar experience at the next three bookshops I visited. I really was beginning to feel that nobody wanted the book. But I decided to go to one more bookshop before giving up. It was just as well that I did. "That's just the book we've been looking for. We'll take 70 copies for our Christmas table . . . And what's the next title in the series, as we'd also be interested in that!" I felt elated. It is exactly the same with fundraising. Your next approach might be your big success! So keep trying.'

Source: Michael Norton on his book Colour in Your Environment

Turning a NO into a YES

I asked a group of fundraisers who were approaching charitable foundations to telephone them after they had received a letter of rejection to find out why they had been turned down, and to see whether there was any possibility of their application being reconsidered or whether there was anything else they might apply for. What was interesting was how many eventually succeeded in getting a grant. If you are a donor receiving hundreds of applications, there is a tendency to say 'no' as an immediate response to any request. It is far harder to say 'no' to someone who feels that they have a good project which you really should be interested in and who has the courage to come back and try to enter into a discussion with you.

What to do if you are turned down

- Telephone to try and find out why they decided not to support you this time.
- Ask about the possibility of submitting another application.
- Discuss what you are doing and try to find out what aspect of your work they might be interested in supporting.
- Ask for a meeting, so that you can put your case in person.
- Suggest that they come and visit your project to see the excellent and exciting work you are doing.
- Tell them that you will keep in touch and that you will send them regular information on your work and news about progress.

Truthfulness

The fundraiser has to be truthful at all times. The need to persuade people creates a pressure on you to tell only partial truths and to claim more for your work than is the case. The very complex factors that create poverty today are a good example. If you are raising funds by writing a short letter to a potential supporter, how can you hope to describe what lies behind the poverty? And can you give a proper explanation without straying into the politics of the situation, however contentious that may be to the donor?

There is also a tendency to present the beneficiary as a victim. It makes it easier to get a donor's sympathy and support. This is as true for people with physical disabilities as it is for refugee families. The beneficiary may see the fundraising material and even be represented on the boards of your organisation, and may be really offended at how the cause is being presented. The need to present a sensitive but truthful case, while making it powerful enough to persuade donors to give, can cause conflict within the organisation. Frontline workers want the situation to be portrayed realistically. Fundraisers need to ask in a way that will elicit support. To resolve this dilemma demands sensitivity and understanding.

Social skills

A good fundraiser needs confidence, patience and tact. Confidence, because a confident appeal is harder to refuse. Patience, to deal with the particular concerns of donors (for example, when they ask for the third time about the income ratios of your organisation). Tact and sincerity, to ask a supporter face to face for a legacy, or to suggest a variation in a will. A good fundraiser should also like meeting and dealing with people. It is often said that fundraising is not about *what* you know, but *who* you know. There is a great deal of truth in this, as good contacts can help you get money. But it is also true that successful fundraising depends on *who you are*. Your enthusiasm, the impression you make on others, your ability to make friends and earn the respect of others, your cheerfulness and positive attitude will all help you in your fundraising. Some people are born with good social skills, others will need to work hard to acquire them.

Dealing with your donors

'A fundraiser should never give up. Much depends on his (or her) approach and personality. To ask for financial or other support for people who are in need does not mean that you should look unhappy. Your appearance, open smile, courage and challenge should light a beam in the heart of your donor. Your belief in the future for the people you are helping should convince the donor. It is useful to remember that the donor is also a human being who lives in the same world as you, and is anxious to do his bit to improve the community. My modest experience in fundraising says that it is very important to create feedback with your donor. Generous people do not necessarily need to be praised up to the sky, but they will be delighted to know that their support has helped improve something or made a better world for somebody. We have become close friends with many of our donors and try to build long-term relationships with them.'

Source: Ekaterina Kim, Contacts-I, a group with disabilities working for people with disabilities in Moscow

---

Organisational skills

Fundraising often involves keeping in touch with thousands of supporters, all of whom imagine that they are special and that you have some personal relationship with them. Good organisation is essential. Fundraisers have to keep accurate records of correspondence and information on donation history for each donor. All this must be organised so that no past event or piece of generosity is forgotten. A good memory for faces helps too.

Imagination and creativity

Fundraisers who come fresh to an organisation will find that imagination is an invaluable asset. The task may be to dream up new activities that will inspire existing supporters, or to create events that the public is going to be enthused by, or to present your work in a more exciting and imaginative way. You will also find that circumstances are continually changing and new opportunities will be emerging. Fundraisers need to identify new approaches and new techniques, and not simply rely on what has been done in the past.

Contacts and the ability to make contacts

The fundraiser who already has a number of useful contacts will have an enormous advantage. But this is not a prerequisite. A good alternative is to have the confidence to find people and ask them for what is needed. You should have the ability to make new contacts, and you should have the good sense to ask others to help you with the fundraising by providing you with their contacts or even doing the asking.

Opportunism

You need to grasp every opportunity that presents itself. For example, when a well-known supporter is awarded libel damages, would it be a good idea if your letter asking for support were in their in-tray next morning? Or if a leading company has just announced a major hike in profits or has been awarded a major construction contract in your area, it might be responsive to a cleverly constructed appeal for funds.

If there is a feature in a newspaper which focuses on your cause or describes the work of your organisation, an appeal for funds through an advertisement placed in the paper on the same day should be successful (provided of course that the editorial coverage is supportive of what you are doing). So if you know you are going to get coverage, then consider paying for an advertisement; better still, ask the journalist to add a request for support at the end of the article, with a reply address where donations can be sent – or if this is not possible, then at least an email contact.

The calendar provides opportunities at various times of the year. For example in Christian communities, Christmas and the New Year provide an extremely good fundraising opportunity, and other faiths have similar points in the year. And then there are anniversaries or centenaries which can be used as a basis for a major appeal.

Zubin Mehta and the Shalom India-Israel Centre in Mumbai

How Zubin Mehta, the Indian-born international conductor and Music Director for Life, became involved with the Shalom India-Israel Centre in Mumbai: 'Having nurtured the dream of an India-Israel Centre, I visited Israel in 1991, tramping the offices of umpteen cultural institutions, following up on every tenuous connection, meeting with Israeli government officials. Finally on my way back to the airport, I felt the kind of empty fatigue that comes with carrying a load of promises but nothing tangible. I knew we needed a respected and powerful patron, and many names came up, including Zubin's. But it would have needed both contacts and courage to access such a famous person. Back in 1991, I'm not sure I had either. Suddenly, there was Zubin in front of me in the bustling airport. On impulse I went up and congratulated him, and said that he had done every Indian proud. He thanked me politely, then it was over. 'In that crowded place,' I anguished with myself, 'I could have done more.' Two hours later airborne, I noticed Zubin up front, reading glasses perched on his nose. I mustered the courage to send a polite note requesting to talk to him. From that and many subsequent meetings I realised that I was with a very special human being. Zubin's warmth and easy accessibility, his ability to get as excited as a child with an idea, astonished me. Here was something he had always wanted to do – to bring the people of the two countries he loved together culturally.'

Source: Salome Parekh, Hon Director and Trustee, the Shalom India-Israel Centre, Bombay

---

2.3 Who should do the fundraising

Who, then, should actually be doing the fundraising? There are several options to consider:

The management committee/management board/trustees of the organisation

These are the people legally responsible for ensuring that your organisation has sufficient funds to carry out its work and does not become insolvent. They have to see that the fundraising is done effectively and on time. But that does not mean that they actually have to do the fundraising work. They may employ a fundraiser to do this, although in many smaller organisations it is the committee members who will be doing most of the fundraising.

The chairperson

The chairperson occupies a special leadership position within the organisation. Part of the responsibility of heading up the organisation may be to deal with major donors, along with the executive director, and to attend meetings with foundations and businesses where this will be helpful.

A fundraising committee

Where the fundraising is being done by committee members, it is important to remember that some people don't like asking for money or are no good at it. This leads some organisations to appoint committee members for their fundraising skills and personal contacts – if they know the 'captains of industry' and the Great and the Good, they may be in a position to bring in the money. This is not always a good idea, however, as your committee needs to include people with a range of skills and standpoints because it has a wider responsibility for the proper management and strategic direction of your organisation as well as ensuring that it has sufficient funds. It might be better to form a fundraising committee or development committee with people who are interested in the organisation and also keen to help raise money for it. This group can then be charged with overseeing the fundraising, and even undertaking much of the fundraising work.

The executive director

The executive director is the senior staff member of your organisation. As such, he or she is in a good position to do the fundraising – with an expert knowledge of the work being done and sufficient seniority to be an effective persuader. Fundraising can also be an extremely creative process. For if you are dealing with donors, you will be testing out new ideas and getting feedback, negotiating different forms of support and having to think creatively about how to turn people's goodwill into support. All this is extremely useful for a successful chief executive.

One problem, though, is lack of time, which means that the fundraising might not be given sufficient priority. One solution is to give the executive director sufficient administrative assistance so that the fundraising part of the job can be done well.

A professional fundraiser

Organisations that are of sufficient size or which give fundraising a high priority may decide to create a specific post of fundraiser. This will ensure that a person with the time and skills needed to do the job properly is responsible for fundraising.

However, it is all too easy to delegate a job that nobody really likes doing and then forget about it. There are many instances of organisations appointing a fundraiser and telling them to get on with it, only to find a couple of years later that the person is no good and nothing has been achieved. So even if you decide to delegate the job of fundraising to a professional, both the executive director and the management committee need to keep management control of the process, setting goals and monitoring progress, providing active support where needed and giving encouragement.

A volunteer

Yet another option is to find a part-time or even full-time volunteer who is prepared to do the fundraising. Some organisations have been able to do this successfully. Someone recently retired or wanting to return to creative work after taking time off to bring up a family might find this a challenge.

Volunteers are more often given responsibility for a particular aspect of the fund-raising, such as organising a reception or a gala film evening. This has the advantage that a slice of the fundraising work can be handed over to someone else who takes full responsibility for it; but the volunteer should have the skills and commitment that the task demands. They need to be set targets and held accountable for their performance, if the arrangement is to be a success.

A fundraising consultant

There is a new breed of person thriving in Northern countries and just beginning to emerge in the South – the fundraising consultant or consultancy organisation. These may specialise in major appeals, event organising, direct-marketing campaigns or corporate sponsorship. They can be quite expensive since you are paying for their expertise as well as their overheads. But particularly where you are developing a major initiative, they can provide an extremely useful input of experience and knowledge which can add value to your fundraising efforts. It is rarely the case that you will hand over all of your fundraising to an external consultant.

When you need to employ a fundraiser

If you decide you need to employ someone as a fundraiser, the main consideration is a financial one. Can you afford it? And what effect will it have on the administrative overheads of the organisation? Not many organisations are lucky enough to obtain sponsorship for their fundraiser, so you will have to consider the costs involved when deciding whether now is the right time to employ a fundraiser. On the other hand, can you afford not to? Will not having a person to do the fundraising mean that you will fail to raise the money you need, which will in turn create a financial crisis or mean that you are unable to expand as you have planned?

As a rough rule of thumb, to employ a fundraiser will require a full-time salary plus as much again in overheads – needed to cover such things as office costs, equipment, internet, telephone, stationery and duplicating, postage, production of brochures, and so on. To justify such an expenditure, you should aim to generate at least five times as much a year in extra income as a result of this appointment – although you will find that it can take some years for the income to build up if you are just starting to fundraise seriously, and many organisations find that they are not able to achieve this fivefold return.

In the early days it may appear that the fundraiser is doing little more than raising the costs of his or her own salary. When appointing a fundraiser for the first time, you need to take a long-term view, as it will take several years to develop the full potential of the post. The appointment of a fundraiser should be seen as part of the organisation's longer-term development strategy, and targets should be set for the amount of money to be raised in each of the first few years of the appointment.

If you do not want to commit yourself to hiring a permanent full-time fundraiser, there are several other options. The first is to consider whether you have a volunteer with the time and skills to be trained up as a fundraiser. The next is whether a part-time appointment might be more appropriate. Alternatively, you might want to look at a fixed-term contract for, say, one year. You can always reappoint or extend the contract if things are going well, but you will not be committed if they are not.

Some organisations would prefer to pay the fundraiser by results, perhaps giving them 10 per cent of everything they raise. While this means that you reduce your risk, it poses some problems. If you are asking a donor to give you $10,000, of which $1,000 will go to the fundraiser as commission, the donor really ought to be told – and if they are told, they may be less prepared to give. Offering the fundraiser performance bonuses for targets achieved largely gets over this problem.

Fundraising to pay for your fundraising

Some donors are showing an interest in giving organisations funds to help them develop their fundraising. For example, Oxfam funded NESA (New Entity for Social Action), a vibrant network of people's organisations in southern India, to help it develop its own fundraising as well as to impart fundraising skills to its own members. It did this because it wanted to see NESA develop as a viable and sustainable organisation after a period when it had provided direct support for NESA's work.

So if you want to get started in fundraising and would like to have the costs under-written for the first two or three years before significant sums of money start to be generated, you could think about developing a fundraising proposal to this effect. Include in your budget the costs of setting up a fundraising office, employing a fundraiser, and actually doing the fundraising work. Then approach your major funders and discuss this idea with them. You could describe it as an 'investment in your organisation's future' that will enable your organisation to continue to operate sustainably with local funding. You could show this as the next logical step in your organisation's development.

Recruitment of a fundraiser

Once you have decided to recruit a fundraiser, you should consider the following:

Objectives

What are the objectives of the fundraising post? Is it to develop alternative sources of funds to replace grants which are known to be coming to an end? Or to launch an expansion programme? Or to run a major capital appeal? Or to develop a corpus fund or endowment? Or to develop independent and local sources of funding? Or to create a large and active membership? Or to develop corporate support? Or to organise high-profile events which will raise awareness as well as money? Or something else? Set out some clear objectives. This will help you write a 'job description' and a 'person specification', so that you can recruit someone with the experience and skills needed.

The objectives you set should be realistic. They should take into account the fund-raising needs of the organisation and the opportunities that exist, but should not be so ambitious that they present an insurmountable obstacle to success. There will also be an inevitable learning process at the start when nothing much happens. The fundraiser will need to familiarise himself or herself within the work of the organisation and begin to build experience and contacts. But it is important that some money should start to come in, even if the sums are quite small initially, as this will show that things are beginning to work.

Budget

The budget for the fundraising should cover more than just the salary costs of the fundraiser. A sensible budget needs to be set aside to resource the post and pay for all the promotional work that is needed. This should include the costs of equipping the fundraising office and paying the fundraiser's salary, as well as the costs of actually doing the fundraising work – for example producing brochures and other printed materials, building a website with an online donation facility, organising fundraising events, plus PR and other ways of promoting your organisation and the wonderful work it is doing.

Recruitment

So you've decided on your objectives and written a job description. Where do you find this special person that you are looking for? You will need to identify someone with the right:

- **Experience** and **expertise**.
- **Personal skills** and the qualities needed to do a good job.
- **Ethical values** and **commitment** to the cause.

Of these, the last two are really important – especially so in countries where there is as yet little experience of local fundraising. Expertise can be acquired and experience can be gained, but the personal skills and ethical stance come with the candidate. The personal skills required in a fundraiser are discussed in some detail in Section 2.2.

When you decide to recruit someone, there is always a chance that the arrangement will not work out – that they will be the wrong person for the job despite having got through the job interview and selection process. You may want to have a six-month probation period for the newly recruited fundraiser which will enable you better to assess their abilities and potential.

Where to recruit a fundraiser

- Circulate information about the job opportunity to your staff. This post might be something that a current member of your team could do well.
- Circulate information about the job opportunity to your existing supporters and volunteers. They already have some commitment to the organisation. One of them might be just the right person for the job.
- Advertise in the local newspaper, the business press and in marketing journals. These will reach the sorts of people you are looking for.

In many countries, it may be hard to recruit an experienced fundraiser, as there are few people with real experience of fundraising; so you will need to look for someone with the right personal skills and attitudes, who is excited about your organisation and its work. Someone with experience of marketing or customer relations might be just the person you are looking for. Another idea is to apply to an overseas volunteering programme, such as VSO, for a skilled fundraiser to come and work with you for up to two years to help you develop your fundraising and to transfer fundraising skills. This is what Leila MacTavish did for the Kenya Society for the Mentally Handicapped in Nairobi from 2000 to 2002, which helped KSMH to get started in fundraising.

Induction

The fundraiser will be 'selling' the organisation to donors. The induction process is therefore important. It might include:

- Meeting the **management committee.**
- Meeting **senior staff.**
- **Site visits** to projects to see the organisation at work.
- Discussing and agreeing **what the organisation stands for** and how it should be projected to the public.
- Discussing **'no-go areas'**, where the organisation is not prepared to solicit support.
- Agreeing the **fundraising strategy** and the targets for the first year, and sketching out what might be achieved over the first three years.
- Reviewing **existing donor support**, identifying problem areas and opportunities, and being introduced to any key contacts.

Management and motivation of the fundraiser

Fundraising is a tough and demanding job . . . and often a lonely one. Faced with all the difficulties of raising money, and with a steady flow of rejections, it is easy to get downhearted. Proper management of the fundraiser's job means:

Keeping in touch with the work of the organisation

The fundraiser should keep in regular touch with those doing the front-line work, visiting projects to see their activities at first hand, talking to project workers and beneficiaries to get a feel of the needs and the quality of the support being provided, in order to understand the issues and the particular approach and ethos of the organisation. This interchange of ideas also has the effect that those spending the organisation's money learn more about the fundraising process and begin to recognise the concerns and interests of donors.

Setting targets and monitoring progress

Targets should be agreed with the fundraiser rather than imposed. And progress should be regularly monitored. If targets are not being met, this will need to be discussed and the causes identified. Perhaps the targets were over-optimistic in the first place. Perhaps a particular fundraising approach or technique is not working well enough. Perhaps things could be done better or there was a mistake to learn from. A good idea is to create a small fundraising advisory group that will take a particular interest in the fundraising and with whom the fundraiser can discuss issues.

It is also important to keep track of the time and effort put into each fundraising initiative. There is a tendency to spend too much time chasing after sources which are marginal or unlikely, and too little developing those that are really important to the organisation and its future. There is also the problem of organising numerous fundraising events which take up a lot of time but may yield little in terms of money raised. So it is important to find out whether you are using your time effectively – since the fundraiser's time is usually the biggest cost in the fundraising budget.

Finding out about what others are doing

A fundraiser should try to find out how other similar organisations are raising money, and how successful their fundraising is. Here are some simple things to do:

- Visit their websites and look for information about sources of funds, names of donors, and news about their fundraising activities.
- Write for copies of their latest annual reports and accounts. Then see how much each organisation is raising, make a note of its major sources and its major donors (these are often acknowledged), and see how its fundraising is growing.
- Scan the newspapers for mentions of the organisations' work.
- If they have produced appeal brochures or fundraising literature ask to be sent copies. See if you are then put on their mailing lists.
- Telephone to ask about their work – and see how well they answer your call.
- Where you can, participate in their fundraising events. For example, get yourself invited to a gala dinner, participate in a sponsored walk. See how well the event is being run, and how successful it is in raising money.
- Make friends with fundraisers in other organisations. Go on fundraising courses to share experiences.

Giving fundraising due importance

It is important that everyone in the organisation should recognise fundraising as an important function, and that the fundraiser should be given the support needed to do a good job. Fundraising which is just delegated and forgotten about will rarely work well. Fundraising which is starved of resources – it always takes money to raise money – is also likely to fail. So the executive director and the management committee need to have confidence in the fundraising process and the abilities of the fundraiser, and then provide sufficient support to enable it to succeed. And when a fundraiser does achieve success, this should be recognised. This could be through some sort of performance bonus; or better still, just by giving praise.

Training and meeting other fundraisers

There are now courses on aspects of fundraising being run in most countries, and the Resource Alliance runs active training programmes worldwide *(see box)* as well as annual conventions. These are good places to brush up on basic skills, to share ideas and experiences, and to meet and network with others doing a similar job.

But some of the most creative fundraising comes from thinking about what you are doing, chatting to people about your ideas, meeting people and talking about your work (with no immediate intention of asking for money, but to develop a contact and a relationship). Under the pressure to raise money, it is often this 'creative time' which gets lost. The successful fundraiser will make sure that he or she has sufficient time to do all of these things by building them into the work schedule.

The Resource Alliance

The Resource Alliance was originally founded in 1981 as the International Fund Raising Group (IFRG). What began as a modest gathering of fundraisers from Europe and North America organising a workshop to promote best practices in fundraising is now a truly international not-for-profit organisation, dedicated to strengthening the voluntary sector's ability to develop broad domestic popular support.

Over the last 28 years this original gathering of fundraisers has grown into the annual International Fundraising Congress (IFC), which now attracts nearly 1,000 people from more than 60 countries. It is acclaimed as a unique forum for skills sharing, international networking and exchange of ideas for fundraisers worldwide, and is oversubscribed every year.

In the 1990s, the Resource Alliance began to expand its training into Asia, Africa, Latin America and central and eastern Europe, in response to the growing demands for skills in local resource mobilisation, communication and enhancing accountability, and overall organisational effectiveness of voluntary sector organisations. Working with local partner organisations, the Resource Alliance enables regional training workshops to take place in Asia Pacific, south Asia, eastern Africa, southern Africa, central and eastern Europe, Latin America and Middle East regions.

The Resource Alliance organises an annual International Workshop on Resource Mobilisation, which focuses on the needs of Southern organisations and organisations working in the South. In each of these workshops, regional and international, the focus is on sharing cutting-edge skills that enhance organisations' ability to mobilise local support for their causes and increase public confidence in the voluntary sector.

Foundation courses in fundraising have been set up in a number of countries. These are run in partnership with local business schools and universities and involve around 20 days of teaching. NGO of the Year awards have been established in Malaysia and India to promote good standards of management and transparency, and Resource Alliance provides training and advice services, working directly with local trainers to build the fundraising confidence and skills of local organisations.

In addition to training and networking events, the Resource Alliance has developed a unique website, part of it in Spanish, to promote sharing of local resource mobilisation techniques. The need for knowledge generation and sharing also led to the creation of the widely acclaimed e-zine, *Global Connections*. This is published as a monthly e-newsletter and contains case studies, research articles, opinion pieces and regional news bulletins to subscribers in over 135 countries. There is also a Spanish language newsletter, *e-Noticias*, which is published three times a year.

For more information, contact the Resource Alliance, 56–64 Leonard Street, London EC2A 4LT, UK. Tel + 44 20 7065 0810; Fax + 44 20 7065 0811; Email contact@resource-alliance.org; Website www.resource-alliance.org

2.4 Equipping a fundraising office

You will need some items of equipment to help you do the job properly. Not all are essential by any means, and you should be able to find some way of organising the fundraising whatever the resources available to you. The following are some of the things to consider getting. You may not want to rush out immediately and spend large sums of money. Once the fundraising has started to develop, this may then be an appropriate time to invest in the equipment which will make your work easier.

1. Computer and software. A good computer with decent software will be the most important piece of equipment. You will need to write letters, keep donor records, draw up budgets and prepare visual materials to accompany your presentations. You will need to access websites to get information on donors and download application forms. And you will be conducting a good deal of your business by email. Computers are becoming cheaper each year, and specifications are also increasing all the time. You will need programs such as Word, Excel, Powerpoint, Outlook Express (usually bundled together as a package by Microsoft), or the equivalent in free software (Open Office and FireFox). You may want a virus detection program (such as Norton Antivirus) and a database program (such as FileMaker Pro or an off-the-shelf program specially developed for fundraisers). You will need a reasonably good printer (but check the relative costs of ink cartridges) and a scanner. A laptop is useful if you travel and if you also work from home. If there are power supply problems, you will also need equipment to regulate voltage levels and prevent surges, and to provide backup if the electricity goes off.

2. Desktop publishing (often referred to as DTP). This will enable you to design simple leaflets and communications material in your office, rather than sending it out to a design studio. Now that the software is available, and if you already have a computer, you might consider getting your design work done in house. The programs you would need include PageMaker, Adobe InDesign or Quark Xpress, and PhotoShop for playing around with digital photographs and integrating these into your text.

3. Telephone. The telephone is an essential tool. It can be used to find out names and job titles and to confirm the addresses of the people you are writing to; to follow up on an application letter to see if it has arrived and whether more information is required; to check the progress of the application; to thank donors for their support, or to see whether you can change their mind where you have had a rejection; to inform donors of progress; and in many, many more ways. Voicemail will enable people to leave messages for you if you are away from your office (and there is nobody to take a message). Alongside a landline in your office, a mobile phone will enable you to make telephone calls and receive messages wherever you are. You will need to budget for the cost of the handset, the monthly subscription charge and the cost of calls. If you need to be in regular contact with people overseas, then consider using Skype, which is a Voice Over Internet program (Voice Over Internet Protocol or VoIP) that enables you to make phone calls for free.

4. Internet connection. The internet is now an essential communications medium. You will use email for sending letters and newsletters. You will want internet access for getting information about donors and downloading application forms. You will need a reliable Internet Service Provider (ISP) and an easily remembered URL for your website and email address. How you handle this depends on (a) what you can afford and (b) what's available in your own country. If it's available, get broadband (which will give you much faster access) rather than a dial-up connection. You will need to develop a website for your organisation, so that donors and supporters can find out more about what you are doing. Your ISP will provide you with the space for this, but you will also need a good website designer to create the website and to help you keep it up to date.

5. Fax. A fax is becoming really useful, particularly where postal services are uncertain and you need to provide someone with a hard copy of information that you might also email. If your computer has a fax program, this will enable you to send and receive faxes electronically.

6. Photocopier (and a supply of paper). If you are in the business of writing to hundreds or thousands of donors, you will definitely need some photocopying capability – either your own or access to a local copy bureau, or perhaps even reach an agreement with a local company to use their facilities (at cost or *pro bono*).

7. Annual reports, brochures and other project information. Most large donors, such as aid agencies and foundations, will want to see a copy of your latest annual report and accounts. The annual report should be carefully written and neatly, though not necessarily expensively, produced. You should also have a simple brochure, perhaps a single letter-sized sheet of paper (A4) folded once or twice, which gives basic information about your organisation, and includes a reply coupon so that people can respond. You may also want to produce some simple information sheets that describe the various projects your organisation is undertaking or give case studies that show how you are helping people.

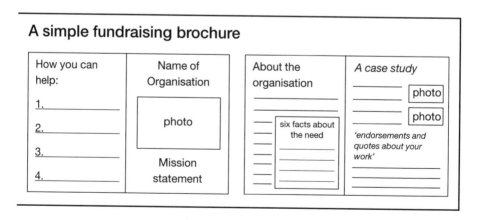

A simple fundraising brochure

8. Books and practical information on fundraising. A simple fundraising library will include grant guides and other directories (providing information on international and local donors and on companies), practical handbooks outlining the different fundraising techniques, and technical information on tax and giving with which you should be familiar.

9. Tax exemption and permission to receive foreign funds (where this is required). It is also important that all the legal requirements for fundraising are complied with.

10. Cash collection facility, which can include a bank account and also an online facility for receiving funds (such as PayPal). When you ask for funds, you must also be able to tell donors how they can pay you. If you hold substantial cash balances, you will want to place your funds in high-interest accounts, both to protect against inflation and to earn a return. You may also need such things as collecting boxes for house-to-house collections, and procedures for collecting the money raised and transferring it to your bank account.

11. Letterheads and compliments slips for correspondence. These will state the name and contact details of your organisation, and could also include its logo, its legal status, any charity or company registration number, the names of the committee members and the executive director, any affiliations, and even a slogan or strapline explaining your 'mission' in a short sentence. It is up to you how much information you provide. But make sure that your stationery is neatly designed. A letter might be a first point of contact with your organisation for many of the people you are approaching, so it should offer an image of a lively and successful organisation.

12. Display equipment for exhibitions. Exhibiting at fairs and conferences can be an effective way of introducing your organisation to a wider public as well as meeting new supporters. Creating an attractive display so that people notice you and want to come and find out more will help you do this. A short video showing the work of the organisation can also be useful, and can also be streamed from your website or on YouTube.

13. Basic office furniture. You will require a desk, a filing cabinet, chairs and a table for meetings – just the basic furnishings that any office requires.

14. Displays for your reception area. Your reception area is where people first arrive when they visit you. If you are inviting donors to your office, you will want to make a good impression. Why not have a display of photographs of the organisation at work on the walls, so that any visitor to your office can see what you are doing? You could also create a comfortable waiting area stocked with promotional literature and annual reports for visitors to read, and copies of your publications available for purchase. First impressions *are* important.

15. A digital camera and camcorder. This can be used when you go on field trips. Case studies with pictures will show where you are working, the problems and needs, who you are working with and how you have been successful. A digital camera and camcorder will enable you to capture images and use them in your promotional material extremely cost-effectively. You might also want to invest in a projector so that you can make PowerPoint presentations.

Setting up a fundraising office will cost money. You could try asking suppliers to donate equipment or give you a big discount. You can also ask supporters to donate equipment they no longer need, or to lend it to you. Make a list of everything you need, and see how much of this you can get donated. Try approaching the following:

- **Management committee members** and **volunteers**, who might have just what you need.
- **Local companies**, who might give furniture and equipment that they no longer need, donate their products (or at least give you a discount on list price), or allow you to use their facilities.

2.5 Engaging a fundraising consultant

You may wish to consider buying in expertise by hiring a consultant. There are a number of people with experience of running an NGO or successful fundraising who have set themselves up as independent fundraising consultants, and are available to advise you in return for a fee.

There are three main sorts of work that such freelance consultants might do for you:

1. Make an **appraisal** of a particular area of your fundraising and advise you on what to do about it.
2. At the same time, be involved in the **implementation** of your fundraising programme, for example by giving you continuing advice, by writing fundraising proposals for you, or by actually doing some or all of the fundraising work.
3. Help you **write and design** effective brochures and other fundraising literature.

You must decide on what sort of help or advice you really need. Each consultant will have their own particular strengths which you need to identify. Some have specialist skills, such as expertise in corporate giving, sponsorship, direct marketing, advertising, promotion, design and print, producing annual reports or videos. Others will have more general skills, or managerial and strategic experience to offer.

Since consultants are expensive you need to ensure that you get good value. If at the outset you are not certain of what value a consultant (or consultancy firm) can bring to you – or of how much you can afford to pay them – you might suggest a feasibility study first. This should be a short, paid investigation of the major issues involved and a preliminary indication of what might be achieved by the consultant. Such a study would imply no further commitment on your part.

Payment by results

Many charities think that it is desirable to hire a consultant on a commission or payment-by-results basis. Although this is done from time to time, it is not generally considered a sound basis for remuneration. Beware of fundraisers who offer this sort of deal. Particularly where the commission levied is high, they will be remunerating themselves at your donor's expense. For most consultants there is sufficient incentive to succeed without linking pay to results. And from your point of view, selecting the best person is what is most likely to lead to success.

Selecting a consultant

Whoever you choose, there are a number of steps to go through:

1. **Be absolutely sure of what your problem is** and what sort of service you actually need. Do you need someone to help you devise the strategy only? Do you need both the strategy and help with its implementation? Or do you have some specific task you need doing, and require someone to do it for you? Or do you just need advice?

2. Write a **good brief** and **clear job description**. This should cover what needs to be done, the timetable, and the specific objectives.

3. Wherever possible, make sure you have a **good selection** of people or companies to choose from – so as to ensure that you choose the best.

4. Agree the **basis of remuneration**. Is the budget acceptable? What control over success and failure will you retain? How will expenses be charged? How much notice is required to terminate the arrangement if you are dissatisfied?

5. Get **references** and follow these up to find out the quality of their work for other, similar organisations. If you do not get good – or indeed any – references, proceed only with the greatest caution.

CHAPTER 3

Fundraising strategy

3.1 Developing a fundraising strategy

Your fundraising strategy is the backbone of your fundraising. Getting it right demands a good deal of attention at an early stage. Not thinking through what you are doing can waste your time and efforts.

Outlining the needs

The starting point for any fundraising strategy is to define the needs of the organisation. This can be done at three levels.

1. Just to keep going

What are the financial requirements if the organisation is to continue its work programme at the present scale of operation? How much money is already assured and how much will need to be raised to meet spending requirements? What level of reserves do you need to plan for, just in case the money does not come in as predicted? If there is a cash crunch, this can precipitate a financial crisis when it is probably already too late to rescue the situation.

These calculations will usually take the form of annual and rolling budgets for the short and medium term (say, up to five years ahead).

2. To expand to meet growing need

Most organisations will say that they are only scratching at the surface of the problem, that if they had more resources, they could do much more to meet the need. And alongside this, the need may be growing or the problem getting worse. Starting with the human or societal needs being addressed by the organisation, you might ask the following questions:

- What exactly is the current level of **unmet need**?
- What are the **consequences** or **implications** of this for the future if nothing is done?
- How are the needs growing and what changes do you foresee happening over the next few years?
- **Who else is doing anything** to meet the need?
- What should you be doing to **respond to the challenges** of the future?
- How does what you plan to do **fit in with what others are doing**?
- Is what you propose to do an **effective way of addressing the need** given the limited resources that are likely to be available?

All these questions should be asked and answered. Future plans should be discussed and developed. Is it just a question of expanding what you are doing? Or will you need to develop different mechanisms for addressing the problem? If the need is not important and your role unclear, developing a good fundraising 'case' can become very difficult.

3. The future development of the organisation's work

Most organisations do not stay still. There is often a momentum to expand and develop. Success with one project not only gives the organisation a feeling of confidence, but will also throw up ideas for other things that the organisation might do, and it brings greater credibility with funders and public bodies who might wish to create closer working partnerships.

What developments will you want to consider for the future? What new services or projects will you want to run? Will you want to export your work into other regions? Will you want to enter into major collaborations with your funding partners to extend your work? Will you want to enter into partnerships with governmental authorities, working with them on a much wider scale to address the problem?

Then, if you are a development organisation, there is the relationship with the people you are helping. Are you empowering people to help themselves? And if you are, how will you be planning to operate once local people have the structures and skills to organise their own development? Will you extend your work and maintain your development role? Or will you devise an exit strategy?

The future of your organisation starts with what you want to do. It is up to your chief executive to plan this, with input from other senior staff and from you, the fundraiser. Then it is up to you to get the resources that will be needed to put the plans into action.

How the organisation itself will develop

Besides funding the work, you will also need to fund the organisation and its future. There are several factors to consider:

1. Capital developments

What are your capital requirements for the future? Will you be developing a training centre or a school? Will you be buying land or acquiring property? Will you be extending or improving your existing facilities?

2. Corpus funds

Many organisations plan to develop a corpus fund or an endowment – that is, a capital reserve which can be invested to produce a regular income for the organisation. Some approach major donors for contributions to this fund. Others set aside some of their income each year for this fund. Either way, it will impose a short- and medium-term fundraising need on the organisation.

The development of 'corpus' fundraising

One recent trend in India has been the development of 'corpus' fundraising to create an endowment. Examples of this are: PRADAN, a rural development agency headquartered in Delhi, which had been able to raise a corpus from its US funder; and SEARCH, a training and information agency based in Bangalore, which has moved towards a more commercial basis for providing training and consultancy to NGOs and community organisations, and has been allowed by its funders to accumulate any surplus income into a corpus fund.

3. Reducing dependency and developing independent sources of funding

There is a fundamental difference between an organisation that receives all its money from one source, and an organisation that has developed a wide range of sources each contributing towards the total requirement. Too much dependency on one source can give too much control to the donor in dictating how the organisation should be working and where it should be going. Such dependency can put great pressure on the organisation to meet the agenda and objectives of the donor, rather than standing up for what it wants to do (where this is different). It can create a risk of failure – that the organisation will not be able to survive if the grant is cut back or withdrawn.

It is for this reason that many organisations seek to extend their fundraising base, bringing in other major donors and developing new sources of funding. You need to decide whether your organisation's funding base is too narrow, and if so, how you are going to broaden it. You will need to think about all the possible sources of funding, and decide which are the most sensible for your organisation to develop.

4. Developing a membership and a supporter base

This is another aspect of financial independence, where the organisation attracts large numbers of individual supporters. This not only brings in money, but also strengthens the organisation by:

- Creating **a constituency** of support (the number of people who support you matters).
- Building **a local base** for your organisation (relationships with the local community will be different if the funding is drawn from it rather than obtained externally).
- Creating **opportunities for further fundraising**. Each donor can be asked to give regularly and to give more generously. They can also be asked to recruit other donors, to volunteer their time and skills to help the organisation, to donate items of equipment, or even to leave a legacy when they die. The more people who support you, the greater the opportunities.

5. Long-term sustainability

One way of looking at the development of your organisation is to see the funding as an 'investment' in your future, and to plan that future so that your organisation can run itself without major external funding after the development phase has been completed.

The organisation and its core work are then sustainable – they will not collapse if external funding is withdrawn. And any fundraising can be used to invest in new developments.

This approach is in contrast to the more usual one of using fundraising to cover running costs. It requires the organisation to plan for a sustainable future, which can come from:

- Designing **services which pay** (either wholly or very largely) **for themselves.**
- Creating **income-generating initiatives** which will fund the organisation's work.
- Forming partnerships with governmental bodies (such as education services, forest departments), where the programme is paid for from taxation.
- Creating **a corpus fund** or **an endowment.**
- Developing **independent and assured sources of funding** (such as a large membership or a successful fundraising event which can be repeated to produce an income year after year).
- Devising **self-help solutions** and **more economical ways of working,** which require less professional support.
- Using **volunteers** and **donated technical help** to work alongside the paid professional staff.

Sustainability

Stan Thekaekara, founder of ACCORD, a community development project working with tribal people in South India, says: 'We should be talking about the sustainable community, rather than the sustainable NGO. This means developing plans which invest in the community to give it a secure future, and not simply pay for processes or services or support. Donors are not used to giving capital; they prefer to pay for projects, and have developed elaborate systems to deal with this task. And communities are not being asked to develop plans which ensure a continuing life for the community organisation and the community institutions were the funding to be withdrawn.'

The development of sustainable funding strategies is an area where much more creative thinking is required. This might include:

- Seeing aid as investment in a development process, rather than a subsidy for work done.
- Using aid to build income generation into the community, so that it will have more resources of its own eventually to invest in its own future.
- Building institutions and other capital investments in the community, which give the community control over resources and an ability to generate income.

Looking at the progress towards financial sustainability made by ACCORD in Gudalur will illustrate these points:

- It partly funds its health programme (including the running of the hospital and the employment of doctors) through a commercial insurance scheme linked to an insurance company, where the local families pay regular small contributions. This is very similar to the mutual aid health schemes which flourished in the UK prior to the introduction of a National Health Service.

- It has negotiated with government to give the community a role in both education and forest conservation, and the resources to back up this role.
- It has set up families in agriculture so that they are no longer forced into low-wage and uncertain day labour, and in particular has introduced tea growing; a lucrative crop.
- It is looking at adding value to the tea-growing activity, and within the community organisation has set up a tea nursery, has joined the tea planters association collectively marketing their crop, and has purchased a tea estate for the community organisation, run commercially to generate an income as well as create employment for local people. It is also developing direct marketing initiatives for its tea, coffee and pepper within India and in Europe, and has barter arrangements with other communities that produce items it needs, such as textiles.

Identifying the sources

In constructing a fundraising strategy a useful starting point is to identify your likely funding sources. These might include:

- Support from individuals through **membership** or **donations**.
- **Major lifetime gifts**, plus **legacies** receivable on death.
- Support from **major fundraising events** such as public collections, entertainments, and participation events such as sponsored walks.
- Smaller-scale **local fundraising events** that involve the local community.
- Support from individuals giving their time (as **volunteers**).
- **Gifts in kind** (by individuals or from companies).
- Income generated through **fees, charges and sales**.
- **Investment income** from corpus funds or the interest on cash deposits.
- A grant from a **central government department**.
- A grant from a **nongovernmental agency**.
- A grant from a **local authority** (town or city, district or province, region or state).
- A **contract** with one of the above to provide services.
- A grant from an **international or national donor agency**.
- A grant from an international or a local **foundation** (or from another source).
- Support from **companies** (by donation or through sponsorship, by providing you with expertise or facilities).

Assessing the opportunities

The above is a fairly comprehensive list of the sources of money that might be available to you. When deciding which to develop, some of the factors to take into account are:

- **Past experience.** The results of your fundraising so far provide a good indication of where you are likely to succeed and what is likely to be less successful.
- **Your natural constituency of support.** Who do you think should be funding you? Who has a stake in the problem you are addressing? Government? Business? Local people? A religious network? Can you get them to share in the solution by becoming an investor in your work?

- **The type of organisation you want to be**. Do you want to be membership based? Or supported by prestigious international donors? Or linked closely to business? All this affects the style of your work and how people perceive you.
- **The style of your work**. Are you radical or conservative? Young and fresh, or established and mature? Innovative and at the leading edge? Every organisation will be able to identify individuals and institutions which share its vision and outlook.
- **The resources and skills available to you.** If you have a good events organiser, that's a good reason for putting on an event. If you have lots of volunteers prepared to do house-to-house collections, that's also something to consider. If you are already experienced in direct mail, why not develop that source of income further? If you're small and under-resourced, you will have to acquire the skills and resources you need.
- **Your existing funding base**. Starting from where you are and building on the sources you are currently dealing with is a priority. They already know about your work and have demonstrated their commitment to you. You need to assess how your donors feel about you, whether they would like to become more closely and more substantially involved with you and what their current interests and priorities are. It is always far easier to build on your existing support than to develop new support. Talk to your current donors. Share your plans with them. Identify areas of common interest. See how you can extend their support and increase their commitment. And with your supporters, conduct some simple market research to see what they think about the organisation and its work, whether they would like to become more involved, and what is preventing them from doing so. This can be done by questionnaire or through interview, or just by chatting to the people you meet.
- **Local practice**. Every country has existing mechanisms for mutual aid – such as harambees in many parts of Africa – which are widely used to raise money to meet a community need. This means that people are already used to being asked for support, although in a different context from NGO fundraising. If you can create fundraising activities that resonate with local practice, you may find a willingness to give.
- **Religion**. Most religions have mechanisms for giving, as well as times of year when giving is particularly encouraged. For example, Islam has zakat, where adherents are encouraged to give a proportion of their income for charitable purposes, and giving is particularly encouraged at Id, which occurs at the end of the Ramadan festival each year. Christianity also encourages its followers to make charitable donations, and before Christmas is a particularly important time for giving. If your organisation is part of a religious network (and many development initiatives are), or if the community you are working with has a dominant faith, this might provide opportunities for fundraising.
- **Other opportunities available to you.** A major company expanding in your area. A new government programme. A chance meeting with the director of a major foundation or aid agency who seems interested in your work. If there are particular opportunities available to you, seize them!
- **Who you know**. Contacts are important. If you know prominent philanthropists, industrialists, politicians, film stars or media personalities, you will find access to grants that much easier. Some people have a knack of forming relationships with the people

they need to help them succeed. But all organisations have some contacts which could be mobilised. It is worth sitting down with your management board, staff and volunteers to see whom you know or whom you can reach who might be useful to you.

The importance of a long-term perspective

Some funding sources are essentially short-term, while others can develop into long-term relationships. If your organisation is going to continue for the long term, you will need money not just for this year, but for next year, the year after that, and into the future. If you raise short-term money, you may meet this and next year's fundraising targets, but you will be looking at a deficit after that.

It is sensible when fundraising for your future to consider the long-term potential of each source of funding:

- If you receive a major grant or are involved in a contract to deliver a service, can you negotiate a long-term arrangement for continuing support (subject to meeting performance targets)?
- If you are attracting funds from individual donors, how can you negotiate regular and increasing support from them? It will not be just a question of soliciting support, but of managing the donor base that you develop.
- If you are organising a major income-generating event, can you plan to run it again next year? And the year after? And do it better and better each time you run it? And raise more and more money from the event?

Short-term and long-term funding sources

Short-term
- A foundation grant for a project, which may be for two or three years and not renewable.
- A one-off donation or sponsorship from a company.
- A house-to-house collection.
- A time-limited grant from a government source.
- An emergency appeal following a flood or a famine.

Long-term
- A long-term funding partnership with a donor agency.
- A major fundraising event that can be repeated each year.
- Membership subscription income.
- An annual appeal to your supporters.
- A long-term contract from a government agency to provide a service.

Identifying the constraints

There will always be a number of constraints on what you can do. Some stem from the nature of the organisation and what it stands for. Some are internally generated. Others are externally imposed. However they arise, you need to take them into account in planning your fundraising.

National or local

Are you a national or a local organisation? And if you are local, is what you are doing of national significance? Most national and international funding sources will want to support national projects or what they consider to be the best local projects – work which is at the leading edge. They are unlikely to respond to requests from local projects they've never heard of.

Local sources will usually support local projects. Local people will certainly be more interested in supporting projects on their doorstep. And companies will only want to support local projects in those areas where they have a business presence or some other connection, or where they are planning to start up.

Appropriateness of the source and 'no-go areas'

Some sources are completely inappropriate because what the donor stands for goes against what the charity stands for. The most obvious example of this would be a cancer charity receiving support from a tobacco company or a peace initiative funded by an armaments manufacturer. Every organisation should decide what sources are inappropriate for them – either for ethical reasons or because they will cause controversy among supporters – and then designate these as fundraising 'no-go areas'. These decisions can then be developed into an ethical fundraising policy that sets the boundaries for your fundraising. Ideally, this policy should be discussed with the senior management of the organisation and agreed with the management board before you set about asking, otherwise you will create problems for yourselves afterwards.

Many businesses use charitable support to enhance their image. Oil and mineral extraction companies, for example, are active supporters of environmental projects. Yet these businesses also have an impact on the environment through their operations. You have to decide whether an association with them is appropriate – who knows, you may even see an opportunity of influencing their behaviour through your association with them!

The Resource Alliance Ethical Statement

The Resource Alliance seeks donations and sponsorship from companies that:

- Embrace social responsibility and show a history of community involvement and work to improve society.
- Demonstrate a history of support to the charitable sector and related causes.
- Have a positive public image compatible with the Resource Alliance's organisational values and good reputation.
- Demonstrate positive employment and safety practices
- Improve the lives of the constituency our key NGO audience serves or cause our key NGO client base works for, through their business, product or service.
- Provide quality products and services that are of long-term community benefit.
- Are committed to the conservation of energy and natural resources.
- Are committed to the ethical treatment of animals.

The Resource Alliance does not knowingly seek nor does it knowingly accept funding or other resources from companies engaged in the following activities or industries:

- Armaments, weapons manufacture and sale.
- Tobacco manufacture.
- Commercial and sexual exploitation of children.
- Pornography.
- Perceived to be involved in unscrupulous business practices.
- Environmental pollution or degradation.
- Animal testing of cosmetic or household products or their ingredients, exploitative factory farming methods, blood sports, fur farming and trading.

The Resource Alliance will take all reasonable steps to ensure that off-limits companies are not solicited for donations or support.

In addition, the Resource Alliance will not accept any funds from governments, companies or individuals, which it perceives to have policies or activities that violate human rights.

The attractiveness of the cause

Some causes are instantly attractive to donors; others have to work hard to make themselves attractive. And some will appeal only to certain types of people who share your outlook. A good example is the Medical Foundation for the Victims of Torture based in London. This is a world-class organisation doing invaluable work. Its instant appeal is only to those with a concern for human rights. But, through clever presentation of case studies and clearly explaining what it is doing, it can appeal to anyone who is concerned about fairness and admires people with the courage to stand up against injustice. But it will never have the glamour of a large hospital appeal or a children's rescue charity.

You need to think about whether you are radical and campaigning, or safe and conservative. Most companies and many 'Establishment' sources will not want to support anything that is too 'political' or controversial. This can impose a constraint on who to approach, or a constraint on what you can do if you accept money from a particular source.

The scale of your need

If you need large amounts of money, there is no point approaching someone who can only give a little – unless it is a major campaign where you intend to recruit large numbers of small donors. Nor is it sensible to spend a lot of time organising a fundraising event which will only generate a small sum. Equally, if you are just looking for some modest support, there is no point approaching a huge international foundation. Horses for courses!

The resources available to you

The resources available to you determine what you can and you can't do. You will need to decide whether you have:

- The **people** to organise the activity.
- The **skills** and experience you will need.

- The **money** to invest in the activity.
- The **capacity** to respond to requests.
- The **contacts** with prominent people or star personalities that might be needed.
- The interest and **commitment of supporters** to get involved.
- The **credibility** as an organisation that will make people want to be associated with you.
- The **time** available, as well as sufficient lead time, to organise the particular fundraising activity.

Then you can decide what sorts of fundraising activity are possible, and which are completely inappropriate.

What other organisations are doing

It is important to look at what other organisations are doing – rival organisations engaged in similar work to you, as well as major fundraising initiatives which are likely to draw away support and media coverage from you. A major hospital appeal, for example, might involve all the leading businesses in your area – which might subsequently be reluctant to support any other initiative for the time being.

Legal constraints

Are you able to receive foreign funds? Are you registered as a charitable organisation so that you can receive tax-exempt donations? Will gift tax be payable? There is a whole range of legal and taxation issues which need to be sorted out before you apply. Some will determine from whom you can receive funds; others will ensure that you get the best tax advantage from any support you receive.

Determining your strategy: some simple techniques

The strategic planning process enables you to think through your options, make informed decisions on the best approach, plan the next steps, and carefully consider the resource implications. There are a number of simple techniques that you can use in strategic planning. Here are two you might find useful:

SWOT analysis

A SWOT analysis identifies the **strengths**, the **weaknesses**, the **opportunities** and the **threats** to the organisation and its fundraising. By doing this analysis you will be able to:
- Develop fundraising approaches which build on your strengths.
- Avoid areas of weakness or find ways of compensating for them.
- Seize the opportunities that present themselves.
- Develop ways of dealing with the threats that appear on the horizon.

Here are some examples of strengths, weaknesses, opportunities and threats that a SWOT analysis might identify:
- **Strengths**
  - An established and active supporter base.
  - Good contacts with local industrialists.
  - A well respected organisation.

- An active group of volunteers who are happy to run fundraising events for you.
- Good relationships with a major company and an important international foundation.

■ **Weaknesses**
   - No current fundraising experience.
   - Nobody available to do the work.
   - Poor promotional material.

■ **Opportunities**
   - A major company has just located in your area.
   - A new funding programme is due to come on line.
   - Your twenty-fifth anniversary.
   - A TV documentary on your work is about to go out.

■ **Threats**
   - Your major supporter is beginning to refocus priorities on other types of work or other areas.
   - Structural adjustment will lead to price rises which will affect your supporters.
   - You are confrontational with the government, which is leading to adverse publicity.

SWOT analysis

Strengths	Weaknesses
Opportunities	Threats

Developing a fundraising strategy: a case study

The following shows how the fundraising consultants to the UNESCO/Bolshoi Theatre partnership developed a fundraising strategy in Moscow.

Until quite recently there was no modern tradition of charitable giving in Russia, as the regime made this unnecessary by providing all the required funds. There is also a general distrust of 'charity' and some organisations are perceived as corrupt.

Strengths
- The beauty and popularity of the theatre, its importance to the culture of Moscow, and its international recognition.
- Pockets of extreme wealth in modern Russia, and particularly Moscow.
- The fundraisers' will to succeed.

Weaknesses
- Lack of fundraising and marketing experience and resources.
- No tradition of charitable giving among the newly rich.
- An unrealistically high expectation of instant results by the Bolshoi management.

The fundraisers also undertook a stakeholder analysis, and reviewed their potential target audiences for fundraising:

- The Russian public.
- Newly rich Russians.
- The expatriate community.
- Local companies in Moscow.
- Foreign-owned companies in Moscow.
- The media to run an appeal targeted at the general public.

The fundraisers also considered the range of possible fundraising activities:

- **A mass appeal via the media.** Despite the popularity of the Bolshoi Theatre, the fundraisers had limited access to the media, and the poor postal and banking services made it nearly impossible for people to reply with a donation.
- **Social fundraising.** Activities like sponsored walks and coffee mornings are unknown in Russia. To organise such events among the expatriate community, though culturally more feasible, would have little financial impact.
- **Trading.** The Bolshoi has a small, well-hidden shop with a limited range of goods. The fundraisers felt it would be great fun to develop this, but the logistics, poor infrastructure, lack of capital and limited potential returns made this an unrealistic fundraising option.
- **A Big Gift Campaign.** This would capitalise on Moscow's civic pride and the love of ostentatious display among the newly rich. Local and expatriate companies as well as individuals could be targeted, but there would still be a need to convince the donors of the benefits of donating.

Limited resources would allow only one activity to start with, so a Big Gift Campaign was chosen, to be launched with a gala evening at the theatre. Trading activities and a media appeal could be developed later if the resources and infrastructure made this realistic.

These conclusions took the fundraisers several days, much coffee and even a little vodka to reach. A Big Gift Campaign seemed like an obvious choice, but having done a thorough strategic review, they also knew it was the right one. It offers them a clear direction for future activities and the skills needed to reassess the situation when this is required.

Source: Karen Culver, fundraising consultant

Stakeholder analysis

Stakeholder analysis identifies funders and agencies with an interest in your organisation's work, and explores why they might be interested in supporting you through funding, the provision of other resources, or some form of partnership.

You need to think as creatively as possible. For example, for an organisation working with tribal people in a forest area, potential stakeholders would include the governmental body charged with protecting the forest. It would be interested in projects to generate income and to develop forest resources on a sustainable basis, both of which would reduce the need for local people to cut down trees; and also in schemes for protecting the forest that involved the participation of local people as 'forest guardians'.

Identifying stakeholders and understanding the reasons for their interest – and the strength of that interest – is a good starting point for developing some form of relationship. You need to answer two questions:

- Who do you think should be funding you?
- What is their interest in doing so?

Deciding your funding mix, planning your future

Having read through this chapter so far, considered all the factors discussed, and related them to the circumstances of your organisation, you are now in a position to start sketching out your plans for the future. One useful tool for doing this is to display the percentages of your funding coming from different sources on a bar chart, and then to show how these will change over a three- or a five-year time span. This will illustrate:

- **The major sources**, which is where you should be putting a large part of your fundraising effort.
- **The major changes**, where you will need to focus your time and energy to make sure you succeed.

The example in the box that follows shows how this can work.

Deciding on your funding mix: an example

You are a research and campaigning organisation working to reduce child-bonded labour. At present, 90 per cent of your funding comes from international donors, with the balance of 10 per cent coming from sundry gifts and donations. You decide that you want to move away from such dependency on large international grants and develop your own fundraising. Ideally you would like to generate at least half your funds in your own country, through developing a strong membership base that will contribute to your work and through local community fundraising in the town where you have established a training project for the children rescued from bondage, as well as through the sundry income you will continue to receive. This can then be displayed as follows:

Now

90% International donor agencies

10% Sundry income

Future

50% International donor agencies

20% Membership

20% Community fundraising

10% Sundry income

Some other strategic principles

Be cost conscious

Do everything possible to save money, both in your organisation itself and in your fundraising. There are two good reasons for this: you should be asking supporters only for what is really necessary; and as much as possible of what you raise should go to support the work of the organisation. Anything you can beg or borrow, any discounts you can negotiate, any ways of saving money – such as volunteers delivering newsletters by hand – will help you run a 'tight ship'.

Relate your fundraising effort to your priorities

If you have a grant from one source which accounts for 70 per cent of your annual income, you must invest time and effort in developing good working relations with that source, rather than simply complying with any reporting requirements that are a condition of the grant. There is a tendency for fundraisers to concentrate on finding new sources of money, and to spend a lot of time on fundraising efforts which are quite marginal to the overall budget. The amount of effort you put in should be proportionate to the importance of the income to your organisation – not just in securing the money in the first place, but also in ensuring that it continues.

Develop your fundraising over time

Unless you are part of a very large organisation with substantial resources to invest in fundraising, it is unrealistic to expect that, after paying all your costs, you will be able to generate substantial sums immediately. Successful fundraising takes time to develop. Your first 100 donors are the hardest to find; finding the next 100 is much easier. You need to invest time and energy in researching the possibilities, developing contacts, and building your organisation's credibility. You will also do better as you progress, learning from experience. So it is best to set quite modest (but still challenging) targets in the early years, and to raise these as time goes on. Setting too ambitious targets will only lead to disappointment.

Be cost-effective

All fundraising activity should adhere to some cost-effectiveness ratio. What is acceptable will depend on the technique being used. Selling Christmas cards will obviously cost more than soliciting a major donation or winning a contract with a public authority. Getting repeat support from donors who have already supported you is far more cost-effective than finding new supporters. But for most fundraising you should try to aim at a cost ratio of between 10 and 25 per cent of the amount raised. The subject of cost-effectiveness in fundraising is covered more fully in Section 3.2.

Avoid risk

Some fundraising is high risk. For example, if you are planning a gala evening at the local arts centre, you may have to pay for the venue and the performers, pay to publicise the event and lay on a reception. The expenditure for all this has to be committed before you see any money coming in. If nobody attends, you will lose a substantial sum. This does not mean that you should not run the event. If you think it will work, do it. But can you find some way of reducing your exposure to risk? Get a local business to sponsor the whole evening. Or find ten supporters each of whom will guarantee to bring along 20 people. Or include a cancellation clause in your contract with the venue, so that you have the option of calling it off if things look as if they are going badly.

Someone has to pay

Remember that for everything that your organisation does, somebody has to pay the cost. It may be the beneficiary paying for or contributing towards the service; it may be an external funder or sponsor; it may be volunteers giving their time and effort free of charge. Or it may be a mixture of all of these. If you are to continue the work you are doing, you need to continue raising the money to support it. That's your job as fundraiser.

3.2 Testing, evaluation and control

Keeping control of your fundraising is essential. Donors, supporters and board members will scrutinise your results periodically and will want to know why your results were what they were. High fundraising costs can be the worst kind of advertisement for new donors.

Fundraisers must know exactly what is going on and how they can improve their performance. Control of fundraising centres on the need to generate the maximum of funds while consuming the minimum of resources. Ideally your fundraising strategy should consist only of those elements which are going to be most cost-effective. The first issue then is to identify which fundraising methods are actually going to prove most cost-effective for you. This is where testing comes in. Demonstrating what is cost-effective requires some measure which relates the effectiveness of one form of fundraising against another. Finally, you have to keep track of what you are doing and compare your performance with what you achieved in the past and how others are doing.

Measuring fundraising effectiveness

You can use various measures of effectiveness. The most important is the **fundraising ratio**: the income raised by a particular fundraising method divided by the cost of doing it. Costs include any direct expenditure on the fundraising, plus the cost of your organising time as well as an appropriate share of the organisation's overheads (rent, electricity, telephone and management costs). This gives the best indication of the costs needed to raise a given amount of money. The higher the ratio, the better the method. Many organisations use a guide ratio of 5:1. This indicates that if all income is raised at this rate, 80 per cent will be available for the organisation and 20 per cent to meet the cost of fundraising. It is a useful measure since it relates directly to what appears in your accounts. The actual ratio you aim to achieve will very much depend on your organisation and cause. If you are starting up a fundraising programme, the ratio you achieve may well be lower than 5:1, as it is harder to raise new money than to get existing supporters to continue giving. If you have a large endowment generating an income, a well-established legacy income flow or large government grants, you would expect a much higher ratio.

An alternative approach is to use the **net income measure**. This is the amount you actually receive from your fundraising initiative. A mailing to a small group of people may have a good fundraising ratio, but produce very little money. On the other hand, a successful event may have higher fundraising costs but produce a substantial income. Which is better? It is only the net income you have raised which is available to support the work of your organisation. Simply concentrating on achieving a high ratio may produce only a small income, even though it has been raised very efficiently. But concentrating on net income only may lead to inefficiency and show your organisation as having a high fundraising cost in its annual accounts. The net income measure may be more appropriate in certain circumstances – for example, trading in shops and local activities – where it is deemed that local fundraising costs are not really within the control of the charity anyhow, and only the net income from the activity appears in the accounts. Organisations which use both measures to assess each part of their fundraising will be able to make a judgement as to the effectiveness of the fundraising and the value of the income generated to the organisation.

Measuring your success

The following are some ways of measuring the success of your fundraising:

- **The fundraising ratio.** The ratio between the income raised and the cost of raising it. Donors do not like to see a low fundraising ratio.
- **Net income raised.** The amount you actually raise after all the costs of fundraising. This is what is left for your organisation to spend – and you need to achieve your income targets for the year.
- **Response rate.** The percentage of those you approach who actually respond. The higher the rate, the more supporters you recruit.
- **Average donation.** The amount given on average by each donor. The total raised will depend on the response rate *and* the average donation.
- **Recruitment cost.** The cost of recruiting new supporters, which is then compared with the expected stream of income from these donors should they continue to support you.

When assessing your cost-effectiveness, always consider the value of the efforts put in by your volunteers. Although this does not show up in your costs, it is a resource, and you need to be sure you are using their time effectively. There may be other things that your volunteers could be doing that would raise much more money for you.

For mass fundraising campaigns, you are likely to need two other measurements. The first is the **response rate**. For mailings, house-to-house calls, collections and other fundraising methods where you are asking a large number of people to help, it is important to know how many of those people respond positively. The response rate is simply the numbers responding divided by the numbers approached.

This measurement will help you to decide whether your approach is better than last time: if you can improve on it, you will also increase the amount of funds you receive. But your success also depends upon the amount each respondent gives. This measure is the **average donation**. The two figures together can be satisfactorily combined into the yield, which is simply the money raised divided by the number approached.

In situations where you are more interested in getting people to support you over a number of years, you should consider the **cost per new donor**. For a mailing to people who have never supported you before (a 'cold mailing'), for example, the cost ratio is usually very high. This does not mean that the method has no value. Far from it: it means that you are measuring the present value of something that is expected to have a future benefit – perhaps yielding a stream of support over many years, and even a legacy on death. Ideally here you should also have a measure (or estimate) of the average lifetime value of a supporter. This can then be compared with the investment needed to find such a person. Even if you cannot accurately estimate their lifetime value, you should attempt to measure the effectiveness of this sort of fundraising on a cost-per-new-donor basis.

Controlling your fundraising effectiveness

Controlling the effectiveness of your fundraising requires two pieces of documentation. The first is a realistic plan. Control then centres on ensuring that you stick to your plan, that the costs are as budgeted, and that the sums which appear in your bank account are what you predicted they would be.

Clearly the first essential ingredient here is a budget both for your costs and the income you plan to generate. Fundraising budgets should be based on past experience as much as possible. If you do not have the experience, you should ask the advice of other fundraisers rather than expose your organisation to the risk of getting your predictions completely wrong. You should also be cautious in estimating the yield from new fundraising methods not tried by your organisation before, or perhaps test out the method before investing large sums in it.

Annual budgets should be broken down into monthly budgets (quarterly for smaller organisations) which take account of inflation, the growth of the organisation and the support it is attracting, new developments, and any seasonal factors (such as the Christmas period in Christian communities). Projected income and expenditure should be shown separately for each period. Results should be calculated for each period and compared against the original budget. If there is a problem, this should be discussed, including the reasons for the poorer-than-expected performance or the higher-than-budget costs, and action taken accordingly.

If you are running any large-scale operation, you will want to know whether there is some other organisation fundraising more effectively than you are. The easiest way to find out is to get hold of a copy of its annual accounts and do a rough comparison of its figures with yours.

CHAPTER 4

The sources

4.1 Individual donors

There is a wide range of possible donors who might be interested in supporting you. Each has different characteristics, different motivations, different preferences for how they might support you, and each will have a different pathway by which they can be reached and communicated with. It is important that you have a clear idea of who you plan to approach and how you propose to attract their support. Possibilities include:

- The **institutional donor** as well as the **individual**. Institutions might include Rotary Clubs and other similar philanthropic groups of local business people, schools and colleges, trade unions and so on. Individuals include anyone you can find or persuade to support you.
- The **less well-off people** as well as the **rich people**. It is often said that poor people are more generous. K. S. Gupta, who ran an eye hospital in Delhi, deliberately set out to target the professional classes rather than the seriously rich, as he felt that this would be more successful.
- **Young people** through to **elderly people**, and everyone in between. People have different interests at different stages in their lives. When they are young, they may be more concerned with the environment or human rights. When they are elderly, it may be medical causes (such as cancer) which will attract them more.
- Those who are members of **religious networks** (including especially Muslim, Christian and Hindu faith communities).
- Those that are **affected by the problem** or in some way involved with it to those who are only **mildly interested**. A parent of a disabled child will have a different interest in disability from a member of the public who has no such direct connection.
- The **general public** through to those with a particular perspective (such as lawyers, doctors, scientists or teachers).
- The **whole of the country** to those living in a **particular city** or **region**, especially those who live alongside the areas where you are working or where your organisation is based.
- **Family and friends** of existing supporters. Many people support charity simply because they are asked. And if they are asked by someone they know well, it becomes quite hard to refuse. You can use your existing supporters to bring in new supporters.

The more clearly you can specify who is likely to be interested in your cause, the more successful you will be in reaching them. To find out about who you might approach, you can:

- See who is already supporting you – perhaps also carrying out some simple market research to find out *why* they support you.

■ Test different audiences to see how they respond. You may find that a wider range of people are interested in supporting you, and for different reasons, than you had at first thought.

The different ways of giving

There are not only different audiences, but also different methods of obtaining people's support. A donor can support you by:

■ Giving a **one-off donation**. This type of support is welcome, but you should remember that there is a cost involved in getting it, which can at times even outweigh its value. What you want are donors who are . . .

■ Giving **continuing support** on a regular basis, perhaps through some type of formal commitment, such as a membership scheme. A useful measure of your effectiveness as a fundraiser is to compare the total support you will receive from a donor while they continue to give to you with the cost of obtaining that donor in the first place and then keeping in touch with them.

■ Making a **major gift** to an appeal or towards a project. Your aim is to encourage people to give more as well as more frequently.

■ Leaving a **legacy** to you when they die. This is the only form of giving that does not cost the donor anything, as it is paid not by the donor but from the donor's estate.

■ Making a **gift in kind**. This can be anything you need, from offering you office space to giving you items to sell at a charity auction.

■ **Purchasing a gift item** (such as greetings cards) or promotional material (such as T-shirts or posters).

■ Supporting an NGO **fundraising event**. There are many types of event which can be used to raise money successfully.

■ Participating in **lotteries** and **raffles**, where a supporter purchases a chance to win a prize (although some organisations are reluctant to encourage gambling for ideological or religious reasons).

■ Raising money from **family** and **friends**. This is the basis on which events such as sponsored walks are organised.

■ Giving their time as a **volunteer** to help you (from simple administrative tasks, delivering newsletters and helping to organise fundraising activities, through to assisting in the organisation's core activity). Many organisations benefit very substantially from the time and effort put in by their volunteers – and mobilising this support can often be more important than the fundraising.

Why people give

If you understand why people may want to give, it makes it easier to gain their support. However, it is difficult to make generalisations about why people give. The cause you are addressing and the sort of organisation you are will affect the motivation. Possible reasons for giving include:

■ **Concern**. This is probably the single most important reason why people want to give. A person may be worried about the environment, whether this is the increasing levels of pollution in cities or the continuing destruction of the countryside and the natural habitat. A parent may be horrified by sexual harassment of children and want to make some kind of response. An individual may see the pitiful faces of starving refugee children on the television news and want to make a donation. Giving offers people the opportunity to do something significant for a cause about which they are concerned.

- **Duty.** This probably comes a strong second as a motive for giving: the idea that we are rich and they are poor – or the feeling that life has been good to us, we who have a house, a job, an income and a comfortable life. People may want to respond to their good fortune with some charitable act (giving their money or their time). Many religions promote the concept of charity. Some even recommend that their members allocate a certain share of their income for this.
- **Guilt.** This encourages people to give in the hope that the problem (and you) will go away. But if people give out of a sense of guilt rather than duty, it is unlikely to lead to any long-term involvement with your organisation.
- **Personal experience.** People who have themselves experienced cancer, heart disease or some other illness, or whose families have been affected, are likely to be especially motivated to give to these causes. Likewise, people who have children at school will want to support the school or anything that helps their child's education. All research indicates that personal connection with the cause is one of the most powerful motivations for giving.
- **Personal benefit.** Many people like the status or recognition that comes when their generosity is publicised. They may also like to meet prominent people associated with your organisation. If social ambition and access to celebrities are important to people, then giving to charity can be one way for them to achieve these objectives.
- **They are asked.** The main reason for most people *not* giving is that they have never been asked! Research demonstrates this again and again. Your job as a fundraiser is to give people the opportunity to give.
- **Peer pressure.** If people know that their friends and colleagues are giving and that they have not yet given, or if friends and colleagues are asking them to give, this can make it harder to refuse. One way of exploiting this is to get people who have already given to you to ask all their colleagues and contacts to contribute.
- **Tax**, and in particular the ability to save tax on gifts made for charitable purposes. Tax is not usually the prime motivator for giving, but can be an important factor in encouraging people to give and to give more generously. The tax concessions that are available on donations to NGOs vary from country to country.

It is important for you to understand why people want to give, and more specifically why the particular person you are approaching might be interested in giving to your organisation. This requires an understanding of human psychology, but also some good research before you approach individuals for support. This will then enable you to tailor your message and create an approach which makes it much harder for the person to refuse.

It is equally important to understand why people might *not* be interested in giving. Reasons might include: they are just not interested in your organisation and what it stands for; or they may have recently given to a similar cause. Bad publicity, high administration costs or a feeling that little of what they give will actually reach the intended beneficiaries can also make people reluctant to give. The problem may be so big that it appears hard to make any impact. People may feel that it is the government's job to do something, and that the matter should not be left to private charity. And then there is the fact that while some people are by nature very generous, others will always be looking for an excuse not to give.

Your Concern is Our Concern . . .

Share your concern for the socially and economically deprived with us. And we'll make it possible for you to reach out and touch their lives and futures.

You can participate in any one of our fundraising schemes. Or you can simply contribute your skills, expertise or even your spare time.

Every little bit counts. Because every little contribution adds up to make a big difference. Here are some examples of how a small amount can amount to a changed life:

- Only Rs300 per month provides complete day-care for a young child, which includes nutrition, health care and education.
- Rs1,200 can educate a child for a whole year.
- Rs1,500 a year pays the fees of a young man or woman's vocational training.
- Rs180 sponsors the education and training of a mentally disabled person for a month.

What is most precious to us is not the size of your contribution, but the start of your involvement with our cause. We see it as the start of a lifetime of changing our concerns into opportunities.

Source: leaflet produced by Concern India Foundation

Getting in touch

To be successful in getting money, you need to do six things:

1. **Identify likely supporters**, then . . .
2. **Create the right message** that is likely to appeal to them, and then . . .
3. **Direct that message** to that person, and . . .
4. **Ask for their support**, and . . .
5. Provide them with an **easy way of making a donation**, and . . .
6. Support your fundraising effort with **good public relations**.

Fundraising is that simple!

The right people are those who fit the picture you have constructed of your potential supporter, whose background and motivations make it likely they will want to support your cause. Careful thinking, with possibly some simple research, will help you identify such people and their characteristics.

The right message is the one (although there may be several) that builds on the motivation of the potential donor, starts from their understanding of the cause, and takes account of people's natural hesitations or the reasons they might have for not giving. A good understanding of your cause and why it might appeal to people will help; and you might want to undertake simple market research to refine your message.

Equally importantly, you will need to find an easy way of reaching your target audience. At the same time as you define your target audience, you should also define a way of reaching it. For example, if senior business people are your target, there are all sorts of channels you can employ to reach them, including using the business press, obtaining the addresses of major businesses and writing to them, working through Rotary Clubs, Chambers of Commerce and other business associations, using businessmen to invite other businessmen to small receptions where you can give a presentation, or asking them to ask their colleagues directly for support.

You also need to make it easy for them to give. Their interest may be aroused, but if they do not know how to give or where to send a donation, they may end up not giving. For example, you could provide potential donors with your address and contact details, pledge forms, bank details so that they can transfer money to you, or stamped and addressed reply envelopes in which to send you their donation.

And finally, people will be more likely to support you if they have already heard about your organisation and its work, and about the importance of the need you are addressing. This is where public relations come in. It is often said that good PR is an essential ingredient of successful fundraising. So you need to spend some of your effort promoting your organisation and publicising your work – see Section 8.8 for advice on this.

Some tips for PR

- Keep a **list of media people** to whom you can send your promotional material.
- **Make friends with journalists**, including those on local papers and radio, and keep them in touch with what you are doing.
- **When you have a 'success', publicise it** by sending out a press release. Follow this up with a phone call to encourage journalists' interest further.
- **Use your beneficiaries to talk about your work**, either through interviews or by quoting them in your press releases.
- **Issue a press release with your annual report**, and try to get publicity for it.
- **When you win a substantial grant**, or if you get support from a government body or from an important company, try to get publicity for this. You might be able to get the cheque handover photographed.
- **Use 'stunts' to generate PR**, especially those that illustrate the need you are addressing or the support that your cause is attracting. A stunt is an event specifically designed to attract publicity – for example, going on hunger strike to draw attention to poverty or starvation, or throwing money into a crowd to protest against corruption.
- **When you produce and publish research, try to get a feature written about it** to coincide with publication. Or find a way of making it newsworthy so that journalists will want to cover it, and then issue a press release highlighting its news value.

The chart below is adapted from the *Charity Household Survey* carried out in the UK. It shows how people in Britain rate the various causes that they might be presented with. The higher the number, the greater the importance they give to that cause. In the UK, causes which relate to helping people – including children and people with handicaps and disabilities – appear to rate the highest. Arts, education and the environment are far less popular.

Recent studies in India and Singapore show similarities and differences. According to a study conducted by Invest India in 2007, disaster relief and education were the most popular causes among donors, while HIV/AIDS was the least popular. For Singapore, the 2008 Individual Giving Survey published by the National Volunteer and Philanthropy Centre shows religious organisations as the most popular cause (63 per cent), followed by social services (35 per cent), health (31 per cent) and education (27 per cent). The least popular causes were environment/animals (5 per cent), sport (4 per cent), heritage (1 per cent) and arts and culture (1 per cent).

The culture and circumstances of countries will of course be different, but in every country there are likely to be causes that generate an extremely positive response and causes that are less attractive. The less attractive the cause, the more important it is to target your appeal at those more likely to support it.

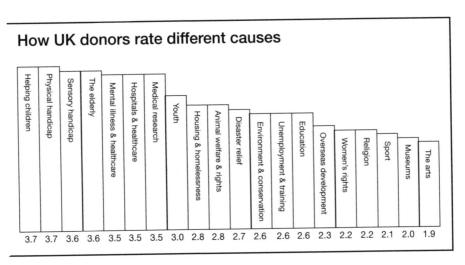

How UK donors rate different causes

Helping children	Physical handicap	Sensory handicap	The elderly	Mental illness & healthcare	Hospitals & healthcare	Medical research	Youth	Housing & homelessness	Animal welfare & rights	Disaster relief	Environment & conservation	Unemployment & training	Education	Overseas development	Women's rights	Religion	Sport	Museums	The arts
3.7	3.7	3.6	3.6	3.5	3.5	3.5	3.0	2.8	2.8	2.7	2.6	2.6	2.6	2.3	2.2	2.2	2.1	2.0	1.9

Six good ideas when fundraising from individuals

1. When approaching individuals, always try to identify precisely **how much money you need to raise,** and then show them how their contribution can play an important part in your plans. Don't suggest something so big that it seems unattainable, but try to make people feel proud to have done something significant to help you.

2. In making the appeal, try to **express the need in human terms**. Give graphic images of the problem and how your work actually helps individuals. Try to avoid giving abstract statistics unless you are using these to emphasise the points you are making. It is said that:

- One hungry person next door to you is equivalent to . . .
- One hundred hungry people in a nearby town, who are equivalent to . . .
- Ten million hungry people in some far-off country.

The nearer you make people feel to the problem and to how it connects with their concerns, the more successful you will be. If they feel that by helping you they are helping to solve a real person's problem, they will be much more likely to give than if asked to support a general cause. One good example of this is KIVA, which is a website linking donors directly with individuals in developing countries who need a loan to help them develop a business which will get them out of poverty. You lend to one specific individual to help them with one specific enterprise. Find out more at www.kiva.org

3. **Ask for exactly what you want**. Prospective donors will not know the size of the contribution that they are expected to make. They don't want to give too little (and thus be seen as mean), and they don't want to give too much (and thus feel exploited). One way of overcoming this is to suggest a range of levels for a donation, and to ask the donor to choose their own level. Sometimes you can show what the different amounts can achieve, linking the amount to outputs (for example, to feed or educate one child for one year) or to outcomes (for example, to redeem one child from bonded labour and return him or her home).

4. **Give examples of success**. This will help people understand what you are doing and how their money will be used to bring about real change. For example, UnLtd India makes grants to social entrepreneurs to help them turn their ideas into successful organisations. Showing how this helped ToyBank, started by two young women to collect donated toys from middle-class families and manufacturers and distribute them to children in need, or Reality Tours, started by two young men to develop tours of Dharavi, Asia's largest slum, will be far better than talking generally about the idea of making small grants to social entrepreneurs.

5. **Repeat the message** that you need their help, and that with their help you can achieve something. Repetition reinforces your message. It is good communication practice to:

- Tell them what you are proposing to tell them. Then . . .
- Tell them. Then . . .
- Tell them what you have just told them.

6. **Target your appeal as carefully as you can**, and make your message as personal and as relevant as possible to the prospective donor. If you are approaching existing supporters, then refer to their generous support in the past and what you have been able to achieve with it. If you are approaching doctors, tell them about your work from a medical perspective. If you are approaching local people, show the local benefits that will be achieved by your work. The more closely you target your message, the more successful you will be. People will feel that you are speaking to them personally, and they will respond far better when you do this. In planning your fundraising, you will have already identified those categories of people who are more likely to want to support you.

Getting started

It is far easier to develop donations income from a base of existing supporters than it is to start from scratch. But many organisations are in the position of having no existing donors. If that is the case for you, then what can you do? Here are some possibilities:

1. **Produce a simple leaflet** that explains your work and shows that you are looking for money. This should have a reply coupon with space for anyone interested to fill in their name and address so that you can include them on your database. To find out their interests, you could ask them to tick a number of boxes (these could show that they are interested in, say, giving money, becoming a member, or volunteering their time). This leaflet need not be anything more than a letter-sized sheet of paper (A4) printed in two colours and folded to make four pages. Try to include photographs of the organisation at work.

2. Get **press coverage**. This might be a feature article about your organisation in a newspaper or a magazine, but make sure that it includes a website URL so that people can find out more, or a reply address to which anyone who is interested can write.

3. Think about **exhibiting** at a fair. At the Zimbabwe International Book Fair, various library development projects, women's writing workshops and other projects took stands. This gave them an opportunity to create interest and win support. If you do this, you will need to have an interesting display and leaflets about your work that people can take away. The stand should be staffed by friendly people who are prepared to enter actively into discussion with visitors and try to capture their interest. Have a box for people to leave their business cards, and you can then add them to your mailing list.

4. Find an appropriate **mailing** list to which you could send a simple appeal – for example, your leaflet and a short covering letter could be sent to doctors and health workers. The APD, a disabled people's organisation in Bangalore, mailed the membership of the Bangalore Club and received a surprisingly high response rate and some quite large donations.

5. Think about **house-to-house collecting**. Remember that most people say that they don't give because they haven't been asked. House-to-house solicitation gives you an opportunity to ask, and also ensures that your organisation and its work get known locally. Have some form of **membership scheme** so that you can enrol those who are interested. This personal approach will always work better than a written appeal, but obviously takes much more time and effort. You need to strike a balance between ease and effectiveness.

6. And once you start recruiting donors, **try to keep them** for life. Getting the most from your donors and supporters is covered in more detail in Section 7.4. And then beyond the end of their life – getting legacies is covered in Section 6.7.

4.2 Government grants

Government funding includes:

- Being funded **nationally** by central government.
- Being funded **regionally** or **locally** by regional or local government.

For some organisations government funding is the mainstay of their work. For others it is marginal or just one of several sources.

The scale of the funds available from government sources is potentially extremely large, and is likely to increase steadily as government moves away from providing services directly to the purchase of services from another body (often under some form of contract), which could include anything from the distribution of condoms to the running of village health centres. Government working in partnership with NGOs to provide services has now become an accepted mechanism in many countries for the delivery of a wide range of services, including social welfare programmes, environmental conservation, community development and refugee relief.

Voluntary organisations as part of civil society

The availability of government funding for voluntary organisations depends in part on the relationship between the two parties:

- Government may see voluntary organisations as a **threat**, since some exist to expose need and failings in society and to campaign for change. As such, their objectives may run counter to those of the government.
- Government may see voluntary organisations as a **mechanism for delivering services efficiently**, with the added benefit that they might be able to draw in outside money and mobilise volunteers. As such, the voluntary sector may become a valued partner, with government seeking to create an environment where non-governmental organisations and community-based organisations are able to thrive.
- Voluntary organisations may be seen as an important **part of a civil society**, whether they criticise the failings of government or act as a delivery partner. In India the strengthening of local democracy through the panchayati raj reforms which encouraged organisation at the village and community level and the establishment of a government-voluntary sector forum at national level are both manifestations of this civil society dimension.

Often the relationship between the two sides is complex, and perhaps contains elements of all these three approaches.

National government

National government will relate largely to national organisations, and will do this in a number of ways:

- It may want to offer funding to support **national organisations** in dealing with issues of concern: for example, population, environment, rural development, watershed management. In this way it will benefit from the energy and ideas that voluntary organisations will bring to discussions on policy.
- It may wish to bring voluntary organisations into **policy formation** – to draw on their expertise and their experience of mobilising people and creating change.
- It may seek to deliver **national development programmes** using the voluntary organisation to undertake the delivery – as a matter of expediency (because the structure is there) or of efficiency (because they are more cost-effective).

Most governments in poor countries are strapped for cash and find it hard to run educational, health, welfare and environmental programmes without some form of international support. But the government as a whole, and specific departments and ministries, is responsible for these matters and does have money available through the annual budget allocations, which include donor-provided assistance as well as local taxation, and it should be encouraged to face up to its responsibilities; it should be offered the possibility of investing in 'solutions' to the problems people face.

Fundraising from government requires persistence, pressure, lobbying, the involvement of local MPs – who can ask questions in parliament and use their influence to get financial support for their communities – and even the use of the law. But with persistence, you can achieve results. For example, a Delhi-based activist, M. C. Mehta, went to court and got a judgment that the air pollution by public service vehicles was an unacceptable removal of a fundamental right to clean air, with the consequence that the city authority had to oversee the replacement of diesel and petrol engines in these vehicles with engines that used environmentally friendly compressed natural gas.

In some countries, organisations are reluctant to become associated with government because it raises issues of corruption and co-option, or because of mistrust, or possibly because they have never bothered to think about the opportunities. Your concerns might be valid, but you should set them alongside the idea that working *with* government is one way of creating change.

Government grants: five steps to success

1. Do your research to find out current government interests and priorities, and then refine your project idea so that it can be presented in a way that matches these.
2. Find out application procedures and deadlines. This can require advance planning of at least one year.
3. Write and submit a good proposal.
4. Lobby and get as much publicity as you can, to try to influence the decision.
5. Achieve success – and if and when you do succeed, see this as a starting point for a long-term partnership.

Local government

Local authorities will be responsible for the delivery of a wide range of local services, whether at regional, city or village level. The functions for which local and regional government is responsible will vary from country to country, but are likely to include health, education, social services, recreation and leisure services, transport and housing.

It is within the areas of their own particular responsibilities that local authorities are most likely to make grants, for many of the same reasons that national government supports voluntary organisations. Giving support may also provide good publicity for government and a feeling 'that something is being done' about an issue of public concern.

Support might be given in a number of ways, including:

■ **A grant.** The local authority may have an established programme of offering grants to voluntary organisations.

- **A fee for a service** provided under a contract. Here the money is related to the work done – work for which the local authority is responsible – where it has been deemed more cost-effective to pay a voluntary organisation to undertake the programme.
- The giving of **services** or **support in kind**. Local authorities can assist in many ways, for example through the provision of premises or property.
- Some form of **partnership** where a voluntary service is run alongside a statutory service, adding to it or complementing it: for example, a cultural education pro-gramme for tribal minorities provided alongside the mainstream curriculum education in schools.

The five stages of a successful application

The process of getting a government grant is often slow and extremely tortuous. It can take years (or longer) to succeed. The outcome can depend on a whole range of factors, some of which will be outside your control, such as the time of year, the political climate and the state of the economy. To get a grant, you will probably need to go through the following stages:

1. Research

- Research the **structure and responsibilities** of government. You need to know who is responsible for what and how decisions are made before planning your approach.
- Find out about **current policies and priorities**, and how your work can advance their agenda. Look at official policy, published reports, and statements made by government and politicians on particular issues.
- Find out what's currently on offer and what sort of **funding** has been made to voluntary organisations in previous years. Identify and match possible funding programmes with aspects of your organisation's work. In some countries, directories of government funding are produced. You can also talk to councils of NGOs and other umbrella organisations operating in your sector.
- Find out what, if any, **links** you have had previously with any government bodies, and whether any of your trustees or members have good personal contacts with any decision-makers.

Approach potential funders not just to tell them what you are doing and what support you are looking for, but also to find out about their requirements and discuss how you might be able to meet their objectives cost-effectively.

2. Application procedures and deadlines

- Find out about the **application procedure**. You need to find out the deadlines for when you can apply (there may be an annual cycle for the submission of applications, and if you miss the deadline you will have to wait until the next year), and how to apply (whether there is an application form, what information you will need to supply, how the work has to be evaluated, and what referees you will need).
- Find out **who is responsible** for making the decision, and get to know as much as you can about how they operate and how they might be influenced.

3. Submit your proposal

- Write a **confident and well-argued** proposal in the format that is required.
- Be as **factual** as you can.
- Show that you will be effective and efficient in the use of their money – they are publicly accountable to see that it is well spent.

Advice on writing an effective fundraising proposal is given in Section 8.2.

4. Lobbying and publicity

- Back up your application with **lobbying**. Government and politicians respond to pressure. Make sure that everyone important knows about your application and the benefits that it will bring. Get experts and prominent people on your side. Try to reach everyone who will play a part in coming to a decision on your application.
- Get **media coverage** for your organisation, its work and the ideas behind your proposal.

5. Say thank you

- If you succeed in getting support, then **thank** as enthusiastically as you can everyone who was involved in the decision and has helped you in any way.
- Give them as much **good publicity** as possible for the support that they have given you.
- **Report back** regularly, and be accountable for the money you are spending. Sometimes this will be specified as a condition of the grant.
- If you fail to get support, **don't give up.** Think about how you might approach them next time, and what you could do to improve your chances of success.

Four good ideas for statutory funding

1. Don't be shy about **making friends** and chatting up the people who will be making the decision on your application. But make sure you chat up the right people, which are those who can help you or can bring influence to bear on the decision. Who you know (and what they know about you) can be extremely important.

2. Consider whether it is a useful ploy to ask for **funding on a matched basis** – that if they support you, then you will find another funder to contribute a proportion of the total you need. The matched sum could even come from your own organisation out of its existing resources or against the value of the volunteer time that is being put in. Matched funding can be an attractive proposition to many funding bodies.

3. Make sure your applications are **relevant to funders.** Link them to themes they are currently interested in and concerned about, and show them how your work will help solve *their* problem. Find out their agreed priorities and show how your work fits in with these. Show how cost-effective you are in doing the work – you may be able to show that they can achieve much more by working with you than by going it alone. They are particularly interested in performance figures – how much work you will do for how much money. But remember that cost-effectiveness is not the only criterion. The quality of your work is also important.

4. Publicity is important. Government departments and agencies are sensitive to political pressures. So if you can, mobilise public and media support to help your cause. But beware of appearing to be applying extreme pressure through your media coverage, as government can sometimes react against it rather than respond to it.

4.3 International grant aid and development funding

International grant aid falls into several categories:

- Support from overseas government aid programmes. This is known as bilateral aid – country-to-country aid programmes, such as USAID and the DFID overseas aid programme.
- Support from international agencies such as the United Nations, the World Bank and the European Union. This is known as **multilateral aid**.
- Support from **international development agencies** (such as ActionAid, Oxfam, Care, PLAN and WorldVision) who raise money in the North to fund development programmes in the South. Sometimes these agencies obtain bilateral or multilateral aid; sometimes they fund their own directly implemented programmes; sometimes they work in partnership with local NGOs they are funding.

Many Southern countries receive considerable amounts of foreign funding, which can be the largest single source of funding for development. The World Summit on Sustainable Development (Johannesburg 2002) and the G8 Summit in Edinburgh (2005) both highlighted the importance of increasing the flow of overseas aid in order to eradicate poverty and narrow the differential between the rich and the poor countries of the world. In addition, the debt relief programme requires highly indebted countries whose debts are being forgiven to allocate the benefits to health, education and welfare programmes, which provides an additional source of funding for development. In order to gain access to this source of money, you need to:

- Understand the **issues**.
- Check whether there are any **legal requirements** necessary for you to receive foreign funds (e.g. registration as a charitable organisation locally, or getting permission to receive foreign funding), and ensure that you meet such conditions.
- **Research** what is available and for what purposes, and whether it is available directly to NGOs on application or whether it is channelled through government or some other agency. You will also want to find out about the application procedures, whether counterpart funding is required, and any other strings that may be attached.
- Develop **contact** with the grants officer or field officer who will be assessing your application. If you are intending to apply for a major sum, then allow a lot of time to build the relationship and to enable them to visit you to see your work.
- **Apply** in the required way.

Some questions to ask when considering international funding

■ What **criteria** seem to be used in deciding which countries and regions get support?

■ What **forums** are there in your own country for discussing development priorities?

■ What links are there between development and anti-poverty work in the North and the work being supported in the South? And are these links all one way?

■ What is the **gender and ethnic balance** of the donor agency's board and staff?

■ If the donor agency has representatives and **staff in your country,** where do they come from? And is there a decision-making board in your country to decide priorities and grants? And if there isn't, why not?

Questions like these are not often asked, but they should be. Besides these questions, ask for a copy of the agency's latest annual report and funding criteria. Do you fit? Do you want to fit? Too many people just see that money is available and apply for it. Such questions and the dialogue that might ensue could become an important step towards what is grandly called a 'partnership'.

Some of these issues are discussed in *New Internationalist*, a magazine dealing with global aid issues on a regular basis and in a readable way. This is available from Tower House, Lathkill Street, Market Harborough LE16 9EF, UK; tel 01858 438896; email newint@subscription.co.uk; website www.newint.org

Source: Murray Culshaw, former Director of Oxfam India.

Issues in international funding

The primary focus of this book is on the generation of national resources from governmental bodies, charitable foundations, the corporate sector and the general public (all discussed in the following sections). However, while pursuing and developing national resources, it is important to understand how international support might either assist or undermine your attempts to raise support nationally. If the key issues are understood, international assistance could make a real input into your overall funding strategy. There are also some fundamental questions to ask yourself before you start:

1. Does the funding come with a political agenda?

'Political' in this context refers to aid given by governments to other countries very often under the banner of 'helping the world's poorest'. Allocation is often decided by a geopolitical agenda. The two countries which for a long time have been receiving the largest percentage of the US government's international aid are Israel and Egypt, and more recently Iraq and Afghanistan – not because they are the poorest countries in the world, for very clearly they are not, but because of the strategic interests of the USA in the region. On the other hand, the Scandinavian countries of Norway, Sweden, Finland and Denmark are generally considered to be the least political with regard to aid allocations. Whether or not there are strong geopolitical priorities, humanitarian concerns sometimes impinge on the consciousness of governments, particularly where there is public pressure through media reports and from lobbying groups. An example of this is the large amount of money channelled into the Horn of Africa during the famine years of the mid-1980s and into Rwanda in 1993–94 as a result of the sufferings of millions in the conflict.

There is another factor, which is difficult to prove but appears to be the case, that governments and NGOs in 'receiving' countries do not *invite* assistance from the economically stronger countries, but are on the receiving end of *offers* of assistance. And with the offers come conditions: trade linked to aid, pressure to vote in a certain way in a United Nations debate, to 'open up' the economy, to receive an expert or to work in a particular way.

Support given by the international nongovernmental donor agency system is perceived to be – and is – much less political, being based more on humanitarian concerns. But the situation is not quite that simple, as agencies have other influences that affect their decision taking. They naturally reflect the attitudes and ideologies of their founders, their current leaders and their supporting public – and strong links to countries with their 'colonial past' are common. Support to predominantly Christian groups in particular countries (whether Catholic, Protestant or Evangelical) is another example of the influence of 'mandates'. And with large-scale disaster and emergency aid, which a number of international NGOs specialise in, their own funds (raised from the public) will often be supplemented by government funds, as the agencies may represent the most effective way for a government to deliver its support.

Remember too that almost all the international NGOs set policies, establish procedures and make decisions in their home country, or on the advice of the representatives they have placed in 'receiving' countries. There is usually little or no public discussion in the countries they have decided to assist on what the priorities and approaches for spending the money should be.

International aid and development funding is complex. It is important that you understand how it works – and what conditions are attached – before proceeding. This means asking questions – and getting answers that satisfy you.

2. Do you want to be supported by overseas funding?

You may feel that your country should try to support its own development rather than rely on outsiders, and that you should be trying to find ways of mobilising local energies and resources. The receipt of large sums of overseas funding can limit your local fundraising work – because overseas funding may be simpler to obtain, you may not put enough energy into developing local fundraising, and this may create a long-term dependency. The relatively easy availability of large amounts of money from overseas can also mean that you grow too large and create an unsustainable organisation. International donors are not based in your country, and their interests or geographical focus may change rather more quickly than you might imagine. Their funds may be readily available now, but might not continue to be available into the future. What will you do then?

Another problem is that the relationship is almost private. You get the money from them and do the work – and hopefully some people benefit. That's it. But if you fundraise in your own country, then you have to go out to the public, raise public awareness of the problems and the need for change, and explain the issues and why things remain as they are, before you can get support. This public education and mobilisation of the public is important if you are to build real pressure for change in your own country.

For example, some years ago I was at the South Asian Coalition on Child Servitude (SACCS), one of the leading campaigners in India against child-slave labour. They were largely funded by a grant from Scandinavia, and were not actively seeking support from within India, and had no membership or supporter scheme (at that time). You might ask yourself if it was possible to end child labour in India without the support of the Indian middle classes and the Indian media. Fundraising within India would facilitate both of these.

3. Competition with Northern NGOs

Another issue is the changing way in which overseas funding is being delivered. Many of the large international donors have regionalised their giving, and now make funds available through regional or country offices direct to NGOs in those regions and countries. Many of the larger international development agencies have regionalised their own structures in response to this. They have established their own regional and country offices and encouraged them to raise money in their country and region.

These Northern development agencies have now placed themselves in direct competition for funds from international sources with indigenous Southern NGOs, and because they are known and trusted by international donors, they will have a much better chance of getting the money. This poses a challenge for Southern NGOs to create a convincing case that the funding should go directly to Southern NGOs (rather than to branches of Northern NGOs) and to develop their organisational credibility and their fundraising skills in order to achieve this.

The issues of dependency and sustainability

These issues should be discussed carefully. Here are some possible responses:

- Build into your development plan a strong element of **public communications and fundraising.** This will not only raise money, but it will also generate public support for what you are trying to do.
- Ask the donor agency to **invest in your fundraising strategy** over a number of years, either to help you become less dependent by diversifying your sources of income, or as part of an agreed phase-out strategy.
- Get the donor agency to support **'capital' developments** as well as paying for the running costs. This way, there will be something left when the money runs out.
- Suggest the idea of **matching funding** for your local fundraising efforts. On the other hand, international aid money is there, and it can become an important component of the funding of your work.

Multilateral aid

This is mainly the aid channelled through UN agencies (see table). It is called multilateral because many governments provide the money for these programmes. The agencies may also be looking for bilateral funding from particular countries for specific projects they want to run.

Usually multilateral aid is used to fund government-run programmes. But increasingly the agencies are looking to cooperate with NGOs. An NGO may be able to get funding from one of the agencies, either directly or channelled through the national government.

Approaching an international agency can be very time-consuming. If you are interested in exploring the possibility, make enquiries by visiting or sending a short letter to the agency that is working in your field of interest (such as WHO for health matters, FAO for agricultural matters, UNESCO for literacy and so on – see table for list of UN agencies and their fields of work). The agency may well have an office in your country; you can obtain the address from the telephone directory for your capital city. If the agency doesn't have an office, then approach the UNDP, which may serve as the focal point for all UN agencies working in your country.

Each agency has its own particular relationship with the NGO community. For example, UNHCR on the whole has a very positive relationship because of the need for active cooperation in refugee situations; whereas at the opposite end of the spectrum, the World Bank has a more complex relationship because many NGOs are critical of the Bank's economic and development policies, and are often fighting the consequences of structural adjustment policies. So before you start, do some homework. Find out about programmes in your own country, visit some of the projects that have been supported, and meet NGO people who know something of the work being done. Once you know the background, you can decide whether it is worth proceeding.

Some United Nations agencies

Food and Agriculture Organisation (FAO) promotes farming, forestry, fisheries, water and land management and rural development. FAO, via della Terme di Caracalla, 00153 Rome, Italy (www.fao.org).

International Labour Organisation (ILO) supports projects that promote income generation for the rural poor, vocational training and manpower development. ILO, route des Morillons 4, CH-1211 Geneva 22, Switzerland (www.ilo.org).

Joint United Nations Programme on HIV/AIDS (UNAIDS) leads and supports a response aimed at preventing the transmission of HIV, providing care and support, reducing the vulnerability of individuals and communities to HIV/AIDS, and alleviating the impact of the epidemic. UNAIDS, 20 avenue Appia, CH-1211 Geneva 27, Switzerland (www.unaids.org).

United Nations Children's Fund (UNICEF) supports formal and non-formal education programmes, and maternal and child health programmes. UNICEF, 125 Maiden Lane, New York NY 10038, USA (www.unicef.org).

United Nations Development Fund for Women (UNIFEM) provides financial and technical assistance to innovative programmes and strategies that promote women's human rights, political participation and economic security. UNIFEM, 304 East 45th Street, 15th Floor, New York NY 10017, USA (www.unifem.org).

United Nations Development Programme (UNDP) supports rural development and infrastructure projects. UNDP, 1 United Nations Plaza, New York NY 10017, USA (www.undp.org).

United Nations Educational and Scientific Cooperation Organisation (UNESCO) promotes education, science and culture, and supports literacy, libraries, and educational and cultural development. UNESCO, 7 place de Fontenoy, F-75700 Paris, France (www.unesco.org).

United Nations Environment Programme (UNEP) encourages caring for the environment, including promoting the Billion Trees campaign and the Climate Neutral Network. UNEP, United Nations Avenue, Gigiri PO Box 30552, 00100 Nairobi, Kenya (www.unep.org).

United Nations Population Fund (UNFPA) supports family planning, maternal and child health, and population policy. UNFPA, 220 East 42nd Street, New York, NY 10017, USA (www.unfpa.org).

United Nations High Commissioner for Refugees (UNHCR) is responsible for welfare and aid to refugees. UNHCR, Case Postale 2500, CH-1211 Geneva 2 Depot, Switzerland (www.unhcr.ch).

World Bank is the major institution channelling loans for development. The small grants programme supports policy analysis, dissemination, publications and conferences. World Bank, 1818, H Street NW, Washington DC 20433, USA (www.worldbank.org).

World Food Programme runs food for work projects and provides food to vulnerable groups. World Food Programme, via C G Viola 68, Parco dei Medici 001458 Rome, Italy (www.wfp.org).

World Health Organisation (WHO) promotes health development and prevention work. WHO, avenue Appia, CH-1211 Geneva, Switzerland (www.who.int/en/).

These are some of the main agencies of the United Nations making support available for development work. They work largely through national governments, but some operate grants funds which support NGO work.

Overseas government aid programmes

Most Northern governments make aid available to the developing world. The suggested norm is 0.5 per cent of gross national product. Most countries fall well below this norm, although the most generous country per capita is Norway. The most significant aid giver is USAID, the aid agency of the United States government – although recent political changes in the US and the ending of the Cold War are bringing into question the purpose, direction, objectives and scale of US aid.

The UK Overseas Aid Programme

The priorities are to:

- Eradicate extreme poverty and hunger
- Achieve universal primary education
- Promote gender equality and empower women
- Reduce child mortality
- Improve maternal health
- Combat HIV/AIDS, malaria and other diseases
- Ensure environmental sustainability
- Develop a global partnership for development.

Assistance is concentrated in the poorest countries of sub-Saharan Africa and Asia, with poverty reduction and sustainable development in middle-income countries, including those in Latin America and eastern Europe, also supported. Full details of the specific grant programmes are available on DFID's website (www.dfid.gov.uk).

Government aid is:

- Often **government to government**, where all aid is routed through the national government. An NGO wanting to receive funding will have to get approval from its national government.
- Sometimes **tied to trade**, particularly in the case of major infrastructure projects.

A recent trend is to acknowledge that problems can only be solved with the participation of the people involved. This means that mechanisms for developing programmes in partnership with local people need to be designed; and this in turn means that government agencies need to work closely with NGOs and people's organisations, which means developing partnerships, supporting empowerment, economic development programmes and so on.

A second trend is to make support available directly to NGOs. This can be done in one of four ways:

- As part of the government's aid programme. For example, much more direct support for the UK's India programme is planned by the Department for International Development, which has moved the administration of this part of its aid programme from London to New Delhi. You need to find out the geographical focus of the programme (in India, DFID works only in selected states), the priority areas and how the support is made available.
- Through major foreign NGOs acting on an agency basis. For example, the UK government might work through Oxfam or Save the Children to channel disaster relief to tsunami areas or Somalia. Sometimes these NGOs will want to work with other agencies to implement their disaster relief programme. If you feel that you have a role to play, make contact with the country office of the particular agency.
- Through foreign NGOs co-funding the projects, with the government providing anything from half to all of the funds. If you are to access these funds, you will need

to do it via a partnership with an NGO in the donor country. The first step is to find an NGO which is prepared to work with you.

■ Through small grants schemes run through the embassy. The British High Commission in New Delhi and the Deputy High Commission in Bombay both make small grants to voluntary projects. This helps keep staff in touch with what's happening in society, as well as providing opportunities for good publicity and photo calls for the High Commissioner.

European Union Funding

In addition to the giving by the governments of the 25 member states, the European Union provides support for work in the developing world. Initially the only areas supported outside the EU were the former colonies of member states in Africa, the Caribbean and the Pacific region (ACP states), although this has now been extended to cover developing countries throughout the globe.

EU funding is complicated. The EU has 24 different agencies (called directorates-general) which between them have around 300 different programmes running at any time. These programmes change quite often and full information can be obtained from the EU's thorough website (www.europa.eu.int). The website can be quite daunting, containing as it does over one million pages in 11 different languages, although the funding pages do provide plenty of information on each of the programmes. It also contains downloadable copies of all guidelines and advice publications and should be the first port of call for all interested parties.

Grants are generally for a percentage of the total cost of the project rather than a specific amount, with different maximums for different programmes. While the EU can give out very large grants, the administration of the grant and reporting back can be very time-consuming. It is for this reason that many organisations are deterred from applying and those who do get a grant appoint staff to cover the increased workload.

Two of the agencies will support NGOs that work outside the EU, as long as the application is submitted by an organisation with a presence within a member state. They are:

ECHO (European Commission's Humanitarian Aid Office) provides emergency assistance and relief to the victims of natural disasters or armed conflicts to ensure that goods and services get to where they are most needed as quickly as possible. As well as providing urgently needed food, fuel, housing and medical equipment, ECHO can fund the costs of transporting the supplies (including increased staff costs) and training and studies in the humanitarian field. In 2007 it gave 60 million euros in humanitarian aid, food aid and disaster relief.

EuropeAid aims to reduce poverty in developing countries with a view to its eventual eradication. Main areas of work supported are: the link between trade and development; regional integration and cooperation; support for macro-economic policies and the promotion of equitable access to social services; transport; food security and sustainable rural development; and institutional capacity building. Other areas of work funded are human rights, the environment, gender equality and good governance.

Useful websites

http://europa.eu – official website of the EU, with details of all the funding streams available.

www.ecas.org – European Citizen Action Service, which empowers civil society and European citizenship.

www.welcomeurope.com – a Dutch, French and German information service providing thorough details of all EU funding issues.

www.bond.org.uk – Bond produce detailed analysis of EU funding on their site.

Overseas NGOs and donor agencies

There are a large number of foreign donor agencies, which might be divided into the following categories:

- **Volunteer-sending agencies** such as Médecins Sans Frontières (France), Voluntary Service Overseas (UK) or the Peace Corps (USA). When these programmes started, the aim was to send usually younger people overseas to 'give service'. Today, many of these agencies now send people with specialist skills requested by local NGOs, who are often required to contribute something towards the cost of the assignment. Two interesting UK agencies are BESO, which provides retired executives looking for a new challenge, and Engineers without Borders, which sends people with specific engineering skills, including retired engineers. There are also a number of agencies which send young people on short-term assignments, where the benefit is likely to be more for the young person than for the receiving organisation. Typically, these are 'gap year' schemes for young people after they have left school and before university or a job. But today, volunteers don't have to travel to you. They can be virtual volunteers, providing their help online. The UN runs a website for virtual volunteers: www.onlinevolunteering.org. Another online volunteering initiative is www.naabur.com where volunteers adopt a village or a community, and then undertake tasks on its behalf.

- **National and global NGOs** which raise money from the public to support development projects in the developing world. In Europe, these include Oxfam, Save the Children, Christian Aid, ActionAid, PLAN, Brot für die Welt, Radda Barnen, Aide et Action, HelpAge International, International Planned Parenthood and so on. Some of these are generalist agencies, some have a particular perspective (children or elderly people), some are connected either closely or loosely with a religious denomination. They will usually have a country office or even a regional infrastructure in the countries where they provide support, whose function it is to identify 'project partners', assess project applications, account to head office for the money donated, offer technical and infrastructural support to project partners alongside the financial support, and participate in policy analysis and development. In recent years, another function has been added: local resource mobilisation, either through accessing large grants from international donors that are available in the region or country, or by seeking to raise money directly from the public (as Oxfam India has been attempting to do). The support given to project partners is often long term. Sometimes there is child sponsorship, community sponsorship or project sponsorship, where the individual donor providing funds to the donor agency ties their support to a particular project, a particular community or even a particular family or child, and where the donor expects to be kept in touch with progress.

- **Specialist NGOs** which deal with such matters as intermediate technology, leprosy relief, blindness, deafness, family planning, water management. These include agencies such as ADD (disability rights), Marie Stopes International (family planning), LEPRA (leprosy relief) and SightSavers International (blindness) that have created an international network of affiliated organisations, as well as agencies such as WaterAid (water and sanitation) and Practical Action (intermediate technology) that work with local partners.

- **Smaller specialist NGOs,** usually set up through the vision and enthusiasm of one individual to pursue a particular idea or address a particular need. Organisations such as Farm Africa, Send a Cow, Tools for Self Reliance, Book Aid International, SOS Sahel, Green Deserts, African Prisons Project, Excellent Development (building sand dams) and PEAS (Promoting Education in African Schools) show the diversity of the initiatives now being developed. Typically, these organisations will have no fundraising base of their own, but will be raising money from foundations and international aid sources for their work. Their work will usually be confined to one or two projects, simply because of their small size. But these will be used as 'demonstration projects' to illustrate new approaches and possibilities.

- **Support groups for local projects.** These are often set up on their return home by someone who has visited your project or a volunteer who has worked with you. They set up a fundraising initiative to support your work by raising money and channelling it to you. This may start as a fundraising committee, but can develop into a charitable institution. For example, Sisters of Mercy (Mother Theresa) in Calcutta has many local support groups raising money for her work across the world. The Karuna Trust in the UK supports an orphanage in Pune. And the Social Entrepreneurs Trust supports UnLtd India to invest in early-stage social entrepreneurs. One strategy for raising money for your organisation is to get enthusiasts, family members and returning volunteers to set up support groups for you in their own countries of residence.

- **Denominational initiatives.** Many religious denominations channel support to the developing world through their affiliate churches and religious institutions across the world. The money can come from the religious body itself and the foundations it controls, or it can come from public subscription. Sometimes this aid is purely for welfare, education and development. Sometimes there is an evangelistic agenda or religious objective behind the provision of the aid.

A good source of information is OneSiteEurope, www.euforic.org/about/en/onesite. htm, an online database giving details of over 8,000 development NGOs.

How new donor agencies start

There appear to be several stages in the evolution of a development agency. As a wild generalisation this would start in the Gambia (or next year's fashionable tourist destination), where an individual or group would go on holiday. There they would see the high levels of unemployment and poor living standards from their hotel balcony, and talk to Gambians about the problems and challenges they face. This would lead them in turn to realise that the local school was not able to teach for lack of basics like pencils.

On their return, our holidaymakers would rally support in their own community to send a package of pencils and school books. This would lead to more requests. Once a second package had been sent off, and a third, our holidaymakers begin to realise that it needs more than just pencils, and the next step might be skills training to address unemployment in the Gambia. It is only a matter of time (and sustaining their enthusiasm) before the group of returned holidaymakers has transformed itself into a development agency.

Source: Will Day, Africa Grants Director of Charity Projects until 1994

A good example of this is TOMS Shoes (Shoes for Tomorrow) created by Californian Blake Mycoskie after holidaying in Argentina. He noticed that many poor people were shoeless, and that the local espadrille was the most comfortable shoe he had ever worn. On his return, he designed and started making a range of espadrille shoes based on the Argentine design, and sold them on a 'buy one, give one free' basis. For each pair of shoes purchased, another pair is donated to a poor person, originally in Argentina, but now extended to other countries. TOMS Shoes is now a successful social enterprise: www.tomsshoes.com

How donor agencies raise their money

Many donor agencies recruit regular supporters who make a commitment to give a certain sum each month. Many donors are keen to offer their support if this can be linked with a particular aspect of the organisation's work. There are two main ways of doing this. One is through 'project sponsorship', where the support is linked to a particular project, and progress on this project is then reported back to the supporter. The other is through 'child sponsorship', where the supporter is linked to a particular child, and can chart his or her progress over the years through progress reports received from the donor agency and correspondence with the sponsored child. This form of support has its critics, but is extremely successful in fundraising terms – as people feel that their money will really make a difference to someone. PLAN International is one of the major users of child sponsorship, with over 830,000 sponsors around the world, helping more than 8 million people in over 30 countries. This is how PLAN International recruits support:

How a nurse from Guildford gave a boy in Kenya the chance to go to school . . .
When Helen Taylor decided to sponsor Ben, an eight-year-old boy from Kenya, she didn't realise how much difference her help could make. Now with the help of PLAN International sponsors, Ben's village has a school where he's learning to read and write. And a mobile clinic where every child can be immunised against disease. PLAN International has also

helped the community to improve its own farming methods, so that the land is more productive and no one need go hungry. For Helen, sponsoring Ben has been one of the best and most satisfying things she has ever done. She knows from the regular reports she receives from his village, how much difference her help has made.

THINKING OF SPONSORING A CHILD?

Read how for just a small monthly amount you can bring health and opportunity to a child in a poor community.

Children like these need your sponsorship today . . .
Diabe Cisse, aged 11, Senegal. The village where Diabe lives lacks even the most basic health care. Neither Diabe nor her brother and two sisters can read or write. The Cisse family live in a mud compound which they share with relatives. It consists of 20 huts, along with a cookhouse, granary and animal shed. The Cisses rely entirely on their own resources. The soil is poor – if the rains fail the crops fail too.

'We know that we cannot really help the world's poor by giving them handouts, or imposing preconceived "Western solutions" on them. Our approach is to help people solve their problems in their own way.'

PLAN was the first charity to use child sponsorship as a fundraising technique. You can read about the origins and development of child sponsorship by visiting the Showcase of Fundraising Innovation and Inspiration (www.sofii.org).

Dealing with a donor agency: twelve steps to success

Here are twelve recommended steps in identifying, approaching and attracting funding from donor agencies. They have been developed in discussion with Murray Culshaw, former head of Oxfam (India), and now a successful fundraising consultant working in India.

1. Research
To find out about donor agencies that might be interested in receiving an application from you, you could:

- Consult a **funding directory** if one has been produced in your country (for example in India, the Voluntary Health Association of India has published a directory of funding agencies supporting health development programmes).
- Identify a **similar organisation** to your own, and then find out from whom it is receiving funding. This might lead you to one or two sources you had not previously considered.
- Ask your **existing funders**. There may be an informal network of donor agencies, and they might know which other funders could potentially be interested in supporting you, and might even put in a good word for you.

- If you belong to a religious network, **ask around the network**. If you are interested in receiving money from a particular country, ask its embassy for any contacts it has.
- Ask **your supporters** in a particular country to research potential sources in that country, or put out a request on www.onlinevolunteering.org for a volunteer who is prepared to do this for a specific country, region or even worldwide.

From all this research, you will want to get the name of the donor agency, its address and telephone number, the name of the person to write to (with job title), and a brief description (if you can get it) of its funding policy.

2. Finding out more

At this stage you will want to find out as much as you can about the agency to see whether it is worth your while approaching it. A good first step is to go to the agency's website. If it doesn't have one (unlikely) or if the site does not have the information you need, either contact the agency via the website or write a short letter of no more than a page. It is better to write, as donor agencies are being plagued with people phoning or emailing. Many will have little or no capacity to deal with such enquiries. On the other hand, your letter will get put into the in-tray and be dealt with in due course. If you don't get a reply within a month, then you can try phoning.

In your letter ask the agency to send you a copy of any statement of policy it has for supporting development work, and for a copy of its latest annual report.

3. Selecting a number of donor agencies to approach

At this stage you will want to draw up a shortlist of donor agencies which you will then approach in a systematic and professional way. This shortlist should take into account the donor agency's:

- **Origins, motivation and bias** (political and religious). You will want to know if the organisation has religious affiliations, for example, and any implications for you if you accept money from them. If you are a democracy organisation, then you will want to know the motivation and political viewpoint of the funder before accepting support.
- **Size.** You will need to know the level of the agency's grantmaking, and whether it is sufficiently high to support your project.
- **Interests.** You will want to know the agency's grant policies and focus areas, the types of organisation it supports, the types of grant it gives and the sorts of project it likes to help.

4. The first approach

At this stage, it is best to send a letter, even though you might have had no previous contact with the agency. The last thing that any donor wants is someone turning up at the door asking for money. And if you were to ring in, they would only tell you 'to put it in writing'. A letter makes it easier for the donor agency to respond as it will have the information it needs to hand. Donor agencies are always looking for good projects to support, so they will want to hear from you.

Your short introductory letter should not be more than two pages long (one page is even better!). Do not send a long and detailed proposal at this stage. You need to introduce yourself and see whether there is any interest in your work, and therefore whether there is any point in your investing a considerable amount of time and effort into developing a full project proposal for the donor to consider. In your short letter, you will:

- **Introduce the organisation.**
- **Describe the project.**
- **Highlight any special features** of your work or your plans, and anything you are planning of an innovative nature.
- **Indicate the approximate scale** of your financial need, the contribution that you will be making to the project (including funds that are at your disposal and which you can mobilise, any technical skills and expertise, assets and equipment that you bring, partnerships with others, and so on) and any other funding sources that you plan to approach.
- **Provide endorsements** for your work and for the project that you are planning to develop. If an acknowledged expert in the field likes what you are doing, this will carry weight.
- **Mention any previous funding.** Oxfam found that when its project partners approached other donors, they stood a better chance of getting support if they mentioned that they had received funding from Oxfam. This provided a point of reference for checking on the quality of the work, and also some assurance that the work was worth supporting. Many agencies belong to an informal network of donors, where they can share thoughts and 'find out the gossip' on organisations they have not had contact with before.

5. Wait for their reply

The donor agency should reply within a month or two, indicating whether your project falls within its mandate and current focus, and whether it has the resources to support you. The funds available to most donor agencies are small in relation to the demand. The agency will indicate whether it is worth your while submitting a proper application, and give any deadline for receipt of this. It will also tell you whether it requires you to complete an application to a prescribed format, or whether you can submit a proposal in your own preferred style. Sometimes it will arrange to visit you or send a representative to check you out first. If you have not heard within six weeks, send a reminder or ring up.

6. Write a project proposal

This will set out your proposal in detail, and will be the basis on which your project will be assessed. It should be prepared with great care – far too many shoddy applications for often quite large sums of money are received by donor agencies. Many donors offer guidance on how they want their applications to be submitted, and you should read this with care. Some require the applicant to use a 'Log Frame' format, which provides a highly structured way of setting out your plans.

Typically your proposal should run to between six and twelve pages plus attachments. Details of how to write an effective application are given in Section 8.2. The following are some important things to consider:

- **A needs assessment.** Nobody wants to support something that is not needed! The donor agency may require evidence of participatory research, participatory appraisal, baseline studies, and other fashionable techniques for needs assessment.
- An indication that the **community and the project staff** have been involved in shaping the proposal, and that it is not just a good idea submitted by the director.
- An indication that support has been obtained from experts during the planning stage, where **specialist expertise** is important.
- Clearly defined objectives that appear to be **achievable.**
- A commitment to **monitoring and evaluation**, measuring the results and outcomes.
- A degree of **creative thinking** about the problem, or innovation in the way you are attempting to tackle it.
- A solid **evaluation of your past work** and a **knowledge of other programmes** of a similar nature to that which you are proposing.
- A long-term **strategic framework** for the project, with thoughts about its longer-term financing – or for a time-limited project, an indication of the period over which the project will run and be completed.
- Some evidence of a **capacity to raise public funds** or to build a constituency of **local community support.**

You will then attach:

- Your latest **annual report** plus an audited statement of accounts.
- A copy of your **constitution** or anything else which confirms your charitable credentials and legal status.
- **References**, where appropriate.

You will type your application neatly (on your computer if possible, as this enables you to send similar applications to several donor agencies, each tailored to that agency's particular needs). Then you send it off, bearing in mind any indicated deadline for its receipt.

If you are a small organisation or do not have sufficient experience of project preparation, then it could just be worth hiring a consultant to help you.

Remember too that most agencies prefer to make substantial grants rather than scatter their money in lots of small grants. They also want to 'invest' in the project over the long term, and even to put in more money if the work is going really well (they like backing a winner).

7. Project assessment

The donor agency will then think about whether it wants to consider your proposal, or whether it wants to reject it at this stage. If you have done your research well, you should not fail at this point. The assessment procedure will almost always require a visit from a project officer or from a consultant. Much will depend on the size and staffing of the donor agency, your location and whether they can easily reach you, and whether the proposal calls for specialist knowledge that it does not have.

8. On the visit

The following are some tips for handling the assessment visit:

- **Plan** the visit carefully, but be flexible enough to respond to the donor agency's needs and interests.
- Show something of your past **successful and unsuccessful work**. Most people try to avoid showing the mistakes of the past. But assessors can sense when something is wrong – they are visiting so many projects that they get an instant 'feel' for your work. Be honest about failures; don't be defensive. If you are prepared to learn from experience and generate new ideas from work which has not succeeded, assessors will respect you all the more.
- The director should stand aside to allow other members of **staff and community representatives** to take part in the discussion.
- **Invite board members** to be present, and brief them beforehand. This provides evidence of a participating and strong board.
- Ceremonial displays and welcomes are *a real bore*. **Show them your work**; you are not there to entertain them.
- Everything should be **tidy and ordered** – but then it should always be. If you appear sloppy and disorganised, this will create the wrong impression.

9. Awaiting a decision

The assessment process will normally take between four and six months. How the decision is made and its speed depends on the size of the proposal, whether it is central or peripheral to that agency's main interests (the more unusual it is, the longer the decision period will be), and the agency's own decision-making procedures. Most agencies delegate discretionary authority to their project staff to make grants within certain guidelines.

10. Saying thank you

If your proposal has been supported:

- Send a short, courteous letter of thanks . . . without frills or gimmicks!
- Read and understand the terms and conditions of the support. Many donor agencies will send a contract for signature confirming your acceptance of the conditions of grant.
- Accredit the donor agency as required by it. For example, PLAN International supports some major projects in India, which then have to be described as a '*PLAN-Deepalaya Project*', for example.

11. Reporting back

You will be required to report back at least annually – some donor agencies require a quarterly report of progress. You will need to:

- Set up a **schedule** for coping with the reporting obligations.
- **Make someone responsible** for seeing that this reporting is done, and that it is done on time. There will also be an expectation that you will turn up at partner meetings organised by the donor agency, attend certain seminars and 'free' training events that it organises for your benefit – which also enables you to network with others – and entertain donors and visitors that it sends your way.

- Ensure that your organisation's **financial reporting** system is able to cope with the financial information that you are obliged to provide. And it is standard practice that your accounts should be professionally and independently audited. You will also need to report any variations on budget and any changes in plan that require the funder's approval. Most donor agencies want to know before significant amounts of money are shifted from one budget head to another. As a general rule, variances under 10 per cent are normally not a problem; above 10 per cent you will need to consult with the donor first.

There is a danger that the original proposal becomes a rigid framework for the project. Circumstances may have changed; you may be learning from experience as the project proceeds. Nobody minds changes made for good reason. If development was an easy process, then all the world's problems would have been solved by now.

Donors seem to have become more demanding in their reporting requirements, and reporting back can become a major burden on your organisation's resources. The implications of this should be taken into account in budgeting for the project, so that you are not out of pocket.

Try to give facts and figures in your project reports, rather than whole pages of generalisations; and try to measure performance against the objectives you originally set for the project in your proposal. For large projects, you may want to build some form of external evaluation into your project plans, both at mid-term and at the conclusion of the work, and the cost of doing this can be built into your project budget. If you can demonstrate your project's success, this can help the donor agency with its own PR or with its fundraising (if it gets some or all of the money from a third party).

12. Maintain good working relations with donor agency staff

Remember that donor agency staff are human beings who are (usually) genuinely interested in you and your work. A project officer will typically be dealing with 10–20 projects, usually in one geographic area rather than on a thematic basis – but this may be changing as development work becomes more technical. The project assessment work involves constant travel, often in difficult conditions and with continuous work pressure. Some project officers may have done a great deal to ensure that your proposal got supported in the first place, and will be as committed as you are to its success. Remember too that distributing money is not an easy job. Difficult choices have to be made, and it is the personal relationships with project staff and the tangible evidence of progress and success that make their job worthwhile. So do make sure that you:

- **Keep in regular contact** with donor agency staff.
- **Give evidence of success** and achievements, not just to agency staff, but also for inclusion in the supporter newsletters – both in your own country and in the country from where the money has originated. Getting to know newsletter editors, sending news releases when there is news to report, and providing photographs with captions are all ways of getting news about your project into print.
- **Be honest about failures,** or where the project is not going quite according to plan. If the project is proceeding more slowly than expected or in a different direction, seek a meeting to discuss progress and what to do next.

If you visit the donor agency's own country:

- **Visit its offices** to meet project staff, and also fundraising staff (if they are raising money), to tell them about your work and your successes. Tell them three months in advance that you are coming.
- **Offer to speak to supporters** or at fundraising meetings that the agency might organise for you. If you can spare a week (or whatever time you have available to do this), it will be much appreciated. The donor agency should be able to cover your out-of-pocket expenses during this time. These meetings are not opportunities to ask for money, but a time to tell people about your work and to say thank you for the support you have received. If you can, prepare a video or an illustrated PowerPoint presentation which shows the work actually being done.

What a donor agency likes to see

- **Proper accountability** for the money given, and up-to-date reporting of income and expenditure.
- **Monitoring and evaluation** of progress, as agreed when the grant was made.
- **Evidence of achievement and success.** The agency is particularly interested in innovative ideas or ways of working that you are developing.
- **Impact on the community** in creating real and lasting change for the better.
- **Evidence of enthusiasm** from the community for what you are doing.
- **Case studies** that demonstrate how you are succeeding.
- **Newspaper and media coverage** of your work.
- **Mobilisation of financial support** from government programmes and from the community to add to the funds it is providing.
- Progress towards operational and financial **sustainability**.
- Your own **continued enthusiasm** for the work you are doing.

4.4 Foundations

Foundations are independent grant-making bodies, deriving their income from an endowment or some form of continuing fundraising. They come in all shapes and sizes, including the very large foundations established by successful business people and large companies, to smaller foundations linked to religious institutions or established by a family to pursue the philanthropic interests of members of that family. Each will have its own policies and priorities, together with its own mechanisms for considering applications.

Foundations (sometimes also known as 'trusts', as many are established with the legal format of a trust) can be a very important source of support, as they are set up with the express intention of giving their money away for charitable purposes and community development. Much will depend on whether there is an established tradition of foundation giving in your country, and whether your work is the sort of thing they are interested in supporting.

One role that some foundations adopt is the promotion of innovation and new ideas. Many emerging organisations owe their existence to the support from the outset of clear-sighted and progressive foundations that were prepared to shoulder whatever risk there may have been at that stage of the organisation's development.

Background information

Foundations come in all shapes and sizes:

- From **very large** institutions such as the Ford Foundation to **tiny bodies** with just a few hundred pounds or dollars a year to distribute.
- From an **international** remit (such as the Aga Khan Foundation) or **national** remit (such as the Rajiv Gandhi Foundation) to operating **regionally or locally** (such as the Bombay Community Public Trust).
- From supporting a **wide range of activities** (many are set up for general charitable purposes) to **specialising** in support for a particular type of work (such as bursaries for tertiary education).

The structure of the larger foundations is highly professional and likely to include a secretary or director (the title varies), who is in executive charge of the grants programme, possibly with administrative staff and, for the very large foundations, a team of specialist or regional grants officers. They will report to a board of trustees, which is ultimately responsible for policy and for seeing that the foundation operates effectively. The trustees will usually take or ratify the final decision on where the grants go, basing their decisions on the recommendations of their professional staff. There may also be local advisers or experts in specialist areas who will be asked to assess the larger grant applications.

Smaller foundations are often run by the family or the individual who set them up. They may be administered by a firm of lawyers or accountants. They are unlikely to employ professional staff to assess grant applications. Many have difficulty in distributing their income – either through lack of expertise or energy, or simply because they do not receive enough applications from organisations looking for support. With the smaller foundations, good contacts with the trustees or some form of personal connection is extremely important.

How a foundation works

The donor

The money for a foundation can be provided by:

- A rich individual.
- A legacy that establishes the foundation on the donor's death.
- A company.
- A public collection or appeal.
- Continued fundraising to top up the endowment or increase the annual income available for distribution.

The trustees

This money is then invested, and the income from the investment is distributed in the form of grants to the beneficiaries. The trustees are the group of people who are responsible for:

- Managing the foundation's investments.
- Ensuring that the fundraising work is done, where the foundation has to raise all or part of its grants budget.
- Distributing the foundation's income in the form of grants.

The beneficiaries

The foundation will have a constitution which sets out who can benefit. This is known as the foundation's 'objects'. It may also state the geographical area where the money can be spent. This is known as the foundation's 'beneficial area'. The trustees decide on the policies and priorities of the foundation. However, they are not permitted to support activity that falls outside the objects or takes place outside the beneficial area of the foundation.

The applicants

Most foundations decide on whom to support through having written applications submitted to them. There is no point applying to a foundation if your work does not match the foundation's current policy and priorities, or if you fall outside the beneficial area.

National and local foundations

In every country there will be some local foundations which give support for national or more local projects. These may have been set up by a prominent industrialist in the colonial era (such as the Beit Foundation, which operates in countries of southern Africa). They may have been set up more recently (such as the National Foundation for India and the India Foundation for the Arts). They may have ongoing public fundraising programmes (such as CRY, Child Rights and You, which funds child rights programmes in India).

There may be a tradition of individuals establishing foundations to support public institutions such as eye hospitals or orphanages, or to support some religious project (a temple or mosque, and associated good works). And in recent years, with the growth of many economies in the developing world and the emergence of a 'super-wealthy' class, many successful individuals and families may have established a foundation either personally or through their company (often these support projects or initiatives in the village or region from where the individual has come).

Establishing a foundation will usually require registration, and procedures will vary from country to country – in most countries foundations will register nationally. But registration does not imply that there is a central bank of publicly available information on foundations. And in most countries there is no published information on foundations either – although in some, attempts are being made to compile information for use in fundraising. Where there is no ready source of information, you will find out about foundations:

- Through personal knowledge and contact.
- By finding out how other, 'rival' organisations are being funded.
- Through keeping your eyes open – there may be articles in the press for example which refer to the support of foundations or the philanthropy of rich individuals.

International foundations

At the other end of the geographic scale are the international foundations. Most of the larger ones are situated in the USA (including the Ford Foundation) and the UK (including foundations with a remit to give support in the Commonwealth), but there are many in Europe and a few in Japan which give internationally. Some of the very large international foundations have established country offices in the main countries where they are making grants.

The main sources of information are:

- The literature produced by the foundations themselves. Many will have their own website. Only the largest will publish **reports or guidelines for applicants**, and these may not always be in a language that you understand; and
- A number of **grant directories** published by information and documentation centres.

Raising money from an international foundation is difficult, unless it has a specific focus on giving grants in your country – where it will have developed a mechanism for receiving and assessing applications – or unless you have a good personal contact. You are a long way away, and it may not even have heard of you – even though you are a reputable and successful organisation in your own country. The foundation's view of the world and its priorities may be completely different from your own (there are a large number of US foundations, for example, promoting 'democracy' defined in different ways according to their political stance). And it will prefer to give in its own country to organisations it knows, even if the purpose of the grant is to provide help in your own country. But there are opportunities:

- Undertaking **work which it is particularly interested in**, where you can demonstrate your track record and expertise. For example, the Bill and Melinda Gates Foundation and the Clinton Global Initiative are both seeking to solve some of the main barriers to achieving the Millennium Development Goals.
- Where there is an **international dimension** to your work, or international interest in it. There may be many people interested in supporting the intellectual property rights attached to tribal and traditional medicines in face of the attempted patenting of such remedies by the multinational drug companies. Equally, rainforest preservation has attracted interest and support from around the world.
- A **bilateral or multilateral** project, comparing approaches and practice in different countries, where you can make a joint approach with your partner.
- A **joint venture** between you and another organisation which is addressing similar issues in the home country of the foundation. The foundation will have heard of your partner organisation, which can then act as a conduit for the money, a source of technical and other aid, and even a guarantor of the project's success, as it will be ultimately accountable for the grant. This is certainly a sensible strategy if you are serious about getting support from a US foundation, as most grants given by US foundations for international purposes go to US-based organisations. It is a requirement for the UK's two largest sources, Comic Relief and the Big Lottery Fund.

Five don'ts in dealing with overseas foundations

1. **Don't assume** that because they are rich and philanthropic they will want to support you. They have plenty of other calls upon their resources.
2. **Don't write a begging letter out of the blue.** You either will get no reply at all, or a certain rejection.
3. **Don't ask for money for your existing work.** Try to find a project which has some international aspect or dimension and which the foundation should be genuinely interested in.
4. **Don't leave it to the last moment.** You will need plenty of time to make contact, discuss your ideas with the foundation, even meet, before submitting a full proposal.
5. **Don't assume that the foundation has heard of you and your work.** You will have to build your credibility. Getting world-renowned experts to endorse your work can help. Good literature clearly explaining the problem and how you work will help. Meet people at international conferences, and follow up on these contacts. If you travel abroad, set aside some time to develop contacts with larger foundations in that country. Just telephone the director's office in advance and ask to visit, or even telephone them on your arrival to try to arrange an appointment. If you make yourself sound interesting or come with good credentials, they may really like to meet you.

Fundraising from overseas foundations: some lessons from experience

The following advice is given by Nilda Bullain of the Civil Society Development Programme in Hungary following a US fundraising trip when a group of CSDP staff visited 12 foundations in four cities during a three-week period, and succeeded in raising a major part of CSDP's budget:

'We found it vital to have good references and to be well informed about the foundation. During the trip, we prepared carefully what we would say and how we would say it – about our project and about ourselves. Among other exercises, we practised our introductions and the presentation we had prepared. We measured the time this took and helped each other with constructive observations. We also had to be aware of the weak points of our proposal. We brainstormed the possible questions that might arise and allocated who would answer each question. We tried to put ourselves into the foundation officer's shoes and imagine how they would see our proposal from their standpoint and what questions they might want to ask. We also prepared our own list of questions so that we could get all the information we needed about procedures, deadlines for applications, the possibility of further contact, etc. We knew exactly what we wanted to accomplish at each meeting, and were usually successful in sticking to our agenda. We always made sure that there was some subsequent follow-up (a telephone call, etc.). For us it was well worth the time and cost of meeting donors personally, and it is part of our fundraising strategy to develop and keep good working relationships with programme officers in foundations.'

Information on international foundations

United States

The Foundation Center publishes a wide range of grant directories, including an *International Foundation Directory*. You can turn up at its offices (or at any of the documentation centres it runs) and access information on particular foundations, including grants lists from previous years and current policies and priorities. The Center also publishes The Foundation Directory Online, a web-based subscription service detailing over 70,000 grant-makers (http: //fconline.fdncenter.org). Note, though, that most US foundation funding for international purposes goes to central and southern America, and more recently to eastern Europe and the former Soviet Union. They are not big funders in Africa and Asia (although there are exceptions), and they will have their particular interests and priorities. For example, they are much more likely to want to give support in South Africa than to the other countries of southern Africa.

CAF America, an affiliate of the Charities Aid Foundation in the UK, publishes newsletters and other information on foundation and corporate giving.

The Foundation Center: 79 Fifth Avenue, New York NY 10003–3076, USA (http:// foundationcenter.org).

CAF America: King Street Station, 1800 Diagonal Road, Suite 150, Alexandria VA 22314–2840, USA (www.cafamerica.org).

United Kingdom

With its historical links to Commonwealth countries, the UK is potentially an important source for funding in south Asia and Africa. International funding is largely directed towards those countries where there has been some historical connection, although more recently media interest in famines and disasters has drawn attention to the needs of countries such as Ethiopia and Rwanda where there was no colonial connection. A particularly interesting foundation is Comic Relief, which is able to fund in Africa because of its highly successful television fundraising spectacular. Good documentation on international funding by UK foundations is provided by the **Directory of Social Change**, which publishes *The International Development Directory*, covering UK-based voluntary organisations working in the developing world, together with details of funding sources for such work.

The Directory of Social Change: 24 Stephenson Way, London NW1 2DP, UK (www.dsc.org.uk).

Some major UK foundations supporting work in other countries

Comic Relief

5th floor, 89 Albert Embankment, London SE1 7TP (www.comicrelief.org.uk).
Supports causes in Africa relating to women and girls, people affected by conflict, people with disabilities, people living in towns and cities, pastoralists, hunter-gatherers and people affected by HIV/AIDS.

The Diana, Princess of Wales Memorial Fund
The County Hall, Westminster Bridge Road, London SE1 7PB (www.theworkcontinues.
org).
Supports work assisting people whose social exclusion, poverty or displacement is due
to conflict, especially in communities affected by landmines or other explosives.

The Gatsby Charitable Foundation
Allington House, 1st floor, 150 Victoria Street, London SW1E 5AE (www.gatsby.org.uk).
Promotes environmentally sustainable development and poverty alleviation through
selected programmes supporting basic agriculture and other enterprise in selected
African countries.

The Paul Hamlyn Foundation
18 Queen Anne's Gate, London SW1H 9AA (www.phf.org.uk).
Supports local projects in India, run by Indian organisations, for development, to
strengthen NGOs or assist disadvantaged children.

Joseph Rowntree Charitable Trust
The Garden House, Water End, York YO30 6WQ (www.jrct.org.uk).
Supports work in urban and rural settings, especially conflict resolution in southern Africa.

The International Small Grants Programme of the Big Lottery Fund
1 Plough Place, London EC4A 1DE (www.biglotteryfund.org.uk).
This programme (currently closed for applications) funded projects that tackled the
causes of poverty and deprivation and brought about a long-term difference to the lives
of the most disadvantaged people.

Foundations in Europe

The European Foundation Centre in Brussels keeps information on European
foundations and can provide informal advice. Just as the UK directs much of its overseas
support to Commonwealth countries, so projects based in Francophone countries will
have equivalent close links to France and French foundations, and projects based in
Lusophone countries to Portugal and Portuguese foundations.

*Brussels office: European Foundation Centre, 51 rue de la Concorde, B-1050 Brussels,
Belgium (www.efc.be).*

Commonwealth grants

There is no published grants guide to sources of Commonwealth grants, but you may be
able to get advice from the **Commonwealth Secretariat** based in London.

*The Commonwealth Secretariat, Marlborough House, Pall Mall, London SW1Y 5HX, UK
(www.thecommonwealth.org).*

These Commonwealth foundations support travel, exchanges and community
service:

The Commonwealth Foundation

Marlborough House, Pall Mall, London SW1Y 5HY (www.commonwealthfoundation.
com).

Has programmes in arts and culture, civil society, commonwealth understanding and professional exchange

The Nuffield Commonwealth Programme

The Nuffield Foundation, 28 Bedford Square, London WC1B 3JS (www.nuffield foundation.org).

Supports initiatives that bring about long-term improvements in health, education and civil justice in eastern and southern Africa and fosters North-South partnerships.

The Commonwealth Youth Exchange Council

7 Lion Yard, Tremadoc Road, London SW4 7NQ (www.cyec.org.uk).

Aims to develop young people and their communities as well as promote international understanding throughout the Commonwealth through reciprocal exchanges.

The Prince's Charities

Clarence House, London SW1A 1BA (www.princescharities.org).

Charities associated with the Prince of Wales, which include The Prince's Trust and the International Business Leaders Forum, some of which support overseas programmes.

Foundations in other countries

Other countries, such as Australia, Canada, Japan and South Africa, have 'foundation centres' which act as focal points and publish information on foundations operating in their country. For further information on foundations in Canada see the *Canadian Directory to Foundations & Grants*, available from Imagine Canada, 2 Carlton Street, Suite 600, Toronto, ON M5B 1J3, Canada (also available online at www.imaginecanada.ca). For information on South African foundations, see the *Donor Community in South Africa: a Directory*, available from the Institute for International Education, 809 UN Plaza, New York, NY 10017–3580, USA (www.iie.org). And for Japan, contact the Foundation Library Centre of Japan, 4–4-1 Yotsuya, Shinjuku-ku, Tokyo 160–0004, Japan (www.jpf.go.jp).

These are some major international foundations supporting work in other countries:

The Ford Foundation

320 East 43rd Street, New York, NY 10017, USA (www.fordfound.org).

Works to strengthen democratic values, reduce poverty and injustice, promote international cooperation and advance human achievement worldwide. It gave support totalling US$685 million in 2007.

The Rockefeller Foundation

420 Fifth Avenue, New York, NY 10018, USA (www.rockfound.org).

A knowledge-based global foundation with a commitment to enrich and sustain the lives and livelihoods of poor and excluded people throughout the world. It gave US$176 million in 2006.

Bill and Melinda Gates Foundation
PO Box 23350, Seattle, WA 98102, USA (www.gatesfoundation.org).
Addresses major global challenges in health and education. In 2007 it distributed $2.01 billion

The Clinton Global Initiative
Clinton Global Initiative, 1301 Avenue of the Americas, 37th Floor, New York, NY 10019–6022, USA (www.clintonglobalinitiative.org).
Combats disease and malnutrition, takes action on global warming and supports microfinance. Since its inception in 2001, CGI has entered into commitments totalling US$30 billion aiming to improve the lives of over 200 million people.

These are very major foundations with wide-ranging grants programmes. Details of what they do can be obtained from one of the international foundation directories. There are also many smaller foundations, especially in Europe and North America, that make grants for international purposes.

The Aga Khan Foundation

The Aga Khan Development Network, PO Box 2049, 1–3 avenue de la Paix, 1211 Geneva 2, Switzerland (www.akdn.org).

The Aga Khan Foundation is a private, non-denominational development agency promoting creative and effective solutions to selected problems that impede social development in the low-income countries of Asia and Africa. Part of the Aga Khan Development Network founded by the Aga Khan, spiritual leader of the Shia Ismaili Muslims, the foundation encourages initiatives in culture, health, education and rural development. Grantees are selected without regard to race, religion, gender or political persuasion on the basis of their ability to address important issues related to improvement in the quality of life in their communities.

Established in 1967, the foundation has its HQ in Geneva, Switzerland and has operations in 24 countries. Although the foundation is decentralised, its units pursue common objectives. The majority of grants are to grassroots organisations interested in testing innovative approaches in a variety of settings, which if successful offer the possibility of replicability. The heart of the foundation's approach is the cross-fertilisation of ideas among these grassroots projects, often linked closely with national and global resource organisations operating in the same field that can offer training, research, networking opportunities and the possibility of disseminating any results.

Religious foundations and missionary work

In some Southern countries, much of the early development of health and education was undertaken by missionaries with support from church bodies and religious foundations, and this influence has often continued after independence. A distinction needs to be drawn here between:

- **Evangelism**, which is the promotion of religion; and
- **Development work** carried out by a religious body, where the work is to do with social or educational provision rather than religion, and which may be for the benefit of everyone or just for co-religionists.

Some religious foundations are only interested in funding evangelistic work, while others support the social development work carried out in the name of their religion. Some have a specific agenda – for example, relating to contraception and birth control – which affects what they are prepared to support. There is usually a close link between the country and the project. For example, German foundations will be closely linked to projects run by the German Lutheran church, and Norwegian foundations to projects established by Norwegians with Norwegian support.

How foundations give

Foundations are constrained by their founding constitution and by a requirement to support charitable work. This does not mean that they can only give to organisations that are constituted and registered as charities, but that the work they support must be of a charitable nature (for example, political campaigning will normally be excluded).

Most foundations simply make cash donations. These can be a one-off grant or a regular grant over a number of years. Even if a one-off grant is obtained, it is possible that the same foundation may be willing to support another aspect of your work in future years.

Most foundations do not want to be committed to supporting a particular project indefinitely. So it is important for the fundraiser to be clear about the long-term goals and funding strategy of the organisation, and to show how the grant proposal fits into this. Where the proposal is for a building or to purchase a piece of equipment, the application should try to show how the facility will be used and how the running costs will be met. Where it is towards running costs, the application should try to show what will happen when the grant runs out.

Besides grants, some foundations may be prepared to make interest-free or low-interest loans. But this will require an ability to repay the loan at some future date, which can only happen if there is some return expected from the project.

Every foundation has a different approach to grantmaking. Some prefer giving start-up money, while others prefer to support the development of more established projects. Some preclude money for capital projects, while others will only provide support for these. Some prefer to support safer, more conservative work, while others are radical and pioneering. Some want to make a large number of smaller grants, while others prefer to concentrate on a few major projects. The least popular area of support is the salaries and overhead costs of the organisation (core funding – which is often what organisations most require); most foundations prefer to support specific 'projects' and 'initiatives', where they can feel that their support is having some impact.

All this can be ascertained from the foundation itself (either by speaking to the director or by reading its literature – if it publishes anything). It is extremely important that you use all available intelligence to ensure that you send only appropriately targeted appeals to foundations, which match:

- **Their policies and priorities.** There is no point sending an application to a foundation which has no interest in your sort of work.
- **Their scale of grantmaking.** There is no point approaching a tiny foundation for a large grant. Or a major foundation for a small item of expenditure.
- **Their ethos and approach.** You will have the greatest success with those foundations that share your outlook and values.

What foundations like to fund

On the whole, foundations like to fund 'projects' – which are particular aspects of an organisation's work that they can identify with and feel that they are having some impact on. Here are two projects supported by the Paul Hamlyn Foundation, which demonstrate the different sorts of initiative likely to be attractive to a foundation:

Chintan: While there is much discussion among environmentalists and policy-makers in India about the need for recycling waste, there is little recognition of the fact that recycling is already a large (and unrecognised) industry, at the bottom end of which are the rag pickers. These are people who go to solid waste dumps, pick out what can be recycled, and sell it to intermediaries who recycle and then remarket the matter. Rag pickers, on the lowest rung of society because of their occupation, and facing harassment from police, municipal authorities and society at large, provide the crucial link in the chain that makes recycling possible. Chintan was set up in 1993 to address the difficulties that rag pickers face in their work. The project has enabled rag pickers to get identity cards from the municipal corporation and set up cooperatives, has intervened in their difficulties with police and authorities, and has linked them with government development schemes. The Paul Hamlyn Foundation has supported Chintan from 2003, initially funding legal literacy camps for rag pickers and later workshops that enabled them to interact with the local police. The work has been recognised and institutionalised by Delhi Police.

Kutch Navnirman Abhiyan: KNNA is a coalition of NGOs based in Kutch (India's westernmost district, in the state of Gujarat), providing a range of services and advice. Using a grant of £33,750 over one year, the Village Development Fund aims to provide 24 selected panchayats, village-level political institutions at the grassroots of Indian democracy, with a grant of 100,000 rupees each. The panchayats decide how the grant is used, on condition that it benefits the weaker sections of the village and that the planning and implementation processes are participatory, honest and transparent. It is hoped that the project becomes a model for strengthening the panchayats' ability to undertake social development activities, and that some of the processes carry over to the panchayats' use of public money. The foundation provided additional resources to KNNA to disseminate information about the project and create, in time, a network of other comparable initiatives being implemented in India.

Getting started

1. Do **research** to find out which foundations are making grants in your country, including national as well as international foundations, and smaller as well as very large foundations. Get as much information as you can from them, including any

reports on their grantmaking, their guidelines for applicants and their application forms (if these are needed). Visit their website (if they have one).

2. First of all, find out what, if any, **previous approaches** you have made to foundations, and whether any have been successful. And for those that have failed, try to establish reasons for your rejection. Those that have supported you once are more likely to want to support you again – especially if you have done a really good job with their money. Those that have turned you down are also likely prospects for future support. You have already identified them as being potentially interested in your work – but as yet, you have failed to convince them of the value of supporting you. Try to find something really interesting for them to support, and present a better case. Most foundations work on an annual grants cycle, which usually means that you can approach them each year.

3. Then find out whether any of your trustees or members have good **personal connections** with any likely funding sources. Personal contact can be an important ingredient in your success.

4. Identify and **match possible funders** with various aspects of your organisation and its work. The more you can match what you want to do with what they want to support, the better.

5. Remember that foundations are unlikely to give very large grants to organisations they have never heard of. If you are looking for large sums, it may be more sensible to **apply for something small** now, and then when you have made a success of that, go back for something more substantial. Another strategy is to work in partnership with a larger, well-established and well-known organisation. Their partnership with you will, in effect, vouch for your credibility.

Making contact

Getting in touch with trusts should be a several-stage process. It might include the following:

1. **General PR** to make people aware of your organisation and its work, so that when you approach trusts, they have already heard of you and understand the importance of what you are doing. Ways of doing this include: sending out copies of your annual report or relevant publications well before you intend to raise money; getting coverage of your work and achievements in the press, and sending photocopies of any printed articles to people whom you think might be interested; and being asked to participate in radio or TV discussions.

2. **A phone call** to make contact. This can establish whether there is a best time in the trust's year to apply, whether a trust is able to support your type of work, and if so, the procedure for applying for a grant. You may also be able to get a clearer picture of the sort of work that the foundation is likely to support. An important thing to find out at this stage is whether an application form is required. There is nothing so maddening as having written a 'perfect application' only to find that the foundation requires all applications to be submitted on a standard form.

3. **A written application** setting out your request. Paper is the medium in which most foundations deal, and is how your request will initially be judged. Make sure that you

attach a copy of your latest accounts, and an annual report (if you have one) or some other description of your organisation and its work. Make sure you read the foundation's guidelines carefully, and that you provide it with all the information it needs. There may be specific requirements, such as a limit to the number of pages or words that you can submit; if there are, make sure that your application conforms to them. See Section 8.2 for advice on writing a fundraising application.

4. You might then **telephone** to see whether your application has arrived, and to ask whether any further information is required.

5. You might try to arrange to **meet a representative of the foundation**. This could be at your premises if there are people or things to see, at the foundation's offices, or on neutral ground. This encounter can seal the fate of your applications, so try hard to get to meet your potential funders face to face.

6. If you have **contact with particular trustees** or with the chair of the trustees, you can try to discuss your proposal with them and enlist their support before the matter comes up for discussion.

How to be more successful in fundraising from foundations

1. Thoroughly **research** your application from the available information and by making contact with the foundation concerned.

2. Present a concise but complete **written proposal** setting out your needs. This should include an introduction to your organisation and a background to your proposed work; what you intend to do and how you intend to set about doing it; how the work will be effective and cost-effective, and what long-term impact it will have; the budget you require, what support you are requesting from the foundation, and how you plan to organise the funding of the project after the grant finishes; and any references or other information which will build the credibility and show the success of your organisation.

3. Ask for an **appropriate amount**. You can find out from your research typical levels of grant that the foundation makes.

4. Try to get representatives of the foundation, whether they be staff or trustees, to **visit** you. It will considerably enhance your chances if someone has visited the project. But make sure that everything is working well, that the premises look well kept and well used, and that they meet some of your clients and beneficiaries who can speak enthusiastically about your work and the help you have given them.

5. Remember one **picture** is worth a thousand words. Have photographs taken of your project at work, showing people and not just buildings.

6. Very often foundations will back the **ideas and energy of a key individual** in your organisation. If you have such individuals, make sure that their strengths are clearly being promoted in your proposal, include a CV, and try to get that individual to meet the foundation representative.

7. Invite foundations to consider **matching** their support with that of another foundation, company or individual. For example, if you are seeking support to produce a brochure, getting the foundation to pay for the design and paper costs, and getting a printer to donate the printing might be an attractive way for both to give their support. Many donors warm to the idea of their gift effectively being worth double its face value.

There is of course a risk that the second donor will not respond and you lose the first donation, but this is quite unusual.

8. If you find you have raised more money than you need as a result of approaches to several foundations, **be truthful** and go back to them with alternative suggestions. Offer to extend the project or improve it rather than have to repay the grant. They will almost always agree.

4.5 Company giving

Why companies give

There is no particular obligation for companies to give their money to charity or to support projects in the local communities where they operate. But many companies do both of these things. The main reason for their giving is often said to be enlightened self-interest, rather than pure altruism. And the following are some of their reasons for giving:

- **To create goodwill**: to be seen as good citizens in the local communities where they operate and as a caring and environmentally responsible company by society at large. But also to create goodwill among employees, who will get a good impression from the good works that the company supports.
- **To promote their products and services** and to create brand awareness. This would provide them with a direct business benefit.
- **To encourage employee volunteering** and **to support the interests of their employees**. This can be done informally, through 'matched giving schemes' where the company matches what employees raise, or through supporting projects with which employees are volunteering.
- **To be associated with certain causes**. Mining and extraction companies, including the oil majors, often like to support environmental projects, pharmaceutical companies health projects, banks economic development projects, and so on. This may be in order to enhance their image, but it could also help them get another perspective on matters that interest them.
- **Because they are asked** and it is expected of them. Companies also don't want to be seen to be mean. If a major bank supports an important cultural project, then other large banks might also want to do the same, each wanting to be seen as generous and caring through their giving.
- **Because the chairman or other senior managers are interested** in that cause (and perhaps support it personally).
- **Tax**. Giving to a charity can often attract tax **relief**. This will usually be an added benefit for the company, but seldom the determining factor.

It is the shareholders' funds that the company is giving away. For privately owned companies or companies that are largely owned and controlled by one family, giving by the company will be little different from personal giving. But public companies will always want to be able to justify the money they are giving away by providing a good reason for doing so. So when you approach them, you can tell them not just why you want the money, but why they should want to support you and what they will get in return for their money.

Companies always appreciate thanks, recognition and good publicity for their support, whatever their motive for giving. You can provide this by acknowledging their support in newsletters and in your annual report, and by trying to get press or media coverage for the project they have supported – which mentions their support, of course.

The sorts of project that companies like to support

Companies support all sorts of projects, but here are some that they might be particularly interested in:

- Important **local projects** in the areas where they have a significant presence.
- Prestigious **arts and cultural events**, especially those that involve TV personalities and film stars.
- **Sporting events** and competitions, especially those that attract keen public interest and those that involve sports stars.
- **Activities that relate to their product**. For example, an ice-cream manufacturer might want to support children's charities.
- **Economic development projects** – because they believe in enterprise and that a flourishing economy will benefit business.
- **Environmental projects** – because these days everyone needs to be seen to be environmentally aware.
- Initiatives which have the **backing of very prominent people**.

Looked at from the fundraiser's point of view, this can provide an interesting insight as to what sort of company to approach and how to make that approach.

Company support in India

ActionAid carried out a survey of corporate giving in India. When it asked companies to spell out the issues and causes they particularly liked to support, the four most popular causes were:

1. **Rural development**, including adoption of surrounding villages (48 per cent)
2. Support for **the disabled** (33 per cent)
3. **Education** (31 per cent)
4. **Health and sanitation** 25 per cent

The fifth was medical benefits and welfare of employees, which was seen as a philanthropic activity.

The main reasons for choosing an area of support included:

1. **Concern** for that particular group (49 per cent)
2. To build **corporate image** (24 per cent)
3. **Family tradition** (21 per cent)
4. **Company tradition** (19 per cent)

When asked what benefits they expected in return, they gave the following main reasons:

1. Satisfaction of fulfilling **social responsibility** (45 per cent)
2. Improved **credibility** (28 per cent)
3. Increased confidence among staff (19 per cent)

It is also important to know what companies are unlikely to support. Experience suggests that most companies will not give to:

■ **Local appeals outside those areas** where they have a business presence.
■ **Purely denominational appeals** for religious purposes, although this does not preclude support for social projects run by religious bodies. This would not apply to family-controlled companies where the family has a strong religious commitment.
■ **Circular appeals**, which are printed and sent to hundreds of companies. These usually end up unread in the wastepaper basket.
■ **Controversial causes**, which might bring the company bad publicity. Companies prefer to play safe – few are interested in supporting active campaigning bodies.
■ **Overseas appeals** – although companies do support disaster appeals, such as providing relief to the tsunami-affected areas, because they feel this is the sort of thing their staff would like to see supported.

What companies give

There are a variety of ways in which companies can support NGOs:

■ **Cash donations.**
■ **Sponsorship** of an event or activity.
■ **Sponsorship** of publications, reports and educational materials.
■ **Joint promotions**, where the company makes a donation to the NGO in return for each product sold, as a way of encouraging its own sales.
■ Making **company facilities** available, including meeting rooms, printing or design facilities, help with mailings, etc.
■ **Support 'in kind'**, by giving company products or office equipment that is no longer required. Giving things rather than money is often far easier (and cheaper) for a company.
■ **Secondment** of a member of staff to work with the NGO. Under this arrangement, an employee will help the NGO on a specific task for an agreed period of time while remaining employed (and paid) by the company. This can provide a challenge for the employee, or serve as a way of utilising staff when the workload is low or they are in the run-up to retirement.
■ Contributing a senior member of staff to the NGO's **management board**. This can bring an interesting additional perspective and provide useful contacts.
■ Providing **expertise and advice** – anything from legal advice to help with strategic and business planning.
■ Encouraging company **employees to volunteer**. This could be done by allowing an NGO to give a talk at lunchtime or after work, set up an information stand in the

entrance to the office or factory, or place a feature on the work of the NGO in the staff newsletter.

- Organising a **fundraising campaign** among employees. This could be via payroll giving or some fundraising event held to raise money for the NGO.
- **Advertising** in charity brochures and publications, which could be done for good will rather than strictly business purposes.

British Airways collects money from passengers

Change for Good, an in-flight initiative with UNICEF, was launched in 1994 at the suggestion of staff, and has raised over £23 million to date. An envelope is circulated to passengers so that any small unwanted foreign currency can be donated, and the message is reinforced by an appeal on the in-flight video or an announcement by a member of the cabin crew. Staff also donate and run local collections for the fund.

There are two points that you should bear in mind:

- There are very **many ways in which a company can help** you. This is an important difference from other funding sources, as most other funders can only give you money. So think carefully about the best way in which the company might help you. You may find that it doesn't give very much at all in cash donations, and that it will be far easier (and less costly to the company) for it to support you in some other way. You may also find that if you ask it to do something quite small to start off with, it will get to know you and perhaps decide to give greater support in the future.
- There is an important **difference between donation and sponsorship**. With a donation, the company gets nothing back except some form of thanks and acknowledgement. With sponsorship, the company aims to get a real return for the money it is spending. This could be some form of publicity for the company, or it could be an opportunity to entertain customers and others (for example at a prestigious cultural event which is being held in aid of an NGO).

The different sorts of companies that give

International and multinational companies

Multinational companies may well have an established programme of charitable giving in their home country. This will be particularly true for US companies (whose giving is documented by the Foundation Center) and UK companies (whose giving is documented by the Directory of Social Change). A trend in recent years has been for companies to extend their giving beyond their headquarters town and home country into the other territories where they have a business presence, and also into countries where they are considering starting up (for example, American Express supported projects in Vietnam as a prelude to opening up for business in that country).

Some multinational companies have an international structure for managing their giving, with budgets set for each country and a common policy for the sorts of activity they are interested in supporting. This is the case, for example, with CitiGroup and BP. Others may give each country a small budget to spend on charitable projects within a broad policy. This has been the case with companies such as Microsoft and Google. With others, the giving is left purely to a local decision.

Leading national companies

Most leading national companies will also be giving something to charity. This is partly in response to what overseas companies are doing, and partly because it often makes good sense to give. Attempts are now being made in some countries to document the giving of top companies.

Where multinationals give

If you look at the geographical breakdown of a multinational company's giving, you will find that:

- most money is spent in the **headquarters town or region**.
- most money is spent in the **home country** of the company. For example, Microsoft spends most of its budget in the USA, but it has a strategy of trying to spread its giving into other countries where it does business.
- the **North gets more than the South**. BP gives most in the UK and Germany, for example

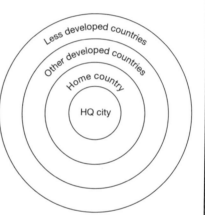

The circle of giving. The further out you are, the less you can expect to get.

Larger local companies

In any city or region there will be large companies who are important to the local economy. These companies will often feel a responsibility to do something to support voluntary action and community initiatives in those areas, and value the good publicity that this will provide. If yours is an important project, it should be part of your fundraising strategy to develop some form of relationship with the larger companies in your area.

Smaller local companies

If you are mounting a general appeal, you will want to approach smaller companies for their support. And they can often also be persuaded to give support in kind.

Some BP initiatives supporting communities

In Trinidad and Tobago: Think Healthy, Act Healthy is a preventative and remedial health awareness programme. It was set up in 2006 by a clinician at the Cascade/St Ann's Community Medical Clinic, in response to local health issues associated with obesity, hypertension and diabetes. At the heart of the programme is a nine-month self-help process that provides local people with instruction on diet, food preparation and community-based exercise. Think Healthy, Act Healthy is all about taking action to change one's lifestyle. Participants attend twice-weekly exercise classes and are encouraged to do 'exercise homework'. Programme co-ordinators provide encouragement and advice. The benefits of the programme are regularly assessed by measuring body mass index (BMI), blood pressure, the demand for medication and diabetes indicators.

For disaster relief: Through the BP Foundation, the company committed $2.1 million in 2007 to humanitarian aid. We supported relief efforts for the victims of the earthquakes in Peru, Japan and Sakhalin, Russia, the cyclone in Oman and the California wildfires. We have disbursed funds through agencies such as Save the Children, Red Cross and locally based relief organisations. We also continued our longer-term support for recovery in areas of the USA affected by Hurricanes Rita and Katrina.

Encouraging charitable giving by employees: When BP employees choose to support charitable activities, the BP Foundation's Employee Matching Fund matches their personal donations, volunteer time or – under specific circumstances – fundraising. In 2007, employees gave around $6.3 million to charitable organisations worldwide, volunteered time and raised funds for charities, and this was matched by grants of around $8.3 million from BP.

The British Petroleum Company (BP) spent $135.8 million worldwide in 2007 on community and environmental projects. Of this, $77 million (56 per cent) was spent in the USA, $24 million (18 per cent) in the UK, $2.9 million in the rest of Europe (2 per cent) and $31.9 million (24 per cent) in the rest of the world.

Source: BP annual report 2007

Who decides and who to write to

Practice varies from company to company. Many multinationals will have a manager at head office with responsibility for dealing with and deciding upon charitable appeals – although the local top management may also have some say in what is supported. Sometimes decisions are made by an international donations committee based at international headquarters. For larger local companies, the decision on what to support will usually be taken either by the chairman or managing director personally, or through some form of donations committee which meets regularly to consider applications. Large companies may also employ specialist staff (rather like a foundation) to assess applications and make recommendations on what should be supported. Some large companies operate an independent foundation, where the foundation and its trustees will set policy and decide on applications: for example, the Vodafone UK Foundation. With medium-sized and smaller companies, it is nearly always the top person who decides.

The important point to note is that you should try to write to the person who has responsibility for receiving and dealing with charitable appeals. Check who this is, as you don't want to write to the wrong person, let alone someone who left the company ten years ago! And make sure that you have the spelling and job title correct.

Some questions companies are likely to ask . . . with some suggested answers

Why is giving relevant to my company?

- Business cannot operate in isolation from society.
- Having a social vision is integral to the success of the business mission.
- A social investment strategy is a must for any progressive company.
- Qualified professionals increasingly prefer to work for a company with a social commitment.
- Customers show preference for doing business with companies that are environmentally conscious and socially driven.
- Communities and government expect companies to be good corporate citizens.

Why should I be supporting it? Shouldn't this be the responsibility of the government?

- We already receive substantial government support (if you do), and the money we are looking for is to enhance or develop our work.
- Government doesn't always have the capability or the resources to do everything.
- There are some things best done by NGOs and local people.
- There are some sorts of support and expertise that only companies can provide.

How do I make sure that my money will be well spent?

- Select a project that meets your criteria and has clearly defined objectives and the right development approach.
- Route your support through a credible development agency, if you think that this will be better than supporting the project directly.
- Insist on feedback.
- Even think about visiting the project.

I don't have any spare money, so how can I contribute?

- You can give material resources, such as company products, old furniture and unwanted equipment such as computers.
- You can provide technical know-how, financial and management skills, help with PR.
- You can help implement schemes, such as the construction of low-cost housing or toilets, by providing expertise, donating materials or equipment, or encouraging staff to volunteer.

I can't contribute the whole amount, so how will you make up the shortfall? Or will my money be wasted?

- We will find the balance from other sources; you could even make your gift conditional on us doing that.
- You might be able to help us here by introducing us to other businesses whom you think would be interested in providing a share.

If I give to one project, won't I be flooded with requests?
- Have a budget for the year and a stated policy on giving. That way you can support those projects you wish, and have a good reason for turning down the other requests.

Source: Adapted from a 'tick list' for corporate fundraising prepared by the Concern India Foundation

Getting support in kind

Giving things rather than money is often easier for a company. Here are some practical tips on how to set about getting support in kind:

Make a list of everything you need – this is called a 'wish list'. It can include services as well as products (such as the design for a leaflet you plan to produce).

Go through the list and try to **identify companies** that might have what you require. Personal knowledge is fine. But you might also want to use business directories.

Make contact. Writing a letter does not work well. It is best if you can make either personal or telephone contact. State your request, saying that it is for an NGO and indicating how well-used the donated item will be and how important it will be to the success of the project and your organisation's future.

If the company refuses to donate the item, it might be able to give you a hefty discount (perhaps half-price). This is worth asking for, as it will mean that you will need to raise less money. It can be a fall-back position in your discussions.

Be positive and enthusiastic. It can be very difficult for companies to refuse if they know what you want and how important it is for you. It will always cost them far less to donate the item than it would cost you to purchase it.

Say thank you. Report back subsequently on the difference the donation has made. Send the company your annual report. Try then to recruit it as a cash donor.

Some examples of support in kind

Hewlett-Packard: Education is essential to economic development and to creating prosperous communities. Information technology (IT) benefits education by improving access to information, supporting innovative and engaging teaching methods, and increasing student academic achievement.

HP donates products and cash and provides technical and professional development support to improve teaching and enhance student success in educational institutions. In 2007, the company became the leading sponsor of the Clinton Global Initiative's education programme. This aims to place more than 350,000 out-of-school children into educational programmes and improve learning for an additional 650,000 students. HP will employ its expertise in mobile technology to bring classroom learning to students living in remote areas.

Source: Hewlett-Packard Global Citizenship Report 2007

Anglo American plc: In sub-Saharan Africa (where it has large mining interests), the company has established a comprehensive strategy to minimise HIV/AIDS infection among its employees. High priority is given to working with local communities on projects to: widen awareness; encourage condom use, including among sex workers; promote treatment of sexually transmitted diseases; involve traditional healers in combating the epidemic; and create income-generating schemes that provide women, in particular, with the means to alleviate poverty.

Source: Anglo American Community Brochure 2002

Novartis: Malaria continues to ravage much of the world. Novartis, through the Roll Back Malaria initiative, and in partnership with the World Health Organization (WHO), provides its malaria medicine, Coartem, to the developing world.

HSBC India: Staff organised an open day in Delhi for the Butterflies Children's Development Bank initiative, where project managers and street children from different countries were able to see how a 'real bank' operated and compare this with their own microbank.

Microsoft India: This was an opportunity not taken. Pravah is a leading organisation that encourages young people to do something positive in the community. Microsoft had opened its India HQ near to Pravah's offices. Pravah was holding a training session in its new training room. But a request to Microsoft to use its boardroom would have been difficult to turn down (if the room was available at the required time), and could have been a first step in developing a really productive relationship with the company.

Where to find out about company giving

There are two aspects to this:

1. Finding out **what companies operate in your area**. There are several ways of finding out about local companies:
- Through the **local Chamber of Commerce** (if there is one).
- Through **other business and industry associations**.
- From the **local press**.
- By **knowing the area** where you live.

   And nationally and internationally, there may be:
- **Business directories** listing the top companies, and for international companies, *Fortune 500* and *Forbes Magazine* may be useful. These can be found in most business school libraries.
- The **national and international press**, especially *The Economist*, which carries news on international business affairs.

2. **Finding out what these companies are interested in supporting.** To find out what a company gives to is not always easy. Large companies tend to have a website or publish a report which details their policies. Most smaller companies don't, and for these it is the interests of the chief executive or chairman which are likely to be important. So if the chairman is passionate about cricket, he may wish to sponsor a cricket competition for

local schools. Or he may have an orphanage which he strongly supports. Any contact you have with the company at a senior level can be used to try to find out what it currently supports and what it might be interested in giving to. Another possibility is to identify one of your board members, volunteers or supporters who is employed by the company and ask them to find out for you.

Keep in touch with company news and events. This can often generate interesting ideas and opportunities. For example, if a plant is closing down or a new branch opening, the company might want to support some sort of initiative which will benefit the community. Read the papers: the business press, the national press, the local press.

And finally, try to get hold of the company's annual report, which will help you understand its business and identify its interests.

Getting started

There are three things you need to do to get started; once you begin to generate money, it all gets a lot easier.

1. First find out what, if any, **previous contact** you have had with what companies, and what previous fundraising approaches you have made, and with what success.
2. Through **research**, identify and match possible funders with various aspects of your work. In particular, try to find any local companies that are known for their generosity and might be interested in supporting your work.
3. Then find out whether any of your board members, staff, volunteers or supporters have any **personal contact** with any of the companies you plan to approach.

As for getting in touch, a personal approach will usually be best, if you can find a way of organising this. In smaller companies there is usually no staff member responsible for giving, and therefore approaches will have to be at board level. As a first step you might telephone the company to find out the following:

Who is responsible for dealing with charitable appeals.

■ Their **name**, correctly spelled, and **job title**, so that you get it right when you write to them or speak to them on the phone.

■ What **information they can send you** about their company. They might have a brochure which gives information on its charitable support programme. They certainly will have a company annual report, which will tell you about its work. Much of this information may be on the company's website.

■ Any **procedure** or **timetable** for submitting appeals.

■ Whether a representative might be interested in **coming to see your organisation** at work.

Meetings are useful when discussing bigger donations with larger companies, but will be difficult to arrange for anything small. Visits to see your projects are also a good way for a company to understand what you are doing; but it will be hard to persuade senior company executives to visit your projects until they have supported you. Business in the Community in the UK, which promotes corporate giving, organises Seeing is Believing days for senior business people. They find that when people visit projects and talk to organisers and beneficiaries, they get really excited about the idea of giving their own and their company's support; and any support that you do get is likely to be more substantial and longer term.

Almost certainly your proposal to the company will be in the form of a letter. Make your letter as personal as you can, as well as short and to the point. Circular letters will usually be put in the bin. Letters should therefore be directed to a named individual and written to them personally. A brief letter of no longer than a page is much more likely to be read and responded to than a longer letter (and you can attach supporting information to your letter). Because companies receive too many appeals, their first instinct is to say no, so they may not even read the letter. You may find that when you send an invitation to an open day, you receive a standard letter of rejection – even though you didn't ask for money – simply because the letter came from an NGO!

Getting companies to advertise in your publication

Companies are often prepared to support you by taking an advertisement in a publication: for example, your annual report and the programmes produced for fundraising events. This is known as 'goodwill advertising' as it is paid for to create goodwill for the company rather than sell more of its products. Companies like it because they can treat the expenditure as a business expense rather than as a charitable donation, because it gives them publicity in return for their support, and because they are being asked to give a specific amount that they can afford.

Here are some practical tips on getting companies to advertise:

1 Prepare a **rate card** which gives the different rates for a full page, half-page and so on, calculating the charges so that they are affordable to companies, but at the same time will generate a good surplus for your work.

2 Outline the sort of **audience** your publication will reach, and the kind of benefits the company can expect by advertising in it (for example, reaching a select audience of decision-takers, or being distributed widely among your supporters).

3 **Approach companies** that you think might be interested. These would include: those that have advertised in your publications previously; your suppliers; local companies who might be keen to be associated with your organisation; and companies where there is some connection between their business and what you do.

4 Follow up your original communication by **telephone**, and point out that other companies have agreed to advertise. Once one company agrees, this makes it much easier to persuade others to do the same.

5 **Offer to design the advertisement** for them. This is particularly useful if you are planning to approach smaller companies. You can make a small charge for doing this.

6 Always show the company a **copy of the proof**, and get someone there to sign it as 'approved'. In this way, if there is a mistake, you cannot be blamed.

7 Send the company a **copy of the publication**, with a note telling it the page on which its advertisement has been printed.

8 Make sure you **get paid** . . . and remember to say **thank you**.

9 Keep in touch. Tell the company about the success of your fundraising and what you have been able to achieve with the money. Perhaps it will be prepared to advertise again.

Raising money through working with companies: a case study

Dream a Dream is a small NGO based in Bangalore, India. Founded in 1999, Dream a Dream empowers children from vulnerable backgrounds by developing life skills while at the same time sensitising the community through active volunteering, leading to a non-discriminatory society where unique differences are appreciated.

Dream a Dream provides children from vulnerable backgrounds with non-traditional educational opportunities designed to allow them to explore, innovate and build important life skills.

The dream that started with a small group of young people wanting to make a difference in their Bangalore communities has developed into a professionally run NGO serving over 700 children through a strong base of volunteers.

Throughout its history Dream a Dream has been imaginative and resourceful in its approach to fundraising, preferring to rely on local support rather than foreign grants. One of its first ventures involved asking local bars to work with it to host parties on evenings early in the week, normal a quiet time for the bars. Dream a Dream volunteers sold entry tickets to friends and the bars made money on the extra drinks sold – a win-win for everyone. As well as bringing in funds, the parties also resulted in more volunteer helpers.

Another scheme has involved working with a group of restaurants. Each restaurant has a 'dream table' which can be booked by customers and the proceeds from which go to Dream a Dream. The promotion brings in new custom for the restaurant as well as supporting the charity – again a win-win.

Schemes like these are labour-intensive and raise limited funds; useful as a starting point but not a way to fund growth. One of the charity's latest initiatives is an annual seminar for company executives run by a leading figure in the corporate world who gives his time for free. Business people pay a sizeable fee to attend, resulting in a good level of income, and the event is relatively easy to organise.

Dream a Dream is a good example of how small-scale, volunteer-run activities can help raise profile and support which in turn opens up further opportunities. Working with businesses to help deliver benefits to them as well as to the charity has been key to their success.

Source: Vishal Talreja, CEO Dream a Dream. You can read more about the restaurant partnership by visiting the Showcase of Fundraising Innovation and Excellence (www.sofii.org).

Eight ideas for getting support from companies

1. **Put yourself in the position of the company.** Why should a company want to give its shareholders' funds to you? Why should it choose to support you, rather than another appeal? Think about the benefits the company may get from supporting you. And

mention these in your appeal letter. If you are looking for sponsorship, these benefits will be at the heart of your proposal.

2. **Suggest something specific for the company to support**, which you think will be of particular interest. In your letter state why the company should be interested. It is often best to think of something quite small if you are approaching it for the first time.

3. **Use all the contacts you have in the company** to help get a positive decision. Do you know the chairman, the managing director or any other senior member of staff? Or their spouses, who may be able to put in a good word for you? Or if you telephone, can you get into conversation with the chairman's secretary or personal assistant so that he or she becomes interested and enthusiastic and will put in a good word for you? Do you have any volunteers helping you who also work for the company? They may be able to help you 'from the inside'; and it will do you no harm if you mention that they volunteer or fundraise for you in your appeal letter.

4. **Think of all the different ways in which the company could help you.** Cash might not be the best way. Might it be easier for the company to offer staff time or give you some expertise you lack? Or the use of a vehicle or a piece of equipment? Or access to company staff to promote your work? Most other appeals will be asking for cash, but the company may find it easier to give in kind. And once it has given in kind and got to know you and your work, cash support may be possible next time.

5. **Consider whether there is a senior executive of the company** (the more senior the better) who might become a board member of your organisation or serve on a development committee, thus bringing new ideas, good organisation and a wealth of business contacts to your organisation that will be worth many times the value of a donation. If this level of involvement is too much, a request for advice may succeed.

6. **Don't assume that every company will give.** Make parallel approaches to several or many companies.

7. **Consider who might be the best person to make the approach or sign the letter.** It may not be you. It could be a senior businessman who has already given you generous support.

8. **Every time you buy anything from a company, ask for a discount.** This will save you money. But it could also be a first step in getting it to support you.

4.6 Business sponsorship

Sponsorship needs to be carefully defined. It is not simply a gift from a company which is publicly acknowledged. It is an association between two parties (the company and the NGO), each with quite different interests, who come together in order to support a particular activity for two quite different motives.

The NGO is looking to raise funds for its work. The sponsor hopes to improve its image or to promote its products or to entertain its customers – and thereby sell more of its products. The sponsor's contribution does not need to be money, though usually it is. It could also be a gift of goods (such as a car), or services (such as free transport), or professional expertise (such as promotion or marketing consultancy), or staff fundraising (to raise money for the charity), or the use of buildings (such as an exhibition centre), or free promotion (in a newspaper or broadcast), and so on.

An additional benefit of sponsorship is the way in which the link with the sponsor can be developed subsequently – depending on how the original sponsorship goes. If all goes well and they get to like you and admire your professionalism, you might look for further sponsorships on a larger scale, and possibly also for a donation from the company charitable budget, being able to use company resources and facilities (such as a training centre or meeting room) free of charge, getting employees involved in the work of your NGO or senior management to sit on your management board. These are all things you might expect to flow from a successful sponsorship.

One of the future directions of corporate giving is through sponsorship – as companies want to get more back for their money than a simple acknowledgement. In recent years, sponsorship has extended from sport and the arts into the environment, education and social projects. Many companies will give much more as sponsorship than they would as a donation, as they can see the benefits that they will gain for themselves. Developing links with the major national and local corporate sponsors – even if this effort comes to nothing – could be an investment in your future that is well worth making now.

Who sponsors?

Most sponsors are commercial businesses, including state-owned industries. But government departments, public authorities, utilities, hospitals, universities and other institutions sometimes undertake sponsorship if they can gain some benefit by doing so. There are four main opportunities for sponsorship:

1. Companies **anxious to promote themselves,** to create a better image of themselves, or to generate a public awareness in the local communities where they operate. This includes companies with an 'image problem': for example, mining and extraction companies associated with the destruction of the environment who want to project a cleaner, greener image by being associated with a conservationist cause.

2. Companies with a **particular product or service** that they wish to introduce or promote. This could include a new brand of toothpaste or beer, or a supermarket which is opening in the area. Public awareness is important if a product or service is to get accepted. So companies may be open to any proposal that gives a particular product or service more exposure.

3. Companies looking for **entertainment opportunities** where they can seek to influence customers, suppliers, regulators, the media and other opinion formers. This could be a prestigious concert, theatrical event, art exhibition, horse race or sporting event. It would provide them with an appropriate entertainment opportunity plus the chance to mingle with celebrities.

4. Companies that are **committed supporters** of your organisation. They may find something that they would like to sponsor, even if it is partly for 'philanthropic reasons' – just because they admire what you are doing and are happy to be publicly associated with it.

Banks and financial services companies are particularly keen to sponsor, and often sponsor the prestigious cultural events. Foreign airlines and companies might be interested in sponsoring exhibitions and events that are based on their home country culture. Major international companies, and also those just expanding into your country, may have well-developed international sponsorship programmes. Breweries are often active sponsors.

To be successful in getting sponsorship, you need an appropriate event as well as a good understanding of why companies like to sponsor.

Why companies like sponsorship

- It helps them **get their message across.**
- It can enhance or change their **image.**
- It can reach a **target audience** very precisely.
- It can be very **cost-effective advertising** or **product promotion.**
- Further **marketing opportunities** may develop from the sponsorship.
- It generates **good publicity** for the sponsor, often of a kind that money can't buy.
- It generates an **awareness of the company** within the local community in which the company operates and from where it draws its workforce.
- Sponsors can **entertain important** clients at the events they sponsor.

What can be sponsored

An extremely wide range of things can be sponsored, the more popular of which include:

- **Cultural events,** such as theatre productions, film premieres and art exhibitions.
- **Sport and sporting events,** such as football teams and championship matches.
- **Mass participation events,** such as a marathon run.
- **Social programmes,** especially those that address major national problems in an innovative way.
- The **publication of a report or a book,** with an attendant launch.
- The production of **fundraising materials,** leaflets and posters, or even the sponsorship of a complete fundraising campaign.
- **Vehicles,** where the acknowledgement can be painted on the side.
- **Equipment,** such as cars or computers, produced by the company.
- **Competitions,** awards and prizes.
- **Scholarships,** bursaries, travel grants.
- **Conferences and seminars,** especially to specialist audiences (such as doctors) where the sponsor's promotional material can be displayed.

Some examples of corporate sponsorship

Kenya Breweries sponsoring social programmes: Kenya Breweries Limited is a subsidiary of East Africa Breweries Limited and is now one of the largest businesses in east Africa. For a long time it has supported education, sport, water projects, famine relief and barley farmers (who provide a main ingredient for their beer). These are some of the programmes it has sponsored:

Through Guinness, one of its brands, the company launched a scholarship scheme with Strathmore University. It donated Ksh8 million each year to cover education costs for ten students for a four-year degree course at the College. Under the Chevening Scholarships scheme, Guinness also offers two graduate students scholarships to study in the UK. The company also supports IT training in secondary schools to try to bridge the digital divide in Kenya. In 2000, it launched a Ksh20 million Computers for Schools programme which donates computers to schools in poorer communities.

In 1999, the company introduced the Water of Life programme, which began with the Rumuruti water project in Turkana District. In 2003, it entered into a partnership with AMREF to extend the water programme across the country. This aimed to develop and equip shallow wells and gravity water schemes to supply safe drinking water to households.

Through Kenya Maltings, the company has since 1947 been supporting barley farmers by investing in research, seed production and malting. Since barley farming is capital-intensive, barley farmers occasionally require loans. Kenya Maltings has been guaranteeing loans up to Ksh450 million each year.

The company also engages in joint promotions. For example, it donated 25 cents for every bottle of Tusker purchased to Turkana famine relief. The Ksh5 million raised was channelled through AMREF.

The company is now focusing on sustainable development, supporting programmes that have long-term impact on the community.

CitiBank sponsoring financial literacy: Encouraging young people to manage their money properly and save for their future rather than spend, spend, spend is seen as important. For this reason, many banks have been supporting financial literacy programmes in schools by sponsoring the development of course materials.

CitiBank in the UK has gone one step further. It has supported a public-speaking competition in some of London's poorest schools, where students have to speak on topics such as 'Needs and Wants'. CitiBank provides funding to run the programme, cash prizes for the winners and opportunities for its staff to volunteer. The finals are held with a reception for students, teachers and volunteers at CitiBank HQ. The programme is implemented by SpeakersBank, a relatively new NGO that encourages young people to Speak Up and Speak Out on issues that concern them by providing inspirational speaker training.

Awards for social entrepreneurs: UnLtd India is an offshoot of a foundation in the UK which provides cash awards and support to emerging social entrepreneurs. Each award made costs around $3,000. Award winners might be developing sports activity for the youth of Mumbai slums, photography programmes in blind schools or free websites for NGOs. This provides a really good opportunity for sponsorship, as a company can sponsor one or a group of awards linked to an activity that relates to its business, and then be kept closely in touch with the progress of the award winners they are sponsoring. ICICI bank is sponsoring the programme as a whole by providing running costs for the first three years, and awards are being sponsored by accountants KPMG and others.

Identifying possible sponsors

First you should decide what your proposed activity has to offer a sponsor. Is it a target audience? Or the opportunity to meet stars and other celebrities? Or a prestigious event where the company can entertain its customers and suppliers? Or an event to coincide with the completion of a residential development or a new shopping centre? Only when you have done this can you begin to think about which companies might be interested. They may be national companies looking for national publicity, or a major company located in your area, or a purely local concern looking to develop local awareness. Remember that if you are looking for a lot of money, only the larger companies will be interested.

Then you should draw up a list of potential sponsors that you plan to approach. You will need to do a bit of research. Find out what the company has sponsored before, what are its current interests and concerns, and what sort of sums it might provide. The next step is to prepare the written proposal, which will outline the project and highlight all the benefits to be gained by the sponsor. You will put a price on the sponsorship – which will as much reflect the value of the benefits to the company as your own fundraising need.

You will need patience. Sponsorship can take a long time to negotiate; so it is best to plan well in advance. Start discussions at least a year, and possibly even longer, before the activity takes place.

Sponsorship involves a close working relationship between the company and the NGO. You need to think about the ethics of a charitable organisation working closely alongside a commercial organisation. It is one thing when an NGO accepts money from a company about whose activities it has some reservations; it is quite another when it is actively involved in promoting the work of such a company, as it will be doing through a sponsorship relationship. For example, if you are promoting environmental awareness or tree planting, would you want the programme sponsored by an extraction company whose business may be adding to environmental problems? It is strongly recommended that you develop a sponsorship policy before you apply for any sponsorship – agreeing in advance which types of company you are happy to approach and which you are not.

The sponsorship package

Once you have reassured yourself that you are happy to work with a company, you will prepare a sponsorship proposal which will set out:

- The exact nature of **the project or activity**, and how it will work.
- The **audiences** to be reached and the publicity to be obtained. These should be quantified as far as possible (how many column centimetres of coverage and in which newspapers can be expected, how many and what sort of people will attend the event, how many posters will be displayed, and so on). If you have been involved in sponsorship before, what you were able to achieve then will provide a good indication of what you might be able to achieve now. Remember that the company will be primarily interested in reaching those people who are its target audience.
- The **geographical coverage**. Is it a national or a purely local activity?

- The **image** that will be projected through the event, and how this will fit in with what the sponsoring brand or company might be looking for.
- The **specific advertising opportunities** that will be available on poster hoardings, the sides of vans, in the event programme, on TV, in the press, and so on.
- The **other benefits** that the sponsorship will offer the company. This includes benefits for staff, business contacts, and relations with government.
- The **amount of the sponsorship** – and the value that you estimate for the sponsorship benefits, and how this compares with other ways of reaching the target audiences or achieving the same promotional objectives.

All this should be produced in a professional (though not necessarily expensive) way, and include photographs and selected press coverage from previously sponsored events, plus brief background material on your organisation and its work, showing why it is a credible partner for the company.

Sponsorship plan of action for a Royal Charity Golf Tournament in Malaysia

- Sponsors for each hole to pay RM5,000, and a placard with the name and logo of that sponsor to be placed at that hole.
- An automobile company to sponsor the insurance cover for the Hole-in-One prize.
- Donors required for 27 useful and practical prizes.
- A donor for the tonic drinks to be distributed to the 60 participating golfers at the Halfway House (after nine holes) whilst the tournament is in progress.
- Donors for golf balls and other items as gifts in souvenir slingbags.
- Free printing of sponsorship cards
- In addition, each participant was required to raise sponsorship of at last RM1,000 to be able to play. The net proceeds from the event amounted to more than RM100,000.

Source: Malaysian Red Crescent Society

Making the approach

Having identified a potential company and developed your sponsorship proposal, you can approach the company in a variety of ways.

It will be best if you can make an appointment to visit the company, or a PR agency used by the company, to give a presentation of your work and discuss the sponsorship opportunities. Only then will you be in a position to find out what the needs of the company are and how you might be able to meet them. You must make sure you are approaching the person who is able to make the decision. For product promotions, this will be the brand manager. For corporate PR, it may be a senior director.

If you are not able to arrange a meeting at this stage, a telephone call to the marketing department can elicit a wealth of information about who to send the proposal to, and what sort of sponsorships they are likely to consider. Then send a summary proposal to see if it sparks any interest, and follow this up a few days later with a phone call to try and arrange a meeting.

Larger, prestigious NGOs may want to employ an advertising agency or marketing consultant to introduce sponsorship opportunities to sponsors. They will charge you a fee for doing this, which could be based on creating a successful outcome.

Some more examples of corporate sponsorship

Coca-Cola. In the mid-1990s, as part of its marketing strategy for establishing itself in India, Coca-Cola sponsored the World Cup international cricket series, which was being held in India. Cricket is India's national sport and attracts huge television audiences and press interest.

Barclays PLC. Early in 2000, Barclays established an alliance with Africa Online by sponsoring the opening of a number of free internet cafés across sub-Saharan Africa. On-hand help was provided to encourage people to build up skills and confidence in using the technology. Barclays also ran educational programmes, helping to bring the e-world to Africa.

Cadbury Schweppes plc. Cadbury's encourage various local initiatives throughout the world centred around education and enterprise, health and welfare, environmental support, and sport and recreation. The shape and focus of its programmes are usually determined at country or business-unit level to ensure local relevance. Examples of sponsorship by the company have included: the promotion of anti-crime education in schools in Mexico; lifestyle awareness promotion in Nigeria through support of the Cope Breast Cancer television campaign; and the celebration of regional dance and poetry as part of South Africa's Sunrise cultural festival.

The Hunger Site. Every time someone logs on to this site a donation is made sufficient to feed a family for a day. This is paid for by a group of sponsors who have banner advertisements and links to their websites. The money goes to America's Second Harvest (for hunger relief in the USA) and Mercy Corps (worldwide). Other similar sites have now appeared for other causes, including The Rainforest Site and FreeRice.com.

Contractual issues

Because sponsorship involves your giving something in return for the money you are receiving, it is advisable to agree terms through some form of contract, which can easily be done in the form of a letter. A number of important issues need to be settled when negotiating the sponsorship:

- **How long the arrangement will run.** Is it for one year, thus requiring you to find a new sponsor next year? Or can you get a commitment for three or more years? And what happens at the end of this period – does the sponsor have a first refusal on the following year's event? Most successful sponsorships run for several years, and the benefit builds up over the sponsorship period. But companies don't like being tied to sponsoring something indefinitely – their sponsorship programme would begin to look a bit stale.
- **The fee to be paid,** and when instalments are due.
- **What benefits are to be delivered in return for the fee.** These need to be specified as clearly as possible, so that you know precisely what you are contracted to deliver.

- **Who is to pay the costs.** This is something that is often forgotten. Who pays for the additional publicity that the sponsor requires or for the prestigious launch party? There needs to be a clear understanding of who is responsible for what, so you can ensure that everything is covered and there are no misunderstandings later on.
- **Who is responsible for doing what.** Who will do the public relations (will it be you, or will the company's PR department be able to help)? Who will handle the bookings? Who will invite the guests? Whose staff will receive the guests? Plus all the other details that need to be clarified.
- **Any termination arrangements** in the event of the activity having to be cancelled.
- **Who is responsible for managing the relationship** – on both sides.

If everything is written down in the agreement, there are less likely to be problems later on – and it will also ensure that everything has been properly thought through at the outset.

Joint promotions

For larger NGOs, commercial promotions which involve the NGO in helping to market a commercial product can provide another opportunity for working with a company. This is often known as a 'joint promotion'. The arrangement can bring in large amounts of money relatively painlessly and expose the name of the NGO to millions of people for little or no cost. The same technique can also be used by local NGOs through local promotions.

A joint promotion is rather like sponsorship, but the relationships are reversed – you are linked to the company's products, rather than they to your cause. Commercial promotions can include on-pack and licensing promotional deals, competitions and awards, the use of phone lines, and self-liquidating offers. What they have in common is that they present an opportunity to raise money for your cause and to project your NGO to new audiences. But they require that you work with the company on their terms to achieve this.

Some examples of commercial promotions

- For every new mobile phone subscription from one of your supporters, a telecoms company will make a donation. There is huge competition to attract subscribers, and companies are looking at all sorts of ways of attracting customers.
- For every Pizza Veneziana purchased, the restaurant will make a donation to the Venice in Peril Fund. Pizza Express, a UK chain, has raised millions for this fund, which was launched in the 1970s when Venice flooded. Deepalaya in India did a tie-up with a local fast food restaurant chain so that each customer's bill included a donation during the month of the promotion (which customers could opt not to pay).
- Loyalty credit cards, which are offered in partnership with agencies such as the WorldWide Fund for Nature and the RED American Express Card (which supports the World Food Programme), where a donation is made on joining and a small percentage of all the subsequent transactions on the account is then donated.

On-pack promotions

There are many variants of the on-pack promotion. They start with the need of a manufacturer to promote a product or service at a particular point in time – the promotion may be to the wholesaler, to the retailer or to the consumer. The basic mechanism is that with every purchase of the product and for every label or coupon returned, the manufacturer will give a specified sum of money to the NGO, sometimes with an upper limit on the total to be given. Good practice requires that the amount to be donated is specified on the pack.

Manufacturers like this sort of arrangement as they can predict quite accurately what it is going to cost to achieve sales at a given level. Fundraisers like it, since it presents their cause to literally millions of shoppers, and because they can usually expect to raise a substantial sum. Variations on this theme include the consortium promotion, which includes a galaxy of well-known NGOs included together in one promotion. Local and smaller-scale promotions are also possible. For example, a local Indian take-away restaurant in London donates all the proceeds of the sale of a lentil dish each Friday to selected charities supported by the owner.

Licensing

When an NGO has become a well-known household name, manufacturers of consumer goods can become interested in developing an association with the NGO to enhance their sales. A company uses the NGO's good name to endorse its product. Out of this is born the licensing deal. The promotion is likely to involve a fixed number of uses of the charity logo or name over a given period in return for an often substantial fee. Precisely how it is used will be set out in the licensing agreement. NGOs such as the WorldWide Fund for Nature and Save the Children are able to generate substantial incomes in this way.

Competitions

Another variant is the on-pack promotion that involves a competition. This is usually a prize draw, more often a game of chance rather than a game of skill (to encourage as many people as possible to enter), and may involve a tie-break question (for example, describe in 20 words why you like Brand X).

For the fundraiser, competitions offer several benefits. The promotion can be related in some way to the NGO and its cause. If it's a charity working overseas, the prize could be a trip to that country. If an environmental cause, the competition questions could be designed to create a better understanding of that cause. Money will accrue to the NGO either through a contribution for each entry sent in, or from an agreed fee for the use of the NGO's name.

Self-liquidating offers

The self-liquidating offer is the rather grand name for promoting one of your own products so that its costs are recovered from sales. You offer one of your products – say an attractive T-shirt, with a design by a well-known designer – to a manufacturer to feature on the back of a pack. Consumers are invited to send in for this at the 'special offer price', which is set low enough to seem excellent value, but high enough to recover costs.

There are several advantages to such an arrangement. Depending on how you price the product, you could end up making a profit on a large number of sales – something that NGOs seldom manage by marketing the same product themselves. Whether or not you do better than recover your costs, you can certainly expect to distribute a large number of items bearing your message. There is also the possibility of retaining the mailing list of purchasers for subsequent direct mail fundraising. And finally, there will be an extremely large number of people who will see the promotion but not buy – which creates additional good publicity and name-awareness for your cause.

Getting started with promotions

Promotions of this kind are quite difficult to arrange. It is an area where professionalism is needed, so you may want to discuss the possibilities first with a marketing or advertising agency, possibly on a *pro bono* basis.

The first step is to decide whether you are the sort of NGO which can expect a commercial link of this sort. Usually national 'brand name' NGOs and those addressing 'popular' causes, such as helping children, are more likely to benefit from this area of fundraising than the less well-known NGOs and those addressing difficult causes, such as torture or slavery.

Then you need to decide whether to wait until companies or their promotional agencies contact you (they may not), or whether to take the initiative yourself and contact companies you think might be interested. You need to be absolutely clear about the extent to which you are prepared to associate your NGO's good name with a particular industry, a particular company and a particular product. For example, if you are working with children, do you want to be promoting confectionery or sugary beverages?

Ideally, you need to research the industries, companies and products that are likely to make good partners for you. What are their marketing objectives? Who are their competitors? What might they gain through an association with you? With this information, it is worth trying to meet the marketing director to present the possibilities for working together and the advantages of an association.

It is preferable at this stage not to have too detailed a proposal in mind, so that you can react to what you find to be the company's own preferences and needs. You should take along examples of how other companies have benefited from an association with you – though this will not be possible if it is the first promotion you are arranging.

If you are approached by a promotional agency pitching for business, this does not mean that anything is certain. They may be working independently, hoping that a good idea involving your NGO can then be sold to a company. In nine out of ten times, these approaches will come to nothing, and you may find you have put in considerable effort without getting any payback.

Issues

Commercial promotions bring NGOs face to face with a range of dilemmas – just as with sponsorship, but perhaps more so since the relationship is with a specific product and that much more public. It is important that there are no ethical problems for you in being closely associated with the particular company or product, and that the product in question is good value and does not fall to bits. As with sponsorship, you are strongly recommended to develop your own policy on what commercial associations you are prepared to enter into.

How much you should expect to receive from a commercial promotion is also a difficult question. Your name is effectively being sold to the company to enhance theirs or their product's. It may be worth a great deal to them to be linked with you. Any negotiation should start from what you think the association is worth to them and whether it is worth your while to enter into the promotion at that price.

4.7 Other sources

Giving by other institutions

There are many different types of organisation which might be interested in supporting your organisation in some way. These include:

1. **Trade unions**, especially where your work is to do with employment rights or some other matter of interest to them. Trade union giving will normally be an extension of their political stance. For example, many unions contributed to the fight against apartheid by making donations to the voluntary organisations concerned with combating apartheid, in pursuance of resolutions at annual conferences. The structure of giving can be through the Congress of Trade Unions, a union HQ, or one of the local branches, or by being allowed to send your appeal to the membership at large.

2. **Membership bodies** such as the Women's Institutes, Young Farmers, Round Tables, Chambers of Commerce, business and trade associations, Rotarians, Lions and other similar organisations (the range of groups that exist will vary from country to country) can provide important opportunities for fundraising. Usually they don't make large grants themselves, but will encourage their membership to support charity. This can be by adopting a particular appeal – such as literacy or health education. Or it can be by inviting different organisations to address their lunches or dinners – where you will have the opportunity to talk about your work and to circulate information about what you are doing and your need for support. So find out what organisations exist in your locality, make contact and suggest that you be invited to address them. Many organisations have been able to develop significant support from this source.

3. **Embassies.** Many embassies have small grants budgets to create goodwill, but also to create opportunities for their ambassador or other senior diplomats to meet and greet people. This is in addition to any aid budget from that country. It can be worth your while trying to make contact with the person responsible for the grants budget. This is much easier if your organisation is based in the capital city – although the embassy may have a special interest in a particular region of the country or an office in another city. Try to find out as much as you can, and then make contact with the appropriate person.

4. **Schools and young people.** Engaging young people through schools, colleges and universities also provides an opportunity for local fundraising. There are three good reasons for wanting to do this:

■ Young people represent **the society of tomorrow**, and should be encouraged to engage with the issues of development and social change.

- Education on **the issues of development** (whether it is AIDS/HIV, global warming or the impact of globalisation) can go hand in hand with fundraising, and asking young people to fundraise can be a good starting point for getting them further engaged.
- Schools, colleges and universities are **easily reached**, and it only requires the agreement of the teacher or the principal for a fundraising initiative to take place.

Although young people can't give much, lots of people giving small amounts of support can quickly mount up to being something quite useful. All sorts of devices are now being used to mobilise support from young people:

- Sponsored **participation events,** such as walks and fun runs (see Section 6.2).
- **Events that involve young people,** such as 'dress-down days' where pupils are allowed to come to school not in uniform if they pay a small sum, or parties and discos with a small entrance fee being donated.
- **School links** with schools in other countries, where both sets of pupils do something for the cause.

School fundraising is covered in more detail in Section 6.9.

Religious bodies and faith communities

In many countries, religion plays an important role in local life, and religious institutions and networks are well established. This includes especially the Christian, Muslim and Hindu faiths, plus other, smaller religions. These religions all place an emphasis on charitable giving, to the church, mosque or temple so that it can function and to support its wider role in the community, or to the community and the poor. Some religions set a norm for giving, such as 10 per cent of one's annual income (tithing for Christians, zakat for Muslims). Although few people actually achieve these levels of giving, these religions encourage their congregations to give generously. In addition to this, some religious institutions are extremely wealthy in their own right, through endowments and legacies given to them over the centuries; and others are linked to aid agencies established in the North by religious bodies – such as Christian Aid (the Anglican Church) and CAFOD (the Roman Catholic Church) – or missionary movements which brought education and health care to the South alongside their evangelical work.

You need to consider the opportunities for fundraising that religion offers alongside the possible negative impact of sectarianism and religious fundamentalism. Each fundraiser will have a view influenced by the particular environment in the countries where they are operating and the cause they are promoting; so you will need to make up your own mind.

If you do decide to proceed, there are two main possibilities:

- If your organisation has a religious connection, this will provide an entry point into the development aid system linked to that religion or denomination (see Section 4.3).
- In the communities where your projects are taking place, you may be able to harness local support. This could be through local people giving money, but it might also be through their giving time as volunteers, giving support in kind (expertise as well as

other things) and giving moral support. The point of entry would be through a religious leader or a member of the congregation with whom you have a close connection. At a time when development is seen as something done for poor people with money from the rich world, this can create a means of engaging the local community more actively in the process.

Rotary International

Rotary International is a worldwide organisation of 1.2 million people in business and professionals who unite to provide humanitarian service, and build peace and goodwill. It has the following programmes:

- The Rotary Foundation to promote international understanding, grant education awards and sponsor international projects.
- The End Polio Now programme supports immunisation and polio eradication.
- A variety of education and youth programmes to promote understanding by bringing young people together and to develop youth leadership.

www.rotary.org

International Association of Lions Clubs

This is the global organisation for Lions Club members. The Lions Club International Foundation support includes disaster relief – including reconstruction of schools, hospitals and other institutions – vocational assistance and training, and projects that assist blind and deaf people – including glaucoma screening clinics, eye banks, rehabilitation institutes, and auditory equipment for deaf people.

www.lionsclubs.org

Tourism and tourists

For many countries, tourism is an extremely important contributor to the national economy. And because of the structure of the international currency exchange system, the tourist pound or dollar can often go an extremely long way – so that what appears to be a modest sum of money to the tourist can have an enormous impact on your organisation and its work. Some tourists are on tightly organised schedules and never stray from their group, but others are more adventurous and may well be tempted to share in some interesting experience which you can devise for them. And then there are people who are already interested in what you are doing and make a point of visiting you – here you have a special opportunity to engage their support. Here are some ideas:

Visitors to your project. These can be people passing through who have heard about your work, or people coming on a tour organised by a donor agency for its committed supporters to see some of the projects they are helping. You have a chance here to show them your work, to engage their interest, and perhaps to get them to support you. They are clearly interested.

Attracting tourists to come and see you by arranging events and activities at your project (with transport laid on if required). Many tourists would like to do something 'out of the ordinary' during their stay which brings them closer to the life of the country they are visiting. Visiting local craftsmen at work (and perhaps buying some of what they are producing), seeing a rural development project, being shown round a museum with a talk from an expert, visiting a prison and talking to prisoners . . . the opportunities are endless!

You could try to place a display panel or leaflets describing your organisation and its work in local hotels, together with advance notice of events and activities you are organising. You might even try to be extremely inventive by designing special events such as a cycle tour of the city, or a visit to see parliament in action, even where this bears little or no relation to your work – you will be doing something interesting that tourists want to participate in, and this will give you the opportunity to explain your work and to gain their interest.

Getting visitors to support your work

ACCORD is a tribal development project in south India supported by ActionAid. It runs a hospital and a community health service as part of its work. This is supported in part by an insurance scheme where families pay a small monthly contribution. It aims to be as self-sufficient as it can. But there is always a need for money to cover running costs, to purchase equipment or for new developments. ACCORD receives a steady stream of overseas visitors. The project has developed a sponsorship scheme, whereby a visitor can sponsor the hospital and health work for one day at a cost of US$50. ACCORD will then write to you and tell you what happened on that day, what it was able to achieve with your money: how many babies were born, what operations took place, what lives were saved, and so on.

Banana Box in Nairobi's Sarit Centre sells Kenyan handicrafts, but unlike other curio shops it operates on fair trade principles when dealing with local artisans. Banana Box supports a project that trains Kenyan street children to make and hand-print recycled carrier bags and gift packaging. The money they earn helps them to live and several of the older boys now run their own business producing the carrier bags and in turn train and use more street children. They are mentioned in the Lonely Planet guide. Getting into the guidebooks (particularly the Rough Guide, the Lonely Planet and the Spectrum Guide) and having displays at hotels encourages people to visit.

Attracting tourists in and exploiting tourism

The **Multi Environmental Society** (MESO) is a non-profit organisation in Tanzania working to improve the quality of individual and community life and of the environment in which people live. MESO was established in the mid-1980s as a loose association until its formal registration on 24 January 1995.

MESO arranges eco-cultural trips around Karatu and the Rift Valley regions of Tanzania. Its eco-tours serve as an alternative to traditional park safaris, although it does tailor individual trips to incorporate popular game viewing attractions. The project's main focus is to promote environmental and social responsibility, while providing the opportunity to visit natural sites and learn about local culture and tradition. In addition to this, MESO offers the opportunity to participate in village 'homestays', allowing tourists to penetrate the lives of local individuals and observe numerous aspects of daily life in rural areas.

Eco-cultural tours offered through MESO are structured in such a way that environmental impact is minimised; the conservation of valuable resources is of primary concern. Furthermore, the organisation aims to re-establish natural areas and provide visitors with further information to help preserve and protect these areas for generations to come. This process is facilitated through experienced guides who have acquired in-depth knowledge of the indigenous wildlife and landforms that exist in these areas. Surplus income generated through the programmes is distributed among local residents to improve their economic power, or is re-invested into the organisation to develop and maintain the programmes.

Returned volunteers

Many organisations have foreign volunteers working with them for a summer, for a year, or for a longer period. When these volunteers return home, they can be extremely helpful to you in your fundraising. They are already enthusiastic about your work, so your job is to build on that enthusiasm. You can do a number of things:

- Suggest that they form a **local support group** of interested people back home, who will raise funds for you. Give them a project to raise money for (or several projects). You will be surprised by how much money they can raise, and they will be surprised at how much you can do with it. A direct link between donor and project is a far more efficient way of raising money than working through an established aid agency (with its attendant overheads). Give them projects to fundraise for which have some real long-term benefit to the development of the community, which involve improving the lives of people, and where the results are obvious for all to see (for example, providing a well or building a new classroom). You will need to keep in regular contact, so that they can see how your work is developing. They will need literature, which you could provide or which they could have printed. A set of photographs, a short video, leaflets and a PowerPoint presentation will all be extremely useful in helping them gather support.
- If they are going back to paid employment, they might like to make **a regular and substantial financial contribution** to your work. They may not have thought of that. So discuss the possibility with them before they leave.
- They may be able to **help you access sources of money** in their country, particularly from foundations and from national and multilateral aid programmes. If you were to apply directly, you would almost certainly get rejected – not because your project is no good, but because they have no way of assessing your application from such a distance or because they require the applicant to be resident in their own country. If

they agree to work with you and you then apply, this will give you an opportunity to access their funds.

- They may be able to **link you with other organisations** – for example, a school in their country which can adopt your project and fundraise for it; or a voluntary organisation which has just the expertise you need.

There is also the possibility of getting your supporters in other countries to come and visit you, and even volunteer for you. When they have visited you and seen your work at first hand, they will return as even more passionate supporters. Kiva.org, which provides people with the opportunity to make small loans to grass-roots entrepreneurs in developing countries, also has a volunteer programme enabling people to visit communities where money is being loaned, meet the local entrepreneurs (who might include a widow setting up a beauty parlour, or a small farmer investing in digging a well) and provide reports on progress for the Kiva website. UnLtd India runs 'Learning Journeys' that enable people interested in social entrepreneurship to meet leading social entrepreneurs in different regions of India. They may go on to support the work of UnLtd India or to get involved in setting up something similar in another country.

Creating links between two communities

The Marlborough Brandt Group (named after Willi Brandt, who produced an important report on North-South issues) is based in Marlborough, a small town in southern England. The town through the group has 'adopted' a town in the Gambia. This involves a range of activities linking the two places and peoples, including: sponsoring students to train in England, fundraising, development education projects involving schools in both countries, sale of craft items made, and so on.

Just Change India is promoting cooperative buying and selling of produce between poor communities in several states of India (including Tamil Nadu and Orissa). Some of the communities grow tea, and this is being marketed by Just Change UK, which is based on the Marsh Farm housing estate in Luton. The aim is to link the tea growers and the residents of Marsh Farm, not just to sell tea but to explore together the issues of poverty and disadvantage.

Non-resident communities

With the increasing globalisation of business, and as people engage in economic or political migration and travel to seek out educational opportunities, there are more and more non-resident communities abroad. Whether it is the British or Indian expatriate community in Saudi Arabia or non-resident Indians in the United States and Europe (these are now so numerous that they are referred to as NRIs), or refugees from Sarajevo in Germany, they retain strong family links with their home country and culture. They represent an obvious fundraising source for charitable and development and relief work being done in their country of origin.

But how do you reach them, and what do you ask them to do? HelpAge India tried direct mail to mobilise the support of NRIs in the Gulf States. But this did not work well. However, CRY, an Indian development agency working with children, includes an appeal with bank statements sent to NRIs abroad who hold rupee accounts with selected Indian banks. This seems to bring good returns. IndiCorps in the USA and UK organises year-long volunteering and leadership development courses for young people of Indian origin in India. Likewise, Asha for Education (also based in the USA with a branch in the UK) raises money from the NRI community, which is spent on projects identified and supported by Asha members, which they visit on their trips to their country of origin.

There are two possible approaches to consider. The first is general publicity to get your cause known to the non-resident community at large. The second is to find an individual who is interested and wants to help by organising the fundraising for you locally. Here are some ideas to help get you started:

- **Contact the embassy** for details of business and community groupings, wives' associations and so on.
- **Use personal and family contacts.** It is surprising who you can get access to if you think about it or ask your friends. Many people when approached to do something useful are surprisingly keen to do it! So ask.
- **Go through your files and visitor book** to see if there are any addresses of people you can contact. If there are quite a lot, you could try to arrange a meeting for them to hear about your latest work and your plans for the future.
- **Undertake a preparatory visit** – not to raise money, but to make contacts and to see if you can find people prepared to help you. Bring along plenty of explanatory brochures, even a short video showing your work. Give a contact point so that people can get back in touch with you if they are interested. Follow up on every lead. Be persistent.
- **Organise cultural evenings** or similar events. Many non-residents are homesick and would welcome New Year parties or Diwali evenings when they could get together.
- **Get coverage in the émigré press.** There will often be newsletters or newspapers circulating that keep people in touch (with one another and with what's going on at home). Try to get your work covered in these, or write a letter asking if anyone is interested in helping start your fundraising initiative.
- **Publicise your work in the local press,** focusing on a local person who is doing something significant to help you.

CHAPTER 5

Generating income through self-financing

5.1 Self-financing – the poor relation

The Resource Alliance was until 1996 called the International Fund Raising Group, and this name change illustrates a conceptual issue in relation to resource mobilisation. Many organisations that specialise in the process of financing non-profit and charitable activities have the word 'fundraising' in their title (for example, the Fund-Raising School of the University of Atlanta, the Association of Fundraising Professionals). Fundraising has been the dominant concept in the world of financing voluntary organisations for a very long time. Many people involved in this field are proud to call themselves 'fundraisers'. It is therefore important to make it clear that we are talking about something different in this chapter.

Fundraising is based on the concept that disposable income exists somewhere 'out there', and that it is possible and valuable to influence people and organisations so that they give some of their disposable income to the good causes that the fundraiser represents. The disposable income may come from an individual's great wealth (or alternatively from many individuals' pittances); from organisations professionally set up to disburse money from governments; from businesses who can see some advantage to themselves in such giving; and from a variety of other individuals or organisations who occupy cracks between these large categories. Non-profit organisations try to access other people's or other organisations' wealth by a variety of creative techniques that educate, amuse, entertain, and in some cases simply offer an opportunity that people have been looking for.

The important corollaries of fundraising are fiscal responsibility, trust, accountability, public education, and constantly renewed innovation in techniques and ideas – both to compete with other fundraisers, and to tickle the public's jaded palate. The governance of fundraising involves transparency, a good understanding of what the donors will tolerate as acceptable levels for administrative expenditure with the funds raised, and a rule of law that is prepared to address issues like 'breach of trust' or 'improper disclosure'.

Generating income through self-financing is very different. Here the potential fundraiser says, 'I am not interested in trying to persuade you to give me of your wealth; I am interested in creating wealth for my organisation by asking you to buy some goods or service that my organisation produces.' It is based on the entrepreneurial approach that opportunities to create income exist if you look for them, and that there is no reason why such opportunities should only be used by those who work for profit-making entities. This approach tends to attract people who are put off by the atmosphere of 'begging' that often colours fundraising, and who want a relationship of equality between those working for organisations and those who support their work.

Income acquired from self-financing may come from business ideas that reflect the main work of the organisation, or from products and services in completely different fields. The enterprise may sell goods and services to a variety of clients including – but not limited to – the organisation's users, other local people, government, the business world, or foreign markets. The important corollaries are business acumen, entrepreneurial risk-taking, innovative market research, and sensitivity to public (and government) opinion about the organisation's business activities. The governance issues are concerned with making sure that the income generated supports the organisation's mission (and not the other way round) and nimble footwork in dealing with the complicated legal and fiscal position of a non-profit that tries to make a profit (see later for this red herring).

There are, I think, two reasons why so few organisations in the South presently use income-generation and self-financing techniques:

- The first is that traditionally and culturally most financing of nongovernment and charitable activities came from fundraising from local supporters. Such local fundraising was often associated with the impetus to support religious or charitable causes, rather than to support social development or advocacy – which are the purpose of increasingly large numbers of Southern organisations in the 21st century.
- The second is that since the 1970s very large numbers of funding agencies from the North have, in effect, put up notices in the South to say, 'Come and ask us for money – we are in business to support local organisations. You don't need to raise anything yourself – come and ask us to be your funder.'[1]

There is a third reason – which is that few Northern donors have even conceptualised income generation and self-financing as something that they should encourage, let alone support. As we shall see later in this chapter, many actively discourage it, as likely to impact negatively on an organisation's mission. There is comparatively little donor support for the policy changes that governments of the South need to adopt to create a supportive environment for self-financing of organisations – indeed, the IMF encourages departments of taxation to tax anything that moves, and warns them about organisations that may open cracks that subsequently become loopholes.[2]

It is surprising, in an era in which the market has become so elevated an institution, that more donors have not been persuaded to encourage organisations to become market-orientated (although in 2009 perhaps, the market's primacy has been diminished).

5.2 Profits for non-profits – the red herring

Without doubt, one of the conceptual stumbling blocks with income generation and self-financing is that we are often talking about the apparent contradiction of non-profits trying to make profits. It is astonishing that this continues to cause a problem since it is only an apparent rather than a real contradiction. Unacceptable behaviour by some organisations which only generate income for the staff to 'eat' (as the Kenyans say) has prejudiced many people's perception of income generation by non-profits. Part of the problem comes from confusion about the large number of different players in the development business in the South, of whom some are non-profit, some are for-profit, and some are one masquerading as the other. But because this question continues to be a stumbling block for non-profit people, as well as governments and donors, it is necessary to unpack it and explain the inconsistencies.

A charitable or development organisation which has been formed for a social purpose – either to benefit its members (such as a village association, a cooperative or a union) or to benefit the public (or identified groups of the public, such as disabled or illiterate people) has both similarities to and differences from for-profit enterprises. On the one hand, the organisation is not owned by anyone – under most legal systems it is held in trust by an elected or appointed voluntary board, trust or committee, and on the other hand, it has income and expenditure just like a business.

A business that has been formed for a private or institutional purpose of generating profits for owners (individuals or shareholders) has a different kind of income and expenditure, however. Once its income has covered its costs, then what is left, calculated annually, is profit, and this profit is legitimately divided and distributed among its owners. Individuals can own businesses, as can other businesses. Owners can also be staff of the business and can pay themselves salaries for the work they do, and decide what the rate of such salaries should be, and even pay themselves bonuses. Profit (if they make any) is income over and above their salaries.

Once a charitable or development organisation covers its costs, however, what is left over is not *profit*, since it is not available to be distributed to 'owners'. It is simply income that is kept and ploughed back into the ongoing work of the organisation. The staff may indeed get salaries (and they become part of the costs of the organisation, which, in a well-governed organisation, are clearly stated and known). An excess of income over expenditure does not result in a higher salary for the organisation's staff, nor does it result in bonuses being paid to them. This is an important difference between for-profit and non-profit organisations, and needs to be regularly clarified and underpinned by policies and regulations.

Those who 'masquerade'[3] muddy the water for the rest. If a for-profit organisation tries to get non-profit status in order to import goods tax-free, for instance, it should be investigated as to whether it is owned by an individual(s) or organisation, and whether its purpose is the perfectly acceptable one of creating profit. If it is, then the organisation is not entitled to special privileges. This distinction should be clearly drawn. To complicate the picture, however, there are also perfectly admirable for-profit organisations that compete successfully (particularly in terms of quality) with non-profit organisations in such fields as water drilling, micro-finance, building, and management training.

The reason why organisations with a social mission are often allowed tax benefits or other advantages by governments is in recognition of the fact that they are helping the government to deal with problems that the government would otherwise have to deal with by itself. In return for this, non-profit organisations are usually registered under different regulations, which allow for different governance systems, which distinguish them from for-profit organisations. Unscrupulous for-profit businesses that try to avail themselves of these non-profit-specific advantages lead government officials to be unclear about the world of non-profit organisations, and frequently suspicious. For instance, Mari Alkatiri, prime minister of East Timor, the most recently created country in the world, referred disparagingly to 'lucrative NGOs' in a speech to donors in Dili in December 2002. By this he meant NGOs set up to make money for their employees: in a poor country, simply having a wage is a very attractive position to be in, leaving aside any putative profit.

Many tax departments of governments in the South do not seem to understand the points made above (or at least claim not to do so in order to avoid the cracks/loopholes problem mentioned above). 'How can a non-profit make a profit?' they cry. 'This must be an attempt to avoid taxes.' The question is phrased incorrectly – it should not be 'Is this non-profit organisation making a profit?' but 'Is this non-profit organisation distributing income to shareholders or not?' There should be no confusion between a business making a profit and distributing that profit to its owners, and a non-profit organisation that uses any income over its expenditure (and expenditure includes salaries of staff) to advance the mission of the organisation.[4]

A further and more complicated issue is whether non-profit-owned businesses should pay tax. The consensus among most observers of this field is that they should, because otherwise there is an unfair competition between them and the other for-profit businesses that may be operating in the same field of work. BRAC, the largest NGO in the world, based in Bangladesh, and which manages many self-financing enterprises, has always made a point of paying legitimate tax demands. It should also be noted that government demands for tax payments from non-profit organisations have, in some countries, been used as punitive measures to restrict the organisations' work.

Government officials see that very many non-profit organisations in the South derive their income from foreign funding. In many cases they are jealous, feeling that the organisations are competing with them for donor funding. It would seem, on the face of it, that governments would welcome non-profit organisations that do not compete with them, but create income for themselves and are self-financing. In very many countries, however, the laws that govern such organisations' ability to finance themselves through enterprises are unhelpful and restrictive.[5] In turn, very many non-profit organisation workers feel that there is something wrong about a non-profit running a business to earn money, and shy away from the idea. The question should be posed in this way: 'Would you rather be dependent on funding from a foreign donor or be supported from income that you have generated yourself?' There are important aspects of independence, self-respect, and dependency involved here.

5.3 Amateur night or social entrepreneurs?

The worlds of business and non-profit social development organisations rarely overlap, and people from one rarely inhabit the other – to the detriment of both [in my opinion]. Most people in the world of non-profits come from a background in academia, religious organisations, civil service, trade unions, occasionally from the professions – rarely from the world of small (or large) businesses. Fazle Abed of BRAC in Bangladesh is an exception – he held a senior position in Philips Electrical before the Bangladesh War of Independence ushered him into a second career in the world of non-profits, and this probably explains his amazing achievements through self-financing enterprises.[6]

Because of their backgrounds, many people in non-profit organisations do not feel comfortable with the idea of a business – producing goods or services that others will want to buy, and from whose sales they can expand the work of the organisation. Some feel ideologically opposed, some feel incompetent and worried that that they will lose their organisation's mission, some feel that they will not be supported if they invest in such an idea, and some feel the risks outweigh the possible benefits. Let us look at each of these.

Ideology

In countries where most businesses succeed by unprincipled exploitation of labour and natural resources, it is not surprising that many people in non-profit organisations (who are distinguished by having a social mission) will feel uncomfortable about wanting to be part of such company. They claim that they see businesses paying below minimum-level wages and supplying no or few benefits, fiddling their taxes, damaging the environment, abusing their workers, and using unsafe methods and equipment, and they feel that they do not want to be associated with such practices. If there are few, if any, examples in a country of capitalist, profit-making organisations that are run by moral and responsible people, non-profit people will think twice about being the pioneers to start such risky ventures.

Prejudice and misinformation are, however, often at work here. Non-profit people do not attend Chambers of Commerce (for instance), do not know much about businesses, do not know the difficult decisions that business people have to make to keep paying their workers, and do not understand the benefits that employment and local purchasing bring to a community. They are often scornful about business people without knowing enough about the kinds of work they do. They are also often ignorant about the strong social consciences that many business people have and their desire to use their position to benefit other people.

It is often assumed that 'we are all capitalists now', but many of the politically aware non-profit organisations do not join this chorus. We should not assume that the 'Washington consensus' and the 'supremacy of the market' are doctrines that resonate with many non-profit people. Non-profit people, particularly those in the social activist and advocacy end of the spectrum, are often of a leftist persuasion, and will not easily see that the use of market forces for a social end is ideologically correct. They will need to be convinced that starting an enterprise is part of the solution, not part of the problem.

Mission deformation

One of the more helpful aspects of international funding for Southern non-profit organisations has been the Northern donors' insistence on vision and mission statements as a management instrument to be applied by the organisations that they are prepared to fund. Many organisations in the South now have mission statements, which, to a greater or lesser degree, clarify their core work. Often the production of this mission statement has been a painful process for organisations as they have realised the value, but have also felt the pain, of divesting themselves of marginal and ineffective activities.

Non-profit leaders are now faced with thinking about creating businesses to generate income for their organisation. They see, quite logically, that devoting a substantial part of the work of the organisation to making money in one way or another will have a powerful impact on their mission. This is correct: it will do so, and no one should embark on a self-financing strategy without considerably reworking the strategic plan for their whole organisation. The more the enterprise or business departs from the mission of the organisation, the more troubled it may become, for it is venturing into new territory.

If a literacy or public policy analysis non-profit decides that it will try to finance itself by selling the products of its work, such as the books it has written, this will not be considered a great step. If a community development non-profit considers the possibility of running a small for-profit farm to finance its work, it is not such a stretch – and it has the advantage of demonstrating the value of the advice it gives to others. Possibly an organisation working with HIV/AIDS sufferers would not feel too challenged by selling condoms. But an organisation working with orphans that branches out into novel activities such as starting a restaurant, or a home for abused women that runs an art gallery – these present the organisation concerned with difficult, though feasible, choices about how it should be spending its time and energy.

Many non-profit organisations that may have accepted the idea conceptually feel helpless actually to implement it, and look around for technical advice. Luckily a new breed of non-profit business advisers has started to appear. A surprisingly large amount of work has been done in the environmental field – where environmental organisations have found ways to make money to (for instance) operate national parks, save endangered species and locations, or research local ecologies. The leader has been the Nature Conservancy, which has systematically taught its branches to think entrepreneurially, and backed up such training with manuals (see under Resources at the end of the chapter). Another organisation that has provided its members with training in self-financing is the International Red Cross, while a third organisation, NESsT (Non-profits Enterprise and Self-Sustainability Team), has offered itself as a management consultancy group – providing skills to help non-profit organisations come to terms with enterprise creation possibilities.

If a non-profit organisation does decide to move in the self-financing direction, it may have the further difficulty that it lacks consensus among its staff to do so. The long-experienced childcare worker may not, for instance, take kindly to being asked to sell her expertise as a consultant to make money for the organisation; the social activist may not want to run a training centre for the same reason; and neither of them may be interested in producing, for instance, greetings cards – even though they may well be convinced that it is a profitable idea for the long-term sustainability of the organisation.

One of the best solutions is to separate the mission-directed part of the organisation from the fund-generation side. Recognising that the same people may not be well suited to both kinds of activities, and also recognising that the typical non-profit staffer is unlikely to be good at business, it makes a lot of sense for organisations to set up their income-generation as a separate enterprise with its own staff and its own operating procedures. The important thing is that the profits that it is hoped will come from the enterprise are covenanted to the organisation, and used to support its mission.

Non-profit leaders and their staff can veer from one extreme to another when thinking about starting enterprises – reflecting their lack of experience with business. On the one hand they may be very pessimistic that whatever they produce will find a market at a price and in quantities sufficient to make a profit for the organisation. On the other hand they may have a wildly optimistic idea of the income that they will receive – feeling that all their financing worries will be over once the enterprise is under way.

If it were easy to run a profitable enterprise, many more people would be doing so. Non-profit organisations start with the disadvantage that they are not likely to be business minded, but they also have the advantage that people may be inclined to buy their product or service because by doing so they are supporting the organisation. For some people this argues for a close link between mission and enterprise – an agricultural non-profit offers agricultural produce or services, a health non-profit offers services in the pharmaceutical field – so that people will be reminded of the organisation's work when purchasing the product or service. Others feel that there is little money to be made that way, and that it may require more financial and business expertise than they have. They would rather do something simple but profitable – like renting real estate.

Other non-profit leaders are apprehensive about the big jump, and the equally big risk in moving from dependence on donor support to efforts at sustainable self-reliance. They would prefer not to put all their investment of time, energy, staff, and capital into an enterprise that could fail, leaving them very vulnerable and probably unable to go back to their previous donors. There is no reason why a non-profit organisation should not have many financing options on the go at the same time – for instance, a mixture of foreign donor funds, membership subscriptions, government contracts, and income from a self-generated enterprise. This will lessen the risk, and increase the comfort level for the organisation and its board.

5.4 What are the options?

To give us an idea of the range of self-financing options that are being considered, let us look at NESsT's experience.[7] It offers capacity-building services for non-profit organisations interested in self-financing: this can mean a number of hours of consultation – time spent helping organisations think through their business plans – as well as a certain amount of venture capital. NESsT works in central Europe and Latin America – and a list of its recent awards can illustrate the range of activities that contemporary non-profit organisations are considering. From the *NESsT News* of July/August 2002, we see the following:

In Hungary:
- Bliss Foundation plans to sell alternative communication devices for physically disabled young people.
- Afrika-Aszia Forum, a human rights group, seeks to rent African costumes and instruments, cater African cuisine, and sell African art.
- NIOK, a non-profit support centre, plans to provide web services to non-profits.
- Partners Hungary aims to earn income from its conflict resolution training.

- Open garden, which promotes community agricultural production, is expanding a home-delivery service for organic produce.

In the Czech Republic:

- Transitions Online, which works to strengthen journalism in central Europe, seeks to increase fees from its online articles and news database, and from book and CD sales.
- Tamizdat, which promotes alternative culture and progressive thought in central and eastern Europe, seeks to increase revenue from online sales of music CDs.

In Slovakia:

- Vydra, a natural and cultural heritage organisation, aims to run a buffet and cultural activities for tourists at an environmental museum.

If we try to systematise NESsT's and other organisations' experience and analyse the different kinds of enterprises in which non-profit organisations can be involved, we find that they can be broken into five basic types:

1 Enterprises that capitalise on the organisation's core business.
2 Enterprises that capitalise on the organisation's existing capital.
3 Opportunistic enterprises that fit the organisation's human capital.
4 Purely commercial investments.
5 Collaborative ventures with existing businesses.

Enterprises that capitalise on the organisation's core business

Community development organisations, or organisations that work with specialised groups within the community (such as drug addicts, disabled people, or victims of natural disasters) each have the opportunity to think about what aspects of their work could be turned into a profit-making venture – and be useful to the organisation's target group at the same time. Thus community development organisations working with farmers might sell farm produce, disabled people might construct appliances and equipment for disabled people (such as callipers and wheelchairs), and refugees from floods or volcanic explosions might make and sell their handicrafts – both utilitarian a nd decorative. In each case the enterprise is closely linked to the work of the organisation, sometimes using existing skills of the target group, sometimes requiring training or retraining.

One subset of this is the idea of 'fees for service' whereby non-profit organisations charge for services that they had previously been providing free. This subject is controversial since it has so frequently been conceptually linked to the World Bank's Structural Adjustment Programmes (SAPs). In so many countries of the world people are required to pay for what were previously free education and health facilities – sometimes with the result that poor people cannot avail themselves of these facilities and so have to go without. Where there is a strong possibility that people can pay (and where there is a weak tax base), this makes more sense than an insupportable and unsustainable welfare state, but there needs to be provision made for those who cannot pay, and this can best be handled by cross-subsidies. Non-profit organisations can sustain themselves by selling their services to their clients, but, since such organisations are often working with the poorest, they need to consider their special position. The position of PROSALUD in Bolivia is instructive.

PROSALUD – self-financing health services

PROSALUD's objective is to function without outside support, recovering its costs from the sale of its health services and products. In the health sector, recovering costs by charging fees for health services delivered to low-income families is often considered impossible. Charging fees that are high enough to cover the costs of services appears to discriminate against the very poor, who live on the edge of subsistence and often have no money on hand to pay for services or goods of any kind.

The conventional wisdom, however, seems to be belied by the PROSALUD experience in Bolivia. PROSALUD already has a growing system of health facilities in operation that are self-financing through the fees that it charges. Clients are predominantly low-income families. Services include free preventative healthcare and child survival operations. Curative services are provided free of charge to families that cannot pay (these are between 8 and 13 per cent of PROSALUD's patients). PROSALUD has conclusively demonstrated the feasibility of self-financed primary healthcare services, even in a country as poor as Bolivia.

Some products and services may be more saleable than others: credit seems to be a service that people are always prepared to pay for through interest rates and service fees, providing the rates are low and the service efficient, as we can see from the success of the Grameen Bank and its clones set up around the world under the Grameen Trust. Successful borrowers start their own businesses with the loans and this provides them with enough income to pay back their credit. On the other hand, it is more difficult to see a business opportunity linked to, for instance, a non-profit organisation's work with women who suffer from domestic violence; see, however, the work of HOPE in Zambia. What we learn from these examples is the old business principle of segmenting the market, and the new non-profit business principle of cross-subsidies to deal with the problems of the poorest.

Kara Counselling and Training Trust makes money for itself from HIV/AIDS patients

Kara Counselling and Training Trust worked to provide free AIDS testing and counselling to the public in Zambia, and racked its brains for a way to be self-financing. It realised that there was a premium set by Zambian people on confidentiality and avoiding shame and stigma – some people did not want to be seen coming to their free downtown clinic. It therefore offered a two-tier service in two different locations: their usual free clinic open to the public, and a more confidential service in another, more secluded site – for which people paid.

Enterprises that capitalise on the organisation's existing capital

Here we are asking the non-profit organisation to look at itself from the point of view of a potential investor and consider what among its human, physical, environmental, and relational capital could be turned into a profit-making enterprise.

Human capital

Does the organisation have a stock of skills that others might be prepared to pay for, separately from the practice of those skills for the mission of the organisation? In many cases the answer is that the organisation has skills that others in the development community value, and might be persuaded to pay for. These could derive from their experience – of their core business, or their administration and financial management, or promotional and presentational skills. In many cases there may be staff who have skills only a part of which are used by the organisation – particularly in the IT field.

Physical capital

Does the organisation have a stock of physical plant that could develop a secondary function that would be earning income, separately from the use of that plant for the organisation's main business? This could be their equipment (vehicles, computers, photocopiers) or their buildings and land. Is there spare capacity in any of these fields that it would make sense to turn to another use for people prepared to pay?

Environmental capital

Does the organisation exist in a place where its position gives it a saleable commodity? Could the organisation sell its experience and expertise of a particular place to those potentially interested in it? This could be to do with something singular in their location – specific features of deprivation, specific ecological, environmental or cultural interests, or specific natural beauties. Is there a market for things that the organisation's workers see every day, but had not previously seen through others' eyes?

Making money from your physical location

Some non-profit organisations happen to be situated in an area of great cultural interest – such as Yayasan Tengko Sitoru in Tana Toraja, in Sulawezi, Indonesia. They make money from organising eco-tourism, and bring income to the local people as well.

Organisations in the Philippines and Thailand organise tours for 'alternative' tourists to areas of great deprivation, such as Bangkok's rubbish mountain or landless sugar workers in Negros.

Still other organisations (like TC/DC in Arusha, Tanzania) make money from teaching the local language to foreigners who plan to work there.

Relational capital

Does the organisation know many people, or know a few important people well, or has it developed a lot of knowledge about the important people in a particular field? Is this stock of knowledge something that others are prepared to pay for, whether it is a go-between, a writer of directories, or an interpreter?

INSIST documents its work and sells the books

INSIST is a management and advocacy training organisation in Yogyakarta, Indonesia. It documents the experiences of organisations that pass through its courses, and publishes successful books based on both its training course manuals and its accumulated case studies.

Opportunistic enterprises that fit the organisation's management ability

An entrepreneurial scan of the organisation's existing human, physical, environmental, and relational capital may not turn up too many good ideas, and the organisation then needs to look at income-generation opportunities that fit the competence of their staff and their available time. We said earlier in this chapter that the staff of non-profit organisations are notoriously poor in business skills; it is therefore not sensible for organisations to consider opening a retail business in a competitive world like grocery supermarkets. It is also not sensible for non-profit organisations to enter a commercial field in which their bona fides will be questioned – such as a bar or a nightclub. It could make sense to find a commercially simple activity like renting property, particularly if the property rented already belongs to the organisation, as the Red Cross offices did in Zambia.

Purely local and opportunistic ideas can come from a fashion, an event, a change in population composition, a new industry – and an entrepreneurially minded but commercially inexperienced organisation may find room to make money for its work from such localised and happenstance events.

Zambian Red Cross – successful landlords

In 1991 the Zambian Red Cross asked the Finnish Red Cross for the funds to build an office block to house itself but also with space to rent out. When the building was finished in 1992 the top floor was rented to the World Bank, and this, together with the rental of six flats that it owns, covered 87 per cent of its costs.

Another possibility is serendipity, whereby someone sympathetic to the work of the organisation unexpectedly gives them some capital that could be the basis for an enterprise: a building, land, some equipment, a stock of materials, or a small but running business. Serendipity can be stimulated – by the organisation informing people that it is interested in such resources

The important features of enterprises that capitalise on an organisation's core business are all to do with a business and entrepreneurial culture – features that are standard for practising business people, but which need to be learned behaviour for most non-profit organisations. They comprise:

- An entrepreneurial imagination that can think up original and creative enterprise ideas.
- Close attention to customers and their needs, which will allow the organisation to modify products and services as customer preferences change.
- Good costing to make sure that all costs are covered and a surplus is being made to increase the income of the organisation.
- Attention to business principles, such as adequate working capital that allows the business to build up sales before its reserves run out.

There are two further kinds of self-financing possibilities mentioned above that depend upon the organisation already having, or having access to, business acumen: purely commercial investments, and collaborative ventures with existing businesses.

Purely commercial investments

This section is probably applicable to only a few non-profit organisations, but if the organisation is able to acquire the services of an experienced business person, and has access to capital, making investment decisions for that organisation will be no different from making investment decisions for a business. In such cases the business side of the organisation is completely separate from its core business, with its own staff and its own operating principles and practice, and its only duty is to hand over income to the organisation accruing from the profits of the enterprise. The organisation is unlikely to be able to pay for the costs of an experienced business person, but this is often a role that an active board member can play – often when they are retired from their business life.

Collaborative ventures with existing businesses

Existing businesses might well see a feature of a non-profit organisation's work that is attractive to them, and for which they are prepared to pay. The organisation will need to work out how much this will divert them from their core business (if at all), how much income they can derive from it, and – very fundamentally – whether they want to be seen by the public as being associated with this particular business. Many organisations in Africa have been paid by companies to test and counsel for HIV/AIDS.

NGOs working with African firms on HIV/AIDS issues

HIV/AIDS is a pandemic that is threatening the economic life of southern Africa. The copper mines of Botswana and the diamond and gold mines of South Africa are losing workers at a phenomenal rate and reducing profits for shareholders considerably. Many such businesses pay non-profit organisations to enter their workplaces and carry out safe-sex education in an attempt to reduce the rate of transmission of the disease.

5.5 What does it take to make a success of self-financing?

If we accept that the norm for most Southern non-profit organisations is local fundraising (in the case of religious and charitable activities) and Northern donor transfers (in the case of development, human rights, and advocacy organisations), then we have to be clear that those opting for self-financing and income-generation will be to some extent mavericks, and will not have a large body of experience to draw upon.

Commitment

In such a situation, one of the prerequisites for making a success of self-financing is a commitment to doing so. The organisation must examine the alternatives, think about issues like dependency, public reputation, the use and diversion of time from its core business, the need to educate the public (and particular subgroups of the public like government officials or business people) about its work – and then decide on the value of this approach.

The organisation may also decide to hedge its bets and introduce income-generation as one of a variety of financing strategies for itself – but having decided to go in full or in part with self-financing, the organisation must be prepared to stick with it, and ride out the risks that are a part of any business enterprise. It must also make a commitment to educating potential supporters and sympathisers about the value of self-financing for non-profit organisations – to be proselytisers on behalf of this approach to politicians, government officials, Northern donors, and the general public.

Business acumen

A second and most important prerequisite, cited many times in this chapter, is to recognise that most non-profit organisation are unused to and ill-prepared for work in the business field. Many organisations that have a distaste for business try to pretend to themselves that they are involved in a business that has its own laws and norms, imagining that their enterprises are peripheral and can be handled by amateurs – and this results, typically, in stocks of unsellable embroidery, handicrafts that make losses, tiny profits, and time wasted by all.

Organisations need to be aware of their business deficiencies and be prepared to do something about them – which may involve learning about business practices and principles themselves, bringing in consultants who specialise in their field, using the services of business people who are willing to contribute their time and expertise voluntarily, or costing the time of professionals into the business plan for the enterprise.

The business plan is the crux of the income-generation/self-financing approach. It is a recognition that the organisation is serious, it is a document that can sell its enterprise idea to investors, it is a road map for enterprise development, and it is a tool for monitoring whether the ideas come to fruition and whether the organisation actually makes the income that was planned. Most non-profit organisations are unable to make a business plan without considerable outside help.

Venture capital

A third issue is the venture capital that will be needed for the enterprise to be started. Such venture capital may come from grants, loans, goods in kind, savings, and sweat equity. Let us look at some of these.

Grants

Since so many Northern donor organisations are enthusiastically extolling the virtues of non-profit organisations, and funding so many and such varied examples, it should, in theory, be possible for such organisations to get venture capital for their self-financing businesses from these donors. It does not often happen, however.

On the one hand, few organisations make proposals for such funding to Northern donors, having been conditioned through three decades of Northern funding to asking for operating and development costs as grants. On the other hand, few donors have identified venture capital for non-profits as a line item in their budgets. Many donors will tell cautionary tales of failed attempts in the past, and emphasise the dangers of diverting organisations from their core mission. They also cite organisations' inexperience in business as a reason not to fund venture capital. They **could** take the view that this is a challenge to be met, and one that can lead to the greater good of financial sustainability of organisations, but they seem not to. One possibility is that the staff of donors who deal with non-profit organisations also lack experience of how to analyse and respond to proposals based on business plans.

Another aspect of the possible mismatch between the proposals of self-financers and Northern donors is that, increasingly, such donors think in terms of projects that reflect their own strategic analysis of what needs to be done in a particular country. What we are dealing with in income-generation are ways of sustainably financing a non-profit organisation. If it succeeds in this, it will be able to do what it considers important in the country – which will not necessarily be the same as what the donor would like it to do.

At the same time there are likely to be different parts of the same donor organisation that specialise in helping for-profit small and micro- enterprises, but the experience of such units is rarely made available to non-profits. Northern foundations, so often the pioneers in development thinking and practice, are more likely to be sympathetic to the idea of providing venture capital in the form of grants, and they have given a whole new subset of funding practices the title of 'venture philanthropy'.

Loans

These can be broken down into loans at market rates (which is how most for-profit businesses acquire their capital) and loans at 'soft' or subsidised rates, which is the field of INAISE (International Association of Investors in the Social Economy), a specialised group of credit-providing organisations who generally refer to themselves as social investors (in the USA, 'program related investors').

If it has a good business plan that can impress a bank manager, a non-profit organisation in theory should be able to attract credit with which to start its own enterprise. A frequent problem is the banks' need for collateral, which either the organisation does not have, or which the board or trustees are not prepared to provide because of the risk that the enterprise could fail and take the whole organisation with it. RAFAD in Switzerland has faced this problem by linking local banks to Swiss banks and providing bank guarantees to Swiss banks, against which local banks can advance money to local organisations.

What is social investment?

When a non-profit organisation wishes to implement a project that has a chance of being financially viable and producing an adequate return on capital invested, it may go to a bank to try to get the finance required.

Unfortunately, while many project ideas may well be viable, they may not be bankable in view of the existing rules and regulations of the banks, together with the latter's conservatism faced with new ideas. Organisations need a source of investment finance that is flexible enough to meet their needs, is interested in the social aspects of their work (rather than considering the optimal returns on capital) and is prepared to deal with them. This is the field of social investment (known in the USA as 'program related investment') – that is, bodies that have set up funds to lend money to non-profits that prioritise social and environmental considerations. Such funding bodies broadly share the two following characteristics:

■ They tend to serve social economy organisations and small or micro-enterprises that have social or environmental objectives.
■ They finance sections of the population, projects, sectors, or regions that have been abandoned by the traditional banks or financial institutions.

The funds are not grants – they are social investment funds from organisations that want to support viable and socially responsible work, want to have their investment returned with interest, but who are not investing their money with the prime purpose of maximising their income from the interest to be earned. They are usually, therefore, satisfied with a return on their investment below the market rate.

The organisations involved in social investment are often of the opinion that investment in a project is healthier than making grants to it, and that encouraging organisations to become financially self-reliant is better than allowing them to become dependent on grant funding.

Goods in kind

As mentioned before, the reputation of the organisation may encourage well-wishers to give it not money, but some form of in-kind contribution that could be the start of a for-profit enterprise – for example, land, buildings, equipment, financial instruments.

5.6 Is self-financing a viable alternative to fundraising?

The big picture

We now need to look at the whole range of financing strategies for non-profit organisations and see what part self-financing plays. Self-financing can be undertaken through several different channels:

- Funds from Northern governments
  - directly as bilateral assistance
  - indirectly as multilateral assistance
  - via Northern NGOs
  - via their own governments as bilateral assistance relayed to organisations.
- Funds from Northern NGOs directly.
- Funds from the market
  - from existing businesses
  - from NGO enterprises (including investments).
- Funds from citizens
  - directly as gifts
  - indirectly as support.

A wise non-profit board and manager should look at the range of possibilities and decide which of these eight – or which possible combination of them – is applicable to their organisation. Each will be relevant to different aspects of different organisations in different environments, and their relevance needs to be teased out before deciding on what combination is appropriate for the organisation. The following positive and negative aspects need to be considered:

- Positive factors
  - Links to their own society
  - Their control over the use of resources
  - Variety of resources (thus reducing vulnerability)
  - Ability to design their own programmes
  - Commitment to sustainability.
- Negative factors
  - Danger of distorting their mission
  - Amount of work required
  - The likely return on effort
  - Distaste for certain partners (such as business or government) and concerns about conflicts of interest
  - Difficulty of getting support for their particular cause
  - Lack of skills or experience in resource mobilisation.

The balance of positive and negative factors to be weighed up is far from fixed at any one moment in time, however. An alert and active organisation has to be opportunistic and see what existing and new possibilities there are – even though it had not thought of these originally. A change in tax law (for instance) might make it more attractive for businesses or individuals to support the work of non-profit self-financing; a particular event might allow an organisation to capitalise on the interest generated by its work; a new indigenous foundation might be set up, or a foreign donor start a programme of venture capital for non-profit organisations; a business person with entrepreneurial ideas might join the board and have many suggestions for income-generation. One of the important possibilities will always be income generation for self-financing, and those interested in resource mobilisation will always need to consider it.

Endnotes

[1] *In every country that has moved from a totalitarian to a democratic regime, Northern funding agencies have arrived and aggressively marketed themselves to the (sometimes) very limited environment of civil society organisations. Not surprisingly, within a short time, there are lots of non-profit organisations applying for their funds.*

[2] *The World Bank actively encourages and supports non-profit organisations, and the enabling environment for them, but has never dealt with the problem that other parts of their own organisation, plus the IMF, discourage any exceptions to comprehensive tax collection – and are unsympathetic to organisations' special pleas (source: conversations with the International Centre for Non-Profit Law).*

[3] *This refers to the group called 'pretenders' by Alan Fowler in his essential book* Striking a Balance. *The book provides an exhaustive list of the possible masqueraders.*

[4] *More information on this whole question can be found in* A Handbook on the Good Practices for Laws relating to Non-Governmental Organisations *by Leon Irish, World Bank and International Centre for Not-for-Profit Law (ICNL), 1997 (available on the ICNL website: www.icnl.org).*

[5] *In Indonesia there is a top limit on the amount that can be financed this way: in India only activities linked to the organisation's mission are allowed to be financed this way.*

[6] *A visit to BRAC's web site (www.brac.org) will illustrate the range of businesses owned and run by BRAC, all of which pay tax to the government as businesses.*

[7] *NESsT is at www.nesst.org*

Resources

Publications

The publication which discusses current trends in philanthropy and financial self-reliance, including from time to time self-financing, is *Alliance* magazine. Its editorial policy is such that all contributors provide their email addresses, and readers are thus able to contact those with relevant experience or information. The scope of the magazine is truly global.

Alliance Magazine
76 Sistova Rd
London SW12 9QS, UK
Tel: 44 207 608 1862
(www.alliancemagazine.org)

Alternative Financing of Third World Organisations and NGOs
Fernand Vincent
IRED
Geneva, Switzerland
1995

The Charity as a Business
Clutterbuck and Dearlove
Books for Change
Bangalore, India
1996

The NESsT Learning Series
*The NGO/Business Hybrid: Is the
Private Sector the Answer?* 1997

*The NGO Venture Forum: Profits for
Non-Profits*, 1999

Profits from Non-Profits, 1999

*Sustaining Nonprofits: The Impact of
Merging Mission and Market*, 1999
Produced by NESsT, Santiago,
Chile

Generating Revenue
International Federation of Red Cross
and Red Crescent Societies
Geneva, Switzerland
1995

Grassroots Development
Vol. 19, No. 2
1995
(A journal of the Inter-American
Foundation.)

*A Handbook on the Good Practices for
Laws relating to Non-Governmental
Organisations*
Leon Irish
World Bank and International Centre for
Not-for-profit Law (ICNL)
1997

*Integrated Strategic Financial
Planning*
Patricia Leon
America Verde Publications
2001

NGO Funding Strategies
Jon Bennet and Sarah Gibbs
INTRAC
Oxford, UK
1997

Programme Related Investment
Renz and Massarky
Foundation Center
New York, USA
1995

*Resources for Success:
A Manual for Conservation
Organisations in Latin America
and the Caribbean*
The Nature Conservancy
America Verde Publications
1993

*The Virtuous Circle: A Guide to
Sustainability for NGOs in
International Development*
Alan Fowler
Earthscan
London, UK
2000

'Earning Income through Trade
and Exchange'
Horacio Morales Jr
Chapter 2 in *Sustaining Civil
Society: Strategies for Resource
Mobilisation*
Edited by Bruce Shearer and
Leslie Fox
CIVICUS
Washington DC, USA
1997

*Towards Financial Self-Reliance:
A Handbook of Approaches to
Resource
Mobilisation for Citizens'
Organisations in the South*
Richard Holloway
Earthscan
London, UK
2001

*Trainer's manual of the above available
free for downloading at www.akdn.
org/civilsociety in collaboration with the
Aga Khan Foundation.

Towards Greater Financial Autonomy:
A Guide for Voluntary Organisations
and Community Groups
Piers Campbell and Fernand Vincent
IRED
Geneva, Switzerland
1989

Endowments as a Tool for Financial
Sustainability: A Manual for NGOs.
PROFIT
Washington DC, USA
1993

Filthy Rich: How to Turn your Non-profit
Fantasies into Cold Hard Cash
Richard Steckel
Ten Speed Press
Berkeley, USA
2000

Making Money while Making a
Difference: How to Profit with a
Nonprofit Partner
Richard Steckel et al
High Tide Press
Illinois, USA
1999

Cold Cash for Warm Hearts: 101 Best
Social Marketing Initiatives
Richard Steckel
High Tide Press
Illinois, USA
2004

Organisations

INAISE (International Association of
Investors in the Social Economy)
Rue d'Arlon 40
B-1000 Brussels
Belgium
Tel: 32 2 230 3057
Fax: 32 2 230 3764
Web: www.inaise.org

Inter-American Foundation
901 North Stuart St
Arlington Va 22203
USA
Tel: 1 703 841 3834
Fax: 1 703 841 1605
Web: www.iaf.gov

International Center for
Not-for-profit Law
733 15th St NW (Suite 420)
Washington DC 20005
USA
Tel: 202 624 0766
Fax: 202 624 0767
Email: infoicnl@icnl.org
Web: www.icnl.org

The Nature Conservancy
4245 North Fairfax Drive
Suite 100
Arlington
Virginia 22203–1606
USA
Web: www.nature.org

Non-Profit Enterprise and Self
Sustainability
Team (NESsT)
Jose Arrieta 89
Providencia Santiago
Chile
Tel: 56 2 222 5190
Fax: 56 2 634 2599
Email: nesst@igc.apc.org
Web: www.nesst.org

Contributed by Richard Holloway

CHAPTER 6

Techniques

6.1 Setting up a local fundraising group

Whether you are an established national organisation or a small group just starting out, raising money locally through events and collections can be an important source of income.

But organising a fundraising event or collecting money locally requires time and effort. There are two main approaches: using staff to do the work, or using volunteers. A lot depends on the budget for the event. Using your own staff will cost much more, and only really makes sense for very large events. Using a group of volunteers can make sense, particularly if there are people with the right abilities and enthusiasm prepared to do the fundraising work for you. They will work largely independently, but you will need to provide proper management to ensure that they operate effectively, and some back-up in the form of literature, ideas and advice.

There is another benefit to working in this way. The more groups you set up, the more money you will raise. You can establish local fundraising groups in different towns and cities, or in different areas of the same city. Each will be responsible for raising money in its 'patch'. And there is the possibility of getting a returning volunteer or overseas contact to set up a support group in another country to raise money for your work.

Setting up a local fundraising group takes considerable effort and patience. It can take a long time to get the group established and raising money for your work. But the investment can be worth it. The volunteers you recruit, if properly supported (see Section 7.1), could well stay involved with your organisation for many years.

Getting started

To establish local fundraising groups, you need to:

- **Find people** who are willing to put in the time to raise money for you, and in particular
  . . .
- **Find someone to lead the group** (as the chairperson).
- **Establish the group with a constitution**, which defines how it will work and the relationship with the organisation for which it is raising money.
- Help the group identify **appropriate fundraising activities**.
- **Supervise** and support the group in its fundraising work.

Forming a fundraising group

The following story illustrates how you might set about forming a local fundraising group. The key is to follow up on every idea or contact, and to ask persuasively.

Getting a local fundraising group going

My brief was to form a fundraising group in a large city. Where should I start?

My usual way of working is to check my address book and contact my friends for their suggestions. I knew one person in the area who was worth approaching. It was a priest I had known for 30 years. I felt sure that he would set me off in the right direction. I made an appointment to see him.

The meeting gave me a detailed insight into the social needs of the town, and was a fascinating morning. But I left realising that anyone whom the priest knew was at a loose end would have already been snapped up for the much-needed social work of the parish.

I wrote to a Member of Parliament I had met some 25 years ago, to a businessman from my home city who is on various local boards in the town, and to other luminaries. All wrote back most helpfully, but only one suggested any specific people to visit. I followed this up and it led me to a wives' group which I don't think wanted me to recruit their people as they met for purely social reasons. However, through this contact I did meet one person who said that she would be free to help in a couple of years. Too long to wait, alas!

While driving around the well-heeled suburbs, I felt that there must be someone there longing to help the cause. But who? And when would I find them?

Then I was invited to speak at a Rotary luncheon. My hopes were high. Unfortunately the meal was so delicious and the company so convivial that my allocated time to speak about our charity was severely cut, and the one-to-one cultivation didn't happen (no one 'offers' on these occasions!).

My big break came in a totally unexpected way. I was arranging a visit by a group of people from another town to see a child-care project in the city. I said that I would send them a map to show the location of the project. 'Don't worry,' was the reply. 'I was brought up in the city.' This was my cue to act. 'Do you know anyone who lives here who is at a loose end and could help me form a fundraising group?' I inquired. I obtained the names of a relative and another person.

I set off with new enthusiasm, having ascertained that the first person would probably be in on a certain morning. I knocked on the door, and although the lady had been rung by her relative to explain who I was and that I would be making contact, I received a strict telling off for calling unannounced. I apologised and, grasping my diary, suggested that we might find half an hour for a chat sometime else. 'Half an hour?' was the horrified reply. 'Where have you come from?' I explained, and said it was about 45 kilometres away. It must have sounded like the other side of the world, as I was invited into the kitchen for coffee 'as I was here'. Immediately we got on like a house on fire. We might have known each other all our lives. How easily I could have fled at the first tirade! Names and suggestions flowed, and an agreement that she was willing to be part of the new group in spite of her numerous other commitments.

The visit to the next person was also quite alarming. I was invited into the house. 'I was wondering if you know anyone who would be free to join a fundraising group?' I asked. 'Are you asking me – or asking me if I know anyone?' I kept my cool and said, 'I was really asking you if you knew anyone, but if you are able to help as well that would be wonderful!' Not only was she willing to help, but she thought deeply, and made suggestions of others who might be interested. She contacted them. She telephoned me. I visited most of the people she suggested. Others I just spoke to on the telephone. All agreed to help.

The most exciting introduction was to a person who had that very month given up her job (although still young and very active!). She was an obvious candidate to take the chair. Soon we had twelve people and were able to hold our first meeting over lunch, kindly arranged by one of the group. This is always a highly charged occasion. Are people going to get on well together? (They did.) Is anyone going to offer to be secretary (and be responsible for the dreary organisational work)? But after some undercover work beforehand I had already arranged that three of the people should take on the posts of chair, treasurer and secretary. The democratic procedures can follow once the group is established – at future AGMs! The first fundraising function was fixed for a few months later, and all members worked well together and enjoyed themselves. My initial idea was to hold two functions a year, and also to sell Christmas cards and perhaps to distribute some collecting boxes. The first two events organised within the first 13 months raised £1,200 and £1,400. We were on our way.

Recruitment is the key to success. You may need to find people to serve on committees and fundraising groups or you may be looking for one key person to chair a committee or take the responsibility for a particular area of fundraising. You will want to identify the skills and resources that they will need for the job (time available, use of their homes, contacts, ideas, initiative, enthusiasm, and so on). You should allow yourself plenty of time for this. You can also ask existing contacts to suggest other people (their friends or people who they think will be able to do a good job). As the group begins to organise fundraising events (and to be seen to be successful), you will find that more interest will develop in what you are doing and more people will be prepared to volunteer their time. At any stage good publicity in the local press or radio can bring further support. If you are setting up a local branch of a national organisation or network, ask them for their mailing list for the area. These will be people who are already interested in the cause, so when you approach them you may find them eager to give their support.

What makes a good fundraising leader

1. **Good organisational skills**, so that the work is shared out among the team and everything gets done.
2. **Attention to detail**, so that nothing is forgotten and everything runs smoothly.
3. **Ability to lead**, motivate and manage the team of volunteers who are doing the work.
4. **A good judge of people**, recognising and using the abilities of individual members of the group, and understanding people's strengths and weaknesses so that they contribute their best and enjoy being part of the team.

Constituting the local group

You need the people, and you need something for them to do. But you will also need a constitution, which defines how this group of people will operate and clarifies their relationship with the central organisation (that is, with you). If you are setting up lots of local groups, you will probably want to draw up a model constitution. You will need to decide whether the local committee is:

- Simply a **sub-committee** or branch of the main organisation, with no separate legal identity of its own, or whether it is . . .
- A **separate organisation** in its own right, but with the purpose of supporting the main charitable organisation.

A separate legal structure will be more expensive to operate, but it will hand over full responsibility and control to the local group – who will be completely accountable for what is raised and how the money is spent. Which is the most appropriate structure depends on many things, including the legal and fiscal requirements for groups raising money that exist in your own country, the length of time the committee has been in operation (how well established it is), the amount of money it raises (how successful it is), and the number of local groups around the country who are raising money for you.

Sometimes you may find that an individual or a group decides to raise money on your behalf without your permission. In certain circumstances you may feel that because of the nature of the particular individual who is doing this or because of the fundraising method adopted, the good name of your charity will be put at risk. There is probably little that you can do to stop them raising money for you, but if you are unhappy about what they are doing, you should speak to them about your concerns.

Drawing up a constitution

The following are some of the headings for the constitution of a local fundraising committee:

- The relationship with the charity.
- Support to be provided by the charity.
- Responsibilities of committee members.
- Name of the committee.
- Location or geographical area of operation.
- Objects or purposes of the committee (what it is there to do – to raise money for the parent charity).
- Any ethical values which will guide the committee in its work.
- Organisational structure: officers and membership of the committee, how they are elected and their responsibilities, resignation or termination of membership from the committee.
- Rules for handling money and bank accounts.
- Meetings and the Annual General Meeting, when they are held and any quorum for decision-taking.
- Expenses for committee members (normally they will not be remunerated for their work).
- Powers to alter the constitution or wind up the committee.

Local fundraising activities

There is an enormous range of fundraising activities that local support groups can undertake. To give you some ideas, we list here a few that work well:

- Coffee mornings and other 'socials'.
- Bridge tournaments and other games (whist, chess, and so on).
- Sponsored walks, jogs, cycle rides, fun runs and anything else that can be sponsored.
- Heritage walks or cultural evenings for tourists.
- Craft fairs and sales of work.
- Fashion shows.
- Film premieres.
- Concerts and other cultural events.
- Dinner dances and balls.
- Discos for young people.
- Picnics and outings for families, if possible at interesting locations.
- Auctions of donated goods and 'promises auctions' (where a promise to do something useful or interesting is auctioned off).
- Raffles, lotteries and sweepstakes.
- Competitions with an entry fee to participants.
- Sports events and tournaments.
- New Year's Eve parties, and events on other festive occasions.
- Getting supporters and businesses to advertise in calendars and diaries, brochures and annual reports.
- Sales of greetings cards.
- Public and house-to-house collections.

Organising fundraising events is covered in Section 6.2, organising public and house-to-house collections in Section 6.3, lotteries and raffles in Section 6.10, and getting companies to advertise in Section 4.5.

Supporting and managing the local group

The point of having a local group do the fundraising is that the 'hard grind' of doing the fundraising work is farmed out to a group of volunteers, leaving you free to concentrate on other tasks. It often is not cost-effective for a paid member of staff to spare time organising craft fairs or dinner dances or coffee mornings. But you need to make sure that the group you have established to do this actually does the work, does it well, and does not call unreasonably upon your time.

On the other hand, you will need to support and manage the group to get the most out of it. You will need to:

- Provide the group with some form of **induction**, so that members can understand the importance of the work being done by the organisation, see the staff at work, and meet and talk to staff and beneficiaries. If they can see the work at first hand, it will help fire them with enthusiasm, so that they know what they are raising the money for and can convince those they are asking of its importance.

- Help steer the group towards those **fundraising methods** which are more likely to work. Your experience will help, and you can also research what the local fundraising groups of other organisations are doing.
- Give the group a **budget** (they will need to spend some money to raise money) and fundraising targets to achieve. Don't expect too much too soon. It is best for them to start slowly, and to allow more time than they think will be necessary. If you are too optimistic at the outset, there will be a sense of failure when the targets are not achieved.
- Continue to show your **personal interest** in what they are doing, and acknowledge your appreciation of their hard work at every opportunity.
- Monitor their **progress** and be available to **advise them** if they have difficulties.
- Provide them with appropriate **literature** about the organisation that explains its work clearly and powerfully.

Setting up a local group: some key questions to answer

- **How should a local fundraising group be constituted?** Should it be an independently constituted group with its own separate legal structure and charitable status? Or should it be a branch or committee of the main organisation?
- **Who is legally accountable for the money that is raised** (to see that it is spent for the purpose for which it was given)?
- **What freedom does the local group have** to make statements in public on matters that concern the organisation?
- What role does it have in **the determination of where its money is spent?** Does it decide what to support and any terms or conditions to be attached to the way the money is spent? Or do you (when it is yours without strings attached)?
- **What sanctions do you have** if you feel that the group is bringing your organisation into disrepute in any way?

Setting up an overseas fundraising group

If you are based in one country and want to raise money in another, it is often sensible to do that through a fundraising group you have established in the country where you want to raise money. To do this you will need to:

- Set up and register an organisation with charitable status.
- Find a group of people who are prepared to act as trustees, who will take full responsibility for all aspects of running the organisation, including fundraising, being accountable for the proper expenditure of grants received, holding and attending trustees' meetings, and seeing that the organisation complies with all legal requirements.
- Raise money for your work (which is the whole purpose of setting up the group).
- Get the annual accounts prepared and audited (if necessary).

Money can be raised through normal fundraising activity. You can also use the organisation to raise funds from foundations, who may only be prepared to make a grant to an organisation that is registered and operating in their own country. The local group that you have established fulfils these requirements, so that if they would like to support your work, they can now do so.

You can also use this organisation to raise money from government and other institutional sources who make grants to Southern NGOs through partner organisations in their own country, which should not just act as a channel for transferring funds, but also be able to add some value to the work being done (by bringing skills, mobilising additional resources and participating in the strategic planning and evaluation processes).

An example of an overseas fundraising group

UnLtd India makes awards to early-stage social entrepreneurs in India, to people with ideas for creating better communities or a better world, and who are prepared to have a go at turning their ideas into practice. UnLtd India makes cash awards and provides support to these social entrepreneurs. In order to pay for this, UnLtd India had to raise around $250,000 per annum, which it decided to do in India (where it is based), and in the UK where it wanted specifically to target non-resident Indians.

UnLtd India established the Social Entrepreneurs Trust (SET) in the UK as the vehicle for the UK fundraising, which would remit all money raised to India after paying for the costs of raising it. Money is raised in the following ways:

- Through an annual event that includes a reception and an auction. This is used for thanking supporters and making new contacts, as well as for raising money.
- By getting individuals and companies to sponsor individual social entrepreneurs, with a target of raising $2,500 per social entrepreneur.
- By approaching foundations and government sources for support. In the first year, funds were received from a number of UK foundations established by non-resident Indians. Plans are being developed to approach major institutional sources, including DFID, the European Union, the Big Lottery Fund and Comic Relief.
- SET has a board in the UK which is quite separate from the UnLtd India board, but the two boards keep in close touch. The board brings useful contacts who can be approached for support; and it also oversees a group of volunteers who take responsibility for organising the annual fundraising event.

6.2 Organising a fundraising event

All sorts of events can be organised to raise money for charity. But whether you are planning to hold a concert in your home town, arrange a celebrity cricket match or celebrate your organisation's centenary with a firework party in the park, you need to think not just about the fundraising potential of the event, but about the cost and effort involved in putting it on and also about the possibility of losing money rather than making money from the event. For every event that attracts thousands of new supporters and gives everyone a good time, there is another that collapses, is rained off, or fails because sponsorship was withdrawn at the last moment. While there is money to be made from a well-run event, many absorb a great deal of energy and deliver only small returns.

An advertisement for an event

Just to show that events do not have to be world class to raise useful amounts.

* * * DANCE THE NIGHT AWAY * * * *

**On Saturday 30 September, 9pm to midnight at Founders Hall
a 'Dancing Only' get together.**

*Bring a friend, your best bopping music on tape, snacks,
drink and lots of energy!*

Donation of £1 at the door. Proceeds to Waldorf Kindergarten.

Objectives of the event

An event may be of almost any size and complexity. But what all events have in common is that you will be asking your members, the general public or a selected audience to participate, and you will be giving them something to enjoy in return for their money. You should not just be creating an opportunity to take as much money as you can from those who attend – you should do this, of course, but you should be aiming to give them a good time as well!

You must be absolutely clear about the purpose of the event from the start. Is it for PR, to get your name known? Or is it to raise as much money as you can? Or is it an opportunity to entertain your volunteers and supporters to thank them? Or is it simply to give an enthusiastic fundraising committee something useful to do for you? Or to bring your work to the attention of an influential audience? The objectives for the event will help mould the exact form of the event itself and how you run it. Whatever their precise purpose, events always provide an opportunity to get your message across, even if only in a low-key way (by handing out leaflets to participants or mounting a small exhibition illustrating your work at the event venue, for example).

The five ingredients

Whatever your event, there are likely to be five principal groups of people involved. Get them working together in harmony and you are well on your way to success. These people are:

1. The performers

The performers are the people upon whose skills and appeal the event is centred: the band that is booked to play at the ball; the auctioneer undertaking the sale for you; or the football teams and 'star' players who will be playing in the charity match. They are critical to its success. It is on their performance that the success of the event depends. But they also have something to gain from participating in the event. It could be a fee (although you should always try to get a reduced fee or a free performance). It will often provide them with good publicity, and an association with a good cause – which is good for their image.

2. The sponsors

Sponsors may be underwriting much of the cost, and this makes it possible for the event to be held without exposing your organisation to unnecessary risk. They also have a good deal to gain from the event. They are often interested in reaching your audience (with information about their product) and in being seen by the general public (and by their employees) to be supporting something worthwhile.

3. The media

The media are in business to report events such as yours, especially if they bring genuine talent to the fore or are of particular local interest. Whether the event is genuinely newsworthy depends on its nature and on how creative you are in generating media interest. The media may be interested in being given exclusive coverage of the story in return for publishing a major feature or picture. Or they may be interested in becoming a 'media sponsor', offering you not money but free advertising and press coverage to promote the event in advance, and thus attract an audience.

4. The charity or NGO

The next ingredient is you and your organisation. Your involvement gives the event a focus – the real reason for its happening is to raise money to support your good work. The audience may come because they are your supporters, or because they are interested in your cause. The performers will not come to just any event, because they may have many other commitments. But an event for your organisation could be something that strikes a sympathetic chord with them. The sponsors will decide to back the event because of your reputation and the audience that you can deliver for them. Your contacts with well-known patrons can be a further inducement.

5. The audience

Some people go to a charity event simply because they are interested in attending. Others consider it an enjoyable way of supporting a cause or a particular organisation. But everyone attending knows that it is a fundraising event, and expects to be asked to contribute in some way while they are there (in addition to paying the cost of the ticket). Making sure they enjoy the event is important. But finding ways of raising yet more money from the people whom you have attracted to your event is a critical factor in the financial outcome.

Deciding what to organise

One starting point is to examine your market. Who are the people who will come to the event – the people who are already in touch with you (your donors, your members, your volunteers, the readers of your newsletter) or that you can reach through a particular type of promotion? What are the interests of these people? Are they old or young, active and energetic, particularly interested in your cause? What are you and your helpers interested in – and what contacts do you have (access to performers, for example)?

Sometimes you will want to start from the sponsorship end, and ask a potential sponsor what money is available, what sort of event they might be interested in, and what needs to be done for them to decide to back it.

An alternative starting point might be to think about some of the major types of event and to decide whether any seem appropriate. A short list might include:

- **Sporting events.**
- **Musical and cultural events.**
- **Balls, dinners, auctions** and other entertainment events.
- **Exhibitions, festivals and fairs.**
- **Events involving schools** and young people.
- **Mass participation events**, with the participants collecting sponsorship money.

Most events are run on a one-off basis – although you will always want to rerun the event next year if it is successful, thereby creating a regular source of income for your charity. Some events take place over a period of time – for example, a knockout football competition or a film festival. More complicated (and more risky) events should perhaps be left to when you have more experience.

Depending upon the nature of your plans, you may need some sort of licence (to run the event, to collect money in a public place, or to run a bar). Check the legal requirements with the local administrative authority before you start any detailed planning.

FEBA Radio's fundraising dinner

FEBA Radio, a Christian broadcasting organisation in Kenya, decided to raise money to convert an office into a small temporary studio as an alternative to the expense of hiring studio space.

'Since we had not held a fundraising event before, we chose to host a dinner for about 50 people who already knew us and the work we do. We invited members of our council of management and their spouses, and asked them to invite one couple each to a dinner in a local hotel. We also invited a guest speaker and a couple to sing at the dinner.

'In our planning we decided not to ask the guests to pay for the dinner, believing that they would be more generous as a result. We prepared a presentation for the dinner, including the history of FEBA Radio, our purpose and work, and something about our future plans. We also provided quotes from FEBA listeners showing how our programmes had affected their lives. At the conclusion of the dinner one of the council members talked about why we needed the studio, and its estimated cost (about Ksh 60,000 or £750). He then appealed for cash contributions. The total we raised in cash and pledges was Ksh 100,000. The dinner cost just less than Ksh 20,000.

'Because of the small number of invited guests and the fact that most of them are aware of our work, we did not produce any publicity materials specially for the occasion. We made follow-up telephone calls after sending out the invitations to confirm attendance.

After the dinner, we sent thank-you letters to all those who attended and reminders to all those making a pledge.

'This being our first attempt at fundraising, we felt that it was quite successful in that we raised more than we had planned. One of the contributing factors to the success was that the guests were people who were aware of and sympathised with our work and also personal friends. Also because this was a one-off request, many people would find it easier to make a single gift than a long-term commitment. Finally we were raising money for a specific project, and the amount we needed was not a very large sum.'

Source: Leah Gachegu, Audience Relations manager, FEBA Radio

Management

The ability to run the event well is crucial. It will almost certainly take much longer and involve more effort than you think. There seem to be three main approaches to organising the event: do it yourself; get a professional to do it; or recruit a group of volunteers. All approaches have their drawbacks and their advantages.

1. **Do it yourself.** Perhaps the single most important drawback of doing it yourself is the opportunity cost it will involve. What else could you be doing with the time? How much money could you be raising if you were not stuck with doing the organising? Almost any event will require constant attention to detail, and checking and double-checking at every stage. If you are in the middle of a busy fundraising programme, organising something that requires so much of your time may simply not be feasible.

2. **Engage a professional** to do the organising. Very often the event will be run through some sporting organisation or cultural institution that specialises in this sort of activity. If not, there might be professional event organisers in the musical, sporting and entertainment fields. For a fee or a percentage of ticket income, they can be engaged to take over all the day-to-day administration from you. Alternatively, a suitable public relations or professional fundraising company could be used – again for a fee.

3. **Establish a committee** of volunteers to take all the responsibility for running the event. The key appointment will be the chairperson. This need not be someone who knows how to run an event backwards, but you do require someone with the leadership qualities and the good management sense to link the commercial needs of the event to the requirements of the charity. You will want to select a multi-disciplinary team that incorporates all the skills you will need to make the event work – people with the sporting or musical background to deal with the programme, the accountant who will advise on the budget and ticket pricing, the people with marketing and PR skills. You need to give yourself plenty of time to find the right people.

There are several important aspects to managing the event successfully:

■ **An accurate budget.** It is essential to control costs if you are to run the event profitably. Your budget will also give you an indication of the size of audience you will need to attract and what price to charge for tickets. At an early stage you will need to make an assessment of all the likely costs and the potential sources of income – and just to be safe you should include something for contingencies. On the income side it is worth making a high and low estimate to illustrate what may happen in different circumstances. This will highlight the risk involved.

- **Plenty of time.** Although it is possible to organise an event in a short space of time, the longer you leave yourself the better. The best is an annual cycle, with the planning of next year's event starting just after the completion of this year's event. Booking a venue or obtaining the services of star performers may take a lot longer and be an important factor in how far ahead you need to plan.

- **Legally binding contracts.** You will also need to record the arrangements with performers, the venue and any sub-contractors through some formal written agreement. This sets out precisely what has been agreed and is signed by both parties to confirm the agreement. This avoids disputes later on. It is especially important to agree on: how any money is to be split (both expenditure and income); who has the rights to the recording of the event; who is responsible for what costs; and what the obligations are in the event of cancellation. Where considerable sums are involved, the agreement should be drawn up by a lawyer.

- **Good administration and record keeping.** For your first event, you have to start from scratch. But next time it will be much easier, since you will be building on experience. Keep records of everything, so you will know what to do next time – for example, whether insurance is needed, where to go for it and how much to pay. Immediately after the event, hold a debriefing – find out what went really well, what went wrong or could be improved, and what suggestions there are for doing better or for raising more money next time. All this can be used to ensure that the event is even more of a success the next time you run it.

Reducing the risk

The best way of reducing risk is to have a well thought-out event and good planning, organisation and marketing. But things have a habit of not going to plan, so you will need to think about your exposure to risk and how to reduce it. There are several ways of doing this:

- **Financial sponsorship.** Get all the costs of the event covered by a sponsor, so that there is nothing to lose and everything to gain. An additional advantage is that you can tell everyone coming that all proceeds will go to the cause (since all the costs have already been covered). This can be a tremendous encouragement for ticket sales.

- **Commitments and guarantees.** One way of running a charity ball is to have a committee of say 20 people, each of whom agrees to get 12 people to come to the ball. They take responsibility for selling the 12 tickets, or for paying for them themselves in the event of being unable to find others to contribute. This means that you have an already guaranteed attendance of 240 people – enough to fill the venue or make sure that the event is a success.

- **Cost cutting.** Try to get as much as you can lent, donated or sponsored for the occasion, so that you do not have to pay for all of it. The cost of venues, performers and prizes can all be substantial, and if such costs are too high they can jeopardise the success of the event. Not having to pay, or paying less, is a simple way to get more out of the event and at the same time to reduce risk.

- **Insurance.** It may be possible to insure against public liability, theft or damage (in case something goes wrong), and for an outdoor event, against the possibility of bad weather.

Promotion

Effective promotion can turn an event from being a modest success into being really profitable. First think about who is likely to want to come to the event – this is your target market. And then decide how best to reach them – which you can do through getting coverage in the press and on radio, paying for advertising, displaying posters in the street or in public places, mailing your supporters and other lists of people. All this can be extremely hard work, and some of the methods will cost money. But it is a full house that will make the event a success.

For an important event, try to get **media sponsorship** – the backing of one of the main newspapers or radio stations. They may preview the event or interview those involved. Radio may be prepared to broadcast the event live and make frequent mentions in the run-up to the event, giving the date and explaining how to get tickets. A media link can create its own promotional momentum. Another possibility is to give away free tickets as prizes to be offered to readers or listeners. You could devise a competition of some sort or offer two free tickets to the first 25 people who write or call in.

One way of generating publicity is to use **celebrities** who may be attending the event or performing in it. This will be especially true of sporting or cultural events where the performers will be the main attraction. Or you may be inviting a celebrity to act as compère, to open the event or to present awards. Involving famous people adds credibility and will attract people to the event.

You will also need a strategy for getting people to come if ticket sales are slow, but are not so disappointing that you have to cancel the event. Once you are sure the event will happen, it is important for everyone (those who have bought tickets, the performers and the organisers) that it is well attended. At that stage it is more important to see that people are there than that all the tickets are sold. This means that you should be prepared to give tickets away free to groups who might be interested in coming – through schools and student unions for young people's events, through hospitals and other institutions for other events, or via a media promotion. The people who come will contribute to the success of the event just by being there, but they might also spend money.

How to attract people to your event

- Hold a really attractive event that people will want to come to. And make the event fun for everyone who participates in it.
- Find plenty of ticket sellers who between them will take responsibility for selling all the tickets.
- Target the event at a readily identifiable and reachable audience – your supporters, the business community, local politicians, and so on.
- Everyone should be encouraged to ask people in person or by telephone, rather than just relying on sending out printed invitations.

- Get coverage of your event in the local press – so that people hear about what you are planning. Media sponsorship, posters and leaflets distributed widely will also help promote the event.
- Use celebrities to get publicity. And if you can get them to help you (see Section 7.2), their presence will encourage people to come to the event.

Getting sponsorship

Events are ideal vehicles for attracting business sponsorship – because for businesses they offer a possibility of getting their message to your audience and an opportunity of entertaining staff or customers, and for you because sponsorship brings in money and can help reduce your risk.

Sponsors will need to know a great deal about the event and its expected audience. How many people will come? What sort of people will they be? How will they be exposed to any advertising messages? For example, by having their name and logo printed in the poster and programme and included in any publicity before the event and in the media coverage, by distributing free samples of their product, by donating a prize in a competition, by having a 'name link' with their product – there are all sorts of ways, and it is up to you to devise something that will be attractive to a business.

You should have a clear idea of how much money you are asking the sponsor to contribute and what you are offering in return. Besides the good publicity, you might be offering special hospitality facilities for their senior staff, or for more junior employees, or for clients and customers, with opportunity to meet the celebrities. For more advice on getting business sponsorship, see Section 4.6.

Uzhgorod 'Path to Life' charity concert

In August 2005 Path to Life Medical Rehabilitation and Therapy Centre organised a benefit concert in the small town of Uzhgorod in the Ukraine. The objectives of the event were to raise money to support the centre and to introduce the concept of a benefit concert to the local community. A wide variety of artists performed at the concert and more than 400 people attended; as a result, the entire event was broadcast by regional television. The Path to Life benefit concert is a very good example of how NGOs can provide excellent services and experiences to donors while introducing individual giving to a community.

This campaign was the first of its kind organised by the Path for Life Centre. It's important to note that the concert benefited from a wide range of support from the city's most important social organisations. For example, a music teacher was provided by the regional ministry of culture and the mayor's office allowed the organisation to use the Philharmonia theatre free of charge.

An interesting aspect of the campaign is that most of the advertising was done by word of mouth. Information about the event was passed around via school pupils and friends and relatives of Path to Life staff. The Centre prepared and hand-delivered special invitation cards to regional authorities, local hospitals and other town officials who could spread the word about the event. Concert posters were printed and displayed in local libraries and in the windows of local businesses. Finally, a press release was prepared in English and Ukrainian and the Centre organised a press conference a few days before the concert.

Approximately 400 people attended and the concert generated 910 euros. Subsequently, the Centre received offers from other artists, and on 30 September 2005 it hosted a second benefit concert. Besides organising a concert described as being of the highest quality by the ministry of culture, the first Path for Life concert managed to get both the local community and a substantial number of companies involved for the first time, giving both in-kind support and donations.

In addition to the funds raised, this event generated substantial publicity and helped build many useful relationships for the Centre, many of which will help when organising similar events in the future.

Source: Showcase of Fundraising Innovation and Inspiration

Generating extra income

For many events, such as a dinner dance or a ball, the ticket price may cover the cost of organising the event and not much more. If you want to generate even more money in return for your work, you will have to devise ways of getting those who are attending the event to give or spend more. It is by generating this extra money that your event becomes a real success. There are all sorts of ways of doing this. Here are a few ideas:

- Getting local businesses to take **advertising in the programme**. This is called 'goodwill advertising', and is sold on the basis that businesses are helping a good cause and are being associated with a successful event.
- Running **an auction**, where interesting items are sold off during the course of the evening. A holiday donated by a travel company is often the star item. Alternatively, these items can be prizes in a raffle or prize draw.
- Holding **a tombola** or a **raffle**, in which small gifts donated by local shops and by supporters are the prizes. Each prize is numbered, and each ticket purchased bears a number which either corresponds with a prize or does not win. To be a success, a raffle should offer lots of prizes and a good chance of winning something.
- Distributing **pledge forms** for each person to fill in, and making an appeal during the evening. Or collecting money in a bucket from those present. To make sure that people respond generously, you should say what the money is for and perhaps suggest a level of donation. You might get the performers to say something during the evening.
- **Advertising the appeal** in the event programme. Not everyone there will be an existing supporter or know about what you are doing and why the work is important.

Spin-off for future fundraising

A great advantage of holding a successful event is that it enables you to build up a clientele for future occasions. If you keep the names and addresses of those who have attended, you can invite them to participate next time you run the event – perhaps next year.

You will also want to capture the interest of the people who attend the event, so that they can learn about your cause and understand the importance of your work. This can be done by trying to raise money from them in one of the ways already suggested. But you can also add the participants' names to your mailing list and make sure that they receive any appeal literature you are sending out. You might even make them 'honorary members' for three months to get them used to the idea of being supporters. You could think about organising an 'open day' where they could come and see your work, meet your staff and talk to your beneficiaries.

Organising a particular type of event can help you reach new audiences. For example, if you want to appeal to the middle-class cultural elite, you might consider running a concert or art exhibition. If you are interested in the educational establishment, you might think about an exhibition of children's paintings. Or if you want to appeal to the business elite or top politicians, an event involving leading TV or cinema or sporting stars might be worth considering.

A sports event with a difference

Can Too is a non-profit programme raising money for Cure Cancer Australia. Professional coaches train people to run or swim an endurance event while receiving professional team coaching. It gives people the opportunity to reach a personal goal in a supportive, fun and sometimes crazy environment, while raising money for the Cure Cancer Australia Foundation.So often we ask people to take part in events for us or on our behalf, but leave them to their own devices. What a great way actually to engage your supporters in your cause, support them and help them reach their goal so you can reach yours!

Can Too was created by Annie Crawford, who wanted to combine her passion for fitness with raising money for cancer. The programme is structured so that everybody wins. It is an opportunity for participants to achieve a goal they may never have thought possible, while making new friends and getting support from them. At the same time, participants can 'make a difference for others' by raising funds to support breakthrough cancer research directly, as part of Cure Cancer Australia's vision for 'a world without cancer, nothing less'.

This idea is probably expensive to implement, but the returns are greater and it has been shown that people will come back to do more with you. Can Too and their supporters have raised $1,615,000 since 2005. Often we just take our volunteer fundraisers for granted. This demonstrates that we shouldn't.

Any fundraiser who is reading this should look at the Can Too site (www.cantoo.org.au) and think about adapting it to their market.

Source: Showcase of Fundraising Innovation and Inspiration

Sponsored participation events

Organising a 'sponsored event' is not the same as getting business sponsorship for your event. In a sponsored event, which might be a walk or a swim or a cycle ride, the participants get their family, their friends and their colleagues at work to 'sponsor' them by contributing a certain amount for each kilometre or each lap they complete. Lots of small sums pledged by lots of sponsors, multiplied by lots of laps or kilometres, and multiplied again by lots of participants can generate really substantial amounts of money for your organisation.

Remember, though, that the people are supporting their friends to participate (perhaps to do something interesting or unusual) because they have been asked. The participants may become involved because it is a fun thing to do or a challenge.

Sponsored events are among the most widely used ways of raising money for charity. You can sponsor just about anything! Ideas that have been used include:

- Giving up smoking or drinking (sponsoring the number of days going without a cigarette or a drink, up to a maximum number of days).
- Knitting (how many centimetres knitted during an afternoon).
- A litter pick (how many kilos of litter cleared from a river bank).
- Marathon runs (number of miles raced plus a bonus for completing the course).
- Penalty shoot-outs (number of goals scored if you are the penalty taker, or goals saved if the goalkeeper).

Walks for Millions

The Community Chest in Hong Kong raises money to distribute as grants for community betterment and welfare purposes. Around 15 per cent of its annual income has been coming from three sponsored walks involving around 50,000 walkers. The following are some tips for planning a sponsored walk based on their experience:

- **Best time for the walk:** Sunday morning or Saturday afternoon.
- **Route:** three routes – easy, tough and a family walk – to encourage maximum participation. The assembly point should be easily accessible and spacious enough to accommodate all the walkers. The routes should be wide and flat wherever possible. The finishing point should be accessible to transport so that walkers who have completed the course can disperse. Route reconnaissance should be conducted before a firm decision on the route is made.
- **The walk can celebrate** (say) the opening of a new road or bridge, which could bring additional sponsorship and publicity.
- **Facilities:** first aid, toilet facilities and communications with marshals all need to be in place.
- **Target for fundraising** should be set according to the size of the event. The budgeted expenditure should be kept below 15 per cent of the expected income. Items of expenditure include: media, print and production, awards and souvenirs for the walkers, a reception, photography, temporary staffing, transportation, direct mail to potential participants, site expenses, drinks and refreshment, and sundries. Some if not all the expenses can be met through sponsorship.

- **Supporting organisations**: the police for crowd control and safety along the route; the urban or regional council for the use of public amenities; the transport department for agreeing and announcing road closures; St John Ambulance Brigade for first aid services; Boy Scouts and Girl Guides to help with registration of the walkers on the day; Civil Aid Services for crowd control and radio communications on the day.

- **Printed material required**: route map; poster; sponsor forms; appeal letters; certificate of appreciation for completion of the walk; souvenirs; reply form to enable participants to register.

The start of the 'Walk for Millions'

- **Problems**: the event requires a lot of manpower and detailed organisation; effort must be put into collecting donations and sponsorship from participants; special arrangements for road closure need to be made, unless the event is performed in a park; the event could be ruined by bad weather.
- **Ideas learned from experience**: set up a prize or awards system; plan the walk to include walkers of all ages and people with physical disabilities; entertainments and music can be arranged at the start, finish and along the route to make the walk more interesting; encourage each walker to have their own fundraising target.

Source: Winnie Sek, Deputy Director, Campaigns and Donations, The Community Chest

---

Sponsored event checklist

1. **Choose the right activity.** Something that people will want to do and is novel enough to warrant others sponsoring them – but also something that is relatively easy and inexpensive to organise.
2. **Set a date and venue.** Make sure you plan well ahead to allow time for preparation and for participants to get their sponsorship.
3. **Get any permissions you need** – for example, to use a public place – from the police, local authority or the owner of the property.
4. **Produce sponsorship forms.** Give examples of what amounts you expect, and set each participant a target for the number of sponsors and the amount to raise.
5. **Involve other organisations,** as they can be a good source of participants. You might even think of holding a joint event with another organisation. The more people who participate the better.
6. **Organise local publicity.** Get celebrities to sign up as participants, and use this to publicise the event. Get media sponsorship – which can be another way of getting participants.
7. **Get local business sponsorship,** to cover costs and pay for any prizes being offered. This will reduce your risk, but will also ensure that as much of the money as possible that participants raise goes to the cause.

8. **Prepare for the day.** Ensure that you have all the stewards, equipment and information for the event, that the route is well marked, and that everyone is well briefed.
9. **Tidy up afterwards.**
10. **Thank all the participants,** both for their participation and the amount they raised. Tell them what you plan to do with the money.
11. **Chase up all uncollected pledges.** This is most important. People are not being asked to participate in the event for fun, but to help you raise money.
12. **Add the names on your sponsorship forms to your mailing list,** if the forms include details of the each sponsor's name and address. You will then be able to send them an appeal letter in due course suggesting that they continue supporting your work.

In deciding on the event, find something that will be sufficiently popular to attract lots of participants (the more participants you attract, the more money you will raise) and which is trouble-free to organise. Also, you want something that you can repeat year on year, building on your experience and success to achieve greater returns the next time you run it. A sponsored event can also be used to get across an important message about your cause (an environmental charity could organise a sponsored clean-up, Alcoholics Anonymous a sponsored give-up-alcohol, for example).

You need to take into account what will be attractive to your target audience. Younger people may be interested in disco marathons, but will not be interested in a sponsored knit. For older people, it would be the other way round. If your target audience is young families, can you think of something that will involve them all during the weekend? Family strolls ('strollathons'), fun runs and swimming are all popular – your imagination is the only limit to what is possible. You can expect three types of person to join in:

- **Those who have participated before** and who know it will be a lot of fun; so it is important to keep a record of who has participated in previous years.
- **Supporters** of and **sympathisers** with your cause. So mail your members and donors; they may be interested in doing something to help raise money.
- **People who just enjoy the particular activity** you have chosen (cycling, walking, and so on) and who may not necessarily be interested in your work – although their participation gives you the opportunity to interest them.

A fourth group are those involved in your organisation:

- Members of your **management board** (it is a good opportunity to get them doing something useful!).
- Your **staff** (involvement in a sponsored event can improve morale).
- Your **beneficiaries** (a cycle ride for a mental handicap organisation that involves mentally handicapped people as riders can show that they are 'people just like us' and make the cause seem more relevant to participants).

Organising the event

Organisation takes place in three stages:

Stage One: Before the event

Before the event, you will need to:

- **Decide on the event** and agree the route or the venue; get any permission or insurance necessary.
- **Plan the promotion.**
- **Prepare the sponsorship forms** and **explanatory materials** about the work of your organisation.
- **Provide advice and support to participants** to help them collect pledges.
- **Organise volunteers** to help on the day.
- **Mark out the route.**
- **Welcome participants** on their arrival and certify their completion.

Preparation of the sponsorship forms requires some thought. The form must describe exactly what is being done, but should also say why the money is needed. Then it should list the names and addresses of the sponsors (the participant will need the addresses to collect the sponsorship that has been pledged; you will want the addresses so that you can mail your appeal literature and try to get further support) and the amount pledged. You will want to encourage sponsors to commit themselves to a generous amount of sponsorship. They need to know how many miles (or things) they are likely to be paying for. Is there a maximum number of miles, for example? And remember that you are likely to get more if your sponsorship is per kilometre than per mile. Most sponsors do not know what level of sponsorship is expected, and are guided by what others have written before. Thus you might indicate some preferred amounts in the form of one cent, two cents, five cents or 10 cents per kilometre, or encourage participants to approach their more generous supporters first. Some people may prefer to give a fixed sum. The form should allow for this too.

Ideas for a sponsored event

'As well as the more usual sponsored swims, walks and runs, I have heard of sponsored beard shaves, bungee jumping, chess marathons, and group silences. A group of local churches organise a sponsored cycle ride visiting 60+ local churches each summer. Children attempt hopscotch marathons or carol singing. Knitting groups organise sponsored patches – as well as each knitter being sponsored for the number of patches knitted, you get the most wonderful patchwork blanket to donate to a raffle for further funds. I've even heard of a sponsored vasectomy! And I know one brave leukaemia patient who had a sponsored head shave in public just before he went into hospital to undergo a gruelling period of chemotherapy, when he was told to expect considerable hair loss anyway. But don't stop here. Use the basic outline to work out your own ideas. You are only restricted by the limits of your imagination!'

Source: Sarah Passingham, writing in Tried and Tested Ideas for Raising Money Locally *(2nd edition, published by Directory of Social Change)*

Since the ultimate success of the event depends on the amount raised, it is important to have lots of participants raising lots of money. Once you have got the participants, you can encourage them to raise more money by:

- Setting **a minimum sponsorship** requirement which they guarantee to pay.
- Giving them **a target**, both in terms of the number of sponsors they should aim to get and how much to ask for.
- Having **an entrance fee** for participating in the event.

You will be surprised by the range of sums people raise. And this depends as much on the effort put in by the participant (this can be encouraged by you) as on their financial circumstances.

Stage Two: On the day

On the day, you need to make sure that everything runs smoothly, that there are sufficient helpers, and that they are properly briefed. You also need to ensure that participants are welcomed (especially any celebrities), that newspaper and radio reporters are welcomed and briefed about anything unusual (including anyone participating in fancy dress, any stunts, anything unusual about what the money will be used for), that there is information at the start of the event to advise participants and public what the route is and where the refreshment and toilet facilities are – and for events that involve physical exertion, where medical help can be obtained. At the start point you may want to set up an exhibition about your work – which provides a further opportunity to 'sell' your cause. You will need to have sufficient helpers to staff the various check-in procedures and to mark the route.

Stage Three: After the event

After the event, the key activity is to collect the money from participants and to thank those who actually took part. Collecting the money can be difficult. This must be the prime responsibility of the participants who were sponsored in the first place. Keep a register of all participants. Stress the importance of collecting the money. Give a deadline date. Follow up in person if you can or by phone, or if all this fails by letter. Follow-up letters may be needed too. Offer prizes for the largest amount actually raised – which can provide an incentive for people to collect their sponsorship money.

6.3 Collections

Public collections can be a successful way of raising money – if you have enough people prepared to do the collecting. This can take several forms:

- **House-to-house collections,** where you knock on doors and ask for support. Or leave an envelope and information about your work, and call back next day.
- **Street collections** and **collections in public places** (such as shopping centres or cinemas). Typically here a collector will have a collecting box, and may give some token in return for the donation (such as a sticker).
- **Collecting boxes placed at shop counters** for people to leave their small change, or larger collecting devices outside the shop.

- **Collecting boxes in supporters' homes**, where they can leave their small change or ask their friends to contribute.

The great strength of local collection schemes is that over time they can reach very large sections of the public. Not only does this have advantages in fundraising terms (you will be asking lots of people), it can also have a great educational or publicity impact. Imagine the impact of a national AIDS campaign that contacted every household in your town, not just to raise money but also to provide information. You could provide information on the disease, gain publicity for the organisation concerned and of course raise funds at the same time. Equally important to bear in mind is the reverse situation, where sloppy volunteer work will quickly bring an organisation into disrepute.

Because there is always the possibility of theft or fraud where collections are concerned, it is important to ensure that the collection is conducted in a way which minimises the chance that the money might not reach the benefiting organisation. Points to watch out for, in particular, are proper authorisation of collectors, proper procedures for remitting the money to the organisation and accounting for it, and procedures for returning all unused materials and authorisations at the end of the collection.

House-to-house collections

House-to-house collections are very popular with both national and local charities as a way of asking everyone in a particular area to help. Remember that the main reason why people say that they don't give is because nobody asks them. A house-to-house collection provides the opportunity to ask people on a one-to-one basis with sufficient time to explain the work of the charity and why the money is needed.

Right at the start you need to plan how you will run the collection. Local knowledge will help you decide which neighbourhoods are likely to be most responsive. Consideration should be given to the affluence of the people who live there, but also to the ease of access to each house (apartment blocks are easier than suburban houses with large gardens, where security guards may also present an obstacle).

Another factor is the group of volunteers who will be doing the collecting. Typically you may want one volunteer to take responsibility for one street, either their own or one nearby. If you have a local fundraising group, plan the collection with them; if you haven't, you will need to recruit collectors either from among your supporters or from the general public. The collectors should be given some training. They can be told when to call, what to say (explaining the importance of the work of the charity, what the money will be spent on, how much to give), what difficult questions to expect, and so on. You might do this by arranging a meeting for all the collectors, or by briefing people individually.

The collector's main function will be to deliver an envelope on which there is some message, with an accompanying brochure or letter from the charity. People might want to give there and then, or the collector can return after a short interval (of days rather than hours) to collect the envelopes.

The collector will encounter all sorts of responses. There will be those who decline to help you, and those who choose to be abusive. Most people will be polite. Some will be interested in, or even enthusiastic about, what you are doing, some may have heard of you already, and some may even have supported you before. This is an ideal opportunity to recruit a new member or volunteer, and the collectors should be briefed to supply you with the names of people who seem particularly enthusiastic. For those who just return their envelope, make sure that their name and address is noted. You will want to say thank you. You also have a new donor and will want to keep in touch.

Checklist for organising a collection

1. **Check the date**. Avoid holiday periods or times of the year when there are other collections going on.
2. **Seek any authorisation** that you will require from the police or local authority, and from the landlord (for cinemas and shopping centres).
3. **Identify the areas and locations** for collecting. Go for middle-class housing and busy shopping streets. And think about the best time of day to call (during the daytime if they're not working; or in the evenings or at the weekend if they are).
4. **Recruit your team of volunteers**; the more you have, the more you will collect. Get those who have volunteered to suggest their friends.
5. **Prepare any materials** you will need, including stickers, collecting boxes or envelopes, and leaflets about the work of the organisation and any membership scheme.
6. **Brief the volunteers** about the work of the charity, and provide some basic training in effective asking.
7. **Organise how the money will be received** and accounted for. Bank all proceeds immediately upon receipt.
8. **Thank the volunteers**, telling them how much they raised and how important this will be to your work.
9. **Thank all the donors**, by sending them a letter (with a further appeal). Follow up on those who have been noted as being particularly interested.
10. **Debrief** your volunteers. Find out what went well, and what not so well. Suggest ways of doing better next time. Keep a record of which locations or neighbourhoods did best.

Another option is to take a collecting box with you, and ask for money there and then. This can also be effective. However you ask, some people will offer an excuse for not giving. They do not want to be seen as mean, so try to justify their not giving. You can attempt to persuade them to change their mind. But often they will just make another excuse. In the meantime, you may be missing the opportunity to recruit other supporters elsewhere in the street.

The returned envelopes should be handed in at one central point and opened under the supervision of two people. The money received should be noted. This will help avoid fraud. A local bank may agree to help you with this. Make a note of how much money is coming from each area for future reference – so you know which streets and which areas are more generous and which collectors are the most successful.

There is always the possibility of fraud being perpetrated on your charity by someone carrying out an unauthorised collection in your name. All collectors should be given a permit from you authorising them to collect on your behalf. If you receive any reports of unauthorised collecting, you should investigate this as fast as you can. Any bad publicity will damage your organisation.

Street collections

Running a street collection is more difficult than a house-to-house collection. Volunteers find it less agreeable standing on the street with a collecting box, and you, the organiser, have to provide enough collectors on the appointed day or week, scheduled so that there are people there all the time and every passer-by is approached.

The choice of location is extremely important, and you should aim to give your collectors access to the maximum number of people. The main shopping street in the city centre is usually best, though collecting at supermarkets, out-of-town shopping centres or well-attended events (such as at sports stadiums or cinemas) may also work well. You will want several collection points (both sides of the street, outside the busiest stores, at all exit points of a stadium). Draw up a rota for each collection point. Ensure that volunteers stay for an hour or two and are then relieved by a replacement. They can also be encouraged to visit restaurants and bars in the area (obtaining the manager's permission before they start asking customers).

To make the most of the collection, you need to train your collectors. Collectors should not shrink back from passers-by. The collector who is prepared to rattle the box or tin vigorously, to look people in the eye, to station themselves in the middle of the pavement, and to engage people in conversation will do very much better. Street collection requires a positive attitude. Collectors will need a sealed collecting device which is convenient to carry, convenient for the public to put money into, and easy to extract the money from afterwards. They will also need a flag or a sticker to give to everyone who puts something in the collecting box.

Collecting boxes should be opened in the presence of two people, and the money should be immediately banked. Make a note of those locations which have produced the most money, and those collectors who have done best. All this information can be used to make the next collection work even better. Thank all your collectors.

What you need for a successful street collection

- Lots of enthusiastic volunteers prepared to stand in the street and ask passers-by to contribute.
- Good organisation to ensure that everyone turns up when and where they are required.
- Printed information about your organisation, to brief the volunteers and hand out to passers-by.
- Stickers (or flags or tokens) to offer people in return for their donation.
- Collecting boxes, suitably labelled to advertise your organisation.
- Good local publicity in advance, so that people hear about the collection and know what it is for.
- A proper accounting system for receiving and banking all the cash that is collected.

The Paraguayan Red Cross Society flag day: thirteen steps to a successful fundraising event

1. **Establish an organising committee**. This is composed of the event coordinator, the head of public relations, the wife of the president of the Paraguayan Red Cross Society and volunteers.

2. **Determine the number of fundraising stands** and find suitable locations. In 1991, 68 stands were put up in Asuncion, the capital city, and the surrounding area. This represents one stand per 14,700 inhabitants.

3. **Determine the most suitable date**. The most suitable date is when most money will be raised, and when most volunteers are available. School holidays and long weekends are not suitable, and the event should not coincide with other organisations' fundraising campaigns. In Asuncion, the flag day is held in the first week of May from 7.30 to 12.30 in the morning.

4. **Mobilise collectors**. Cards are sent to various state bodies, clubs, banks and diplomats inviting the wives of important public figures and officials to take the responsibility for one particular fundraising stand. Letters are sent to the heads of secondary schools inviting groups of students to assist at each stand. Each school is assigned up to four stands, and the young people pick up the collecting boxes from the stand to which they have been assigned and cover the area in the vicinity. The young people have to be at least 13 years old, and are properly briefed through an explanatory circular letter sent some days prior to the flag day.

5. **Hold a briefing session**. Once sufficient stand officials have volunteered, these are brought together for a briefing session, and are given a detailed instruction sheet covering location, number of collecting boxes, and which students will be assisting. They are given Red Cross flags to decorate the stand with, and invitation cards so that they can invite their friends and colleagues to visit the stand.

6. **Set a budget**. It is important to set a target for the fundraising drive, which should also relate to the needs that the Society is trying to meet. Costs should be kept as low as possible. In 1991, just over $100,000 was collected in Asuncion, of which 5–6 per cent represented organising costs (obviously these will be higher the first time the event is held). As the Red Cross is well established, publicity costs are practically nil.

7. **Launch the event to create public awareness**. Once the organisational framework has been set up, it is important to launch the event to create interest in the media and among the public. This will include articles based on interviews with staff and volunteers.

8. **Order the materials**. Flags, collecting boxes, explanatory leaflets and display materials will be required. These have to be ordered in sufficient time to be distributed to the stands.

9. **Publicise the event**. The flag day is publicised for 15–18 days prior to the event via television, radio and newspapers. In 1991, 3,131 column-centimetres of space were taken in newspapers, and just under 120 minutes of advertising time taken on two TV channels. A recorded message was also sent to the radio networks. Posters were put up on poster sites donated by a soft drinks company with the slogan 'Service in Action'.

10. **Inform the media of the results**. Once the total amount collected has been counted, the press should be informed. The Central Bank of Paraguay helps with the collection, its cashiers counting and banking the proceeds that are handed over to them by stand officials.

11. **Recovery of material**. All unused material should be returned and inventoried. This provides useful guidance (on the best stands and the best collectors) for next year.

12. **Send out letters of thanks** to everyone who helped, including a report on the final results at the stand for which they were responsible. Suggestions and comments are also asked for.

13. **Hold a debriefing meeting** in order to find out in detail what worked and what didn't go well; draw conclusions from this so as to be able to correct mistakes and improve performance next time.

Source: Paraguayan Red Cross Society

Collecting boxes in public places

Locations for collecting boxes can range from bars and shop counters to cinema foyers – anywhere where people are paying for things. They will usually be on private property or on the street immediately outside a shop. Most airports now have collecting boxes for travellers to place unwanted foreign currency (and some airlines circulate an envelope for the same purpose).

There are two types of collection device. First, those that appeal to children; these need to be visually appealing and have some sort of moving part that is operated when the money is inserted. Adult boxes, on the other hand, need to be functional and have a good design or label which clearly expresses the cause for which the money is being given.

Finding good locations for collecting boxes can be a job for a persuasive volunteer – who has to persuade the owner or manager of the premises. Once the device has been placed, it still needs to be looked after. You need to see that it is not vandalised or stolen, that it is well displayed, that it is not so full that people can no longer put their money into it, and so that you receive the proceeds regularly. One approach is to suggest that the box become the responsibility of the proprietors of the establishment. But it is far better if one of your volunteers has the overall responsibility, as this will ensure that the scheme runs smoothly and that the money is regularly emptied, banked and accounted for.

Trick or Treat for UNICEF

Trick or Treat for UNICEF is a valued Hallowe'en tradition that has continued over the past 50 years with children carrying the Trick or Treat for UNICEF collection boxes on Hallowe'en night. Instead of collecting sweets or candy, children all over North America have collected coins as they go door-to-door dressed as wee witches or pint-sized superheroes. The money they collect is given to UNICEF, often through their schools, to improve the lives of less fortunate children in the world.

It all began in 1950 when a Sunday school class in Philadelphia, USA decided to collect coins instead of candy on Hallowe'en. They sent their inspirational donation of $17 to UNICEF and an idea was born.

Canadians joined in and sent Hallowe'en collections to UNICEF in the United States. Then, in 1955, the Canadian UNICEF Committee was formed. In the first year Canadian children collected $15,000. Since then, millions of Canadian children have raised more than C$90 million trick-or-treating for UNICEF.

Trick or Treat for UNICEF has moved on from coin collection to month-long fundraising drives in schools and at home. In 2000, 31 October was declared National UNICEF Day by the federal government in Canada.

Over the past few years, the US Fund for UNICEF and UNICEF Canada have made the Trick or Treat for UNICEF campaign more engaging, educational and fun for kids, as well as relevant, flexible and easy to implement for parents and teachers. They have also been listening to the concerns expressed by teachers, schools and the public about the logistical and safety challenges of the traditional door-to-door coin collection.

The US Fund for UNICEF conducted market research to discover the national reach and influence of the Trick or Treat for UNICEF programme in the United States and to measure the programme's health in the US marketplace. This survey found that Trick or Treat for UNICEF is the most recognised fundraiser where children help people who are in need.

Source: Showcase of Fundraising Innovation and Inspiration

6.4 Direct mail

Ken Burnett, author of *Relationship Fundraising* (2nd edition, 2002, Jossey-Bass), describes direct mail fundraising as 'One person writing to another person about something they both care about. It is an opportunity for both the writer and the potential donor, for it allows both the chance to do something personally to help.'

Sending letters to people is one of the most flexible and powerful tools in fundraising. Direct mail is just one of a number of direct marketing techniques that are used commercially and have been adapted for fundraising. At a price – and direct mail can be expensive – you can reach out to large numbers of people and try to gain their support. Once you have got their support, you can then encourage them to give at higher levels and on a regular basis.

A direct mail fundraising programme can provide an assured source of income for your organisation, and one that will grow over time if it is managed well. Unless you already have an active and enthusiastic list of existing supporters, you will have to spend time, effort and money to build one up. Direct mail should not be seen as a source of quick income.

The essential feature of this medium is its ability to direct a personalised message of the length you choose to a target audience at a time of your choosing. It requires the use of:

- A **list of addresses** to send the letters to.
- A '**communication package**' – usually a brochure with a covering letter and some mechanism for replying.
- A system for **dealing with the response.**

The principle is to get the following three elements right:

1. **The audience.** There can be an enormous variation in the sort of response rate you achieve. Sending the letter to people who are more likely to respond will reduce the costs of acquiring a new donor considerably.
2. **The message.** What you tell people and what you ask for are also extremely important. A powerful message that will move them to give will be much more effective than a downbeat message. The creative approach – the way you angle the story you are telling them – and the 'offer' – what you are asking them to do – are the two important components of the message.
3. **The timing.** When to send the letter? Some times of the year may be better than others. In Christian countries, the period leading up to Christmas works best, as it is a time when people feel predisposed to give. If there is an urgent reason for the appeal – for example, as a response to a natural disaster – the immediacy of the need and the necessity of demonstrating that you are responding efficiently and effectively means that you should get your appeal out as quickly as you can.

There are three types of mailing:

1. '**Cold**' mailings to people with whom you have had no previous contact.
2. '**Warm**' mailings to your existing members and supporters, where you already know they are interested in your work.
3. '**Reciprocal**' mailings, where you swap your membership list with that of another organisation and use their list to recruit new members for your organisation (they will use your list to recruit for their organisation).

The power of the medium comes not only from the ability to target your message precisely, but also from the ability to send the same message to very large numbers of people, thus offering economies of scale. You also have the possibility of sending slightly different messages to different groups of people. This is called 'segmentation'. You will certainly want to say something to your existing donors that is different from what you will be saying to the people who have not yet given to you and whom you are trying to recruit. And you may want to subdivide even further, treating larger donors differently from smaller donors, those who have supported you consistently over a number of years differently from recent recruits, and so on.

But as a mass communication medium, direct mailing has some dangers. The whole idea is to make the medium seem personal; the most effective letter is one written by hand to a friend. As the number of people you are writing to gets larger, then the opportunity for making the communication personal gets smaller. There is a cost, for example, for producing a handwritten salutation on 5,000 letters, and it is much easier to print 'Dear friend' on every one. This 'depersonalisation' will usually have an impact on the level of your returns.

Ten ways to personalise your mailing

A personal letter works far better than a circular letter. However, if you are writing to thousands of people, you will have to send a circular letter. But you can personalise it so that the recipient thinks it is a personal letter written specially to them. Here are some ways:

1. **Handwrite the donor's name** in the salutation at the start of the letter ('Dear . . .') and handwrite the signature at the end of the letter. With large mailings this can be done by a volunteer. Or **use a word processor** to incorporate the donor's name in the salutation ('Dear Mrs Khan' rather than 'Dear Supporter') and where appropriate also in the body of the letter.
2. Personalisation is not just a matter of name and address. It is also any **personal detail** which might be incorporated into the body of the letter – such as the amount of the last gift and the purpose for which it was given. Such details can often be incorporated using a word processor.
3. **Type or handwrite the address** on the envelope.
4. Use an **ordinary postage stamp** rather than putting the letter through a franking machine.
5. Make **handwritten notes** or **underline parts** of the text of the letter even if this is then going to be printed!
6. Have a **handwritten PS** (postscript) at the end of the letter which reinforces the message. Again, this can be printed.
7. Ensure that the **response form** has the donor's name on it.
8. Use a **reply envelope** that is handwritten with the sender's name, as well as the organisation and reply address, on it (so that the reply letter is addressed to someone and not to an anonymous organisation).
9. **Stamp the reply letter.** Although this will double the postage bill, it should generate much better returns. But keep track of the response to ensure that it is worth doing this.
10. Even think of **handwriting the whole of the appeal letter** – which can be short, with the work of the organisation and the purpose of the appeal being explained in an accompanying leaflet.

Components of a mailing

Typical components of a mailing can vary widely. A well-used model consists of five parts:

1. **An outer envelope** with a window so that a name and address can be printed on the reply device included in the envelope. The envelope can be overprinted with some 'teaser copy' to encourage recipients at least to open the letter.
2. **A letter.** This is the main communication, and should be written as interestingly and personally as possible. Advice on writing appeal letters is given in Section 8.4.
3. **A reply device.** This is what the donor returns with his or her contribution. It summarises what the appeal is for and suggests donation levels. It is printed with the donor's name and address (which appears in the window envelope). And it

may carry a code, so that you can track the response from the different lists you are using (to see which work well and which don't).

4. **A pre-printed reply envelope.** Making it simple for the donor to reply will increase your response considerably. The reply envelope could be stamped or pre-paid. This adds to the expense, but again will improve response rates.

5. **A brochure or leaflet** that reinforces the text of the letter, and illustrates the need and the work of the organisation. If the donor is interested, he or she may want to find out more – and you can suggest ways of doing this.

Another advantage of this form of fundraising is that you can include as much information as you feel you need – in the brochure and in the letter. There are several views about how long the letter ought to be – from a single page to several. It depends on how much you have to say, and whether you can capture the reader's interest. Even the simplest mailing package can include a lot of information. But beware of producing letters and brochures that are too full of words – there is a great danger that they will go unread. Use pictures to tell the story, case studies and quotes to illustrate that you can make a difference, and all sorts of graphic devices to break up the text.

Improving your appeal response

Here are six ways in which you could increase your response rates or average donation values. Before committing yourself to any of these, you should test the idea first.

1. Wherever possible, **personalise your communication.**
2. Mail a different appeal to your **large and regular supporters** that refers to their past giving, recognises its value to the organisation, and asks for a generous response to this new request.
3. Read through your letter and **rewrite** it to **improve its impact**, and introduce case studies of how people are being helped.
4. Try including a **leaflet** with **pictures of your work.**
5. Ask for **specific amounts** to achieve specific things: for example, '50 rupees will buy a new syringe'. Mention this in both the letter and in the response device.
6. Put a **stamp** on return envelopes. No one likes to see a stamp wasted, and the only way to avoid this is to reply to the appeal!

Getting the message right

Getting the message right is at least half the challenge (the other half being sending it to the right people at the right time). For a mailing, there are two key components:

1. The proposition

Each mailing should have a central proposition. This might be '50 rupees can help a child in distress' or 'Urgent action is needed to save the rainforests of Brazil'. The proposition should become the visual and verbal theme used throughout the mailing. This ensures the recipient receives a clear and strong message.

2. Making the request

The essential purpose of the letter is to get someone to support you. It is often assumed that the recipient will know what you want from them. But they don't. You have to ask. You want money, not their sympathy. A good letter will repeat the request for support several times. It will also show how the money will be used to benefit your work – and how many people it will help. It may also suggest various levels of giving for the donor to choose from. Then there can be no mistaking what you are really wanting from the reader.

Warm mailings

Sending letters to people who have already given to you is the most cost-effective way of raising money by direct mail. They have already demonstrated an interest in your work and should be predisposed to support you if you ask again.

The high response you can get from warm mailings is the real reason for recruiting new donors by direct mail in the first place. Response rates will vary enormously – typically from 7 per cent to more than 30 per cent. You can expect to raise up to £10 for each £1 spent in fundraising costs. Writing to your own supporters involves a number of special requirements. Get the message right and you will succeed in raising a lot of money.

There are varying views about how often you should write to your donors. Some feel that more than once a year is an invasion of their privacy, while others want to keep in touch at least once a quarter (and some even on a monthly basis). A test is sometimes the best way to see whether more frequent mailings will be worth your while. If you find it cost-effective to mail more frequently, then do so. Another possibility is to ask your donors how often they would like to receive information from you, and if your list of donors is large enough, you can then divide this into different groups who wish to be mailed at different frequencies

Whatever the frequency you decide, you need to develop a planned programme for the dates when you will mail and the sort of appeal that you will make with each different mailing.

Cold mailings

It's all very well to dream about the returns you could get if only you had 10,000 supporters on a computer mailing list. Somehow these people need to be identified and won over to your cause. One of the main ways voluntary organisations do this is through the use of cold mailings – 'cold' because the person in receipt of your letter has not demonstrated any warmth for your cause before.

The practice, then, is to create a mailing list from directories or to hire lists from another organisation (such as a bank or an insurance company) or from a specialist list broker . And then you should combine these lists with any other promising names you can find to send the appeal package to.

The differences between warm and cold mailings lie in the cost and in the message. Because the people you are contacting are not your existing supporters, you can expect a much poorer response rate. Thus to raise the same amount of money, you may need to mail up to ten times as many people – at ten times the expense. And there will also be the cost of hiring the list.

Because most of the recipients of a cold mailing will not know much about your work, your message will need to be slightly different – a rather more simplistic approach to describing your cause and giving some reassurances about the value of your work. This might take the form of providing endorsements from well-known people; or you might present the answers to frequently asked questions, such as 'How little is spent on administration?'; or you might highlight your achievements and successes.

Not all of the names on the list will be new. Some may be duplicates of people who are already your supporters. Wherever possible you should try to find some way of removing these duplicates – sending two letters to the same person, or an inappropriate message to long-standing supporters can have a negative impact. There are extremely sophisticated computer programmes that do this. If this approach is not possible, you can try to remove duplicates by looking through the list, trying to identify duplicates (which are not always that easy to detect – as names may be misspelled or the surname and first name reversed, and so on).

Though cold mailing response rates may be as high as 4 per cent or even 5 per cent in special circumstances – for example, an emergency appeal following a natural disaster – 0.5 to 2 per cent is the more likely range. Since you have to pay the printing and postage costs, cold mailings rarely pay for themselves – even with the benefit of a few high-value responses. Why do it then? There are several reasons:

- To get new supporters in order to replace lapsed donors (that is, just to stand still).
- To increase your list of supporters (to develop your fundraising base).
- To obtain a source of future income. You are balancing the cost of acquisition against the likely lifetime value to you of those who respond – the total support they will give you over the years minus the costs of continuing to mail them. Once a donor has given, you will get much higher response rates from future mailings to them, and these should more than pay for themselves. If half the donors continue to support you for five years, your list of new recruits is a valuable asset. And some may even go on to leave a legacy. You have to balance the cost of donor acquisition against the 'expected lifetime value' of an average donor to determine what is a reasonable donor acquisition cost.

If you are just starting in direct mail, you may find that the programme only begins to generate a surplus after two or three years. However, at that point, the returns can rapidly build up. The question, then, is how to get started.

Issues in cold mailings

- **Whether to buy other people's lists.** There is a vocal group of the public which regards selling lists as an invasion of their privacy when they receive unsolicited mail. These people will contact you from time to time and complain in the most vocal way. Be prepared with your response
- **It can appear a waste of money.** If only 3 per cent of people respond, 97 per cent will be throwing all that paper away – which is why cold mailing is sometimes referred to as 'junk mail'. It is those who reply, not those who don't, which makes direct mail an

effective fundraising method. But you do have to watch the response rates and postage costs to ensure that you are being effective. But even if you are, those that are not responding will think you are wasting both your money and the world's resources. Using recycled paper can give the right signals, despite its higher cost; and suggesting the letter is handed on to a friend may also help.

■ **It can be expensive.** You must ensure that you have the capacity to invest in this form of fundraising, which requires a large commitment of expenditure, a significant degree of risk and a payback period of several years. If you can't do it properly, don't do it.

Finding the right lists

Your success in cold mailing will depend very much on the list you are using. Some lists will work extremely well for you, others will not. There are several places to look:

1. **Publicly available information**, such as electoral registers and telephone directories. The electoral register (if published) can give you names and addresses in particular areas, and you can then select those which you feel are more likely to give – because of the affluence of the neighbourhood. The telephone directory at least gives you access to everyone who is able to afford a telephone. But not everyone is predisposed to respond to a request sent by post, and these lists compiled from public information do not always work that well.

2. **Lists compiled from directories.** Typically these could include lists of leading business people or the largest companies, which should be treated with care, as you may find that such people are the target of many appeals. But there may be directories available which provide you with just the right list of names to send your appeal to.

3. **Lists that you obtain from other sources.** These may be lists of people who have purchased something by post, lists of account holders at a bank or with a credit card company, lists of subscribers to a magazine or information service, lists of graduates from a university. It depends on what is available.

Questions you will want to ask include:

■ **Does the list have any affinity with your cause?** For example, if the list is of people with an interest in gardening, an environmental cause may be particularly relevant.

■ **How old is the list?** If it is several years old, many people will have moved, so the returns you get will decrease accordingly.

■ **How frequently is it mailed?** Some lists are used regularly for mailings, and recipients may come to expect 'junk mail' which they throw straight into the bin.

■ **How is it held?** Will it be supplied as labels or on disk? If it is supplied on disk, do you have the capacity to merge it with other lists, including your own supporters, in order to remove duplicate addresses (people do not like being mailed twice with the same appeal, as they will feel that you are wasting money – even where it is cheaper to mail them twice than remove duplicates).

■ **How much does it cost?** There is usually a charge made for supplying the list, which will cover the cost of printing out the addresses, but which also reflects the value of the list. You will usually only be given permission to use the list once (which is why the process is known as list rental), and it will often contain one or two addresses inserted specifically to identify any mailings made using the list. The charge for list rental will usually be only a small part of the total cost of doing the mailing, so it can be more cost-effective to pay more for a list that works really well than to use a list which is available free of charge but which might generate a very poor response.

Experience will tell you which sorts of list tend to work better for you. It is important to code your mailings so that you can identify which list the response has originated from. And for large mailings, there is always the possibility of testing a sample of the names on the list first.

Reciprocal mailings

One answer to the low response rates from cold mailings is to undertake reciprocal mailings. The thinking here is that though your best potential donors are the people who have recently given to you (warm mailings), the next best will be those who are giving to similar organisations. These people are likely to be socially concerned and they are known to respond to direct-mail appeals. They may also be happy to support two similar causes. So that if you mail your supporters with an appeal from a similar charity and they mail your supporters, you will both gain. And that's how it usually turns out in practice. Typically, response rates can range from 2.5 to 10 per cent.

The best results will be obtained by swapping lists with organisations that are closest to your own, even though they may be competitors. Before you do so, make sure that your organisation backs you in this. Most organisations will want to devise a simple policy to safeguard their own interests and those of their donors.

Getting started in direct mail

The real difficulty in direct mail is getting started. Once you have a large donor base and an active mailing programme, it is a question of good management thereafter. But before you get there, considerable sums of money will need to be spent – and this means considerable risk. Here are a few tips:

- Find as many ways as possible of **capturing the names of supporters**. People who write to you or visit you. People who have participated in a fundraising event. Volunteers who are giving their time. Keep their names and addresses on a database.
- Get these existing **supporters to suggest friends** who might like to be written to.
- Try to get a **sympathetic organisation** to agree to let you mail its list for free. This is a reciprocal mailing without giving something back in return.
- Acquire **other lists**, but test them first. It is a good strategy to send a small test mailing to several lists in order to see the response; if they respond well, you can mail the rest of the list later on. Dip your toe in the water first – do not dive in!
- Use **directories**. This method does not always work: if, for example, you were to use a telephone directory and target people who lived in a certain area, you would be writing to both responders and non-responders – some people never respond to direct mail. If you wrote to someone else's mailing list, they would all be known responders. This is why people prefer to rent other people's lists rather than compile them from public information.

- **Hand deliver** where this is possible to save costs, and start with a simpler mailing package – though the message must be powerful for it to work at all.
- **Start slowly**, and build up.

Getting started: a case study

The Association for the Physically Handicapped, Bangalore, dredged about 300 names and addresses from its files (including past donors, visitors to the project and other contacts) and sent a simple letter which was personalised and signed by the president of the association. Within six weeks they had received $2,000 in response to the mailing, including a first donation of $65 and individual donations of $300 and $150, which was more than double the target set for the fundraising.

Management

Because a lot of money is involved, direct mail needs good management. Here are some factors to consider:

Costs and budgets. You need to invest money to make money. But you also need to budget for response rates and average levels of donation. In this way you can control your costs, but also set targets for your income. On the cost side, be as cost-conscious as you can. Find a cheap format for your printed material, and get competitive quotes from printers.

Testing. Before you use a large list, test it by mailing a section of it. This will give you a good idea of the response to expect from the rest, and will prevent you from wasting your money on mailings that do not work. There are mathematical formulae which tell you what sample size will give a significant result. But if you are small and not using advanced techniques, a rough guide is to mail 10 per cent of the total – that is, one out of every ten names, to ensure a random selection. In order to carry out a test, you need to code the response – which is easily done by putting a code number on the reply coupon, which tells you which mailing list it has come from.

And more testing. You can test all sorts of other things: the approach, the headline, the amount you are asking for. But never test more than one factor at a time. Otherwise you will not know which is producing the result you are getting.

Segmentation. Perhaps the most important advantage of direct mail is its ability to target different groups of supporters with a different message. Depending on the sophistication of your mailing-list software and the information you are recording, you can subdivide your list into different segments: for example, longstanding members (perhaps those that have been members for at least three years); the rest of the membership; people who have recently made a substantial donation; people who live locally and those who live outside the area; people who have participated in a particular fundraising event; people with a known interest in, say, conservation. Segmentation gives you the ability to address a slightly different message to each group that reflects their particular relationship with you.

Increasing the average donation. If you can find ways of getting donors to give more and to give more frequently, you have one of the keys to success. Just because a donor has already given does not mean that they will not want to give again. On the contrary, they have demonstrated their support for you. So if there is a reason to ask again – for example, you are launching an appeal to purchase a new piece of equipment – ask your existing supporters, even if they have recently made a donation. Try to get them to give to you quarterly or even monthly – they will give much more if they give frequently than if they make an annual contribution. Try to get them to commit in some way to supporting you for a long period of time. ActionAid asks its supporters to give a monthly contribution for ten years – on the basis that if the donor is serious about helping, then it needs a lot of money over a long period of time to have any impact.

The donor pyramid

The aim of direct mail is to get people on to your donor base (which is expensive), and then to move them up to become regular, committed and substantial givers. And possibly to consider leaving you a legacy when they die.

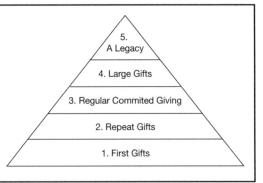

5. A Legacy

4. Large Gifts

3. Regular Commited Giving

2. Repeat Gifts

1. First Gifts

List management

The most valuable resource you have is your own list of donors or members. Guard it carefully. If your list is held on a computer, how safe is it? Have you got a security copy of your file held somewhere else for safety's sake? You should produce regular backup copies of your files. If you lose your list, you may never be able to recreate it without a massive investment of time and money.

You also need to manage your list in various ways. You need to keep it up to date by removing all inactive or deceased supporters. Periodically you should see whether you are holding the names of people who are no longer active donors (say, those who have not given for two or three years). One way of determining this is to segment this part of your list and look at the response. Where the yield is below that of a cold mailing, you should consider removing the names. You can also ask these people if they want to continue receiving information from you. If some reply, at least they are interested and you should keep their names on file.

You need to make sure there are no duplicates. If you are mailing the same person twice or three times each mail-out, this is a waste of money and can cause aggravation. Automatic 'de-duplication' can be a complicated business requiring a sophisticated computer programme. If you are a small organisation, you will have to do it by eye. Remember that a person's name may be misspelled, or their address wrongly typed in, which can easily create a duplicate record.

Lastly, add all new names immediately. The sooner you can do this, the sooner these people will be able to receive further appeals.

The Good Mailing Guide

1. Use **emotion** in your writing.
2. Include **stories** about individuals.
3. **Ask** for money directly.
4. Use **simple language**, avoid jargon.
5. Make all written material **visually attractive**.
6. Portray **your beneficiaries** as 'doers' rather than as 'victims', not as helpless, but needing your help.
7. Catch the **reader's attention** immediately, perhaps with a snappy headline.
8. Use someone specific as the **signatory** – this could be someone well known, your director or chairman, or a frontline worker.
9. Get the **timing right**.
10. **Make the reader give**.
11. Appeal to the **reader's conscience**.
12. **Read what you are sending** before sending it – would *you* give in response to your own appeal letter?

This is a list of success factors drawn up by Oxfam after studying ten years of appeals to supporters.

Advice and consultancy

Direct mail is a highly technical fundraising method. The skills required include:

- Writing effective copy.
- Producing a cost-effective mailing package.
- Knowing how much to ask for.
- Planning a mailing programme.
- Selecting the best lists to hire.
- Testing (and coding) of the response.
- Knowing what response rates to expect.
- Evaluation of your performance.

You may not have all (or indeed any) of these skills. But it is possible to get advice from others, including:

- Other organisations with direct-mail programmes, which might be prepared to share their knowledge and experience with you.

- Professional consultants who specialise in this medium. But you will have to pay for their expertise. So it is as well to know what you want, to brief them well, and to have a contract that sets out precisely what they are expected to do and for how much. Consultants fall into two categories: charity fundraising consultants, and advertising or promotion consultants specialising in direct mail (a technique used for business promotion as well as charity fundraising).
- The Resource Alliance's network of fundraisers and training courses.

Amnesty International pen pack

This is one of a handful of fundraising communications that really broke the mould. It's famous because it was the first donor recruitment pack to include a pen – a technique which was subsequently used to lift response rates by many charities. But it is much more than that. Because of the account of how a pen is sometimes used as an implement of torture, the pack is a moving, intelligent and beautifully put-together case to support one of the world's great causes. The beauty of it is that everything is relevant and sincere. Nothing is gratuitous. This is the standard to which all direct-mail writers and designers should aspire.

Amnesty needed a powerful and effective means of recruiting new donors to their cause. This was it. It was so good that the pack was Amnesty UK's banker for 10 years or more and was copied or adapted by many Amnesty International sections around the world.

This was, as far as we know, the first ever occasion when a free pen was included in an acquisition mailing, in the UK at least. So this was the pack that launched a fashion and a thousand (or more) rather inferior copies. But that doesn't do this innovative and hugely effective pack justice. It is also a beautifully crafted, brilliant and passionately written piece of communication. It is fundraising direct communication as it should be.

You can view the pack by visiting www.sofii.org

Source: Showcase of Fundraising Innovation and Inspiration

6.5 Committed giving and membership

Committed giving

Committed giving is what really makes sense of your direct mail (and indeed your other donor acquisition activities). The donor acquisition process is expensive, and unlikely to cover its costs through the immediate income it produces. But it is the first step in building up a supporter base. The follow-up mailings are what generate the real revenue – for as we have seen, the people who have given already respond much better to an appeal. Your aim is to:

- Get your first-time donors to **continue to give** by sending them further appeals, only removing them from your donor list when you are convinced by their non-response that they are no longer interested.

- **Stimulate their concern** for the cause and their interest in your work, which should then lead to an increase in the level of support they are prepared to give.
- Help them to recognise the **importance of giving long-term support** to your work (work that may take time to yield results, and which needs their continuing support to succeed). And then get them to commit themselves to supporting you on a long-term basis.
- **Make it easy** for them to give on a regular basis. Set up a simple payment mechanism to enable donations to be paid regularly (see below), which offers convenience to the donor and a continuing stream of income for you. You might also want to use some form of 'membership' or 'friends' scheme to suggest levels of giving.
- Encourage donations to be paid in a **tax-effective way** (if there are tax incentives for charitable giving available in your country). Explain the tax benefits available and help the donor take advantage of them.
- Ask them to think about **legacy giving** as the 'ultimate gift'. Legacy fundraising is covered in Section 6.7.

This list of tasks sets an agenda for you to develop your direct mail and donor acquisition programme, and to turn your first-time giver into a committed and enthusiastic long-term supporter.

Standing orders

Setting up an automatic system enabling donations to be paid to you regularly (annually, quarterly or even monthly) by transfer from the donor's bank account will ensure that the support continues until the donor cancels the arrangement, and it will make the process of collecting the money far simpler for you to administer (the money appears in your account on the due dates, and you do not need to send subscription reminders) and far simpler for the donor (who does not have to write a cheque and send off the payment each time).

Various mechanisms can be used for this purpose, including standing order, direct debit, autogiro, pre-authorised checking and EFT. The system you use will depend on the banking facilities available in your country, and the cost of using such facilities.

Promotion

Not every donor will agree to enter into a long-term commitment, but it is important to give each one of them the opportunity to do so. For this reason, a clear promotion strategy is needed. This should include answers to these questions:

- What are the **interests and motivations** of your supporters?
- What are your **financial requirements** – how much income do you need to raise, and how much do you think your donors will be prepared to give?
- How will you **promote a scheme to your existing supporters** to encourage them to make a commitment?
- Are there any **other prospective committed supporters** you can identify?
- How should you **report back** to your committed givers so as to maintain their enthusiasm and support?

- **What else can you do** to get them to feel more involved in the work of the organisation and the cause it is addressing?

The following are some of the promotional techniques you can use:

1. **Approaching active givers.** If you analyse the response to your appeals, you will see that a number of your donors will have given more than once. They may give each year in response to an annual appeal. They may give more than once during the year. They may respond very promptly to the appeal. These people are your priority targets for committed giving. You should contact them, pointing out the advantages of giving regularly and offering them all the appropriate forms. If there are only a few prospective 'targets', you can contact them in person or by telephone.

2. **Member-Get-Member or Supporter-Get-Supporter.** This is simply an invitation to an existing member or supporter to nominate or recruit another. Various incentives (such as a free-entry prize draw or some form of gift) can be offered, either to the original member or to the new one. This method relies on the personal enthusiasm of existing members and their ability to persuade their friends and colleagues. It is a system of membership promotion which works extremely well.

3. **Promoting committed giving more widely to your donor base.** Another strategy is to organise one appeal per year which promotes regular giving and encourages payment by standing order or some other regular payment system. This will mean that you will not get a response from those not in a position to give regularly, but who might otherwise have made a one-off cash donation. A different approach is to mention the value of committed giving in each mailing, but by way of an afterthought or postscript, and to give people the opportunity to support you in this way.

Médecins sans Frontières – regular giving conversion pack

Recruiting regular givers is an extremely difficult challenge for most organisations. However, it is recognised that such givers help to generate long-term growth for the organisation. Existing supporters are the perfect potential regular givers, as they feel an affinity with, and loyalty to, the cause, and may thus be the providers of vital cash injections.

In 2007 Médecins sans Frontières developed a highly successful pack aimed at converting cash donors into regular givers. Specific characteristics of the mailing were:

- Careful segmentation of supporter base to separate cash 'ask' from regular giving 'ask'.
- It tested a new regular giving conversion proposition which recognised that such conversion was about changing behaviour, not attitudes: 'change the way you give'.
- It explained why regular giving is so important to MSF's work.
- The target amount was tailored to suit the 'ask'. The letter said that 642 new regular givers were needed to provide $X guaranteed funds over the coming 12 months. The target amount was then worked out to be their 'ask' amount x 12 months x 642 regular givers.
- Strategic use of images and copy to reflect benefits of regular giving.

- Highly personalised copy that referred to donors by name and acknowledged how long they had been supporting MSF.

The campaign generated 915 new regular givers to MSF and created a strong and successful regular giving conversion pack that can be rolled out.

The total cost of the campaign was $60,916. The pack achieved a 3.5 per cent response rate to the regular giving 'ask', $281,814 first year regular giving income and gross cash income $666,114.

Source: Showcase of Fundraising Innovation and Inspiration

Child sponsorship and similar techniques, where the donor is linked to a specific project, community or family. This works best where the link is with a particular child, as it commits the donor to continuing to give support while the child is growing up, perhaps for 10 to 15 years. In return the donor receives news of the project and the sponsored family, and even letters written by the sponsored child. Such an approach works extremely well in fundraising terms, but has to be handled with care. Problems can arise where the donor really wants to help just one individual child, although most schemes provide support for the whole community, to improve livelihoods, education and health, but show the benefits to the life of one family or child; or where the donor builds up an expectation of a relationship with the sponsored child, which may not be what the family wants.

Keeping in touch, maintaining enthusiasm

A common problem is that once you have obtained the commitment of your supporters, you begin to take them for granted. You know that their contribution is going to arrive, so you don't bother too much about keeping in touch with them or telling them what you are achieving. You must avoid neglecting them at all costs. They are your most important givers. You need to do everything you can to maintain their enthusiasm and support.

You should take every opportunity to keep them in touch with what you are doing – and with any further developments and need for support. You might feel that once a donor has made a commitment it is an indication that they do not want to be asked for further support. A better approach is to view their commitment as an affirmation of the value of your cause. When you approach them, always recognise their commitment, so that they understand you are approaching them precisely because of this commitment. In this way you can appeal to them on a regular basis and ask them to give additional support. This will make particular sense when there is an obviously good reason for the appeal, such as an emergency. Or if your supporter list is big enough, you can launch special appeals which you ask members to support: for example, you want your friends to help you equip an operating theatre or sponsor a new theatrical production, and you need to raise £10,000 from them just to do this.

You will need to report back to your committed givers on what you have achieved with their money. You might ask them to visit you to see your work. You might organise talks and discussions about your work with an expert. These ways of getting the donor to understand the value of what you are doing and to see your work at first hand can only increase their commitment. Such methods are used successfully by many organisations – including overseas development agencies such as Oxfam, who now organise trips for their donors to see projects at work. The payback for this is the increased support you will receive as a result.

You might produce a newsletter or a magazine or send a specially personalised letter from the chief executive. This special treatment can make donors feel important. Committed donors are likely to want to see a minimum of expenditure on 'unnecessary' items, and so they should not be approached too frequently or too lavishly.

Your invitation to join the Hospital Well Wishers

'Well Wishers is a special group of caring people. People who care enough to lend their support to our critically ill children. As a member of this group, you will receive our free regular newsletter. Each issue will bring you news of the latest research and treatment breakthrough and real-life stories of outstanding courage, determination, hope and success. It will give you an insight into the day-to-day running of the hospital. It will also keep you in touch with other Well Wishers.'

After the huge success of the hospital building appeal, this idea for a membership scheme was created to maintain funds flowing into the hospital.

Membership

A membership subscription scheme is the method many organisations use to encourage supporters to get more involved with their cause. But the aims of a membership scheme are not necessarily to raise money. There are several different types in use:

- Schemes that **confer benefits of a constitutional nature** (such as the right to attend and vote at annual general meetings, and the right to receive an annual report). The rights attached to membership will normally be spelled out in the organisation's constitution.
- Schemes that provide more **tangible benefits**, such as free or reduced-price entry to museums or wildlife facilities.
- Schemes that give the donor a **'sense of belonging'**: for example, as a 'friend' of an organisation who is committed to helping it raise money, or as a member of a campaigning group, such as Amnesty International (human rights) or Greenpeace (the environment) who supports the aims of the campaign.
- Schemes that are used as **a mailing list**: typically, a theatre or cultural centre will offer to circulate information on forthcoming productions to this mailing list, and there may be benefits such as preferential booking and discounts on tickets available to subscribers.
- Schemes that are designed to **encourage committed giving**, where donors are made to feel more a part of the organisation. Besides encouraging supporters to give in the long term (see *Committed Giving*), it is also possible to develop a scheme where large numbers of supporters each pledge regular support as part of some sort of friends'

group. Although individually small, these donations can amount to a useful source of income if the scheme is developed on a wide enough basis.

Some membership schemes are aimed primarily at people who are interested in doing something – helping the organisation campaign, attending cultural events, volunteering their time. The aim of these is not to generate an income, although members may be happy to give when asked. Membership schemes of these types may have their annual subscription levels set deliberately low to encourage as many people as possible to join. Then there are those schemes that have a fundraising purpose – their primary aim is to generate an income for the organisation.

You can derive three main benefits from a membership scheme:

1. **Commitment.** A membership scheme offers a convenient basis upon which to obtain committed long-term support for your organisation.
2. **Involvement.** Membership opens up an organisation and provides a mechanism for democratic control through the right to vote at annual meetings (if this is included in the constitution), thereby giving the members some influence over the direction of the organisation.
3. **Money.** The annual membership fee provides an income, and the membership list is an ideal hunting ground for further donations. Members have demonstrated their interest in the organisation, so become likely prospects for obtaining further financial support.

Another important reason for having a membership base is the indirect benefit it can bring to your organisation. If you wish to mount a campaign, your members are the first who can be called on to participate in it. And the number of members you have indicates the degree of public support for your campaign or issue. A large membership can increase your influence and impact.

Membership lists are usually held on computer, but when you are just starting out, the addresses can equally well be held on a card index system. To keep members in touch, they should be mailed regularly with newsletters and annual reports. Appeals to members will be made using standard direct-mail methods – the membership list should generate extremely good returns. Members may be asked to make contributions for special projects or in an emergency. Since they are already contributing their membership subscription on a regular basis, the appeal should be seen as an add-on, a completely separate contribution for a specific purpose.

Standing orders and other systems can be used to facilitate payment of the subscription when it becomes due. But if you raise subscription rates, you will need some system for alerting members so that they increase the amount paid on the due date.

Frequent giving

The value of committed giving or membership subscription income depends on:

- **The number of donors or members.** The more you have the better. Once you have established a scheme, your aim should be to find ways of recruiting new donors or members economically.
- **The annual subscription level.** With a membership scheme, this will depend on your objectives – to make money or to involve as many people as possible. Some

organisations give the donor or member different levels of annual subscription to select from, each with a different name and possibly different benefits or levels of involvement in the organisation. A supporter scheme might have three categories: a 'friend', a 'good friend' and a 'best friend'; or a 'supporter', a 'sponsor' and a 'patron'.

- **The cost of running the scheme.** This includes the cost of member acquisition and of the annual administration, including the cost of communicating with the member and sending information such as newsletters and annual reports. This expenditure should be calculated and budgeted for, so that an organisation has a clear idea of the surplus income that will be generated by each member after the costs of running the membership scheme.
- **The value of any additional income** generated from further appeals to members.

You will also find that the frequency of giving is important. If you ask for a smaller sum on a more frequent basis, you will be able to get people to contribute much larger annual sums. For example, ActionAid in one of its most successful promotions asked, 'Does this child need 50 pence more than you?' It was inviting supporters to give 50 pence per day, which seemed a trivial sum. In fact, it was asking donors to enter into a monthly commitment of £15 (which again did not seem that much in terms of what their money would be achieving for the charity). But if people had been asked outright to give £180 a year, most would have refused, as it would seem far too large a commitment.

There is enormous advantage in seeking frequent payments, as they build up to large annual sums but still sound reasonable to the donor. You can ask people to give once every three months (quarterly), once a term (three times a year, which might be appropriate for a school project), monthly (the frequency of many people's pay) or even weekly (for the real enthusiast!). You might even suggest a certain level of donation and ask the donor to select the frequency (a variation on the usual practice of asking the donor to suggest an amount from a list of suggested levels of giving). The value of frequent giving can be tested quite easily in one of your mailings. The usual outcome is that requests for monthly or quarterly giving will be no less effective, and will produce dramatically higher average annual donation levels for you.

The Malaysian Nature Society membership scheme

The Malaysian Nature Society is a membership-based organisation run by the secretariat, and governed by an elected board of trustees and council. MNS is an avenue where the Malaysian public has the opportunity to be part of a national effort in adding their voice towards the conservation of Malaysia's natural heritage.

Your membership gives MNS a stronger voice, representing civil societies, when we bring forth conservation issues to decisions and policy-makers towards ensuring sustainable development of the nation. MNS membership also comes with attractive perks such as trips, courses, discounts and activities, giving you the opportunity to interact with like-minded individuals. For more information on MNS membership, visit http://www.mns.org.my/

Administration

The administration of membership demands a high degree of organisation, especially if you wish to maximise the benefits of your fundraising effort. There are two key issues:

Membership renewal

How should you invite members to renew their subscriptions? When any fixed-term commitment comes to an end, there is both an opportunity and a need to ensure that as many people as possible renew. The usual way to do this is by sending reminder letters:

- A few months before the expiry, giving them time to renew.
- Coinciding with the expiry if they haven't yet renewed, to remind them that renewal is due.
- A follow-up reminder some months after expiry, telling them that they haven't yet renewed and that their membership will lapse if they don't.
- A further follow-up some months later – which is the final reminder.

The telephone is also a valuable tool. It can be used to ask donors why they have not yet renewed. This reminds those people who have just not got round to dealing with their membership renewal, and it also gathers useful market research information about why members are not renewing.

Membership renewal can be done on a fixed date each year (with annual membership running from 1 January to 31 December, for example). This means that all renewals are handled on one date. But you then have the problem of what to do with the members who join during the year, and especially those who join in the later part of the year – who will feel that they have already paid their subscription. So an alternative method is to make each person's membership expire exactly twelve months after the annual subscription was paid. But this requires more efficient organisation, as you will be dealing with membership matters throughout the year.

Any substantial membership scheme is likely to require a reliable computer system to make it work well. A key point is the ability of the system to identify renewal points so that you can mail not only on the point of renewal but also both before and after to stimulate the highest possible renewal rate.

Maintaining donor records

With your committed givers and members, you have a group of people who will be giving money to you regularly, and possibly also supporting you in a number of different ways. You need to keep track of their support, so that you can identify people who might be able to give you special help when you need it or whom you could invite to special events such as receptions, or simply so that you can personalise as much as possible the appeals you write to them. This means that you need to keep all the information on one record, and that you should avoid at all costs sending duplicate mailings. You need to merge donor information, which is collected when members make additional donations, with their membership record.

It is essential not to keep two separate sets of information – so that you can look up one person in one place to find out how and when they have supported you, and with how much.

6.6 Personal solicitation

Meeting and speaking to potential donors in person provides good opportunities for fundraising. As a technique, it has similarities with direct-mail fundraising. You have to identify people to approach, communicate with them effectively, and motivate them to give.

But there are also significant differences. First, the medium is different: you will be meeting people and asking face to face, or be using the telephone. Second, with direct mail you are approaching thousands or even tens of thousands of people with the same message, which you try to personalise through clever copywriting and by segmenting your mailing list into different categories of donor; whereas with personal solicitation you are approaching one (or a few) individuals in person to put over a message that is personal to them. It is obviously much more effective to persuade people in this way, but it is not very efficient – you just don't have the time to approach the same number of people that direct mail can reach. So it is important to recognise when and how personal solicitation can be used to best effect. Under the heading of personal solicitation we are including:

- **Face-to-face meetings** with existing donors in their homes ('warm visiting'); but face-to-face meetings with people you have never met before to recruit new support (cold calling) is covered in house-to-house collections (see Section 6.3).
- **Making presentations** at meetings – both meetings with outside people you are asked to speak at and meetings with your own supporters to keep them in touch.
- **Street fundraising.** Signing up supporters on the street has proved a highly successful technique in many parts of the world.
- **Telephone solicitation.** Although not as powerful as face-to-face meetings, it is a useful fundraising technique.

Warm visiting

Warm visiting involves face-to-face meetings with people who have already supported you or with whom you already have some form of contact. There are two ways of doing this:

1. A 'soft sell' approach where you visit to talk about your work, to find out more about their interests, and to try to develop a warmer relationship with them, rather than to ask for money. This is an investment in the relationship which you hope might lead to more committed giving (or even a legacy) later on.
2. A harder sell as part of a major appeal, when you really do need their support. And having got the support of your committed donors, you are then in a better position to go public on your appeal.

Some larger charities employ individuals whose job it is to visit all their more substantial donors. Though the visit is ostensibly being made to thank them for their past support, in practice substantial sums can be collected and other ways for them to support the organisation can be discussed.

Since you are dealing with people who already have some relationship with you, you must make sure that you:

- Have **precise information** on the support they have given in the past, so that you can thank them and tell them what you have been able to do with their money.

- Are **well briefed** about the work of the organisation, so that you can talk about current work and future plans in an informed and interesting way.
- Have some idea of **the sort of support you need**, and the sorts of ways in which they might be able to help you – so that if the opportunity arises, you can introduce the idea of some further support.
- Know about **tax-effective giving**, as that can be one excuse for being there in the first place – to tell them how their money can be used even more effectively, by donating it tax-efficiently.

Meeting potential new supporters

Where someone has indicated an interest in giving to you, you may want to meet them personally to 'seal the deal'. At this meeting, you will be able to answer all their questions and suggest things that they might like to support. Such a meeting should be held in an appropriate venue: the charity's offices are not always the best place to meet potential supporters – a site visit where the beneficiaries are present, or a meeting at the offices of an important existing supporter may be better. But if it is at your office, make sure that everything looks well-run and busy – as this gives a positive image of your organisation and its importance. Alternatively, some people might feel more comfortable meeting you in their own homes. For such a meeting you need to:

- **Research the donor** and their capacity to give, so that you know their interests and understand the scale of giving that may be possible.
- Have a **'shopping list'** of projects which they might like to support, so that you can discuss with them what will most interest them.
- Have **good clear information** available about the organisation and its work, including photographs of staff in action and endorsements from prominent people.

Don't be in too much of a hurry. The skilled fundraiser knows when to ask – and it may not be immediately, but later, when the person's interest has been stimulated and they have had time to think about the matter.

Presentations at events

Many organisations have the opportunity to provide speakers at other people's meetings or conferences. This is an opportunity to speak directly to the people present about the work of your organisation. It can also be a good opportunity for talking about the fundraising needs and getting people interested in the idea of supporting you.

The presentation has to be carefully thought out. It must be tailored to the needs of the particular audience. A presentation to young farmers will be very different from one to a group of doctors. The main problem is to work out how your audience can respond to any appeal you make, as it is someone else's event and organisational matters are not under your direct control. After you have spoken, will the audience be leaving quickly after the meeting to move on to something else? Will the audience be circulated with information about your organisation or appeal literature? Will you be able to take names and addresses of people who are interested? Or will you be able to circulate everyone who was there subsequently? Will there be time for questions and discussion – and if there is, will they be friendly or hostile? Can you actually raise money at the event by organising a bucket or plate collection (where volunteer collectors are placed at the door or at the end of each row)?

The good public speaking guide

- Find out how long you are expected to speak for.
- Plan your talk. But remember that it is more spontaneous to speak 'off the cuff' than to read out a written speech.
- Start with a joke or a story, to enliven the proceedings.
- Explain your involvement in the organisation, and inject a sense of personal commitment to the cause.
- Use case studies and personal stories to explain the work. This is far better than a stream of statistics about the problem.
- Do not use jargon.
- Appeal to your audience's emotions – their hearts, not their heads.
- Ask for support if you need it.
- Have business cards, explanatory leaflets and even pledge forms to hand out to those who are interested.
- Tell people to telephone you if they are interested, and say that you would be delighted for them to visit you to see your work at first hand.

Your own events

Other people's events offer you new audiences. But you can also organise your own events for existing and potential supporters. These can be visits, study tours or open days to see your organisation at work, small discussions with an expert speaker so that they can understand the problems you are addressing in greater depth, or receptions of some sort (drinks receptions, dinners, and so on), perhaps at the home of a well-respected donor and possibly with a guest speaker or some sort of presentation afterwards.

Such events can be an excellent fundraising investment. You will make your existing donors feel important, and give them a better understanding of the issues. This may lead to them giving more substantial support or committing some time to your organisation as a volunteer.

Think carefully about your objectives for such an event, and about your audience and the sort of event that will most appeal to them. It is not just organising the event, but having the right event that is important. One idea is to mix existing supporters and people who have expressed an interest at such an event. If you do this, all the new people attending should be told to expect a follow-up visit from you afterwards.

Street fundraising

For many organisations, face-to-face fundraising on the street (or 'direct dialogue' as it is sometimes called) has proved to be the most cost-effective way of recruiting large numbers of monthly donors. After a decade of use in developed economies, however, the signs now are that many fundraisers are looking to other methods of donor recruitment as attrition rates rise and the cost of acquiring donors by face-to-face (F2F) seems set to go through the roof. But some fundraisers, particularly in developing markets, appear well able to make F2F work, perhaps with some adaptation to local circumstances. This is where you can find out about them. CRY in India, for example, has made extensive use of this technique.

Face-to-face is not remote mass solicitation. Its distinguishing feature and great benefit is that it is one on one, as close to your prospect as you can get (within the bounds of decency!). This kind of fundraising requires a range of specialist interpersonal skills that are very much its own. Many NGOs use professional agencies to recruit donors for them. Some train up in-house volunteers to carry out the recruitment.

Greenpeace India – SMS lead generation for face-to-face

Face-to-face fundraising everywhere faces the same problems of high cancellation rates and low retention. This innovative, adventurous approach to pre-qualifying leads for F2F is particularly interesting in that it was first developed and tested in India.

The SMS lead generation campaign is a filter mechanism designed to source 'warm prospects'. An SMS text message was sent to 56,137 people, all qualified as potential warm prospects with an interest in environmental issues. It said, 'Hi, don't you wish your city was cleaner 'n' greener? Begin by planting a free sapling offered by Greenpeace. Reply GREEN to 6363 to get your free sapling. Sender Greenpeace.'

The text message was sent to the mobile phones of prospects in and around the region of Bangalore and Pune. The offer of a free sapling fitted well with Greenpeace's objective to improve the environment, and it allowed recipients to feel they were actively involved in combating the problem. Take-up was much higher than expected.

The objective of the campaign was to increase productivity from Greenpeace's recruiters (paid fundraisers) and thus increase financial support to the organisation. Before the SMS lead generation campaign, GPI used a simple direct dialogue (face-to-face) method of fundraising that involved stopping people in the street and requesting their time to present the aims of the organisation, with the goal of recruiting them as a financial supporter. Using this method, only 17 per cent of people approached agreed to listen to the presentation, and of these only 10 per cent would then go on to sign up as financial supporters. The average productivity of each recruiter was 0.45 sign-ups per day. Those requesting saplings were personally visited by a recruiter and asked to make a donation. So far it has been possible to make three such visits per day, with a conversion rate above 25 per cent.

Many responders turned into donors at a cost that compares very favourably to other recruitment methods. Greenpeace will continue to test different methods of finding prospects for face-to-face fundraising.

The cost was INR 1,200 per supporter (approx US$30). Initial income generated is double this. This approach significantly increased the return on investment and introduced new donors at a high (25 per cent) conversion rate. It exceeded all expectations in terms of responses to the SMS, doubled the productivity of recruiters, and increased the number of financial supporters recruited. However, Greenpeace is still seeking a more effective system to reduce travel time so that recruiters can approach more people each day. Greenpeace also found from this test that it is vital to respond quickly to interest – within two days or interest will be lost.

Source: Showcase of Fundraising Innovation and Inspiration

Telephone solicitation

Asking on the telephone has many of the same characteristics as personal solicitation. But it is much more efficient – you can contact many more people in a given space of time. It is even possible to organise mass telephoning campaigns (either warm or cold calling) using your own volunteers, or even a specialist telephone selling agency. The telephone can be used successfully for:

- **Emergency appeals**, where there is a particular urgency. This could be some disaster, or because you have the opportunity to purchase a property if you can raise the money by a deadline.
- **Large appeals**, where you are trying to get lots of your supporters to give something. The telephone will be more effective than direct mail. But asking people to attend meetings will be even more effective; the telephone could be used here as a follow-up reminder to the written invitation. Or to contact those who could not attend the meeting or did not reply to the invitation – they may still be persuadable. Remember, the biggest reason for not giving is that people are not asked.
- **Discussing tax-effective giving** with people who have given. Here there is a particular reason for telephoning – you have some important information which could save them money!
- **Cold calling** – but remember that the telephone is intrusive, and people being disturbed by an unsolicited call can be hostile or even abusive.
- To succeed over the telephone, you need a confident-sounding voice, a good introduction to your conversation (practising to increase your confidence, and preparing a script help here) and enough knowledge about the work of the organisation to respond positively to any questions that come up. If you are using agents or volunteers to do the calling, you must make sure that they are well briefed about the organisation and its values, so that they can present it properly, and that they know why they are making the call and what they want as the outcome. Using the telephone is discussed in more detail in Section 8.6.

What you will need to succeed

Here are some of the things that you will need to succeed in personal solicitation:

- People who are really **good speakers and presenters**. You may wish to provide some form of training for them in presentation skills and asking skills. You might even try to set up a 'speakers' panel' of people who are interested in speaking about your organisation at meetings – and are also good at it.

- **Donors who have already given,** who are prepared to speak at meetings which potential donors are attending. There is nothing like being able to say, 'The organisation is great, and I've given to it,' to get others to give.
- **Volunteers** with similar skills for warm visits.
- **Good pictorial and other visual material** that can be used to illustrate a presentation. It is important that these show *people*: people helping and people being helped.
- For meetings you may want **visual aids** (for use with an overhead projector or a flipchart) or even a short video (no more than five minutes long).

Any visit should be prepared with care. Although it may seem to be overdoing it to rehearse a presentation that is going to be made to just one person, it can pay off. You should try to predict what questions will come up. Use a colleague or friend to help. You will need to be well armed with written information and visual material. You should leave some prepared material behind when you leave. Most people will not make up their minds immediately, and will be guided or reminded by the material you have left with them – and you can telephone them a few days later to get their response to the meeting.

Throughout the meeting, you should give people the opportunity to put questions. If you are not getting much feel for how the meeting is going, ask them some simple questions. Do they feel it is an important issue? Do they think the project will achieve what it is setting out to do?

At some point in the conversation, you will need to ask for money. There are several different approaches to this. One is to say that you want them to consider helping in any one of several ways, which you then describe (having researched their interests and potential level of giving as well as you can). A more direct approach dispenses with such niceties, explains the urgency of the need, and simply asks for the money – but always try to ask for a specific amount. Probably the most effective way is when someone who has already given support is 'making the ask' and is able to mention what their own donation has been.

And finally, remember that the best person to do the asking may not be you. Someone who has already given, someone known to the donor (peer-group giving) may be more appropriate. The skilled fundraiser will organise the right person to ask that particular donor.

6.7 Legacies and memorials

By the time most people die, they will have decided how their assets (their money, their property, their investments, their belongings) should be distributed. Different societies have different traditions on how wealth is distributed among family members after death. But if someone wants to leave specific instructions on the distribution of their assets, this is done by writing a will, which sets out who should benefit. On their death, their property is then distributed according to their wishes as set out in their will. The people responsible for distributing the proceeds of the will are called the executors.

Normally people leave the greater part of their assets to their immediate family (a surviving spouse, children, close relatives). But many people also take the opportunity to leave something to charity. Some have no family, so leaving their money to charity becomes an obvious option. There are several reasons why people might like to support a charity with a legacy:

- **Their immediate family is already well provided for** and does not need all their money.
- They would like to 'do good' on their death, as this seems an **appropriate gesture** – or possibly a passport to heaven!
- They can help **create a better world** for the next generation.
- The gift can be coupled with some sort of **memorial** to them.
- **It costs them nothing**! They are not there when the money is paid over.

Legacies are often large amounts – and sometimes huge, where there is no surviving family to leave the money to. Legacy fundraising can generate quite large sums of money. You should remember that you will not get the money immediately. Only when the donor dies – and by that time, the donor may have written a new will and changed his or her mind about your legacy. And even then it may take some time before you receive the money. You need to think carefully about the appropriateness of asking for legacies or proposing them as a method of giving. Attitudes towards death, expectations regarding the passing down of wealth from one generation to another, the support needs of the surviving spouse, and the legal background to inheritance vary so much from country to country and culture to culture.

If you do decide that it is an appropriate fundraising technique for you to use, how do you invite people to give you a legacy? Like other forms of fundraising, what you get out depends on what you put in. You need to think about who to ask, the best way of asking them, and what to ask for – and preferably prepare a plan. There will usually be a time-lag of between three and four years before you begin to see any return for your effort. But after that a steady stream of income should develop. It is a matter of investing time and effort now in the expectation of a future return.

Target audience

There are three groups to consider:

1. **Your existing supporters**. Your management board, your volunteers and your existing supporter base is a good place to start. They already have a good understanding of your work and have made some commitment to you. If getting them to give regularly is a natural progression from occasional giving, then a legacy is a natural next step up from regular giving. What is more appropriate than to make their last gift to the charity their biggest and best? This is something you need to suggest to your supporters and encourage them to do.
2. **The general public**. Approaching the general public has the benefit of increasing public awareness of your work, but it is expensive unless it is clearly targeted. You should try to target elderly people whom you think might be interested in your cause. You can use cold mailing, advertising or posters.
3. **Intermediaries and advisers**. Yet another strategy is to concentrate on people who advise on legal and financial matters: lawyers, bank managers or accountants. When wills are written, so the argument goes, these professionals are the ones who advise. They may be a source of information about charities, and will certainly have their own

preferences or prejudices. You can reach them by direct mail or by advertising in professional journals, and tell them about your work and the opportunities for their clients to leave you a legacy. At a local level for a local cause, you can communicate directly through personal contact or by talking at meetings.

Memorial giving

Memorial giving is particularly appropriate for charities with a medical or health slant, or where the deceased is known to have had a strong interest in the cause. Memorial giving is actually giving by the friends and family of the deceased in memory of him or her. Pieces of equipment, rooms in buildings, bursary funds, lectures and planting a garden are all items that could be paid for through a memorial fund.

Nature Conservancy of Canada – legacy mailing

The Nature Conservancy of Canada legacy pack is a straightforward but very good example of a non-profit attempting to access what's been referred to as 'the pot of gold at the end of the fundraiser's rainbow' – the potential over years for developing substantial legacy income from a well-maintained warm donor file. Visit www.sofii.org to view the pack contents.

This mailing attempts to find donors who would consider leaving a legacy – particularly, a gift in their will – to NCC. It is a simple direct-mail appeal with an unusual call to action. The piece has been mailed many times by NCC. As a result, they now have hundreds of donors who intend to leave a gift in their will. At an average of $25,000, this translates into serious money invested in protecting Canada's most precious places.

The pack costs about $2 per person contacted. Initial results were stunning, with about 13 per cent of recipients responding to the initial mailing of 5,000 pieces. And four per cent (180 people) indicated they were interested in leaving a legacy to NCC. Every time this piece is mailed, more people make a commitment to leaving a legacy.

There is immense potential in writing to loyal direct-mail donors, asking them to leave a legacy to a cause they care deeply about. The potential revenue for causes such as the environment, human rights, the women's movement and other 'social justice' causes is astronomical.

Source: Showcase of Fundraising Innovation and Inspiration

Getting started

The first thing you will need to do is to understand how legacies work, and the legal and tax background – there are often estate duty benefits in leaving money to charity.

Next you will need to produce some literature which gives a background to your work, outlines your needs, suggests a legacy, and tells the readers how they can set about leaving you a legacy. Important points to make are:

- Any tax exemptions that apply to legacies made to a charity.
- The importance your organisation places on legacies as a source of income and some idea of how legacy income will be spent.

- The sorts of legacy that are possible (and the legally correct forms of words for a codicil – if there is room to include this on the reply form).
- A pledge form, so that they can tell you what they plan to do – and if they decide to give you a legacy, you can then continue to keep in touch with them through putting them on your mailing list (a special segment for legacy donors).

You may also want to produce explanatory material on legacies. This is something that only very large charities with large supporter lists can afford to do. If you can produce your own material, you might think about getting together a few simple practical books on making a will.

Next you will need a promotion plan. Who will you approach? And how? This should be linked to a budget – as it will cost money to produce the material and run the promotion, as well as your time (which is also a cost).

The value of the legacy income you receive will depend on a large number of factors. The most important is the age profile of your supporters. If they are young, then on average a considerable time will elapse before they die – which means that however successful you are in getting people to agree to leave you a legacy, the prospects of your getting any income in the near future is much reduced.

How do you decide how much to invest in legacy fundraising? If you are starting out, you will have no immediate legacy income against which to calculate a fundraising cost. You could set a target for the number of pledges that you will receive each year. As time goes on you will find out both how many turn into legacies and how much it costs to get a pledge. If you are already receiving legacy income, you might set aside a percentage (say 10 per cent) of your current legacy income for legacy promotion.

6.8 Capital appeals and big gift campaigns

Charities are able to attract big gifts from time to time, but they are a particularly important component of any major building or endowment appeal, or any other sort of capital fundraising campaign. In many ways, large-scale fundraising is just the same as any other fundraising – you have to ask effectively. But because you are asking for a lot of money, it is important to plan your campaign and to put sufficient resources behind it.

The stages of an appeal

There are likely to be several clearly defined phases in a properly planned appeal:

- **The planning phase,** which will include: the preparation of a case document, which sets out and justifies the purpose of the fundraising; a business plan or feasibility study, which sets out the plan and timescale for the fundraising; and research into likely sources and givers.
- **The recruitment of an appeal committee,** and in particular of the appeal chair, who will lead the appeal.
- **The private giving phase,** in which major gifts are sought and obtained.

- **The appeal launch**, when enough major gifts have been obtained to ensure that the appeal will be a success and the charity is happy to go public.
- **The public giving phase**, when contributions are sought from a wider range of people and through public fundraising activity and events.
- **The consolidation phase** when all contacts who have not given are followed up in a final push.
- **The appeal closes** – hopefully when the budgeted sum has been raised.
- **Completion of the project**, which might be accompanied by a thank you and a dedication ceremony.

Working through this process is important, not only to ensure that the appeal is properly organised, but also to allow a feasible timescale for it. It may take at least two years (and sometimes as long as five years for a major appeal) from start to finish. During the initial stages of the appeal, you will be spending money without seeing any return. The whole organisation needs to understand the appeal process, have confidence in the outcome, and try not to panic before the income begins to flow.

A major appeal will be launched very infrequently, so you will need to create the structure specially. But if you run it successfully, there are a number of spin-offs which can significantly enhance your organisation's fundraising capability:

- You will probably have developed a **large donor list** (of people who contributed to the appeal) and the systems to deal with it. You can continue to raise money from this list towards subsequent projects or running costs.
- The **public image** of the organisation should have been significantly enhanced as a result of all the publicity obtained during the appeal.
- The confidence of the management and fundraising staff will have increased as a result of the success of the appeal. And in fundraising, confidence creates success.
- You will have attracted **important people** to the organisation to serve on committees and to lead the appeal. These can be asked to continue their involvement with the organisation.

And because you will not be running another major appeal for some years (if ever again), try to incorporate all your capital needs into the appeal budget.

Planning an appeal

The planning stage will involve a number of separate activities. These include:

1. **Planning the development**, with drawings and costings. You need to be able to justify the development as being important to your work and the future of your organisation. If you can't make the purpose of the appeal sound really important, you are unlikely to be able to persuade others. You should draw up a business plan for the development, to assure yourself that there will be enough money to keep going once the development has been completed. Too often a new building has to close, or a new piece of equipment lies idle, because there are insufficient funds to pay for its running costs. You will also need

to consider the costings and how much you should raise to undertake the proposed development.

2. **Establishing the feasibility** of running the appeal. Many organisations will take on a consultant to advise on how to conduct the appeal. One of the first things a consultant will do is to conduct a feasibility study, which apart from anything else will indicate whether the appeal is likely to be successful. This study is an important process, as it will serve to highlight any inconsistencies or ill-conceived ideas.

3. **Planning the structure of the appeal.** This is likely to require an appeal committee to lead and oversee the appeal. The key appointment in this committee is the chair. The function of the committee is to raise big gifts, and people should be appointed for their asking ability, rather than for any other quality. You may also want to establish sub-committees to oversee the running of events and to attract publicity and media coverage in order to harness volunteer help. A professionally staffed office will provide the back-up these committees need.

4. **Reviewing the likely funding sources.** A vital planning tool is a table setting out the number and size of donations needed. This table lists the gifts that you plan to get, helps you to identify possible donors, and gives guidance on the level of support to ask for. You will need to develop a plan for how you are going to raise the money you need: through soliciting major gifts, via a mailed appeal, or through fundraising events and activities.

5. **Documentation and research** to back up the above actions. For the major gifts, you should undertake at this stage some preliminary research into the possibilities, and you should certainly explore potential government and aid grants.

6. **Preparing the case statement.** This vital document will be the strategic plan for the appeal. It will include sections covering the following:
- A **background to the charity** and its history.
- A description and justification of **the project**.
- The **costs** of the project.
- The individual **components of the project**, costed.
- The **gifts needed** to achieve this target.
- The **plan** to meet the needs and raise the money.
- The **sources of money** expected.

This should be attractively produced as a report, and you may wish to produce some overhead projector slides as visual aids for presentations.

7 **Identifying the people who will lead the appeal**, and asking them if they would be prepared to help. This is usually done by drawing up lists of leading businessmen and other influential people gleaned from a wide range of sources, including personal knowledge and contact. They will meet infrequently, but are there to help solicit the

largest gifts through their contacts and credibility. The chair will also be the public figure leading the appeal, so this is a critical appointment which can determine success or failure.

Table of gifts needed

Number of gifts	Value of gifts required	Total to be obtained
1	25,000	25,000
2	10,000	20,000
5	5,000	25,000
5	3,000	15,000
10	1,000	10,000
25	500	12,500
200	100	20,000
500	50	25,000
748 donors		152,500

This typical table of donations indicates the number of donors and the amount of fundraising and research you will need. You might expect a success rate of one in 10, meaning that you will need to approach 230 people who could give 1,000 or more. In the example given, you will see that the top three gifts account for 30 per cent of the income and the top eight for nearly half. This is typical of these sorts of appeals and illustrates the importance of planning the leading gifts at the right level, and then going out and getting them.

Leadership

The leadership of the appeal campaign is enormously important. There are two important principles to bear in mind:

1. People respond better when asked by people who are at (or above) their own level in society – this is called peer-group giving,
2. People respond better if the person who is asking has already given and given generously. One question they will ask is 'Have you given?' If the answer is no, it is far easier for them to refuse.

The qualifications to look for in the chair and members of the appeal committee are: the ability to give major gifts on the scale you need (either personally or through the company or foundation with which they are associated); the possession of important contacts; and the ability and willingness to ask others to support the appeal, both in person and by letter.

The first stage is to identify people to help you plan the appeal. Since you are simply asking for advice, it is easier for them to say yes. Later on you will be asking them for money! A group of two or three senior people with an interest in your work can be invited to act as a planning group. Their role is either to act as the formal leadership of the appeal or to select that leadership. They should be people who are well respected in the community and who may have not been associated with a similar appeal in the recent past

– if they have, their asking capacity will have been diminished. They should have plenty of contacts. One of their tasks will be to select other people to form the nucleus of the appeal committee.

You need to understand the motivation that will make important people want to work for your cause. Research seems to suggest that almost every motive under the sun will be present. Some people find themselves genuinely supporting the cause; others find the approach from a senior person in the community difficult to resist; others find the link with other business people attractive for their own purposes; some are motivated by the prospect of some sort of public recognition for what they have done; and some just like the challenge of achieving something unusual and worthwhile. Everyone involved at this level is likely to appreciate (and be used to) efficient administration and being provided with the backup they need. This will ensure that they spend the minimum of time in committee and that their time is effectively used.

Many people don't know how to ask effectively, and you may wish to provide some induction into the work of your organisation and its importance, and some training in the principles of effective asking.

The private phase

With all the building blocks in place, you should now be ready to begin the slow but vital task of soliciting the bigger gifts.

The first task is to get the members of your appeals committee to agree to give. It is important that these early gifts are of sufficient size to give a lead to those that follow (who will probably be giving smaller amounts). Most committee members should be aware of the scale of the donations needed. They will have engaged in discussions about what is expected of other prospective donors, and will be familiar with what might be expected of them. If they find it difficult to give the amount suggested, then propose that they give a smaller sum regularly over a number of years – and you can take their total contribution as being the value of their gift.

Once they have made their own commitment, the committee members should move on to the task of approaching others. For this purpose you will have already drawn up lists of prospective donors. They will be able to help by adding new names and deciding how an approach can best be made. The role of the fundraiser is to provide smooth administration; the task of asking for big gifts is best done by the committee member. Once you have identified the best person to approach a prospective donor (and this is one of the prime functions of the committee), a wide variety of methods can be used. The one that succeeds is likely to be the one with which the person concerned feels most comfortable with.

Often, big donations take time to be confirmed (and this is particularly true when approaching public sector sources). A decision should not be expected within the course of a single meeting. What might happen is that there will be a series of meetings – possibly including a reception, followed by an informal chat, even a visit to see the organisation at work and meet some of the beneficiaries. This will culminate in the prospective donor being asked to support the appeal, and being offered a range of possible ways of doing this (but you should try to secure their support at the level of giving you have decided for them). They can also be asked to give support in kind and to suggest other people who might be approached.

The objective of the private stage of the appeal will be to collect promises of between 25 and 50 per cent of the target sum. This will give a tremendous boost to the public phase of the appeal when it is launched. Indeed, you should not actually launch an appeal to the public until you are confident of its ultimate success.

The public phase

The public phase commences with the launch. This can be done in any number of ways. It should certainly include a press conference and might also involve an event, such as a reception, to which you invite prospective donors who have not yet committed themselves.

In the public phase of the appeal, much of the money will be raised from larger numbers of people who make smaller donations. This might be through personal solicitation. But you could also develop a direct-mail campaign, both to existing supporters on your mailing list and 'cold' to people you have targeted as likely to be interested in the appeal. It is important, though, to leave direct mail until towards the end of the process, so that nobody gives a small donation in response to a letter who might have given a bigger one if approached earlier in person. This is, in fact, the biggest danger in running an appeal – that you might get a tiny donation from someone who, if approached properly, would have given you very much more.

A press and public relations campaign is important to give your appeal a continuing profile. Some of the bigger appeals recruit PR committees and involve a range of PR and media professionals on a voluntary basis. You should certainly have someone working hard on public and media relations, as this will underpin your other fundraising activities.

Events are an important component of an appeal, so long as they are organised by a group of volunteers (perhaps an events committee). This will ensure that your time is used effectively – it is too easy to get swallowed up in event administration when the real money is coming through personal solicitation. Events can attract good media coverage, and can thus make a larger audience aware of the appeal.

At this stage, you are well on the way to success. There may be a consolidation phase when you are close to your appeal target, when you go back to the people who turned you down and to those who have already given (particularly the smaller donors) and suggest that just one small effort will see the appeal through to success. And finally there is the business of ensuring that everyone is properly thanked – the volunteers as well as the donors, who together have made the appeal a success.

6.9 Raising money from young people and in schools

Fundraising from children and fundraising in schools are virtually synonymous, since schools are by far the easiest venues to approach children. If you want to reach large numbers of young people and harness their enthusiasm, schools are the best place to start.

But a word of warning: if you are planning to raise money from young people and in schools, remember that you are dealing with a vulnerable and impressionable group. You need to approach them with care and be sensitive to their needs. You should not put undue pressure on them to support you or to get their parents and family to support you. You should try to get them to understand your work, the reasons for it and why it is important. A code of practice on fundraising in schools, produced for fundraisers in the UK by the Institute of Fundraising, sets out the main factors to consider.

What children are likely to have is time rather than money, and access to the support of their families and friends. There is also the link between the nature of your work and their educational interests to consider – the relationship will work very much better if you can build their understanding of the cause or need you are addressing, rather than simply asking them to raise money for you.

To obtain access to children, you will usually need the permission of the head teacher (or the support of a committed class teacher who can persuade the head teacher). You can make the approach directly; or there might be a committed supporter or volunteer who is also a parent or a teacher who could do this for you. Targeting young people will:

- **Help you generate money for your cause.** This will not always be a huge sum.
- **Involve young people in your cause**, giving them a better understanding of the issues involved and the work you are doing.
- **Lay an important base for future support**. If people get involved in supporting charity when they are young, this can influence what they do and choose to support in later life.

Alongside whatever you do to raise money with young people through schools, the school itself will be raising money through fundraising activities with its pupils and their parents. This can either be to raise the money the school needs for its own work (for example, to create a scholarship fund, pay for books, pay for equipment, or improve facilities). Or it could be to support a local good cause.

Some fundraising ideas for schools and young people

- Contests and competitions.
- Discos and end-of-year/graduation parties.
- Quiz evenings, dinners and dances aimed at parents.
- Litter picking and clean-up campaigns.
- Picnics and outings.
- Raffles and auctions aimed at parents, with prizes donated by local firms.
- Dress-down days, when students can come to school not in uniform if they donate a small sum.
- Learning and reciting poetry.
- Collecting and recycling waste materials.
- Sponsored walks, runs and swims.
- A school summer fête with face painting, name the teddy, high-jumping, puppet making, treasure map, book stalls, a tea bar, treasure hunt, tug-of-war and other exciting events.
- A sale of crafts and produce (such as cakes and jams) made by parents.
- Involving tourists: asking them to become supporters or to collect and send educational equipment and books on their return home.

Making the approach

If you are a local or city-wide charity (such as a night shelter for the homeless, a training centre for the disabled, or a family planning clinic), you will want to approach the schools in your area. You will probably be addressing the head teacher in the first instance. A personal visit is best. If this is not practical, a telephone call will be better than a circular letter, which is likely to find its way into the wastepaper basket.

When you are thinking about how to involve the young people, a useful guide is to make your activities:

■ First **fun** – so that they enjoy what you are asking them to do.
■ Then **educational** – so that they learn about the issues (such as poverty, disability, health care, family planning).
■ And only then **about fundraising**.

The usual starting point is to offer to give a talk about your organisation. You will need to make your presentation as attractive and interesting to the children as possible, because this introduces the next step – the invitation to do something to help by fundraising. This will either be taken up by the school as a whole or by a particular class if the activity fits somehow into their educational programme.

For junior schools you will need to develop a simple and very clearly set-out activity for the young people to use in their fundraising. Quizzes for different age groups designed to fit the curriculum is one idea. Competitions are popular, as they give the child the opportunity to learn, and they may be invited to obtain sponsorship from their family and friends for the number of questions they are able to answer correctly.

For secondary schools, the children themselves are in a better position to decide how funds should be raised.

Everyday choices

You don't have to join a voluntary agency to begin making a difference to children's lives. Almost anyone can make a difference by being sensitive, aware and persuading others that it is important to get involved. Below are some simple, easy-to-do suggestions you can undertake at school or college, starting from today.

Students:
■ Place donation boxes in the canteen.
■ Write and circulate research papers on child-related topics.
■ Adopt a slum.
■ Organise street theatre on child-related issues.
■ Organise debates on various issues.
■ Get involved in voluntary groups doing child-related work.
■ Motivate others to get involved in similar ways.

Teachers:
■ Motivate students by organising events and helping them understand issues.
■ Involve students in collecting materials like clothes, toys and books for deprived children.

Source: a promotional leaflet produced by CRY – Child Relief and You, Bombay

---

Publications for schools

A number of the larger charities produce publications for children. These fall into two categories:

1. **School packs** of teaching materials specially designed for use in the classroom (where they must be linked somehow to the curriculum). With many schools chronically short of books, producing good educational material (either for sale or for free circulation) can get your cause into the school. You also have the opportunity to get the costs of doing this paid through sponsorship.

2. **Simple information** aimed at young people. This could include books, pamphlets, newsletters and information sheets. You could send the information to young people in response to enquiries or as a thank you for a donation. You might even consider setting up a junior supporters 'club' to nurture the interests of young people: for example, a junior environmentalists club. These undoubtedly build a strong loyalty to the organisations concerned and are an important ingredient of school fundraising.

National competitions

National organisations and the larger city-wide ones have another opportunity: to design and develop a national award scheme for young people – for example, an essay competition or an art competition.

You will need to offer prizes, either to the young people or to the school – or perhaps both. The prizes might be in cash. Alternatives are books, bursaries or travel opportunities. You will need to reach schools with information about the award scheme – which may require a media sponsor, such as a newspaper. And you will need to have the money to do this. The prizes will usually represent 25 per cent or even as little as 10 per cent of the total cost of running the award scheme, as you will have to pay for publicity, printed materials, the judging, the awards ceremony, and all the administration involved. But competitions can be a suitable vehicle for sponsorship, as they will appeal to sponsors who are looking for ways of reaching young people and of obtaining the good publicity arising from having supported an exciting award scheme.

6.10 Gambling activities that generate money

The big issue: to gamble or not

Organisations with a religious tradition may find the use of gambling as a method of fundraising ethically difficult. For example, Muslims, Methodists and Quakers all actively discourage gambling and would not like their denominational charities to raise money in this way or to accept grants from foundations which generate their income through some form of lottery or gambling activity.

To them, gambling is the issue – it is not really important whether there is any actual link between addictive gambling and buying a lottery or raffle ticket. It is the principle. Does your organisation have any problems with raising money in this way? You need to be clear about the attitude of your trustees before starting to organise any game of skill or chance. Get your management committee to agree a policy on this to ensure that there is no disagreement later on.

Types of gambling used to raise money

There are three main types of gambling activity which charities use to raise money:

1. **The lottery.** This is a sale of tickets where each gives an equal chance of success and no skill is involved. A sweepstake on the outcome of a horse race or a football competition rates as a lottery. A money game (sometimes known as an instant lottery) is usually run with scratch cards, which the entrant scratches to reveal whether the card has the right combination of symbols to win a prize. These all normally offer cash prizes. A tombola or a raffle, where numbered tickets win, usually offers items such as television sets, video recorders or holidays as the main prizes (which charities usually obtain as donations). The running of a lottery may be governed by lottery laws. You should check out any legal requirements in your country.

2. **The game of skill.** This is a genuine competition based on skill or knowledge, where there are prizes for the winners. Competitions with an entry fee can be an extremely successful way of raising money for a charity. There may also be laws on how you can run skill competitions.

3. **The free entry draw,** where there is no charge for entering. This may be part of a sales promotion (often used for consumer products) or offered as an incentive to members. Here anyone can enter for the prize draw simply by replying to you. This is often a good inducement to membership recruitment. Because no stake money is involved, this will almost certainly fall outside any lottery or gambling laws.

Prizes

For many people, the attraction of entering a raffle or competition is clearly the chance to win a prize. The prizes on offer should be things that the audience you hope will buy the tickets will really want.

For most small-scale competitions, the audience is relatively easy to assess. At the school fête you can be fairly sure that parents and their children will predominate – in which case toys, food and drinks are safe prizes. It is in these sorts of events that the prize is least important. People will often buy a ticket for the fun of it (because they are there), because they wish to support the cause, and because there is someone there persuading them to buy a ticket.

For a larger event with a higher ticket price that aims to raise a larger amount of money, the choice of prizes is more important. In a recent Save the Rainforests raffle, the first prize was an Amazon adventure for two donated by a travel company, with a second prize of an expedition to Mount Everest. These were targeted to appeal to an audience interested in the rainforest and in the environment generally. Prizes like this are often easy to get donated – because the travel company is donating an empty place on a tour that is being run anyway, or a hotel company a room that would otherwise be unoccupied. 'New technology' prizes are also extremely attractive: computers, televisions, video recorders, music centres, and so on.

An unusual and imaginative prize will almost always be more attractive than a money prize. And sometimes it will not cost a lot to organise. For example, a museum supporters group might arrange a personal tour with the director followed by a smart dinner. An arts organisation might persuade leading painters to paint a portrait of the winner (free of charge).

Try to get all the prizes donated – both goods and services – or bought using money donated by a sponsor. This reduces the risk of the venture and increases the amount you raise from the lottery. There is a temptation to go out and buy the best prizes, then find that nobody buys the tickets.

If you are trying to get the event sponsored, identify what you can offer a sponsor. Can you put their name and phone number on the raffle tickets? Can you describe the prize they have donated in glowing terms in any posters you produce? Can you mention their generosity in your newsletter? Link this to the number of tickets you expect to sell, and you will have an attractive proposition to offer any sponsor.

Promotion

Everything hinges on selling the tickets. The more you sell, the more money you will raise. If you sell only a few, you may end up losing money. Whether you have a captive audience at an event or are involving a dispersed membership by direct mail, selling those few extra tickets will make all the difference. If you are able to get the prizes donated, most of the other costs of a raffle are in the organisation and the printing of the tickets.

If the prize is appropriate and the price of tickets is not too high, raffle tickets are best sold on a personal basis. First approach your own constituency: your existing supporters, your management board members, your volunteers, your staff. Ask them to buy tickets for themselves; ask them to sell tickets to their family and friends. Give them a date to sell the tickets by and to return any unsold tickets to you. Then there is your supporter list, where you could arrange for a team of volunteers to go round door-to-door to sell them tickets (for their own use and for resale to their friends). Unlike cold calling, you are dealing here with people who already support you.

Your supporters may have access to other networks. Groups of medical workers could sell in hospitals; trade union members could sell to other members; and employees to colleagues at the workplace. This can be very cost effective. Similarly, if you are organising a large public event, you can sell books of tickets at the event by personal solicitation. A small team of volunteers can go around a show ground or a conference hall, and ask everyone they meet to buy a ticket or a book of tickets.

Some organisations are now offering incentives for the sale of lottery tickets. Since it is likely to be your own supporters who will sell the tickets, you need to find a prize that will appeal to them and offer it to the person who sells most tickets. The telephone can be a powerful tool for finding people to sell tickets.

You can also try to sell the tickets by direct mail, sending people on your supporters list a book of tickets, a covering letter and some information about your organisation and why you need to raise money. Though many people dislike inertia selling, mailing raffle tickets to supporters or distributing them door-to-door is just about acceptable and can work financially (although the cost of mailing will be higher than for a regular appeal). On receipt, your supporters will go out and sell the tickets to their friends, buy the tickets themselves, send them back to you, or do nothing. Very few will return them – usually only around one per cent. Most will do nothing or throw them away. In one large raffle run in the UK, 20,000 members of a charity were each sent two books containing 10 tickets each. This resulted in around 100 being returned and a total sale of 96,000 tickets. The result was expenses of £12,000, yielding total receipts of £60,000.

The draw

At any fundraising event, the prize draw for the raffle is a key moment of drama, especially where there are glamorous prizes. The recruitment of a celebrity presenter to make the draw and distribute the prizes can add to the success of the raffle and the event.

It is important to build the timing of the draw into your plans. At the event, it should be announced that the draw will take place at a certain time. This time is critical, because after it people will begin to drift away. It is a fixed point in the programme that most people will stay for. Indeed, it can be a time of great excitement – the opportunity to collect a prize from a celebrity. As the time of the draw approaches, announcements should be made to encourage last-minute sales.

The Botswana Red Cross Lottery

The Botswana Red Cross Society lottery was hailed as a life-saving strategy for the financially strapped humanitarian organisation when it was launched in March 2004. A partnership between the society and Mascom Wireless, the lottery was launched with fanfare in Gaborone by Botswana Red Cross Society president First Lady Barbara Mogae.

The lottery is promoted on Mascom's website (www.mascom.bw/what/redcross_lottery.htm):

This week's cash prize
- 1 Prize – Pula 4,434
- 2 Prize – Pula 1,847
- 3 Prize – Pula 1,108
- 4digit – Pula 782
- 3digit – Pula 522

How to play
Option 1
- SMS your five-digit lucky number to 71117777 or dial 71117777 and follow the voice prompts to enter your five-digit lucky number.
- You will receive by SMS the lottery ticket with your reference number.
- Keep the message with the lottery ticket to claim your prize.
- Three prizes to be drawn weekly.

Option 2
- Subscribers send the word 'LOTTO' to the lottery number: 71117777
- A FULL lottery ticket with a five-digit lucky number (randomly selected by the system), reference number and draw date is sent to the subscriber. The new mechanics will work hand in hand with the original SMS mechanics. The lucky numbers will be saved in the same database.

Two extra prizes have been added to the Red Cross Lottery weekly draw

Players that match the last three and four digits of the first prize lucky number will receive prize money.

Instant airtime prize

On entering the Red Cross Lottery, clients stand a chance to be an instant winner of a P10 airtime voucher. The winner will be sent an additional SMS with the P10 voucher number.

The lottery is open to all persons 16 years and above.

For more information call Mascom Call Centre on 0800 700 111 or 111 from your Mascom cellphone.

6.11 Advertising for support

Paying for an advertisement in a newspaper or magazine can be a powerful way of promoting your cause or of raising money – but it can be expensive. You can raise money 'off the page' directly by making an appeal for money, or indirectly by recruiting members, volunteers or people seeking further information (whom you will later persuade to give to you).

Advertising can be particularly successful in raising money at the time of a disaster or when an issue has hit the headlines. Your advertisement will reach people at a moment when they know that something needs to be done – and you are offering them a way of helping.

You can also use advertising to build awareness of your charity through a promotional campaign about what you are doing. You can sell greetings cards and other products with which you are raising money for your work. A further use is to invite people to support you with a legacy.

Advertising can take the form of:

- **Press advertising.** Taking space in national or local newspapers, through display advertising or small ads.
- **Advertising in magazines and journals** (general interest or specialist).
- **Inserts.** A leaflet inserted in a magazine and circulated with it to its readers.
- **Posters.** This can include billboard advertising and smaller posters displayed on notice boards or flyposted in the street.

Press advertising

There are several key factors governing the use of the press as a medium for advertising. The cost is high, even for a limited space. As a result, the messages you can afford will be relatively short, and so must be more striking if they are to be noticed. Press advertising has an advantage over other fundraising methods in that you can select your audience by reference to the known readership of the newspaper or magazine. You can also predict with some degree of certainty whether your issues are likely to be given editorial coverage – and if so, whether or not the coverage will be sympathetic. You can link your advertising with the press coverage of the issue – for example, when there is a disaster. And you can design and place the advertisement much more quickly than it would take to organise a direct-mail fundraising campaign.

Advertising for donations is expensive and it is easy to lose substantial sums. Whatever response you receive from advertising, you can probably achieve similar results much more cheaply through an effective and well-targeted public relations campaign.

If you decide to advertise, you should always try to evaluate its cost-effectiveness. If you do this, you will learn more about which media work well and which don't. And if you don't, you may be pouring lots of money into an ineffective promotional device without knowing it; many charities advertise because they see other charities taking advertising space and assume that it works. You can evaluate by using a coded coupon, a coded reply address or a special phone number on the advertisement. You will then be able to link every response to a particular advertisement. The coding should be done for the campaign as a whole and also for each separate promotion in the campaign. This is the only way you can find out which medium works best for you. Results can then be measured in terms of:

- **Income raised** in relation to cost.
- **Cost per new donor** recruited.

Disaster advertising

Possibly the most useful aspect of using advertising to fundraise is its flexibility. You can place an advertisement extremely quickly. Thus if a disaster happens one day, you could be appealing for help the next day at the breakfast table.

What is a disaster? It is not what you think is serious, it is what the public is being told is serious by the newspaper itself and by the other news media. Timing is all. One estimate is that 30 per cent of your response is likely to come from launching your appeal immediately. The problem here is getting enough information soon enough to be able to create a truthful advertisement. A famine or a man-made disaster are obvious instances where disaster advertising can be used successfully. SightSavers (the Royal Commonwealth Society for the Blind) used this approach with the Union Carbide chemical spill in Bhopal.

Acquisition advertising

This is all about finding new supporters who can then be put on your mailing list. The acquisition cost, as with direct mail, is likely to be high, but it is the opportunity to capture them on your list and then profitably appeal to them over the years that makes financial sense of doing this. Only under exceptional circumstances will most organisations break even on the initial proceeds of their advertising. They regard it as an investment in developing their mailing list. As an example, the Woodland Trust in the UK takes small spaces in the newspapers to invite you to send £1 to plant a tree. Many of those responding go on to give more substantial sums on a regular basis. You should decide before you start how much you can afford to pay to find a new supporter. The precise sum for your organisation will depend on how much on average you can subsequently expect to raise from each supporter.

Awareness advertising

If no one knows about you or if you want to launch a new campaign, your objective may be to build awareness rather than just raise money or find new supporters. This form of advertising is expensive, and requires you to continue the campaign over a period of time if you are to have any real and lasting impact. It is also difficult to measure. So if you want to know whether there has been any impact, and whether it has been cost effective, you may need to carry out market research into public awareness.

Although awareness advertising is much used by large companies and successful consumer brands, is it the best way of using very limited charitable funds? Many would say that, if done well, public relations will buy a good deal more awareness than any amount of advertising. The advantage of paying for the space is that what appears on the page is exactly the message you want – at the time and frequency you have decided. With public relations, on the other hand, you are in the hands of reporters and editors.

A good example of awareness advertising was the Hungry for Change campaign mounted by Oxfam in 1983, where the stated purpose was *not* to raise money, but to increase public awareness of the reasons for inequality and the need for change. A consequence of such an awareness campaign is that people will send in unsolicited gifts, and they are likely to respond more positively when you do appeal for funds – as they already know about the issues and have heard of you.

Legacy advertising

This is more difficult and demands careful thought. On the one hand, if you can persuade people to support you with a legacy, the monetary value is likely to be very high; on the other hand, you can rarely determine whether the advertising has succeeded – partly due to the length of time that will elapse before you receive the legacy (usually several years) and partly due to the difficulty of linking any legacy you do receive with a particular promotion.

Smaller spaces tend to work best

How big should your advertisement be? This table illustrates what research and practical experience has discovered about the disproportionate impact of using small spaces for your advertising. You should bear in mind that you may be able to get a larger space for a greater discount on the posted rates, and this would improve the performance of larger spaces as compared with taking a smaller space.

Space size	Response
Quarter page (25%)	48% of that achieved for a full page
Half page (50%)	71% of that achieved for a full page
Three-quarter page (75%)	87% of that achieved for a full page
Full page (100%)	100% of that achieved for a full page
Double page (200%)	141% of that achieved for a full page

Source: Commonsense Direct Marketing, *by Drayton Bird, The Printed Shop.*

Loose inserts

One of the main problems with buying advertising in newspapers is the size constraint: the space is very limited, and the cost escalates as you take more. The use of loose inserts gets over half of this problem. Depending on the publication, anything from a small leaflet to a catalogue can be inserted loose or stapled into the publication. There are four important differences between an insert and an advertisment:

1. There is much **more space** available to you – and you can even include an envelope with the insert. There may be restrictions on the weight of the insert imposed by the publisher, and the print cost will vary with the size of the insert. This makes inserts an ideal medium to describe your work and set out the different ways of supporting your organisation. Inserts can work extremely well for membership drives, campaigns for committed giving (such as child and community sponsorship schemes), and appeals that demand space if they are to be promoted effectively.
2. Although the cost per recipient is much higher, inserts can often be extremely **cost-effective**. This effectiveness is a combination of the space available to you, the cost and value for money factors, and the ability to design a powerful response mechanism as part of the printed insert.
3. Inserts take **time to arrange and produce**. Thus they cannot easily be produced to take advantage of topical events in the same way that an advertisement can.
4. They can be **easily detached** from the publication, and without damaging it. On the other hand, they can fall out and get lost, or thrown away.

Inserts can provide excellent opportunities for testing the message or the format of the appeal.

Door drops

Delivering leaflets through people's letterboxes, or using the postal service to distribute leaflets to every household in the neighbourhood, will cost considerably less than doing a cold mailing (see Section 6.4). And you may find that you can obtain a good response by doing this. Try it out and see what happens. Some organisations have succeeded in recruiting a reasonable number of new donors using this technique.

Posters

Posters fit least well into the fundraising repertoire, as it is difficult to get a response to your message, but they are nonetheless a useful promotional medium. Posters can range from the huge 96-sheet billboard hoardings that you see on main roads right down to small handbills produced on a photocopier for use in windows and on notice boards.

The impact of a poster depends on the size of the image and the extent of the coverage. Naturally it requires a great deal of both to get a message across: that is, a large image displayed all over the place. And this is expensive. What charities can do is to use the medium in small bursts to highlight a week or the launch of a campaign, either nationally or in a chosen area. Or they could rent a site for just one day to put up a poster which will generate controversy and media coverage (this is similar to a stunt used to generate publicity).

It is also important to note what posters *cannot* do. By and large they cannot be used in rural areas – most sites are in towns and cities, or along the highways linking them. Perhaps more significantly, posters do not allow for any direct response, except via a phone number. You can't print a tear-off coupon! The time during which people see a poster and read its message is extremely short, whether they are travelling in a car or walking around the town. So the message has to be short, powerful and extremely simple if it is to work. Thus, at best, posters can only act as an awareness-raiser to support other promotional and fundraising activities.

You could ask an outdoor advertising company to give you a free poster site – if they have one available, it would cost them nothing to donate it to you. The things to consider with free sites include:

- **Are sites available** when you want them?
- **Where are the sites** themselves? Are they in the right place?
- Is the **cost of printing posters** (which you will have to design and pay for) too high to make it worthwhile?
- If you do decide that it is worthwhile, would it be useful to produce **cheap run-on posters** in addition to those required for the free sites? The run-on cost is likely to be low, but what would you do with the extra posters?
- Can you **get the posters sponsored**? You can acknowledge the sponsorship very publicly. But will this get in the way of the message?

Handbills

In a different league from billboard posters are the small posters that can be used to publicise almost anything. They are especially attractive for fundraising, since they can be printed cheaply and posted with your mailings to supporters.

Handbills can be targeted at whoever you want. They can be put in the windows of local shops, on library notice boards and in community centres to publicise a local fundraising event. They can be flyposted on walls or pinned to trees. Distribution can be done by volunteers – distributing thousands of your leaflets and creating highly visible campaigns at little cost.

Two issues in advertising

How does advertising affect public perception of your cause?
Advertising requires headlines, images and few words. This means you have to simplify what is often an extremely complicated problem. If you are trying to attract funds, you will want to illustrate the cause in a way that makes the reader want to do something – then and there. This means appealing strongly to the donor's emotions. The question then arises as to the effect all of this might have on public attitudes towards the problem and on the beneficiaries themselves. And whether, in an attempt to improve fundraising effectiveness, the basic aims and values of the organisation are being forgotten.

Free or fee?
Advertising is expensive, and it is not always possible to measure the response that you get from it (although you should always try to do so). Is it a worthwhile use of your funds to pay for advertising? You will have to decide what you want out of it beforehand, in terms of publicity for your cause that will support other fundraising activity, as well as the direct support you obtain in response to the advertisement. If it still seems too expensive, there remains the option of trying to obtain the advertising free. A number of campaigns have been developed using free space as it becomes available. The disadvantage here is that you have no control over the intensity or timing of your campaign. The same approach can be applied to getting the services of an advertising agency. Some will be prepared not to make a profit on charity accounts; some may be prevailed upon to take on your account free.

6.12 Digital fundraising
Contributed by Jason Potts

The world of online giving continues to evolve rapidly, not only in terms of the techniques available – which include internet, email, social media (such as Facebook and MySpace), SMS (Short Message Service – more familiarly known as 'text messaging)', MMS (Multimedia Messaging Service, which allows images, audio and video to be sent from one mobile phone to another), interactive TV, Instant Messenger – but in the range of countries where these techniques are used. The digital media already represent a cheap and low-risk method of recruiting and retaining donors, and are likely to grow in importance.

Whether you are a larger, older charity or a small new one, the lessons are the same. As a donor or supporter comes to expect better service and more transparency, based on their wider experiences online, you need to improve your performance. The donor is better briefed about global issues than ever before and can find information about your organisation from sites like Charity Navigator or Intelligent Giving. Now is the time to see where technology can help you with tasks like administration, transparency and communications with your donor.

The digital world: a brief overview

Internet
In 2008 the internet was available to more than 1.5 billion people worldwide, more than double the number in 2000. Email is still by far the most common reason for using the internet. Although the rate of growth is slowing in some developed countries, largely because most people are already users, elsewhere in the world where penetration is much lower, the growth rate is dramatic (see table that follows) and there is plenty of room for expansion. Much of this future growth will occur in the use of wireless applications to access the internet.

Internet penetration by region

Region	Penetration (per cent of population)	Growth in users 2000–2008
North America	73.1% (247 m)	128.3%
Europe	48.5% (390 m)	271.2%
South/Central America/Caribbean	28.6% (166 m)	820.7%
Asia	17.2% (650 m)	469.0%
Pacific	60% (21 m)	54.0%
Africa	5.6% (54 m)	1,100.0%
Middle East	23.3% (46 m)	1,296.2%

Broadband

Because of the speed of internet access it offers, broadband has considerable potential for online fundraising. In the third quarter of 2007 there were 328.8 million broadband subscribers worldwide: the highest growth rate per quarter was in eastern Europe (10 per cent), followed by Latin America (almost 9 per cent), with the US and Canada (3.29 per cent) and the Asia Pacific region (2.4 per cent) trailing. China alone reported 3.5 million new broadband users in that quarter.

Social media

Social networking websites such as Facebook, MySpace, Hi5, Friendster, Orkut, Bebo and Skyrock are beginning to arouse the interest of fundraisers worldwide. Between them, these networks received 580 million unique visitors in June 2008, up from 464 million in June 2007, an increase of 25 per cent. The regions of highest growth over this period were the Middle East and Africa (66 per cent), Europe (35 per cent) and Latin America (33 per cent), while once again growth flattened out in North America (just 9 per cent).

The single most frequently used social network is Facebook, which grew from 40 million monthly unique visitors in April 2007 to 115 million in April 2008. In August 2008, 63 per cent of Facebook's 132 million users came from outside North America. The site, which had been translated into 20 languages, including French, Spanish and Mandarin, has recently added 69 more.

Second to Facebook globally is MySpace. But although it is the largest social network in the United States and has expanded to more than 29 countries, including India and Korea, in the past few years, MySpace grew only 3 per cent worldwide, from 114 million unique visitors in June 2007 to 117 million in June 2008. The market leader in Spanish-speaking Latin American countries is Hi5, which received twice as many visitors in June 2008 as in June 2007.

Worldwide Growth among Selected Social Networking Sites June 2008 vs. June 2007. Total Worldwide Audience, Age 15+ – Home and Work Locations

	Total Unique Visitors (000)		
	Jun-2007	Jun-2008	% Change
FACEBOOK.COM	52,167	132,105	153%
North America	35,698	49,248	38%
Europe	8,751	35,263	303%
Asia Pacific	3,712	20,712	458%
Middle East – Africa	2,974	14,951	403%
Latin America	1,033	11,931	1055%

Source: comScore World Metrix

Mobile phones

There are now 3.95 billion mobile phone subscribers throughout the world – in other words, 46 per cent of all the people on the planet have a mobile! About 3.5 billion people own one or more phones, 3 billion send text messages (SMS), 1.3 billion send picture messages (MMS), and 1 billion can access the internet via their mobile. In 1998, by contrast, there were only 309 million subscribers, and in no country other than Finland was there more than one subscription for every two people. Today there are more than 60 countries where the number of mobile phone subscriptions exceeds the total human population.

Just to give you some idea of how fast mobile phones have proliferated, it has taken thirty years for personal computers to reach their current worldwide total of around 950 million, whereas more than 1.2 billion **new mobile phones** were sold in 2008 alone.

Interactive TV

Interactive TV has yet to see any real development globally; the UK is still leading the way, and the rest of the world is waiting to see how the market develops. Will interactive TV become a sensible route through which to fundraise, or will the use of web TV and mobile devices makes it unnecessary?

Digital technologies available to fundraisers

Digital technologies have a key role to play in the future of worldwide fundraising. Now that old favourites like direct mail and face-to-face fundraising are showing reduced returns in many markets, trying to develop such techniques further is unlikely to bring long-term growth or stability. If you want to avoid wasting money and facing a steadily more ineffective fundraising future, now is the time to set off in search of new opportunities. There are many valid ways to go: relevant, focused and segmented donor development, market expansion, audience- or territory-specific sub-brands, creative use of online or mobile tools, connecting actions and giving more closely, and experiential or event fundraising for younger donors. All these new activities can benefit from the sharp and targeted use of digital media.

We need to consider digital as a part of a wider toolkit of techniques, including judicious use of print, powerful use of TV, and clever use of advertising, radio and offline events. We must integrate these different tools in order to reach supporters in the modern media world we inhabit. Why? Well, on its own digital will rarely be as effective as when it is playing its part in a wider integrated campaign. And how exactly do social networks and social enterprise and pro-social commerce relate to fundraising and digital? Human interaction and compelling storytelling are still at the heart of all effective fundraising: creating the stories, connecting people to them and enabling those people to interact are all helped by the new social tools freely available around the world.

Fundraising is currently under pressure from a number of different factors: the downturn in the economy, increasing demands for new income, reduced returns from older methods, extra competition within the sector, and often a change to the pace of the organisation. So let's look at what tools and technologies are available to help. Those who have had little to do with digital up to now need not be fearful of the technology – not least because you can enjoy an exciting new world where seriously complicated things like Oracle Enterprise Databases or massive proprietary content or donor management systems exist happily alongside free tools and on-demand services.

Customer Relationship Management (CRM)

At the heart of your fundraising will be the vision of a relationship with individual supporters, be they activists, donors, companies or trusts. They are all seen in the same light and valued in the same way – as positive contributors helping you to achieve your mission. What is very different now from the situation a few years ago is how you *manage* these different supporters. A while ago you might have used a variety of systems based on the interaction these people have with you – or it might just have been an MS Excel spreadsheet and Post-It notes! Now you can use a single, cheap (or even free) system that can grow as you grow, that can help you maintain a single, detailed view of the supporter, and can diversify as you create new types of relationships. Welcome to the world of Customer Relationship Management (CRM) – often known simply as 'our donor database' when it could better be described as 'the place where we store, make use of, and learn from, all our supporter information'.

At the time of writing, the leading tools for CRM are CiviCRM, Salesforce and SugarCRM. By the time you read this, one or two new options may have arrived and better deals may be available to enable the voluntary sector to make use of currently expensive commercial tools.

- **SugarCRM** is a commercial product but 'open source': you get access to a managed system but you can develop it and customise it, and you don't pay a licence for the software as such.
- **Salesforce** is a software-as-a-service solution: you pay to access its tools per month (although most charities would be able to access it for free as part of the manufacturer's widely advertised and easily applied-for commitment to CSR). It is a very clever, robust and adaptable commercial tool to help you manage different types of data, interactions, supporters and partners. With a little initial development to set it up, you're ready to go.

- **CiviCRM** is an open-source solution to managing mainly donors, and can be used with Content Management Systems (CMSs) like Joomla! or Drupal (see below). It is good for small to medium organisations, but perhaps more difficult to optimise for larger organisations. If you use a CMS like Drupal with CiviCRM, you may find you place quite a considerable burden on your serving infrastructure, so your IT people need to be aware of this. Salesforce supplies its own experts – CiviCRM requires you to provide your own.

- If you do have in-house people supporting your technology, each of the solutions listed above will allow them to customise certain aspects of the service. Some (like Salesforce) permit you to build dedicated bespoke applications based on their platform, or they enable you to build extensions in frameworks like Drupal. Whether you want to tinker with the technology in this way is up to you, but larger organisations should think about spending some time and money on optimising the systems to their own requirements – that way you get to use technology to its best advantage.

- Salesforce is a hosted commercial platform, which means that it manages your data in its systems but you own and control it. As in any situation where all your supporter data is in one basket, backing up the data onto another service is really important from the point of view of business continuity and risk management. This applies to all the providers, but is particularly relevant when you are in effect outsourcing the service. Salesforce stores your supporter data in EU Data Protection Legislation compliant data centres and offers multi-language and multi-territory support. These internationalisation/localisation features are to a greater or lesser degree supported by CiviCRM and SugarCRM too.

- Be assured that Salesforce and open-source services are *not* new, fly-by-night offerings that can be ignored because Microsoft has been around longer or because Oracle is a more expensive and hence, in theory, 'better' service. There are indeed situations where it makes more sense to stick with better known or more expensive offerings: perhaps the rest of your technology uses their tools, so that the reporting integrates more easily; perhaps you are getting all the licences and support for free. But it is important to look beyond the stigma surrounding open source and software as a service. True, some of the open source stuff is pretty poor – but then so is a lot of licensed proprietary software. Newer open-source technologies have large pools of developer support. They have online documentation and they rarely lock you into a specific way of working. They are built to embrace a world where different systems should talk to one another and where data needs to move seamlessly from one place to another. If massive multinational organisations as well as tiny start-up businesses are moving towards working in this way, why shouldn't voluntary organisations?

Content Management Systems (CMS)

Not content with changing the way organisations manage their supporter data, the experts have also been thinking up ways to build websites and mobile sites more easily. You can use a Content Management System (CMS) to publish and manage the content you display to people via your sites; it can publish content in many languages, formats and standards, as well as making it available to many different browsers – even phones.

Why is this important? Well, in the past various CMS solutions have been offered, some targeted at the NGO world (as if a charity's website uses an entirely different way of communicating with humans than a commercial product!) and some at the commercial world. The result was a range of complex, inflexible and very expensive tools. A few are genuinely effective – about 10 per cent – 50 per cent are average and the other 40 per cent are actively poor. They actually hinder an organisation in its work. You can't make content changes quickly enough to cope with emergency appeals; you have had the same structure to your home page for years; you can't add Flash assets, video or embed content from places like YouTube; you can't publish content in any language other than 'American'; you can't administer the site in any language other than 'American geek' – the list goes on.

Enter the brave new world of open-source Content Management Systems. These scalable, secure and *free* tools can reduce your technical headaches, increase your responsiveness, and add value to your organisation. Moving to a new solution is never going to be a totally painless experience, but now is the time to get on with it. Your supporters want you to react to international or national events, so you need to be reactive to get your content into the news agenda – and you need to be dynamic to show you are a living and growing organisation rather than a gently decaying one.

You need to look at the most important aspects of your work and how you use content to support them. What sort of a publisher do you need to be? For a start, you could accept that all your staff actually work in 'marketing' and that your digital presence is vital to that function. It is your shop window to a passing audience of over 1.5 billion connected humans. A few more than the audience that watched your latest TV ad perhaps – by a factor of 100 or maybe 1,000.

The content displayed to those people and the way they find you are now more important than ever. Your news will be compared with CNN and the BBC; your donation process will be compared with iTunes and Amazon; your newsletter will be compared with the last one from Avaaz, Obama or The Onion; your online transactions will be measured against your online bank. You're no longer able to shelter behind your NGO status to justify poor usability, design and technology.

CMSs like Drupal and Joomla! can provide you with the framework to build and present usable, large and relevant websites to a global audience. And they're free. So what's the catch? Well, you need to set them up, just as you would with any CMS, and in the case of Drupal you may need a little expert help to make it work well. You need to arrange for the hosting of the service, unless you opt for a hosted solution (from a partner like Acquia in the case of Drupal and a handful of others in the case of Joomla!). Some training will be needed for your fellow content creators/editors/producers and some limited ongoing support. But in view of the fact that the alternative commercial products, even for the NGO sector, might cost between 10,000 and 200,000 euros a year to licence (not counting any costs for template development), you will be saving money as well as getting access to a better and more powerful tool.

As the world moves faster and news is increasingly generated by citizens, NGOs have an important role to play as connectors and enablers. Agency staff reporting from areas of conflict or natural disaster ahead of news crews can provide content that can be syndicated across global media outlets. These developments give organisations a real opportunity to become major players on the world stage. However, to derive maximum value from this situation requires preparation and a willingness to adopt scalable tools. Why have the news available to you but not be able to publish it? Why should your site crash because too many people want to collect the news from you? Would you be happy if your donation page failed because you were too popular? In the past, access to the right tools was often limited, for reasons of budget or complexity – you would have needed a massive bank balance or scores of IT experts. Now there are better options.

A small amount of money and some sharp brains can create technology that is able to scale up to deal with large events and yet still ensure that you deliver a good service to your supporters. What enables you to cope in this way? Usually it is the right mixture of servers, bandwidth, applications and security.

With platforms like EC2 from Amazon Web Services (AWS) and other 'cloud computing' services (i.e. those that provide computer applications over the internet) making it both quick and easy for you to beef up the infrastructure supporting your website, there is no longer any excuse. If you only need to respond when there is an emergency, there is no point in having a huge and costly infrastructure ready all the year round when you can roll one out in a couple of hours. Likewise, why have a tiny infrastructure which can't cope when things get busy? When you only pay for what you actually use, not for the possibility of using it, the charges for hosting your site usually decrease, even though you are increasing its resilience. Along with server capacity, AWS offers several other excellent services, from storage (S3) to content distribution (great if you want to post some Flash assets or PDFs on your site and do not want to worry about how large numbers of people can access them).

A word about partners: with a CMS like Drupal running a potentially very busy site, you need to ask someone to share their expertise with you in how to scale the site up to cope with large numbers of visitors. Similarly, if you want to take a lot of cash on your site or sign up a lot of activists, you need to make sure that any partners supporting this side of things (the equivalents of Authorize.net, Cyber Source, IATS or WorldPay or Advocacy Online) are able to cope too. Another really important part of the solution is the process by which you scale up and down. You need the right experts around and you need to be aware that you want the solution to scale up and then down again – so you should design it with this in mind from the outset.

If you want to cut your overheads even further or focus your resources on new areas, you could look at the tools available free or for a monthly/annual fee from providers like Google. Most of their offers – from Gmail and Google Analytics to Google Apps and Google Sites – are worthwhile, and you can find out more about them in Google Enterprise. Add their solutions to things like Open Office and you can have a working office quickly and cheaply.

Project management and collaborative working

There are now tools for collaborative working and project management available online – including Basecamp, Goplan, LiquidPlanner, ProjectPier and Teamspace – and new ways to run projects and deliver them in a more 'agile' way have also been developed. This type of delivery is not right for every project, but in the areas of website development, application building or most other digital delivery it would be well worth investigating. You can produce and release more frequently, deliver faster and reduce your overheads too. Just do a web search for 'agile development practices' and you can find out more.

Online payments

Recent developments make it easier and more affordable than ever to take donations online – not just directly from a donor but also from their friends and family through peer fundraising tools.

A note on payment security

Donation sites seem to have been the target of a lot of transactional fraud in certain territories and banking partners are aware of this. Hence it is important to work with your payment provider and your supporters to deal with the issue. Newer security measures like 3-D Secure supporting older methods like Captcha can be implemented, together with risk management/rating services from your payment provider, to make fraudulent transactions less of a burden. You need to strike a balance between locking things down to remove all fraud – sadly, the only way to achieve complete success in this is to remove the commercial element from your site! – and letting your real supporters still give you money online in a usable and speedy manner.

For many years PayPal has dominated payment services, due in no small part to its ubiquity in the world of e-Bay. Recently, however, two other services with equal potential reach have been expanding in certain markets: Amazon Flexible Payments Service (AFPS) and Google Checkout. Google has in the past been very generous with transaction charges for NGOs, so it is worth investigating it further. Amazon is more focused at the time of writing on the US market, but has plans for expansion into Europe and further afield. In view of the potential to make payments more accessible and more efficient in terms of price, they are two useful options to keep an eye on in the coming years.

The newer models for donor interaction regarding payment can be divided into two groups: sites that use technology to enhance the donation or micro-lending process, and sites offering to help a fundraiser secure support on behalf of a charity. Services and organisations like Donor's Choose, GlobalGiving, Kiva.org, MicroPlace and theBigGive have shown how technology can help to create a new relationship between donor and beneficiary, using digital tools to report back to the donor and make them fully aware of the value of their contribution. Adding free content-gathering or sharing tools like twitter, blogs and project-specific micro-communities within sites like Bebo, Facebook, Hi5 and Orkut – or setting them up yourself using free services like Ning – creates a tight and meaningful contact between three important communities: the donors, the beneficiaries and the enabler. The role of the introduction service provided by the enabler – for example, Kiva.org – should not be undervalued.

Peer-to-peer fundraising

Another area of growth in the past five years has been in peer to peer fundraising online. There are already various providers on the market, and more to look out for in the coming year: services with better financial models, services that (like Artez Interactive) combine event registration and peer fundraising in the same application, services providing global solutions with multi-language support and mobile. An exciting aspect of these up-and-coming products is their potential to integrate with tools like Salesforce or Joomla! or Drupal or CiviCRM, thus making data management, single sign-on and reporting considerably easier. This will give an organisation a clearer view of its supporters' interactions, thus enabling it to trigger behaviours, provide rewards and incentives, learn more about its supporters, and help them to do more through targeted, short and easily actioned communications using email or SMS.

A current challenge with peer fundraising is how to provide the fundraiser with the tools needed to be an effective advocate on behalf of your organisation. They need to know how to ask for money, reward participation, and give feedback about the outcome of their activity. As more service providers realise the importance of this role, new solutions will probably emerge. The granular communication of Kiva.org needs to be paired with the free availability of content from twitter, YouTube or Vimeo and some creative use of print to make an effective toolkit for event or peer fundraisers. If this does not happen by 2010, peer to peer will decline in effectiveness as supporters begin to tire of continuous demands from their friends with no feedback.

Mobile phones

Mobile phones, now owned by 46 per cent of the world's population, are dramatically changing the environment for fundraisers. The major changes differ between developed and developing countries: in the developing world penetration is still growing sharply, as we have seen, whereas in the developed world it is the diversity of data services available on the handset that is growing, along with the take-up of these services.

The developing world would benefit from the spread of twitter and Tumblr as tools to help people collect content, tell stories, monitor developments and send information to individuals or a central site with just a text or an MMS message. Emergency appeal coordination and information as well as content to drive a news agenda are all just a text message away from your main site – or the main site of a massive news agency if they subscribe to your updates. Another exciting prospect for the coming years will be improvements in connectivity in the more rural areas of developing countries. The leapfrog of wired telephony may be mirrored by a leapfrog of PC-based internet access straight to access via a mobile device. In this case the potential to support storytelling and impact monitoring is enormous.

In the developed world mobile technology will be increasing in complexity and decreasing in price. When everyone you know has a BlackBerry or a smart phone or an iPhone, what do you think is the most likely way they'll check their email? Increasingly likely it will be on a hand-held device. So the trend will be towards the different secure interactions and 'rich media' applications you can access from your 'phone' – which is now becoming more like a small computer. Can you take a donation from a phone? Can a sponsor support one of your fundraisers in the same way? Can you watch a video direct from the centre of an emergency, delivered to your phone as a link in an SMS and take action right at the end of the film to make a real difference? By 2010 – or perhaps sooner – you will need to be able to help your supporters respond to your requests entirely in a mobile environment.

Social networks

The potential of social networks to help you coordinate activity, connect supporters, and act as a 'village green' for free makes them exciting places. As of March 2009, however, this potential is still unrealised: will some organisation find a way to make a million dollars or a million pounds regularly from a social network in the coming years? Hard to say right now, but their role in the next large-scale emergency, war or campaign will be as telling as the role of technology in the success of the Obama presidential campaign. IT people don't win elections on their own, nor do social networks – but the creative use of every outlet, expert, technology, service and channel available to you alongside other tactics will help you to increase your reach, manage interactions more personally and save cash.

Choosing the right digital tools

Here are some points to ponder when thinking about how digital technology can help you:

1. Digital might initially be more useful as a recruitment tool to support campaigns and then as a migration tool to move people into a financial relationship with you later on, rather than simply as a donation tool.
2. Digital can really help you to learn more about your supporters and to optimise their experience of your organisation. By using a range of analytical tools to monitor a user's journey through your digital offering, you can learn more about the parts of your site at which people most often exit. Then you can redesign those pages to help reduce the exit rate. In the case of donations, you can track your conversion rate and drive it from often low single figures into double figures with a little added science and some design help.

Tools like Google Analytics, Urchin and WebTrends for tracking user journeys and Google Web Site Optimizer for testing better conversion paths are all there to help you get the best results from the users you welcome at your site. There is little point in trying to be the media's favourite destination for news if your call to action is unclear, your processes shabby and your technology cannot cope with the traffic. Running a donation page with a conversion rate of less than 10 per cent is nothing to be proud of – it means that you're happy to lose 90 per cent of people with an interest in donating. True, only some of them really *mean* to donate, but it is almost certainly more than 10 per cent of them. Make good use of some free tools and a little science to drive up the conversion rate and you will find that you can make a lot more money.

Having said all this, which *are* the right tools for you? What can you do if you're stuck in a dinosaur of an organisation and want to make change happen? This is not an easy question to answer, as every organisation has unique requirements and pressures, but here are some general suggestions:

- If your organisation is not already using digital technology, pick a small project that can be supported by using mainly free tools and have a go. If things don't work out as planned, at least make sure that you learn from the experience and identify which aspects of it didn't work out – was it the technology, the strategy, the design? Once you have acquired the learning you can transfer it to the next project and ensure that you are making progress.

- If your organisation is already working online, drive conversion harder and engage your users more in the design of assets for them. Support your fundraisers as advocates if you raise money from peer fundraising, and use simple tools throughout this process to increase your returns and gather more insight.

Can digital technology help you to attract gifts? Yes – in many different ways and on every scale or budget. Digital fundraising has hitherto been the preserve of larger organisations that have bigger budgets and are under more pressure to innovate. Now every organisation can benefit from the tools – in fact, every organisation *should* be using them if they are serious about becoming more effective and efficient raisers of money. We live in challenging and complex times, but digital technology is here to help you, and once you have the tools at your fingertips you'll be wondering how you managed without them!

Online fundraising: what people are actually doing

Several recent campaigns are worthy of note and give a good indication of the direction online giving will follow over the next few years.

US presidential election campaign 2008

As did previous US presidential campaigns, Barack Obama's campaign set the standard for online giving and the engagement of individuals using new media channels. Some key facts from the campaign:

- The campaign received 3 million gifts.
- 50 per cent came in online.
- One billion emails were sent.
- 7,000 different types of email were sent.
- Two million personal pages were created on Obama's website.
- 70,000 fundraised via these pages.

Very sophisticated email targeting and the use of engagement through personal fundraising pages are the key features to note from this brilliant campaign.

Virtual market entry

The possibility of entering new markets with an online-only test has been talked about for many years, and in December 2007 and January 2008 the World Society for the Protection of Animals (WSPA) conducted an online fundraising test in Mexico. It used a cost-per-thousand impressions model on online properties such as Yahoo, Weather

Channel and MSN. WSPA simply took its most successful online fundraising proposition from its international website and translated it into Spanish. It also changed the image used from a bear to a dog, as this was thought to have more cultural resonance with Mexicans. The payment system was credit card and WSPA asked for a committed (monthly) gift.

The return on investment for the campaign was 1.2 and 550 donors were recruited over a three-month period at an average gift of 7 euros a month. Break-even was in one year and the net recruitment investment cost was zero.

Various models are available for virtual market entry. The WSPA used a very low-impact approach that minimises risk and investment. A more integrated approach would probably be better, although the WSPA-type test could quickly tell you whether your particular cause, and indeed brand, could build a supporter base in a country or region. It is advisable to have a local country website to support any online advertising initiative, as this builds credibility

Other possible virtual market entry models include:

- **Expanded virtual testing.** This would add other online channels to improve results, while retaining the low-cost, low commitment to infrastructure approach of the WSPA model. To support the banner advertising, other digital recruitment activities would be added, using the same creative proposition(s) and the same look and feel:

- **Google Ad Words.** Purchasing a range of key words/phrases that mirror the fundraising propositions being used in the banner advertisement campaign, in order to drive more traffic to the landing pages. (This could be tested very inexpensively, as the amount of spending per day can be capped and results assessed instantly.)

- **Online PR.** Approaching some of the bigger local websites to carry free content. This is simply a way to build more traffic to your in-country website and to encourage visitors to become donors.

- **Viral marketing (social media).** Creating viral videos and messaging to drop into existing social networks that large numbers of the country's citizens use. This would initially be for the purposes of name capture; you could make follow-up fundraising 'asks' via email or SMS.

- **MS or mobile web browsing.** In countries with high penetration, this can be used as low-level 'ask' fundraising and list building.

Fully integrated new media testing

The third model would include all the activities in the WSPA approach and in expanded virtual testing, and would require the creation of a full website and a full-time web staff in the country. All the other media used in the fundraising would be fully integrated with the online media; for example:

- All direct mail would feature a prominent link to the website for donations.
- Any direct response television activity would use the web (and possibly text messaging) as a fulfilment channel.
- Any face-to-face recruitment would use the web as a fulfilment channel and email as an ongoing communications channel.

This model would most likely require a local office. Though not absolutely essential, an office would make the following activities easier:

- Website building and regular updating.
- Search engine optimisation.
- A full e-communications programme.

Using the social media in peer-to-peer fundraising

Where the practice of asking friends and family for donations is concerned, interesting cultural differences are emerging: for example, the British are more likely to ask other people to contribute if the activity is extreme, such as climbing Mount Everest or running a marathon, whereas Americans or Canadians are more willing to reach out for less adventurous pursuits, such as walking five kilometres or competing in a sports tournament.

However, there are common themes in digital peer-to-peer fundraising that cut across cultures. For example, the 80/20 rule is as true in the Netherlands as it is in Australia: 80 per cent of the online donations will be solicited by 20 per cent of the online fundraisers. Also, online fundraisers perform better when part of an online fundraising team.

How will the global recession affect digital peer-to-peer fundraising? Early evidence suggests that average gift levels in online fundraising campaigns are running at only 80 per cent of their value a year ago. However, overall fundraising levels are up because there are more online fundraisers now than there were 12 months ago.

Mobile fundraising

In 2008 mobile phones became the latest trillion-dollar industry for the planet, towering over air travel, broadcasting and IT, which are all in the half-a-trillion bracket. The industry's income can be divided into two categories: the larger is mobile services (the cost of call minutes, text messages and any premium content we access) and the smaller is the hardware, mostly the mobile phone handsets and the network infrastructure.

The global mobile industry

The global mobile industry is a complicated phenomenon – particularly when it comes to trying to understand why so little of every donation ends up in your organisation's bank account! Here is a brief description of the different players:

- **Carriers/FCC Licence holders.** These include global players such as Deutsche Telekom, Vodafone and France Telecom, and national providers such as TIM in Italy or Vodacom (part owned by Vodafone) in South Africa.
- **Device manufacturers** such as Nokia, Motorola and Ericsson, who are very much allied with the carriers as they rely on them to purchase and distribute their handsets.
- **Content aggregators/providers** such as Global Networks, AOL, Yahoo! and CNN, who provide content via SMS, through carriers and the networks themselves. As on the internet, they offer advertising within their content.

- **Infrastructure.** Providers such as Openwave and Omnisky allow users to access content through their infrastructure, very much like Microsoft and Netscape provide browsers for the internet.
- **Ad networks** such as Doubleclick and 24/7 which, like the internet companies, offer cross-network targeted advertising to mobile users.

All these companies are potential targets for corporate fundraising approaches and with the right deal could prove very lucrative fundraising partners.

The most important recent development in the world of mobile technology has been the rise and indeed near-dominance (certainly in the more developed economies) of 3G ('third generation') devices, notably the iPhone and the Blackberry. With the iPhone in particular, you have the prospect of downloads that can actually provide additional functionality for your phone for nothing or at a small cost. By accident rather than design, this is creating a friendlier environment for mobile fundraising. Rather than adding a donation to your bill – where charities would be lucky to see half the actual amount charged to the subscriber – you can download an application that would mean the charity gets all the money. The mobile suddenly becomes the equivalent of a mobile wallet – the 'cash on your phone' that has existed in markets such as Japan for years but is only just beginning to become a reality in other countries.

This rapid growth in 3G mobile technology means that surfing the web on your mobile and filling in a donation form offer yet more exciting potential for global charities to explore. *More people* on the planet *now access* browser-based content by using a mobile phone (1.02 billion) *than by using a PC* (950 million). The mobile phone is already the dominant method of internet access in countries ranging from the most technically advanced, such as Japan, Taiwan and South Korea, to those that are relatively poor, such as India, Kenya and South Africa.

What can you do with your mobile phone?

In a couple of years, the majority of phones will offer more internet devices than the iPhone does today. Here are some of the things you can do with your mobile:

- The picture messaging service MMS (Multimedia Messaging Service) today has a potential reach (meaning that the phone itself, and the network to which it is connected, support MMS) of over 1.9 billion phones. Almost half of all Asians (48 per cent) use MMS messaging and around 25 per cent of Europeans.
- Text messaging (SMS) has been the biggest data application on the planet for many years now but keeps on growing dramatically. SMS now has more than 3 billion active users (76 per cent of all mobile phone subscribers) and in 2008 was worth 130 billion dollars globally. On average, active users send nearly four text messages per day, although in the Philippines (which has led in this category since national statistics were first reported) the *average* user sends 25! The heaviest users worldwide are young people, who send an average of 100 texts a day.

- The mobile is becoming part of the banking system. In countries such as Kenya, South Africa and the Philippines it is normal for employees to be paid their full salary to their mobile phone ('non-banking') account.

You can also buy things with your mobile:

- In India, you get a five-per-cent discount if you pay your utility bill using your phone, because it is more efficient for the utilities to handle the payment transfers electronically than by using cash payments.
- In South Korea, half the population already makes payments using a mobile phone, as do 17 per cent of Japanese.
- In Finland, 58 per cent of the single tickets sold on Helsinki's trams are paid for by mobile phone.
- In Estonia, the only way to pay for parking is with a mobile phone.

Successful mobile fundraising campaigns

Here are some examples of successful mobile fundraising campaigns from around the world (you can find many more at www.textually.org):

- Using a 'text to help' campaign, the American Red Cross in 2008 raised more than $190,000 to help the victims of disasters such as Hurricanes Gustav and Ike.
- Under the slogan Goal4Africa, a benefit soccer match involving the world's top players will be played in Munich in 2009 and broadcast on TV around the world. The proceeds will go to Nelson Mandela's 46664 Foundation, which supports HIV positive and AIDS infected people. During the game, the charity campaign will be prominently advertised by the broadcast partners. Viewers in 16 countries can text a keyword to a local SMS short code and receive in return a mobile phone wallpaper.
- The Zain Group, the leading mobile telecommunications operator in the Middle East and Africa, donated $85,863 to the Nelson Mandela Foundation from funds raised through an SMS competition in 2008. The competition formed part of a global SMS birthday wishes campaign prior to the 46664 Concert honouring Nelson Mandela at 90 held in London.
- Greenpeace in Argentina has often used mobile phones to encourage its 350,000-strong mobile list to lobby for important environmental legislation. Among its successes was the passage of the Ley de Bosques ('forest law'), where Greenpeace constructed a large database containing both the email addresses and mobile phone numbers of the people who had signed a petition supporting the new law. They sent out text messages to alert people to critical hearings and city council votes, and to coordinate demonstrations and meetings.

Global direct giving portals

The final trend to be described in this section is the continuing growth in global direct giving portals, where the donor is put in direct contact with the beneficiary, often bypassing the charity. In the case of www.kiva.org, this is done through the mechanism of a loan, so that anyone anywhere in the world can lend a farmer in, say, Bolivia a hundred dollars to set up a micro-enterprise. The site also allows donors to see who else has made a loan to that specific project and to engage in some social networking with like-minded peers.

There are already up to a dozen significant sites of this kind, and they are arousing considerable interest because of their transparency and simplicity, and the timely, personalised reporting they offer – for example:

- On Kiva.org, a loan is made every 28 seconds.
- On Global Giving, there have been over $14 million in donations since 2002, involving 1,300 projects and more than 41,500 unique donors.

Online giving: market profiles by region

North America

Although North America remains one of the largest and most mature markets in online giving, the financial crisis that began in 2008 has shaken consumer confidence. Here are the key findings of research into the effects of the crisis on online giving conducted during September and October 2008:

- The amount raised in September 2008 was 34 per cent greater than in September 2007; but the amount raised in October 2008 was only five per cent greater than in October 2007.
- The number of gifts went up by more than 15 per cent in both September and October 2008, as compared with September and October 2007. Despite the distractions of the faltering economy and the presidential election, a significantly larger number of donors gave in these two months of 2008 than they did in 2007.
- However, the average size of gift appeared to decline in October 2008 as compared with October 2007. This may be a sign of the weakening economy, as many donors continue to give online but in smaller amounts.

Overall, then, the news is relatively good: despite the financial crisis and the elections, online fundraising grew in both these months as compared with the previous year. Which raises the question: why has online fundraising continued to grow while many other forms of fundraising have declined in the current economic climate?

Unfortunately, the experts predict that the current economic crisis will get worse before it gets better. So the fact that growth in online giving was slower in October 2008 may be a sign of things to come.

Elsewhere, online political fundraising has become the main learning ground:

- In November 2007, the campaign by Ron Paul, the libertarian Republican presidential candidate from Texas, raised $4.2 million in about 24 hours from more than 37,000 contributors.
- This achievement has now been overtaken by the Barack Obama presidential campaign, referred to earlier in this chapter.

Latin America

Brazil has by far the highest proportion of internet users in the region, but here are the runners-up:

- Mexico (35%)
- Argentina (19.3%)
- Chile (12.4%)
- Colombia (11.4%)
- Peru (8.6%)
- Venezuela (7.9%)

Large numbers of connected individuals in Latin America are now making mature use of online social media. The diagram below shows the level of sophistication of users in the key countries:

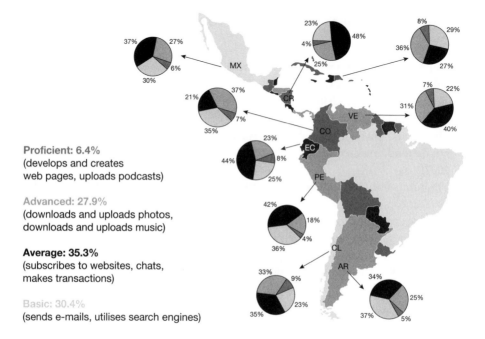

Proficient: 6.4%
(develops and creates
web pages, uploads podcasts)

Advanced: 27.9%
(downloads and uploads photos,
downloads and uploads music)

Average: 35.3%
(subscribes to websites, chats,
makes transactions)

Basic: 30.4%
(sends e-mails, utilises search engines)

Diagram courtesy of www.AvatarLA.com

As the WSPA case study earlier in this section illustrates, the region is certainly ripe for new media campaigns to acquire new supporters. Using the mobile to fundraise or engage individuals in campaigning activity also seems to hold promise.

Western Europe

As is true of most other regions, western Europe is a complicated collection of nations at different stages of development as regards their access to, and consumption of, digital technologies. Some markets in this area are maturing, such as the UK, and some offer emerging opportunities, such as Spain. These two markets are profiled below.

The online fundraising techniques with most resonance across western European include peer-to-peer giving – even in markets that have no real tradition of sponsoring friends to do something (sporting or just unusual) to raise money that is collected online, charities are making this work! Virtual gifts and child sponsorship online are also very strong, as is emergency online fundraising.

The UK, a mature western European market

The UK is a relatively mature market for online fundraising. It can show a range of tried and tested techniques where the return on investment is well known, plus a high volume of activity that is working for some organisations but not for others. The types of organisation that are successful online vary as widely as the types of product that work best for them – for example:

- **Oxfam**'s virtual giving catalogues (Oxfam Unwrapped).
- **Cancer Research UK**'s mass participation event for women (Race for Life), for which most participants now sign up and fundraise online.
- The banner advertising campaigns by the **World Society for the Protection of Animals** (WSPA).

These all share a very strong sense of tangibility around the fundraising 'ask' – much like the trend in the US with websites such as Kiva and Global Giving. Emergencies and adoption (animal and human) are very strong offerings online in the UK.

The tried and tested online fundraising techniques include:

- Adwords (Google and Yahoo!).
- Affiliate programs.
- SEO (natural search).

These techniques benefit from being low risk: with Adwords, you only pay per click and you can quickly change things if the return on investment starts to fall; with affiliates, you only pay on results. SEO of course relies on you having a highly optimised website with a highly usable transaction process.

Less guaranteed techniques but still highly effective if they work are:

- **Pay-per-click banner advertising.** As noted above, WSPA has been very successful with this in the UK with its animal adoption 'ask'.
- **Pay-per-click contextual advertising.** This involves placing ads next to relevant content both on news-based websites and within social networks (such as Facebook's Beacon advertising system, which allows highly targeted contextual advertising within individuals' personal profiles).

The key name-gathering technique for two-stage conversion is:

- **Social media.** Placing content/functionality within social networks to capture data for later follow-up, usually via email.

Mobile giving is taking off in the UK and, if issues with operator fees and cross-network compatibility can be addressed, may become the leading digital acquisition tool for the next few years. The entrance of payment provider PayPal into the mobile market could facilitate this process sooner rather than later. In March 2009 Comic Relief, in conjunction with Radio 1, raised over £1 million in the space of a few weeks by encouraging listeners to send text messages to donate £1.

Spain, a maturing western European market

Here are some key facts about the Spanish digital market as it stood in summer 2008:

- 47 per cent of the Spanish population over 15 years old had **access to the internet** at home or at work.

- The average amount of **time spent online** per month was 25 hours, which is relatively high compared to other European countries (and second only to the UK).

- The year-on-year (June 2007–June 2008) growth in unique **users with access to the internet** at work or home was 15 per cent, from 14 million to 16.2 million.

- The most **popular sites** in Spain were Google (13.9 million unique visitors), MSN and Microsoft group (12.9 million), Yahoo! (7.9 million), Telefonica group (7.2 million) and Orange (6.3 million).

- In June 2008 the **lead social network** in Spain was Tuenti with 2.8 million unique visitors.

- Growth in **visits to social network** sites (25 per cent) outpaced general growth in internet usage (11 per cent), with a rise in unique visitors from 464 million in June 2007 to 580 million in June 2008. Of those visitors, by August 2008 over 46 per cent had visited their social networks using a mobile device; within that group, 70 per cent had visited MySpace and a further 67 per cent had visited Facebook.

- Since June 2008 Facebook has grown considerably in Spain, following an aggressive campaign to recruit translators to support new language options within the network.

- Growth in **broadband subscribers** in June–July 2008 was 15.8 per cent, to a new total of 8.7 million lines.

- The most recent figures for **broadband purchase** in Spain (May–July 2008) show Telefonica leading with 76 per cent of new clients, with other operators capturing 13.7 per cent of the market and cable adding a further 10 per cent.

- During the same quarter **mobile subscriptions** topped 51 million (in a country with a population of just over 44 million people), a growth of over 5.8 per cent on the previous quarter.

- The **mobile market** is divided between three operators: Telefonica Moviles (46 per cent), Vodafone (31 per cent) and Orange (20 per cent). The new entrant in the market, Xfera, has a market share of just 1.7 per cent, but this is predicted to reach 4 per cent by the end of 2009.

- There has been a 44 per cent growth in **e-commerce** between 2007 and 2008, with the chief online transactions being booking flights, hotels and entertainment tickets, and buying groceries, books or music.

- The audience for **e-commerce** is currently skewed towards men, who make up 62 per cent of the users.

- An online user of **e-commerce** is most likely to fall into the age group 26–35.

- Across Spain the speed of **broadband connectivity** can vary by more than 50 per cent, making the experience of users in the Asturias region considerably better than in the Basque and Aragon regions. While this will not affect the use of very light applications such as hotmail, it will hinder people trying to use streaming media (YouTube) or music (iTunes).

Eastern Europe

Much of central, eastern and south-eastern Europe is undergoing a transformation because of the need to meet the requirements for joining the European Union (EU) and the World Trade Organisation (WTO). Markets have been liberalised and incumbents privatised. The region's mobile market, once viewed as underdeveloped, has reached saturation point in some countries and is growing rapidly in others. The impact of increased mobile usage is evident through the substitution of fixed lines by mobile. Fixed-line incumbents, faced with growing competition in liberalised markets, are extending the reach of their networks and turning to broadband as a source of revenue growth. Mobile operators are also turning to data as the saturated markets mean that they can no longer grow easily through acquiring new subscribers

The new entrants to the EU and the rapidly developing eastern European markets are already showing potential for new media fundraising both online and more notably via mobile. The Czech Republic and Estonia are countries that now have more mobile subscriptions than people, and Hungary is not far behind.

Online fundraising in Slovakia

The Good Angel organisation was started in 2006 by two businessmen, Andry Kiska and Igor Brossman. Both had personal experience of cancer and its economic impact on the family, and they wanted to do something to help people in difficulty.

The organisation, a registered non-profit, operates through a website http://www.dobryanjel.sk/ (only available in Slovak). Concerned members of the public make donations through the site and the funds raised are used to pay a regular monthly stipend to families in need. A network of over 200 doctors is used to identify potential recipients of funds.

The founders use their own money to fund the overheads – which are kept as lean as possible through the use of volunteers and smart IT. This means that 100 per cent of the value of donations goes to families affected by cancer. Advertising space (TV spots, billboards) is obtained pro bono through business contacts.

Donors can give as little as 1.5 euros. They can give regularly or not. They can choose to give to a particular family or not. They can choose to be named or to remain anonymous. Donors and recipients of funding are encouraged to share their stories, and can get in touch with each other if they wish. There is no pressure, however: decisions are left entirely to the donors and beneficiaries about the level of engagement they want.

To ensure maximum transparency, each donor has a personal online account which lists the history of their gifts and how they were used. Donors receive a monthly email, updates and appeals. Statistics showing aggregate levels of donations, funds paid out and numbers of families helped are regularly updated. By March 2008 (after 18 months of operation) 1.28 million euros had been raised from 31,870 donors – an impressive achievement in a country of 5.5 million people.

Asia Pacific

Asia is already the world's largest regional internet market, and continues to develop:

- Mobile has continued its strong growth.
- 3G mobile services are being rolled out in the major markets.
- Internet access is rapidly moving from dial-up to broadband.
- Asia continues to be a global leader in broadband roll-out.

The rapid take-up of internet, mobile and 3G services in this region offers great opportunities for fundraising via digital channels. Opportunities in the more developed economies, such as Australia, are much like those in North America and the UK, whereas markets such as Japan and South Korea offer very different opportunities because of their higher usage of mobile for messaging and for consuming broadcast content.

In countries such as Taiwan and Singapore, the infrastructure for digital fundraising is well established, but the public has not yet been sufficiently educated to use this as a giving channel.

Africa

Owing to limited penetration in most African countries, there is little in the way of digital fundraising. South Africa is an exception, with quite a degree of web and mobile fundraising activity. The immaturity of the market means that this activity tends to centre around one-off, high-profile campaigns that include the web and mobile as part of an integrated campaign or corporate partnership. However, the rapid growth in mobile in particular across the region should offer fundraising opportunities over the next few years.

What to do next

When thinking about digital media, the key challenges for fundraisers are: which are the right opportunities to take, and in what order? The global recession can only make these issues all the more urgent.

Here are some important factors to think about when looking for the right opportunities:

- **The value of people.** One of Barack Obama's first actions on becoming US president was to appoint a chief technical officer (CTO) at the White House, a post that had not existed under previous administrations. An essential first step in getting results from digital channels is to have a senior person – a CTO or Head of Digital – who will drive the implementation of digital technologies to create business benefit and raise money. This is a big step up from the usually very junior role most non-profits have traditionally given to the person responsible for the web.
- **Internet speed.** The ability to deliver IT projects quickly and cheaply has increased as technology has improved and become more easily available; open-source or at least open-architecture technologies have been largely responsible for this. 'Agile' project management methods that challenge more traditional Prince 2 techniques have further confronted the *status quo*. The agile approach to delivering all digital projects is vital to achieving success in this fast-paced environment. As opportunities appear and disappear in a matter of days, the successful non-profit will be able to seize the moment at internet speed rather than traditional direct-marketing speed. eBay claims to have an innovation development framework that takes only six weeks from the idea to

going live to the public. This time span, and indeed more quickly in some cases, should be the aspiration.

- **Peer to peer.** The use of applications like Just Giving to enable online peer-to-peer fundraising has been a key trend over the past few years. This trend will continue and indeed intensify: as the economic recession bites, the ability to allow donors to become fundraisers on your behalf will become more and more important.

- **Channel shift.** The use of email and latterly text messages to deliver both fundraising and communications has developed very slowly in markets outside the US. The idea of shifting donors or supporters of any kind from expensive offline channels to lower-cost digital channels has been around for a while, but with recruitment figures for new donors holding steady, there has never been the incentive to make this happen. But the harsher economic climate and the fact that the majority even of older non-profit donors are online will almost certainly make channel shift a key business imperative over the next few years.

- **Social media.** Allowing people to interact with your organisation online, posting content of all kinds, from blog posts to images, and by allowing them to interact with each other is without doubt the future of the internet – and probably the way non-profits will most effectively exploit its benefits.

- **On the move.** For the past few years, mobiles have been at the same time the most promising and the most frustrating opportunity for the sector. Everybody has one, but annoyingly they each have a *different* one – and therein lies the problem. As soon as phones are standardised – at least in terms of the things they can do – and everyone can use them as cash, then watch out! Once these problems have been resolved, it would be hard to imagine a more powerful fundraising and communications device.

- **Usability and analytics.** As online channels become more important to the business of fundraising, so too does the importance of improving the user experience and tracking and reporting on activity. Learning from how people behave will be particularly important now that the challenging economic climate has made it vital to recruit and retain donors cost-effectively.

6.13 Trading

One of the most visible aspects of fundraising by charities – though completely separate from the income generation activities discussed in Chapter 5 – is their trading activity, which is targeted largely at members and supporters. This can include:

- **Sales to supporters through gift catalogues**, especially the sale of greetings cards and promotional materials such as posters and T-shirts.
- **Charity shops** selling donated goods from premises in the town centre.
- **Sales of publications** and other activities directly concerned with the charity's work.

Trading may seem an attractive fundraising option, but in fact it involves a long, hard slog at relatively low margins, a high input of capital, and a considerable drain on management time. Although some organisations, like Oxfam in the UK and CRY in India, find trading an extremely successful method, generating half or more of their annual income, many others lose money from it.

So the first issue to consider is whether to do it at all. Can you actually make a profit out of the trading? Is it the most effective way of using your time, your money and your volunteers – or are there other ways of using the same resources to generate much more money? Too many charities take an over-optimistic view of trading, and end up losing money once they get involved in it.

Beyond large-scale trading, however, there is a range of much smaller-scale trading activities – from running stalls selling old clothing and 'jumble' to making and selling jams and cakes – that are usually undertaken by volunteer supporters and can add useful amounts to an organisation's income. The same principles apply here as in the running of any small-scale fundraising event.

Charity shops

Most charity shops are simply a retail outlet, selling merchandise to generate a profit for the charity. Some aspire to do more than this by being an information point, promoting the cause and the work of the charity, and perhaps recruiting new supporters.

To run a shop, whatever its purpose, requires a considerable management effort. The following are some of the key factors in doing it successfully:

- **Location.** Finding the right location is essential. The shop must be sited in a place that can attract passing trade. It must be near enough for the voluntary helpers who will staff it. And you have to balance these requirements with the rent you can afford to pay.
- **Staffing.** Most charity shops depend extensively on volunteers for their staffing. The usual pattern is to employ one professional manager for a shop of any size, who coordinates a team of 20 to 40 volunteers. Some shops have a separate volunteers' committee which takes responsibility for running the shop. The training, recruitment, supervision and management of this whole group of people is a key determinant of success.
- **The merchandise.** Charity shops tend to sell three types of merchandise: goods donated to the charity by well-wishers in order to raise money (such as second-hand clothing, household items and jewellery); goods produced by the beneficiaries of the charity (for example, in workshops for disabled people and rural development projects); and goods produced by the charity (such as greetings cards). The quality of the merchandise is an important factor – and this is particularly true where the shop is selling donated goods, which should be cleaned, repaired or checked, sorted and priced before they are sold.

Selling promotional items

Here are some examples of promotional items that can carry the charity's name, logo and message and be sold to raise money:

- Greetings cards
- Calendars
- Diaries
- T-shirts
- Address books
- Pens and pencils
- Wallets
- Mugs
- Posters

Catalogues

In catalogue trading, new goods are offered to supporters, usually by mail order or, as in the case of Traidcraft (which sells products from Southern rural development projects to Northern customers), through local agents. Even charities that make a success of trading in this way may earn as little as 10 per cent profit, since the cost of the merchandise, the marketing and the management have to be taken into account. Often it is only the associated donations that purchasers add to the purchase price that brings any profit at all. Here are some key points:

The merchandise. When selling goods in this way, you need to maintain high standards. The items are described in print and have to live up to their description when received by the purchaser. If they don't, there will be disappointment, and it will reflect badly on your charity. The goods should also in some way aim to reflect the values of the organisation – either in the use of materials (recycled paper, for example) or through the design. The items in the catalogue should be conceived of as a range, rather than as a collection of unrelated products, and the range must appeal to the target market. The goods must be available in sufficient quantity to meet likely demand, or a serious loss of confidence will arise. And the cost must be low enough in relation to the selling price to give the possibility of a profit.

Promotion. Unlike in a charity shop, where customers can walk in off the street, a catalogue needs vigorous promotion. The mechanism normally used is direct mail, the aim being eventually to build up a list of regular purchasers which will create an assured market for the merchandise. Although some sales will be made through word of mouth and personal contact, most will be made as a result of sending the catalogue to previous purchasers, to your supporters and to other likely mailing lists.

Control and administration. The management of catalogue trading involves a major buying operation, with all the associated control and cash-flow worries. Also, the warehousing and order processing systems required to support catalogues of any size can be a major logistics operation. Then there are the questions of proper pricing, cost control and good management of what is a business activity, very different from the normal work of the charity and perhaps requiring quite different skills. And finally, there is the question of how to finance such a fluctuating business, where the purchases may need to be paid for well in advance of the revenue actually being received.

Other trading activities

Posters, T-shirts, bumper stickers and other promotional items are often a profitable source of income. Organisations such as Greenpeace find that they can make money and get their message across in this way. The key here is to recognise that it is the design as much as the message that will create success. The ideal approach is to have all the production costs underwritten by a sponsor, so that all the sales proceeds are clear profit. Every effort should be made to encourage sales, whether the merchandise is sponsored or paid for. Losses are often made in this area because of goods failing to sell or over-optimistic production runs.

Generating revenue: a case study

Baphalali, the Swaziland Red Cross Society, raises money from the sale of industrial first-aid training, including the sale of first-aid kits. This not only provides income, but promotes the aims of the society through reducing accidents. A donor provided sufficient funds to launch the programme, which cost 40,000 euros to train the trainer. In the first 10 months 80,000 euros was raised, and the programme is being expanded to meet demand.

Source: Swaziland Red Cross Society

CHAPTER 7

Working with people

7.1 Working with volunteers

The role of the volunteer is important for many charities. Volunteers can be largely or even totally responsible for the organisation's work. The Samaritans, a telephone helpline for people who are despairing or suicidal, is a good example; and many environmental campaigns rely substantially on the efforts of volunteers. Volunteers bring extra expertise, but also save money, as the organisation might otherwise have to pay a member of staff to do the same thing.

Volunteers can also be used to raise money for the organisation, and are especially useful in a range of fundraising tasks, many of which could not be carried out without them – either because the organisation would not have sufficient time or the capacity to do the fundraising in the first place, or because, if volunteers were not being used, the money could not be raised cost-effectively. Volunteers can also assist the fundraiser by providing all sorts of administrative support and backup.

Involving volunteers in fundraising requires more than just finding the people to do the work for you. In order for your organisation to get the best out of its volunteers, they need to be chosen well, placed with imagination, given satisfying work to do which matches their skills and interests, and managed with skill. They are not simply there to be deployed as 'cheap labour' in all the worst jobs. Rather, they can add hugely to the resources available to you, enabling you to do more with less and to do it better.

Types of work that volunteers can do

Committees

Most voluntary organisations are controlled by a management committee, which decides policy for the organisation, oversees its work, and ensures that it meets its charitable objectives. This committee normally consists of volunteers, many of whom also get involved (again as volunteers) in other aspects of the organisation's work.

Committees may also be set up to supervise and develop particular areas of the organisation's work – such as a 'development committee' to plan a major appeal, a 'business committee' to develop links and partnerships with local businesses, or an 'event committee' to plan and run an important fundraising event.

The committees of new organisations usually consist of the founders and perhaps a few friends to assist them. As the organisation develops, there is the opportunity to set out precisely what skills and experience you are looking for in your committee members, and then to go out and find the people that meet your requirements.

Administrative tasks

The administrative office of most organisations is usually an extremely busy place, where there is more work to be done than people can cope with. There are all sorts of ways in which volunteers can help:

- Addressing and stuffing the envelopes for the thousands of addresses you are sending your appeal to.
- Dealing with the response – banking the proceeds, sending thank-you letters, and putting the names of those who responded onto the database.
- Reminding members whose subscriptions are about to lapse that they should renew their membership, either in writing or on the telephone.
- Answering the telephone, acting as receptionist or being in charge of the library.
- Editing the newsletter.
- All sorts of research.
- Organising a public meeting.

Volunteer jobs should match the skills of the volunteers you are using, and the volunteers will need supervision and support if you are to get the most out of them. And you will find, if you ask, that a great many people are prepared to help.

Volunteers who raise money

One of the most important ways in which volunteers can help is by fundraising for the organisation. Again, there are all sorts of ways in which they can do this:

- House-to-house and street collections, where success depends on the numbers of collectors that you can deploy.
- Organising a fundraising event, such as a sponsored walk, a fair or a dinner dance, where a team of volunteers can be entirely responsible for running the event.
- Contacting local companies and shops to get prizes donated for a raffle.
- Selling raffle tickets or Christmas cards.

Much of this work can be done by fundraising groups. Many people really enjoy this sort of local fundraising activity, doing something useful in their spare time in the company of a group of like-minded people. Inevitably, they will be representing the organisation and people will ask them about its work. It is important that they understand what the organisation is doing and share its values, as in a sense they are acting as your ambassadors. Some induction training is helpful, so that they can be briefed about the organisation's work and meet some of the staff and beneficiaries.

Peripatetic volunteers

Another sort of volunteer is someone with time to give, but who wants to help at times more suitable for themselves. It is possible to design volunteer jobs for such people:

- Visiting donors to offer thanks and explain the organisation's work in more detail.
- Speaking at Rotary lunches and other similar events, or in schools.

You will need people for these jobs who are highly motivated and articulate, and who are happy to be given a large degree of responsibility.

Volunteer recruitment and selection

The recruitment and selection of your volunteers is an important task. Exactly as for the recruitment of a new member of staff, there should be a proper job description for the volunteer task, and the volunteers should be selected according to their ability to do that job. You can also be opportunist. If a person arrives on your doorstep and offers to volunteer, you can try to design a suitable job for them to do which matches their particular skills and experience. Recruiting volunteers can be done in one of two ways:

Recruiting people locally

Where you need a number of volunteers in one place – perhaps to help in the office or with a fundraising event – a range of recruitment opportunities exists. People occasionally turn up at your office or telephone you for information. If they seem interested, you could ask them directly if they would like to help as a volunteer.

Your publicity leaflets asking for support could offer the option of giving that support in the form of time as well as cash.

Speaking tours, an article in the local newspaper or your own newsletter, an interview on the radio – these can all be used to make known your need for volunteers.

You might even take paid advertising space in the local newspaper, just as you would for a paid job.

Who volunteers?

- You may find that the people who are prepared to volunteer are those with the least time on their hands. Busy people like to **keep busy**.
- **Middle-class women** whose children are growing up or **recently retired people** may be willing to do something useful and challenging.
- **People who have a particular connection with the cause** may be willing to volunteer out of a sense of commitment. For example, someone whose child has recently died of AIDS might be willing to volunteer for an AIDS charity.
- **Unemployed young people**, such as recent graduates yet to get their first job, might be persuaded to volunteer just to keep active. You can tell them that they will develop new skills and that this can improve their job prospects. The same is the case for people between jobs.
- If you need something done and it sounds interesting, then just ask. If you ask enthusiastically, you may find that people are prepared to help out. It is just the same as with fundraising: the main reason given for not volunteering is because people were never asked!

Recruiting people with specific skills

This needs a rather more directed approach, as you need not just a person but a person with particular skills – such as a financial adviser, an investment adviser, or someone who knows how to write effective promotional literature. Each category will require its own particular recruitment method:

- To find an accountant you could seek the help of the local bank manager or accountancy firm; or for a lawyer, contact a local law firm.
- Professional bodies and associations are a good hunting ground for recently retired people with time on their hands. You could offer to give a talk, or suggest an article or a free advertisement in their newsletter.

If you know exactly what you want, asking people if they know anyone who could do the job might eventually lead you to someone prepared to do it.

Unsuitable as well as suitable people will volunteer. So the next step is selecting from the people you have identified – which you will do through an interview and taking up references, just as for a paid job. Don't lower your standards simply because someone offers to help you. You need to take particular care where people are expected to represent your organisation in public or where they will be involved in handling money.

You will need to agree terms and conditions, and set these out in some form of 'contract' or agreement:

- The **nature of the job** to be done.
- The **hours expected**.
- The **supervision and support offered**, and any training that will be given.
- **Grievance procedures**.
- What **expenses** are paid.
- Any notice to be given on **termination of the arrangement** (by either side).
- All these need to be discussed and agreed.

Before you volunteer . . .

Being a volunteer can be demanding and frustrating. The deeper you get involved, the more the organisation will depend on your contribution. A strong sense of commitment and patience will help ensure that you do not tire too soon and drop out, or grow cynical.

Most issues pertaining to children are complex and must be understood thoroughly by those wishing to help. Plan to spend time talking and reading to understand the issues involved. Also be ready to get involved in whatever needs to be done, rather than going with preconceptions of what you will do.

Here are some suggestions that will help make you a better volunteer:

- **Make a list of your skills and resources** before approaching a voluntary organisation.
- **Be clear about how much time you can spare**. This will help the organisation guide you.
- **Don't expect to be paid**. Voluntary organisations usually do not pay volunteers. Check if they will pay for work-related phone calls, travel and so on.
- **Be prepared to work as part of a team**. Volunteering usually means teamwork.

Source: adapted from advice by CRY – Child Relief and You, Bombay

Management of volunteers

Volunteers work for charities for a wide range of reasons. Some do it because they believe in the cause and want to do something, while others do it because they want to get something out of it. Some will be there because they have nothing better to do or because they desperately crave human company after the death of a husband or wife or on retirement from a job. All can be useful members of your team. But just like the paid members of staff, they will need managing.

- A volunteer should have a clear **job description**.
- You should set them **objectives**.
- There should be an **induction** process, so that they can understand the work of the organisation and meet members of staff (who will also need to appreciate the role and contribution of the volunteer).
- You should **train** them in what they have to do, so that they can do the job effectively, and you should continue to provide on-the-job training as necessary.
- You should ensure that they have enough **information** to do their job, and that they are **briefed** about recent developments in the work you are doing.
- You should **supervise their work**, give them **feedback** on how well they are doing, and congratulate them when they have made a positive contribution. They are just like any other human being striving to do a good job. They need to know what the job is, how to do it, and whether they are doing it properly. But because they are not being paid, they need other forms of **reward** – and recognising and appreciating their contribution is extremely important.

People volunteer when asked

- 55 per cent of people said that they had volunteered in the last three months.
- 55 per cent of people said that they would be prepared to get involved in further volunteering activity.
- 1 per cent of people said that they would not like to volunteer.

Source: Charity Household Survey in the UK

Overseas volunteers

There are basically three types of overseas volunteer:

- Those who apply to and are selected by **overseas volunteer-sending agencies**. These may be young people with energy and enthusiasm, perhaps in a 'gap year' between school and university or after they have graduated, or between jobs. They may be mid-career people with specialist skills. They may be older people who have retired but who have both skills and maturity.
- Those who have **an urge to 'do something useful'** and apply to organisations they have heard about or have some existing contact with.

■ **Tourists and travellers** who arrive on your doorstep wanting to spend a few hours seeing your work . . . and then want to stay on for six months or come back in a year's time.

Each type of volunteer needs to be handled differently.

Volunteers from specialist agencies

A number of countries have agencies specialising in recruiting and placing volunteers abroad. The best known are the Peace Corps (USA), Voluntary Service Overseas (UK), CUSO (Canada) and the UN Volunteer Programme. These and many more specialist agencies are always looking out for volunteer placements. So if you are interested in having someone with a specialist skill, make contact with this type of agency.

Most of these agencies are supported by governments. So choose your country and write to the embassy, which will know if the agency operates a volunteer programme in your country. People coming through such agencies have (usually) been well screened, and so will be professionally competent and sometimes very good. There is the advantage that the sending agency provides a number of support services – such as cultural orientation and language training before volunteers start, visits and meetings during their term of service, assistance with medical problems, and good debriefing at the end of their stay. If something goes wrong, the sending agency can help sort matters out with you. If you know the skill you need, these agencies can usually find someone appropriate. The right person can be invaluable, the wrong person a disaster!

Each sending agency has its own expectation of the support you will be required to provide. This could include accommodation for the volunteer and perhaps pocket money. Contracts are rarely for less than six months, and may well be for two or even three years.

A separate category consists of young people who have just left school. They will have enthusiasm, but perhaps little in the way of practical skills and experience. The purpose of their visit is to do something useful, but also to gain valuable insights into life in other countries as part of their own personal development. They (or their parents) will usually be paying for their visit, possibly raising the cost through some sort of fundraising or sponsorship, and they will usually be working alongside other young volunteers and helping out on more basic work.

People wanting to 'do something useful'

All development organisations based in the North and doing work in the South receive a steady stream of 'offers' from people wanting to do voluntary work in a Southern country. Most are put off with a courteous reply. But there is always the one per cent of them who persists – they may have direct contact with an organisation or have heard about its work.

If you are approached in this way, one response might be that people from the North are not needed to 'do something useful'. If you need something done, you will find someone from your own country to do it. But you might like to be more flexible, feeling that the interchange of ideas between countries can be productive, and that the volunteer will be able to learn about your country and culture while working as a useful member of your project team.

First ask for details of such things as: age, health and mental health, dietary considerations, religious beliefs, interests, skills and experience, hobbies, reasons for wanting to volunteer, timing and length of the visit, financial capacity of the individual to sustain him or herself and so on. Do not hesitate to point out that the volunteer should provide his or her own health insurance, and if you are not in a position to provide accommodation or to pay pocket money, say so. Depending on the response you receive to these questions, you can then make a decision on whether or not to proceed.

People arriving on your doorstep

With the growth of tourism, more and more people with some experience of voluntary work in Northern countries are travelling in Southern countries. When they arrive to see the Taj Mahal in India or the game parks of Kenya, a few wonder to themselves whether it is possible to 'see the real country' or 'meet the real people'. And what better way of doing this than contacting the office of a voluntary organisation they have heard of? And so they turn up on the doorstep of an office whose address they have got from a directory, or from a friend of a friend.

If you can spare the time, such people are often genuinely thrilled to see something of development work and very appreciative of any explanation you can give of the work being done by your organisation. Many will want to make a donation there and then – which of course you should encourage and accept! Some will suggest that when they return to their homes they will raise money for your work from their friends. Encourage them to do this. A very few may want to come back for a longer visit, when they can help out as a volunteer. If you feel that they can really be useful to you, say yes.

7.2 Working with patrons and celebrities

Associating your organisation with a well-known personality could lift you from obscurity into the limelight.

Celebrities can help in many ways. Their presence at any function will draw others. For example, the fundraising dinner, which supporters are paying premium prices to attend, will become very much more attractive if there is a smattering of film stars and media people in attendance. They can inspire members and donors, and can turn your fundraising event into a roaring success.

Probably most important, though, is the media coverage that celebrities can attract. If, for example, a well-known broadcaster is prepared to lead a press conference announcing a new campaign, the press is going to be much more interested than when an unknown charity executive says the same thing. Similarly, picture editors of national newspapers are more likely to publish a photo of a well-known and attractive actress opening some new facility than when a local councillor is doing the same thing.

Many organisations ask well-known people to help them for these reasons, and celebrities are often prepared to give their time to the organisation for precisely the same reasons that anyone else wants to support it – they think it is worthwhile and that their contribution can make a difference. However, it is not just having the celebrities associated with your organisation, but the way you use them that will have an impact.

Finding a celebrity

Celebrities whom you might try to attract to your cause include:

- Sports personalities.
- TV and radio stars.
- Film stars.
- Pop stars and musicians.
- Business leaders.
- Prominent philanthropists.
- Politicians and retired politicians.
- Journalists.
- Writers.
- Academics and experts.

The list can include anyone who has a high public profile and is well liked by those parts of the public you hope to draw support from. Here is an example of how a celebrity can get involved in a cause:

Shabana Azmi is an Indian actress of international repute, having starred in over 100 mainstream, alternative and international films. Apart from her acting, Shabana Azmi is also a committed social activist. She has undertaken a five-day hunger strike for the slum dwellers of Bombay and has opposed slum clearance and negotiated alternative land on behalf of Nivara Hakk, the Mumbai housing rights organisation of which she is a board member.

Using celebrities effectively

You should try wherever possible to find a relevant celebrity. Somebody who has had some direct experience of the problem (if you are working with handicapped children, for example, someone who has a handicapped child) will be a much more powerful advocate for the organisation and the cause.

Celebrities should be matched to your target donor audience. Well-known people can be used in a wide variety of ways – from becoming a patron or joining your board of trustees to appearing in photo calls, launching publications, giving out prizes, or participating in fundraising events.

When asking a celebrity to help, you need to think carefully about how best they might be involved and discuss the matter with them. They will want their association with you to be a success, but the time they can offer might be quite limited.

You also have responsibilities towards them. Celebrities have their own reputations to consider, so they do not want to become associated with bad publicity or with controversy. And they may be used to a level of personal support and attention that is difficult for small organisations to sustain – everything from being given detailed instructions on what they are expected to do to having speeches written for them, being collected by taxi or car and driven back after the event, and being accompanied and looked after while they are there.

Managing celebrities

It is often said that celebrities are the most difficult of people to work with and that their presence can result in major culture clashes. This is undoubtedly true for some organisations, but couldn't be less true for others. Some well-known people demand to be treated as celebrities in all aspects of their lives; others can be deeply appreciative of the opportunity to be involved at all. It is important to build your relationship with such people carefully – as indeed you should do with anyone who contributes to your organisation in any significant way.

Because celebrities can bring you great benefits, you should treat them professionally and politely, and try to make sure that their contribution is meaningful for you and satisfying for them. In an organisation of any size, it is important to control access to your celebrities tightly. This is to help prevent them from being asked to do too many things too frequently, or indeed being asked to do things that they have specifically declined to do.

Where performers are concerned, the question of whether to pay them for appearing at an event may arise. If you want to avoid having to pay large fees in future, it is wise not to start doing so now. Most performers do not expect or want to take fees from charity events, and certainly should not be encouraged to do so. As a general rule, you should be prepared to pay reasonable expenses (but not for a convoy of air-conditioned limos for them and their friends) and only consider paying the most nominal amounts as a fee, and then only in exceptional circumstances and possibly as a donation to a charity of their choice. The possible exception to this rule is the use of musicians at entertainment events.

If you are recruiting someone for an event, they will need to have a very clear idea of what is going to happen and precisely what is expected of them. Is a speech going to be necessary? And who is going to write it for them? Will a car be provided? At what time must they arrive? And when can they discreetly slip away? Who will greet them and look after them while they are with you? Will there be a presentation of flowers or a public thank you? Who will be responsible for formally thanking them afterwards on behalf of the organisation? And so on. They will also want to be told how much their presence has helped: how many extra people have come this year, how much extra money was raised, how many reporters covered the story. Any professional will want to know that they have really been able to help and that you have got the most out of their presence.

Sometimes it is not possible to deal directly with the celebrity. You have to approach them via an agent or personal assistant. Working with an agent can be both a help and a hindrance. They will be more concerned with fees and payments, and may not want their client to do something for nothing. On the other hand, being associated with you can bring the celebrity a lot of good publicity and help create an image of a caring person. So there is some benefit to their client. Attempt to get a direct line to your celebrity supporter as soon as you can. The agent can be helpful in identifying long-range opportunities and availability (diaries are quickly filled up); they can also help you get an idea of what the person concerned is looking for, as well as their likes and dislikes.

7.3 Working with trustees and committee members

Most NGOs need outsiders to provide fresh energy and new thinking, and to contribute their particular skills to the running of the organisation. The obvious place for such people is on the management board or on one of its advisory committees.

In many organisations, management boards are a self-selecting group of people that have more to do with the history of the organisation than with its current needs. They can become stale and out of touch with what's happening, and can soon forget that they have a crucial role to play in the organisation's success. A properly structured, well briefed and motivated team of people can play a hugely important role in the life of the organisation.

One of the roles of the management board is to ensure that the organisation has sufficient resources to carry out its work and that it is doing all it can to meet the need it is seeking to address. This means having a strategic view of the organisation's fundraising potential, and ensuring that there is sufficient expertise and administration within the organisation to raise the money that is needed. So for the fundraiser, it is imperative to get people on to the management board or fundraising subcommittee who will ask the right questions, think long-term, advise on crucial issues, suggest useful contacts, and bring clear thinking to the fundraising.

The management board

The role of the management board

1. **Giving direction to the organisation:** Setting and reviewing the mission of the organisation, developing priorities and agreeing plans, monitoring progress, steering the organisation through good and bad times.
2. **Managing people:** Being responsible for the performance of the chief executive, and ensuring that the organisation is getting the best out of all its people – paid staff as well as volunteers.
3. **Making the organisation accountable**: Ensuring that the organisation is accountable to everyone who has a stake in it, including the community it is serving and those providing funds for its work.
4. **Keeping within the law:** Ensuring that the organisation abides by its governing instrument and fulfils its objectives and purposes as stated in its constitution, and that it operates within the law at all times.
5. **Managing resources:** Ensuring that money and property are used properly and to best effect, and that there are sufficient resources to cover all liabilities and to enable the organisation to keep going and develop its work.
6. **Managing itself:** Ensuring that the board operates successfully as a team, that its meetings are effective, and that all individual members are contributing and involved.

Who to put on the management board

1. **Professionals:** accountants, lawyers, teachers, welfare workers, architects and so on.
2. **Experts** in the service you provide.
3. **Clients** who have benefited from your work.
4. **People drawn from your local community.**

Qualifications required

1. A **genuine interest** in your organisation and what it is doing.
2. **Specialist skills** from which your organisation can benefit.
3. **Contacts** and access to people who will be able to help you.
4. **Time** to devote to your work.

But what do you do if you have a management board that seldom meets, does not understand its role, and has lost interest? There are several steps you can take:

- The staff team, including the executive director and of course the fundraiser, should recognise the **potential contribution** that an effective management board can make to the running of the organisation.
- The matter might then be **discussed with individual board members** who share the concern that the board is not operating effectively, and who are committed enough to want to do something.
- You could then undertake an **'audit' of the skills and expertise** you would like to have among your board members.
- **Fresh people** might be identified and approached who are willing to become involved as board members to bring these skills and expertise.
- **A plan** can then be drawn up for reforming the board, replacing those who have lost interest with new people, setting an agenda for the board, and allocating roles and responsibilities to individual board members.

Fundraising committees

Besides appointing people to serve on the management board, there are other ways in which you can bring outsiders into your organisation. One is through the fundraising committee. There are a number of different models for such committees:

1. **The fundraising strategy committee**, which reports to the executive committee. Its role is to monitor regularly and improve the fundraising across the whole of the organisation. Its role is purely supervisory – this group will not raise money for you.
2. **The fundraising advisory committee**, a looser grouping which may meet less frequently. It consists of 'ideas people' drawn from different walks of life, chosen because of their occupations or talents. It can be a useful source of inspiration for the fundraiser and can sometimes be a means of getting new ideas taken up by the organisation.
3. **The event committee**, which can play a crucial role where any sort of fundraising event is being organised. It is likely to be an *ad hoc* group specifically created for the purpose of running a ball, film premiere or other activity. It has room for both the great and good (useful for the sale of tickets!) and also the unknown but committed (useful for doing all the work!).
4. **The appeal committee**, which can be most effective where individuals are recruited specifically to help raise large amounts of money for a major appeal. Members of this group are chosen because of their ability to give substantial donations themselves and for their willingness to ask others (rich people, important philanthropists, leaders of industry and commerce, and those in charge of government programmes) to give. Meetings are likely to be rare, and the role of the chairman in leading the group and ensuring that the money is raised is crucial.
5. **The local committee**, a group that acts as the local representatives of your organisation. It will consist of the activists in a given area and will usually be prepared to get involved in any activity that is needed, including fundraising, public speaking and media work.

Sometimes the role of the committee has not been clearly thought through. Getting the right brief for the committee is as vital as recruiting the right people. It is much better to start with the correct concept of what the committee is going to do than to try to change the approach or brief once members of the committee are in place.

How to get the most out of your committee members

Collecting a group of skilled and experienced people to help you is only the first stage. Getting the most out of this group and ensuring their continuing interest and involvement is equally important. Here are a few things to consider doing:

- Give each new person a **proper induction**, showing them the work of the organisation, introducing them to some of the clients and beneficiaries so that they understand the impact the organisation is having on people's lives, introducing them to members of staff so that they understand who is responsible for doing what, and giving them printed literature about the work of the organisation (including a copy of its constitution, the latest annual report, research reports and papers, other publications and fundraising literature).
- Discuss with each person how best they might contribute to the success of the organisation and what **personal objectives** might be set for them. It is better to ask for specific contributions and commitments than just to ask people to help as required. And it is better to get people to do something significant for a limited period of time than carry out minor tasks until they grow old. If you set performance targets, they will be able to recognise their achievements.
- Agree matters like **regular attendance** at meetings, remuneration of expenses, training, attendance at conferences, and so on.
- **Review their contribution** (as a group if everything is going well, or individually if it isn't) on an annual basis.
- **Keep them motivated** by continuing to impress on them the importance of the organisation's work, showing them its achievements, involving them in discussing matters of current interest or concern, and continuing to expose them to the organisation's front-line work.

7.4 Getting the most from your donors and supporters

Your existing donors and supporters are a really important part of your fundraising future. They have demonstrated their commitment to you through giving, and you should try to retain this commitment and to develop their involvement in your organisation. In this section, we look at two important aspects of developing your relationship with your donors and supporters – saying thank you and involving them further.

Saying thank you

Saying thank you to your supporters is both an essential courtesy and a piece of enlightened self-interest that fundraisers forget at their peril. And this applies as much to grants from donor bodies (such as government departments or international donor agencies) as it does to donations from individual supporters and participants at fundraising events.

Saying thank you makes donors feel good about their giving; it tells them that their donation has actually been received, and that it is being put to good use; it gives you the opportunity to find out about the depth of their interest, and perhaps some of the reasons why they have decided to support you; and it enables you to tell them more about your work and your future plans. All this will help you to get further support from them in the future. Your best prospects for a donation are those people who have already given you a donation. So the thank-you process becomes crucial. There are many ways of saying thank you:

By letter

Some charities reply to all donations, while others reply only to certain classes or levels of donation. It can be expensive to reply to smaller donations. But there are important advantages in thanking all donors in some way if you can – as a small donation now may turn into a large donation later, or for the donor, what is a small amount of money to you may be a major commitment of money and concern for them. But if you are worried about cost, you might ask donors to tell you if they are not bothered about getting a reply (to save administrative costs).

When you do say thank you, make your reply swift – say within three days of receipt of the donation. Make the letter personal to the donor, and recognise their giving history (the length of time they have been supporting you and their level of giving). A word processor can help here, using standard forms of thank-you letters as the basis, and adapting these as necessary.

Some organisations wait to get the chairperson to sign the letter. This is not necessary – your smaller and regular donors are probably much more interested in building up a personal link with your donations administrator, whom they will be able to contact if they have a query or want further information.

By telephone

For a really fast and personal response, little can beat the telephone. This is not recommended for small donations, but is an important medium for thanking larger donors. As soon as you receive an exceptional gift, ring the donor. Thank them personally. Reassure them that their cheque has arrived safely – donors often feel concerned about committing their generosity to the vagaries of the post. Find out what prompted the gift. Find out what they think of your organisation.

Fundraisers will need to use the evenings to do this, as donors will often be out during the day. When making a phone call, try to create a sense of excitement, enthusiasm and urgency – the money will really help, it is being put to good use immediately, and it will bring real and important benefits.

By visit

Personally visiting donors who are likely to be of importance to the organisation may be a very time-consuming business. But research shows that it can be an extremely worthwhile way of saying thank you. You need to be able to identify those whom it will be worth your while to visit and those whom it is not too difficult to visit in geographical terms. The visit can be made by the fundraiser, by a member of the management committee or fundraising committee, or by a trained volunteer. A preliminary phone call can be made to announce when they are going to be in the area, and an appointment can be set up.

Donors may be wary about the object of such visits until they have actually received one. A simple chat to tell the donor more about your work and to thank them for their gift will often naturally lead on to discussion about committed giving or how they might help as a volunteer – and even about the possibility of leaving a legacy – without your having to introduce the subject yourself or ask directly.

By meeting

Where personal visits are not possible, some charities set up meetings, receptions or open days for much the same purpose. Supporters in a particular area are invited and refreshments laid on. A senior person from the organisation will give a short talk. It is important then to have staff, committee members or other volunteers present to chat to those invited to the event.

One possibility is to hold the event at your office, where all your staff and committees are available. People are always interested in seeing your offices and your facilities. Such events are usually very well received, even when all they are able to see are desks and filing cabinets. Another is to organise a site visit to see the project at work and enable the donors to meet some of the beneficiaries or the local community. It is the people that donors and volunteers most enjoy meeting at such events.

By gift

Some fundraisers offer an inducement or token in return for gifts of a certain size. These inducements have two distinct functions: some are heavily promoted by the charity to encourage a particular type or size of response, while others are tokens of thanks used to build commitment and help spread the message to others.

Paper items of low cost and high perceived value are most frequently used for this latter purpose. A special Christmas card from the president; a certificate for a pledged legacy; or a wildlife print in return for a donation of more than a certain amount. Though giving is often a private matter, some supporters welcome opportunities to discuss their favourite cause with their friends. A thank-you token or certificate of support which they can display in their home can help them do this.

By public acknowledgement

A further way in which thanks can be given is through a public announcement – such as an advertisement in a newspaper, or a mention in your newsletter, magazine or annual report.

The use of the annual report is sensible. Not only are you thus able to thank your donors, but the announcement also sends signals to others that you are interested in receiving donations and will publicly acknowledge the support you receive. If you indicate the level of their gifts, this will create a certain peer group pressure for others to give at similar levels. Perhaps more important is the credibility factor – 'If *they* have given, then it must be a good organisation'. As an organisation grows, however, this becomes no longer feasible, as the number of donors gets too large to be able to list everyone. Even then, the major donors can be listed or mentioned.

Taking paid advertising to thank donors can be expensive but may be worthwhile if there are other messages to communicate (for example that the cause has widespread or prestigious support). Remember always to get the donor's permission before you do this, as most do not expect to see their names publicly in print (and may become concerned that they would then receive an avalanche of appeals from other good causes).

Thanking your supporters

We are grateful to . . .

Arab British Charitable Trust	Britten Pears Foundation
Association of University Teachers	Comic Relief
Austcare	Christian Aid
BandAid	DES. . .

A much-used way of recognising the role of major donors to your organisation is to publish a list of them in your annual report. This is the beginning of a longer list published in the World University Service annual report.

Getting donors involved

The better your donors and supporters understand your cause, the more likely they are to give more generously. If supporters are aware of the issues and policies behind your work – of your difficulties and failures as well as of your successes – they are much more likely to become firmly committed. The effectiveness of fundraising can be enhanced by using a number of devices which give the donor a feeling of much greater involvement in the work of the charity.

Involving your supporters in the campaign

The Anti Apartheid Movement in the UK needed both to raise money from its members and to make a political point about sanctions against South Africa. They invited both their own supporters and those of the Campaign for Nuclear Disarmament to give a donation and to send in a card printed in the shape of an orange and bearing their name. A thousand oranges, each one addressed to the prime minister, were then hung on a huge model tree and taken to the prime minister's official residence. Using this method they not only persuaded more members to give a donation but got more of them active than they would otherwise have done.

	Cash response	Responders sending oranges
AA members	7.5%	20.0%
CND members	3.0%	7.8%

Regular mailings to supporters

Sending mailings to your supporters is a vital form of communication. It keeps them in touch with what's happening. It reports back on your progress and, by implication, how you have been able to use their money. It highlights successes and achievements, including major grants that have been received. It sets out future plans and further opportunities for giving support.

In communicating with your supporters, you will want them to read what you have sent, and you may also want them to respond in some way. Both of these can be difficult in a world where people are constantly receiving unsolicited information from all manner of sources. So you may want to find ways of improving the communication process. Here are some possibilities:

1. **Questionnaires:** If you have many supporters, you can profit from their strength of numbers both to inform yourselves better on what they think (and who they are) and to use their views to make important campaigning points. Sending a questionnaire to supporters in a regular appeal mailing can increase response rates. Some people will be motivated by the appeal and some will be motivated by the request to provide information.

2. **Campaigns:** Asking supporters to return cards to a government minister or to a planning authority, either directly or through the organisation's offices, can achieve much the same.

3. **Competitions:** A quite different way of encouraging involvement is through some form of contest or competition. Competitions where the chief skill required is a knowledge of what your organisation stands for can often develop greater understanding of what you are trying to do. But use this technique with care. Attractive as it may be to get supporters looking at every line of your copy for the answer to a clue, some surveys have indicated that large and regular donors do not respond well to this sort of device, which they might find too childish. But there are other sorts of competitions that you might consider: for example, the best suggestion on some matter that concerns the organisation and its work.

Other involvement techniques

There are yet other ways in which you can try to involve your supporters much more in the work of the organisation. These methods seek to provide greater understanding and to expose the donors to the people behind the organisation (staff, volunteers, clients, beneficiaries and the local community where the projects are based).

1. **Visits:** Most supporters never get to see the work you are doing. You can strengthen their commitment by inviting them to visit you. This can be done in a number of ways. Open days at your office will yield a surprisingly high level of interest, even if the office is remote from the projects you are running. If possible, site or project visits are even better. Overseas development charities have for years organised project visits for their staff, donors and volunteers – not because the much-visited projects particularly want it,

or because they enjoy the administration involved, but simply because the excitement and understanding generated by such a visit can never be replicated through less direct means.

2. **Events:** You can also get supporters more involved by inviting them to events such as annual meetings or celebratory receptions. Try to ensure that you have enough explanatory literature around, and that members of staff make a point of meeting guests and discussing the work of the organisation with them.

3. **Lectures and talks:** You can lay on events specifically for your supporters where they can hear experts discuss the issues connected with your work. This gives them the chance to understand more fully the cause you are addressing, and makes them feel that their contribution is important. You can tactfully introduce the notion that you are looking for support to develop some new initiative whose importance has been highlighted in the talk. But the essential purpose of such a meeting is not to raise money, but to build interest and involvement.

4. **Involving donors in your fundraising:** On the principle that the best person to ask is someone who has already given, you might try inviting donors to accompany you to fundraising meetings, particularly where you know that their support is enthusiastic. If they can convey something of what motivated them to get involved, it can encourage others; but equally importantly, it will cement their relationship with you.

5. **Friends' groups:** By 'enrolling' donors as members of a friends' group or a supporters' club (either free or in return for a subscription) and sending them a regular newsletter which focuses as much on the donors and what they are contributing as on the work of the organisation, you can create a sense of belonging. You can then organise special events for these key supporters. And you can also develop special appeals where you ask your existing supporters to raise a sum of money for a specified purpose. Giving them the responsibility for doing this and a target to achieve will encourage them to donate generously.

6. **Regular giving:** This has been covered in Section 6.5.

7. **Campaigning:** Many voluntary organisations have as part of their brief a message to communicate to the public and government alike. The campaigning is usually spear-headed by the paid staff, but can often be reinforced by volunteers. Involving donors in campaigning can also build commitment. Those who become involved in advocating a cause will develop a much deeper commitment to it. It is exactly these people who are likely to become your best supporters in the long term.

Fundraisers should never allow raising money to become divorced from the advocacy of the cause. Ensure that there are a number of different ways for people to support an organisation: giving money, volunteering, fundraising, and campaigning. Some people will only be able to do one of these things. However, many will want to do more, and by becoming more involved, they will strengthen their concern and their commitment to you.

Challenges for the fundraiser

1 To get the donor to give again.
2 To get the donor to give regularly and frequently, on some form of committed basis.
3 To get the donor to increase the level of giving.
4 To get the donor to give in several different ways at the same time.
5 To encourage the donor to think of giving a legacy.

Recruiting volunteers from your donors

It is sometimes assumed that volunteers and donors are two separate categories of supporter that should not be mixed. Many charities feel that they should not ask their donors to volunteer, and that they should not ask their volunteers to give money. This assumes that people compartmentalise their concern and their response – which is plainly not true.

From the fundraiser's point of view, two things need to be borne in mind. The first is that all those who are giving their time should also be given the opportunity to support the organisation by giving money. If you feel that they should be protected from other requests and encouraged in their existing support for the organisation, you might consider doing some simple market research to find out whether they would like to be asked to give. The second is that donors can be invited to become involved as volunteers in some way. Most will not have the time or the inclination. But some will, and they will continue as donors too. Even if they don't volunteer, their commitment may be reinforced by being told that other local people are working as volunteers for the organisation.

CHAPTER 8

Communication skills

8.1 Developing a brand identity

A few years ago branding may have been regarded as something that belonged firmly in the commercial sector – the preserve of multinational companies with enormous advertising budgets. Indeed, the language of branding and its association with commercialism has often prompted not-for-profit organisations to neglect the issue or even to regard it with hostility.

This is changing. Today the topic of branding is being discussed more and more by fundraisers, as it becomes clear that any organisation of any size can communicate more effectively if it regards itself as a brand. As the American fundraising journal, *The Chronicle of Philanthropy*, put it: 'Most non-profit institutions are a brand already. The question is are they defining, articulating and managing it to their advantage?'

Branding is simply a matter of understanding fully your organisation's essence and values so that you can connect more effectively with the values and needs of your various audiences. Put this way, it means that you can only communicate coherently and consistently if you understand your brand.

Effective brand management need be neither complex nor expensive. This chapter will help you understand, define and manage your brand so that it becomes an asset in your fundraising and communications.

What is a brand?

It is important to begin with a clear understanding of what a 'brand' is. Sometimes people use the term to refer to a corporate symbol or logo, or to the visual images and editorial style used by the organisation.

A useful definition of a brand is provided by Feldwick and Baker, writing in 1999: 'A brand is an entity with which consumers . . . have a relationship based upon factors over and above its functional performance.'

For NGOs, you can replace the word 'consumers' with 'donors', as donors have relationships with our organisations which are based on factors over and above our functional performance.

'Functional performance', which can be measured and evaluated, may also be an important factor, especially for larger donors. For individual donors, personal experience and values will often be a key driver; and these manifest themselves in a wide range of emotions such as trust, hope, compassion, guilt, anger, and personal empathy – all of which can be conveyed through your branding.

Beyond functional performance

Donors engage with not-for-profit organisations for a wide range of reasons, which include rational, emotional and aesthetic elements. This is good news for fundraisers, as our organisations are built on the kind of visions and the urge to tackle specific needs that also have strong rational, emotional and aesthetic attributes. For example:

- At a **rational** level, you can point to the precise achievements of your organisation over a period of time.
- At an **emotional** level, you can engage audiences with the emotive and dramatic stories that can be found in your current work and your past history.
- At an **aesthetic** level, the visual imagery and corporate identity you use will help you express your organisation and its work.

Ways in which you express your brand

- **Your name.** What meaning and impact does it have? Does it sound well established or modern? You may want to convey one or the other attribute depending on the age and attitudes of your audience. Is it memorable? Distinctive? True to your vision?
- **Your strapline.** This is the short phrase you can use to explain what you do when your name is either not yet well known or not immediately descriptive of your work. A few major international brands – Greenpeace, Red Cross, Save the Children – may not need a strapline, but most other causes will benefit from some form of explanatory text. Do keep your strapline brief – no more than five to six words.
- **Printed materials** for fundraising and campaigning. This is important both in terms of the individual items, and in the way they work to reinforce each other. You might use different images and language for different audiences, but they should all feel part of the same family. You will achieve this through corporate style guidelines (see separate panel).
- **Your office or offices** – the way they look and how welcoming you are. This will influence how people perceive you. You don't need to have a plush office, but you should be smart, tidy, welcoming and inspiring for visitors.
- **The way people within the organisation behave** and interact with beneficiaries, volunteers, donors, job applicants, enquirers, and so on. This can be an important way of enhancing (or damaging) your brand.

It is also helpful to take a relationship-based view of branding. This entails seeing your brand as an amalgam of all the relationships that people within your organisation have with people outside your organisation. Taking this approach enables you and your colleagues to see that every person in your organisation – staff or volunteer – plays an important role in communicating your brand. In fact, everything your staff and volunteers do each day will in some way have a positive or negative impact on how other people feel about your organisation.

Why are brands important for fundraisers?

The danger for fundraisers is that short-term pressures – most notably annual fundraising budgets and targets – can lead to short-term thinking. This in turn can lead to the use of fundraising messages that are at best simplistic and at worst misleading, designed simply to generate income now rather than to help build your brand.

The result of this is 'look-alike fundraising' which creates confusion in the minds of the public, who find it difficult to remember just who they have supported and why. You will find it hard to build loyalty from someone who can't even remember why they supported you! John Murphy of the international consultancy Interbrand says: 'Most branding seems to be concerned not with distinctiveness, but with sameness, with camouflaging the brand so that it melts in among all the other brands in the market. To be distinctive, to refuse to follow the herd, takes courage and it can be highly rewarded.'

While there is no magic formula, distinctive branding can certainly help to make your organisation stand out in the crowd by embodying the values and attributes that lie at its heart. Every cause is in some way unique, so a brand-literate approach to communications – one that reveals fully the unique aspects of your cause – will help you to achieve distinctiveness, and this in turn will increase your chances of attracting the attention and support of existing and potential donors.

Strong brand management can give you an edge in many ways. First, within your organisation a well-defined brand will unite people by:

- **Building on your vision and mission**, so that everyone inside the organisation – trustees, staff and volunteers – feels a sense of common purpose.
- **Reinforcing the values that you hold to be important.** These are often taken for granted, especially within small organisations, but need to be formalised so that you don't lose sight of them over time.
- **Identifying how these values shape the way you behave and communicate.**
- Organisational values are just like personal values: they only mean something when put into action.
- **Specifying how this communication will manifest itself** to the outside world. Here you build outwards from the core 'essence' of the organisation to bring the brand to life in the eyes of external audiences.

All of this will create clarity for your internal stakeholders, which can bring real benefits. Take, for example, the issue of assessing creative work. When you look at a design for a new poster or mailing pack, it can be far too easy to make a subjective judgement – you find yourself thinking about whether you 'like' the work. But you should be assessing this objectively, by looking at it not in terms of whether or not you like it, but whether or not it is accurately articulating your brand. Your brand will be a starting point for briefing and assessing all forms of creative communication, and so will help to ensure that all of your communications appear to be from the same family and add value by reinforcing each other.

There can be even more to gain with your external communications. By developing a brand that is well-defined, focused and true to the heart of your organisation, and by applying this consistently to all you do, you have more chance to:

- **Gain attention.** This is the first important step in all fundraising, particularly in direct response fundraising such as direct mail, advertising and so on. Effective branding can give you a competitive advantage.
- **Engender trust.** Consistent messaging will build recognition among donors and the broader public. This can build your credibility, which is a prerequisite for potential donors to decide to give you money.
- **Increase likelihood of donations.** Quite simply, the public are more likely to give money to causes that they have heard of and recognise, and you are more likely to be recognised if you communicate coherently.
- **Generate loyalty.** Too many donors give only once. They may give in response to a particular appeal – such as emergency relief – and then forget the name of the organisation they have given to. One-off donors are more likely to become regular givers and stay loyal if they recognise and trust you, and if you communicate in a way that reflects your core values. This applies to everything from the speed and warmth of your thank-you letters to the way in which you deal with telephone calls and respond to complaints.
- **Make clear decisions** about corporate fundraising or corporate relationships. A well-defined brand will help you see whether or not you feel comfortable working with certain companies. Is there an obvious fit between your brand and theirs? Equally, your brand could help you if you are considering a **strategic alliance** or even a **merger** with another NGO.

Taking all these factors into consideration, you will see that an effective brand strategy can help you express coherently your beliefs and values and so generate higher levels of income, as well as income that is more dependable in the long term.

How do commercial and not-for-profit brands differ?

It is worth understanding some of the differences between commercial brands and not-for-profit brands. For while we have much to learn from the commercial sector, we also need to preserve and promote what is distinctive and valuable in not-for-profit branding.

Commercial branding gives objects or services emotional resonance in order to generate consumer desire.

- This is often achieved through levels of advertising expenditure that not-for-profits could only dream of! In particular, commercial operators will often invest hugely when launching a new brand, or relaunching an ailing brand.
- While the development of commercial brands is informed by the needs of the consumer, it is driven by the need to deliver profit to shareholders.
- Some corporate brands are driven by the genuine and deeply held values of their founders, for example the ethical and social values of The Body Shop. However, the majority of products have 'invented' values, which are established and reinforced by advertising to appeal to the consumer.
- Branding is directed by brand managers, who dictate and control every message regarding their product.

Not-for-profit branding connects your beliefs and values with people's hearts and minds so as to help you achieve your mission.

- The absence of large advertising budgets means that not-for-profit brands are judged much more on what they do than on what they say. For example, Greenpeace is often cited as a strong brand. This is not because it spends a lot on advertising – it certainly doesn't – but because it puts its values into visible, effective action.
- The lack of large advertising budgets makes it very difficult for NGOs to change their corporate identity (name and logo) without reducing their recognition. While this should not be a reason for never changing your name or logo, it should be seen as a risk factor.
- Your cause and brand are driven by the vision and conviction of your founder to address a genuine need – whether this is to eradicate cancer, to save whales, to feed hungry children, to house homeless people or for other causes.
- People don't have a practical need to 'buy' what you do, in the same way that they need to buy food or soap or petrol. So the emotional connection you make with your audience is vital.
- You are having to deal with many stakeholders both inside and outside your organisation. This makes it much more difficult to keep your message focused while avoiding accusations that you are over-simplifying.

The worst instances of commercial branding could be seen as applying a thin veneer of respectability to an otherwise unpalatable organisation or product. This may be true, for example, in the cases of various sportswear manufacturers who have a 'healthy' brand image but have sometimes been revealed as having far from healthy manufacturing processes, such as using sweatshops or child labour. Not-for-profit brands need to avoid such a superficial approach and ensure that they express the *genuine values* that lie at the heart of their organisation.

Connecting personal values

For fundraisers, good brand management means not just understanding and communicating your brand, but doing so in a way that generates donations. This is exemplified by the RNLI – a volunteer service that saves lives at sea and promotes maritime safety.

The recruitment insert emphasises the dedicated and selfless volunteer spirit of the lifeboat crews. The headline, combined with the determined face of the lifeboat man, expresses the same essence and the same values as those that drove the organisation when it was founded in 1824.

Moreover, the values are expressed in a way that connects directly with the values of the target

He'll face 30ft. waves, blizzards, force 9 gales and sub-zero temperatures.

All we ask of you is £18.

audience – older people (65 plus) who place great value on high moral standards and community spirit.

This means that a powerful link is forged between the brand of the organisation and its donors.

How can you define your brand?

The following is a suggested structure for mapping your brand and identifying how it relates to your various stakeholders. Regard this as a framework rather than something set in stone. The important factor is not that you adhere rigidly to this framework, but that you properly understand the various elements of your brand and how they relate to your audiences.

We will look first at a *brand model* and then at the *brand process*. Chart 1 shows a structure for constructing your brand. It is built around a series of concentric circles, which build outwards from the core of your organisation (the essence) through to the external manifestations of your brand (the benefits).

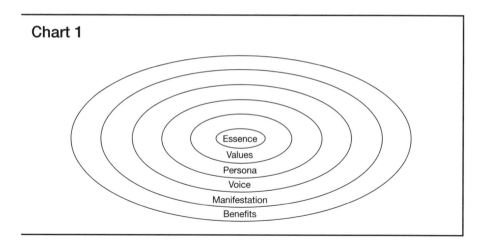

Chart 1

You should aim to develop a single phrase that sums up the essence of your organisation, and then six to eight individual words to encapsulate each successive layer.

- **Essence:** What lies at the very heart of your organisation? This is usually found in the vision of the person who founded it. The essence should not be open to change, and it certainly isn't a temporary slogan. Rather it is a fundamental objective on which your entire organisation is based.
- **Values:** Identify the values that really matter to your organisation. Almost all not-for-profit organisations will include words such as honesty and integrity. This is well and good, though try to identify values that are unique or specific to *your cause* rather than to *all good causes*.
- **Persona:** Try to think of your organisation as a person. What would you look like? How would you behave? Is there perhaps a specific famous person you would like

to resemble? But remember that not every cause can be a Gandhi or a Nelson Mandela! Another useful exercise is to imagine your cause as an animal or a car or a country. Which would you be, and why? This will all help you define a distinct persona.

■ **Voice:** Your voice flows directly from your persona. We all know many people, and each has their own way of talking. Formal or informal? Serious or light-hearted? Stimulating or dull? You may find that the voice you have now is not necessarily the one you would like to have. A brand model can help you to identify both what you are now and what you would like to be.

■ **Manifestation:** How are all the previous layers visible to the outside world? What sort of words, images, slogans and communications do you produce? Do they all appear to be driven, as they should be, by your essence, values, persona and voice?

Collect together all your leaflets and other communications materials. You may find that some look as if they have been produced by a completely different organisation. You can use your brand model for briefing copywriters and designers and evaluating all your future communications so that they become increasingly coherent and mutually reinforcing.

■ **Benefits:** Quite simply, how would the world notice if your organisation did not exist?

Of course, your brand does not exist in isolation. So the next step is to plot how your various audiences relate to your brand. Chart 2 shows how to divide your brand into external and internal audiences. This will enable you to look at how effectively you are communicating with each audience. This will then help you identify the gap between how you want to be perceived and how various audiences actually do perceive you.

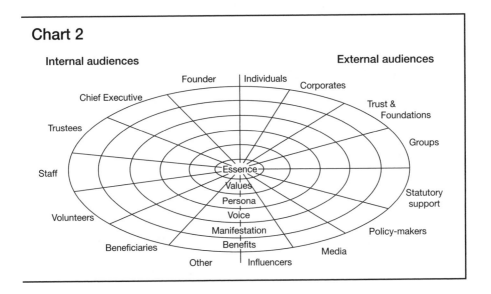

Chart 2

Internal audiences

External audiences

The audiences shown here are merely examples. You need to design this exercise specifically for your own cause. Identify where you think you may be failing to communicate effectively, and use this to inform your future communications strategy.

Developing a brand toolkit

The brand model you develop is just one element of your 'brand toolkit'. You can also develop:

- **A corporate style guide.** This will include all of your editorial and graphic design guidelines, such as:
  - how you use your logo
  - specific colours to be used in publications
  - your preferred typefaces
  - how you use photographs: for example, how you use photography to portray your beneficiaries while also respecting their dignity
  - the editorial style you prefer, including phrases which should or shouldn't be used in describing your work.
- **Short, medium and long-form messages.** These describe your cause (what you do and why you do it) and your ambitions, and may range in length from a single sentence to up to 200 words. By writing down these messages, you will help staff and journalists communicate your brand consistently and effectively.
- **Case studies** – including photographs and videos as well as written material – which portray your work accurately and powerfully, and which again can be used by staff, volunteers or journalists.
- **Key facts and statistics.** Choose three or four key facts or messages that convey the scale, scope and impact of your organisation. These can be woven into all your written materials and verbal communication so as to impress your audiences with the importance of what you are doing.

Making thank you mean more

It is possible to apply your branding to any form of communication. The examples here show a thank-you card sent to Greenpeace supporters.

The outer envelope carries the line: 'WARNING: CONTAINS STRONG LANGUAGE'. Inside the envelope we find two thank-you cards with the words: 'Thank you is one of the most powerful phrases in the whole English language.'

This approach is surprising, creative, truthful, and initially confrontational, but leaves the supporter feeling good – thus reinforcing a range of components of the Greenpeace brand.

The same can be said for the postcard used to raise awareness of the need for legacies: 'When you come back as a whale you'll be glad you put Greenpeace in your will.' This injects a rare burst of life-affirming humour into the serious business of legacy promotion.

The process: commitment from the whole organisation

Branding involves every single person in your organisation. It is therefore essential that any brand development involves a wide cross-section of the people involved. This was the approach taken by Home-Start, an organisation that provides experienced parent-volunteers to support other parents who are dealing with the challenge of raising small children.

The organisation was happy with its name and logo, but felt that it needed to bring greater clarity to the way it expressed its work. It wanted to refocus its brand. This process started with a one-day workshop involving representatives from across the entire organisation, including the PR manager, fundraisers, local project representatives, the chief executive, and the chair of the trustees. While the cross-section of views is important, it is critical that the most senior members of your organisation are involved in this process, so that they 'buy into' the ideas that are generated.

The result of this consultation was then included in a questionnaire that was circulated to all local Home-Start groups. This kept them involved in the process and gave them a chance to add their own ideas. The final result provides the key messages for all future communications.

If you look at your organisation as a brand, you will be able to strengthen your communications by doing so. You may already be communicating intuitively in a way that is right for your brand. But as you grow it becomes more and more important to formalise your branding to ensure that you continue to communicate effectively.

If you manage your brand well, this brings a whole range of benefits, perhaps the greatest of which is that you strengthen your position as a trustworthy recipient of funds.

8.2 Writing a fundraising proposal

Writing a proposal is probably one of the most important skills in the fundraiser's repertoire. The difference between a good and a bad proposal could be the difference between success and failure in getting a grant. The fundraising proposal must communicate the needs of the organisation to potential supporters, and suggest how these might be met. It is largely on the basis of what is written in the proposal that many funders will decide whether they will make a grant.

The advice that follows should not be regarded as a blueprint that will guarantee success. What it does is identify the key points to enable you to produce a proposal which matches the requirements of a potential funder, thus giving you a better chance of success. The same basic approach will apply when approaching any grant-making body, whether central government, a local authority, a trust or a company. Where differences exist, these are identified in the text.

Planning your approach

In thinking about how to structure a proposal, you need to consider who you plan to approach, what their interests and priorities are, how you will make the approach, what procedure they have for selecting and assessing grant applications, what you need to say about yourself and what you propose to do, and when you will be submitting the application. There are several factors to consider at this stage:

- **Application forms.** You should find out whether the donor requires applications to be submitted in a standard format, or if an application form has to be completed. There is nothing more frustrating than having written a really good application only to find that it should have been submitted on an application form or in a required format.

- **How many donors you plan to approach.** If you are sending your proposal to a large number of donors, you should try to make it as personal as possible to each. The simplest way of doing this is by having a standard proposal accompanied by a covering letter. Your covering letter can mention any previous contact and say how the project particularly fits within the donor's guidelines and current interests and (if relevant) whether and how the donor will benefit from supporting you.

- **The size of the donor.** Large donor agencies, major foundations and government funding programmes will need to be given a great deal of detail. They will be receiving substantial applications from a wide range of organisations. They are looking not just for good ideas, but for evidence of need and of professionalism in delivery, and for a clear indication of the sorts of outcome that are expected. Smaller donor bodies, which include smaller foundations and many companies, just do not have the time to read through a mountain of paper. They want everything shortened and simplified – a page or two at the most. If they need any more information, they can ask for it. But you should include all the important points in your short proposal.

- **The likelihood of success.** The larger the grant you are applying for and the greater the likelihood of success, the more it is worth putting time and effort into your application. Conversely, for smaller sums or where the chances of success are low, you need to limit the time you put into preparing your application if you are to be cost-effective. It is a general principle of fundraising that it is better to put more effort into doing fewer things than to scatter your efforts widely. So concentrating on a few applications where you think you stand a good chance of success, and following up your written proposal with a phone call or trying to arrange a meeting will be a better strategy. You can at the same time send a more or less standard appeal to a selection of other donors in the hope that one or a few will respond positively.

Targeting your proposal

Whom you send your proposal to will depend on a number of factors:

- **Urgency:** If you need the money really urgently, the best bet may be to approach those who have already supported you. You have already convinced them of the worth of your work, and they may be willing to support you again.

- **Scale of need:** If you require large sums of money, then you have a choice. You can either apply for a few large grants – or even one grant for the whole amount – by approaching larger donors who are known to be interested in your sort of work (or who have already supported you) or a government source. Or you can mount a wider appeal, seeking a range of large and small donations from a larger number of donors. Remember, though, if you want a large donation, you are unlikely to get all you need if you approach a small grant-maker.

- **How many donors to approach:** Donors are often interested to know how many other people have been asked and whether anyone else has already agreed to give. The general rule is to make a careful selection of those whom you think are likely to be interested. If you mention in your proposal why they might be interested, the recipient is more likely to take it seriously than a proposal mailed out widely. It will also save you a great deal of time if you can cut down on the number of applications you make.

- **Type of project:** New projects and new initiatives are more likely to be of interest to foundations and companies than simple contributions to the running costs of your organisation or the provision of a basic service. There is a skill here in constructing your proposal to make what you are doing seem new and exciting, and to be addressing matters of current concern in an innovative way. This can be simply a matter of presentation.

- **A personalised approach:** You should try to personalise your approach as much as you can, as this is likely to be far more successful than what appears to be a standard proposal sent to a lot of people. Refer to previous contacts and any previous support. Match your proposal to their interests as demonstrated by their stated interests and policies or by the other grants they have made. Try to make them feel that you are writing to them personally. This is obviously much easier to do if you are approaching just a few donors.

Content of the proposal

What to raise money for demands a good deal of thought, and there are many points that you will need to consider. You should decide whether you are seeking support for the organisation itself or for a specific piece of expenditure or project. Once you have done this, you should try to answer a series of questions, which are the questions that the donor will need to have answered before deciding to support you. Here are the questions, together with some suggested answers for a village tourism project that will enable tourists to stay in a local village and experience traditional rural life:

Question: What is the problem or the need that is to be addressed?
Answer: Local economic development. Tourism is among the most important economic development opportunities in the country. But tourism generally has a negative impact

on local communities (see the well-publicised report just produced by Tourism Concern on this subject). Our project seeks to harness the potential of tourism for local benefit.

Question: Are there any particular geographic or socio-economic factors which make it important to do something in the area where you plan to work?
Answer: The particular location of the village is ideal for this initiative (state why). The economic condition and trends in the village and the region, based on our research, demonstrate the importance of this initiative.

Question: What are the aims and objectives of this project?
Answer: To use tourism for local economic development, thereby enhancing people's incomes. To provide a demonstration model for the development of 'sustainable tourism' in our country and in the region.

Question: What working methods will be used to meet these aims?
Answer: Develop a small tourist complex using traditional village structures, which will be owned and managed by the village.

Question: What are the short- and long-term operational plans?
Answer: Open the site in 2010, marketing it through the local tourist industry and guidebooks, through eco-tourism websites and through development NGOs.

Question: What are the expected outcomes and achievements of the project?
Answer: Create a self-sustaining project, which will move into profit by the end of Year 2. Generate an annual income for the village (include income projections), which will be used for social and economic development projects. Produce a report charting the experience of developing the project. Link with Eco-Tourism International to organise a number of conferences and seminars on models for sustainable tourism to spread the ideas more widely.

Question: Do you have a clear budget for the work, and can you justify all the expenditure?
Answer: Yes! See attached budget and business plan.

Question: And what is going to happen when the funding runs out? Will the project continue on a sustainable basis? Or will you be able to identify and develop alternative sources of funding? Or will the project come to a natural end?
Answer: It will continue on a sustainable basis, while also generating an income for the village that will be used to enhance village facilities, including education and health.

Question: What sources of funds have you already identified? And what has already been committed to the project?
Answer: The villagers have contributed an initial sum, and feasibility plans have been drawn up free of charge by a prominent firm of architects who are leading advocates of

the use of traditional technologies. The budget for the project is as stated, and we are looking for support from the following sources.

Question: When do you need the money?
Answer: We plan to start work in September (in nine months' time), and we will need the money in three equal instalments paid over a period of a year.

You need to answer all of the questions as factually and as honestly as possible. This list should provide you with a structure for writing your proposal, and with many of the points you will want to include. You also need to demonstrate the importance of what you are planning to achieve, at the same time as describing your work and telling them about your plans.

Fundraising proposals should try to answer the question *why* as well as explaining *what.* The following are some of the WHYs you need to answer:

- **Why is the need important and urgent?** And what would be the consequences if nothing is done?
- **Why are you the right organisation** to do something about it?
- **Why is the method you have selected the best** or the most appropriate or the most cost-effective?
- **Why are you likely to be successful?** You can demonstrate this by listing some of the skills and resources you will bring, as well as describing your previous successes. You can show your ability to handle sums of money of a similar size to that which you are requesting, and how you have been able to deliver on your promises.

There is also the question of 'leverage'. What will the grant that the donor will be providing achieve over and beyond the actual sum of money given? Factors that are important include:

- What **other grants** can be mobilised to add to the sum being requested from that particular donor?
- Will you be able to mobilise the energies of **volunteers**, and how much value will this add to the work being done? Often this will be considerable, and you can then show how much you can achieve with a relatively small sum of money.
- Will you be mobilising **the local community?** Again, its involvement will make your project that much more effective.
- Will you be **collaborating** with other organisations, enabling you to bring in additional skills and resources? Often, their credibility can add to your credibility.
- Will the project become **self-sustaining** in some way and at some future time? Does the sum you are requesting represent an investment which will continue to bring benefit into the future?
- What are your **plans beyond the project**, to build on the work you are planning for this next phase? You should at least consider this, even if you have no firm plans at the present time.
- If the work is **innovative**, what plans do you have for dissemination? And is it possible that your success will influence how others address the problem?

When dealing with donors that have an application form, what they need to know will be evident from the questions included in their form. Make sure that you answer all their questions as fully as you can.

When approaching companies, an additional factor you should consider is whether and how you can offer something to the company in return. For most companies this will be very important, and for any sponsorship proposal it is crucial. Things to consider are: ways in which you can publicise the company's support (in your annual reports, newsletters, the local press, and so on), and the number of people who will become aware of the company's support; the interest of the company's own employees in your organisation as fundraisers or volunteers; and the proximity of your organisation to any major plant or branch of the company.

Checklist of things to include in your proposal

1. Do you really **believe in what you are doing** and the value of the project?
2. Have you got a **strategy**?
3. Have you **planned ahead**?
4. Have you selected a **good project** which will appeal to that particular donor (where you have a choice of things to fundraise for)?
5. Have you tailored your application to address the **particular interests and priorities** of the recipient?
6. Have you done enough to establish your **credibility**?
7. Have you any **personal contact**? And have you plans for using this to progress your application?
8. Have you prepared a **realistic budget**?
9. Have you been specific (and asked for **what you need**)?
10. Have you a **target** for the amount you need to raise to get the project started?
11. Is your proposal **concise, factual, and to the point**?
12. Have you assumed people know what you are talking about? **Check for jargon**, initials and acronyms, and other things that people may not understand.

Deciding how much to ask for

You will already have found out the typical sums given as grants by that particular donor through your preliminary researches. Very often this will be less than the total sum you need to raise. In such cases, you will need to approach a number of funders, asking each to contribute part of the total. There are several ways of doing this:

■ You can approach, say, three different sources, and ask each to contribute one-third of the total (or an appropriate proportion, depending on their size).

■ You can break down the project into separate components. For the tourist project described above, this might include: land purchase and basic building work; equipping the complex; marketing the project and the running costs for the first year while it gets going; producing the final report and dissemination. Each of these might be made the subject of an application to a particular donor, and in each application you will highlight the particular importance to the project of what you are asking that donor to support – as well as the value of the project as a whole.

Then there is the matter of strategy. Do you approach all your prospective donors at the same time? Or do you approach one of them first, hoping to gain their support, before approaching the others? This is something that only you can decide. If you have a funder with whom you have worked closely in the past and who is prepared to make a commitment to support the project, then the fact that you have been able to obtain their support might encourage others. On the other hand, if you have to wait to get a commitment from one funder before approaching others, this can delay the funding process.

Whatever you decide, it is important to have a funding plan, and to be able to explain to everyone you approach how you propose to raise the rest of the money you need.

Timing

It always takes much longer than you think to prepare a proposal: you should allow up to a month if you have not yet fully formulated your thoughts or if you need to consult others. There may also be a lot of information to be collected, and this will also take time. And after your first draft, some editing may need to be done – and finally you will need to produce a perfectly typed copy.

Then there are the time requirements of the funders themselves. This may mean that some sources cannot respond within the time frame you require. For example, applications for European Union funding may have to be submitted up to 18 months in advance. Government bodies have their own procedures and an annual budget cycle. Foundations may take up to six months, and smaller foundations may meet only once a year – although companies tend to respond more quickly.

There is the question of the length of time you want the money for: whether you require a single sum or continuing support for a number of years. It is frequently said that you only get what you ask for; from this it follows that if you need three-year or five-year funding, you must remember to make this clear in your proposal – although that is no guarantee you will get it.

There is the question of what happens afterwards. If your project is to continue, how will it be funded after the initial grant period? If you are applying for money to purchase a piece of equipment or a building, how will the running costs be met? You may not have all the answers now, but you should at least be thinking about the problem.

Writing the proposal

When writing your proposal, you need to consider a range of factors:

1. **Length:** There is a lot of information you could put in. If you put it all in, your application would be far too long for most funders. For a substantial proposal, this may well be appropriate. For less complicated projects, keep the length to a minimum. A page for some donors or two for others will normally be sufficient. You can also append more detailed information or a photograph or technical information to the proposal, if you feel that this will be of interest to the donor.

2. The key points: At the heart of your proposal, you will describe the needs you are trying to address, the aims of your project, and how you will achieve them. You should include as much detail as is necessary for a person who is not knowledgeable in your area. You should also give an indication as to how you would expect to measure the successful outcome of the project.

3. Your credibility: If the organisation is new or the funder has had no previous contact with you, they may well need to know who you are and why they should entrust their money to you. If this is the case, you have a credibility problem. You can overcome this in a number of ways: by providing CVs of the key organisers and others involved; where you have a well-connected committee or patrons, by listing their names; by mentioning the support you have previously received from other major donors or some government body, which will reassure them. If you have obtained press coverage, you can include the clippings. If you have had an evaluation of your work carried out, that might provide supporting evidence of your effectiveness. If you have received feedback from users, experts or others, you can mention this or include a direct quote.

4. The importance of the problem: If the problem itself is not widely recognised as being important, then references to other respected reports or endorsements by prominent people will help.

5. The budget: Your budget will always be carefully scrutinised by potential funders, and needs to be clear, complete and accurate. Most donors will not be interested in the minor details of your stationery or postage bill. What they will be interested in are the major areas of expenditure and income. You should identify capital or other one-off costs, salaries, overheads and any other major operational costs. Similarly, income estimates should show the money you expect to generate from the project itself or through fundraising. Beyond this, you may have to show how the money you need in the medium term is going to be raised, say over a period of three years. This may require a summary income and expenditure statement and a capital expenditure statement, both spread over a three-year period. Additionally, you may need to supply a more detailed budget and your organisation's audited accounts for the latest year for which they are available.

Getting the budget right

There is a tendency to under-cost proposals. If you do this, you will not raise the money you need to do your work effectively. So you should ensure that:

- You include every item that you expect to have to pay for (travel, training, and equipment may all be required, and should be provided for).
- You put in a realistic cost for each item (based wherever possible on estimates you have obtained from suppliers).
- You take account of inflation. Different funders will have different systems for dealing with this. But you don't want to find that the price of something has shot up just when you need to purchase it.

- Include administrative overheads associated with the project, where this is possible. The organisation needs to function properly if its projects are to happen; and all the costs of running the organisation need to be paid for.
- Include sums for dissemination and publicity, both within the communities where you are operating and to interested parties. Telling people what you are doing can strengthen your organisation and its work.

6. Information on the organisation and its status: It is useful to include the formal and legal information about the organisation on the letterhead. This includes the registration details and the names of trustees, board members and patrons, which can help create the impression that you are well established. This information will answer points of detail which may come up later. Some applicants include their bank account details – optimistically assuming a grant!

7. Language and jargon: Many applications are, frankly, very boring to read. If you have the skill, try to write the application in a lively, upbeat way, concentrating on your strengths, the opportunities, the desirable outcomes and your hopes for the future. This is far better than the flat language that most reports are written in. Your application is a selling document – selling the idea of supporting your project to a potential donor. Points to avoid are: long sentences, long paragraphs, jargon words which mean something to you but nothing to the reader, and waffle. Far better to have short words, short sentences, short paragraphs, bullet points and bold text to highlight key features, headings and subheads to indicate the different parts of the application, and so on. The best advice is to get someone else to read what you have written before you send it off – and the best person is someone who knows little about your work, as that is the position of most of the people you will be sending your application to. They can ask for explanations and challenge assumptions where things seem unclear to them.

8. Facts and figures: It is important to back up your claims – about the extent of the need and the effectiveness of your methods – with facts and figures, rather than relying on generalisations. Everything *may* be 'desperate', 'urgent', 'important', or 'unique', but you need to *prove* this. Try to include a few selected facts and figures in your proposal, and you can, if you want, also provide a wealth of detail in a background paper attached as an appendix to the application.

9. The human story: If you can, include case studies and examples of how people have been helped by your organisation and what they have gone on to achieve as a result of that help. This will demonstrate clearly that you are effective in helping people – which is what interests many donors.

10. Presentation: How you present your proposal is luckily not the most important aspect, but it can make a difference. Different standards and expectations apply to different donors. A sponsorship proposal targeted at the marketing director of a major company will have to have a different feel from an application being sent to a national foundation which is receiving dozens of others each day. And government agencies and international donors will have their own standards and preferred styles. Remember to tailor your style of communication to whomever it is you are talking to.

Fifteen dos and don'ts for your proposal

DO
1. Address your appeal to the right person.
2. Tailor your appeal to the recipient.
3. Include a clear statement of your NGO's functions/objectives.
4. State clearly the purpose for which the funds are needed and the amount required.
5. Break a large appeal down into manageable, realistic amounts for particular elements and items.
6. Include your latest sets of accounts.
7. Offer to go and see the prospective donor, and follow up the letter within a week.
8. Make full use of VIP contacts.
9. Keep it brief.

DON'T
1. Make your appeal letter look mass-produced.
2. Include irrelevant information or large quantities of printed material.
3. Get angry at a refusal – funders cannot support every request, even those which meet their criteria.
4. Be put off by a refusal – try again next year.
5. Feel obliged to offer expensive hospitality to a prospective donor.
6. Leave too little time – it can often take months for your application to be processed and a decision made.

Getting in touch

Skilled fundraisers would not consider sending a proposal out of the blue to anyone but the smallest and most remote foundation or company. To ensure a greater chance of success, you need to know as much as possible about whomever you are approaching. Equally, if the recipient already knows something about your work and reputation, that will be an important advantage.

For example, you will need to know:

- What constraints are imposed by the donor as a matter of **policy** (there is no point applying for something that they cannot or will not support).
- **What sort of things have been supported** in the past (so that you know their particular interests and can tailor your approach accordingly).
- **Who to write to** (their name and job title), but also who makes the decisions and who they are advised by (so you can plan any lobbying).
- Whether they expect to get any sort of **recognition or benefit** in return for their support (so you can think about this before you write your proposal).

- Their **decision-making cycle** and the best time for applications to be submitted.
- Whether proposals must be written to a **set format.**

Some reasons for refusal

A large number of applications are rejected because they fall completely outside the funder's guidelines. The Commonwealth Foundation has a series of standard letters it sends out in reply to inappropriate applications, giving these reasons for refusal:

1. The Foundation cannot support students at any level.
2. The Foundation cannot support non-Commonwealth citizens.
3. The activity is being held in a non-Commonwealth country.
4. The Foundation cannot help with general appeals.
5. The Foundation cannot normally support activities limited to one country.
6. The proposed activity is outside our terms of reference or priority areas of interest.
7. The Foundation cannot support research activities.
8. The application has arrived too late – the Foundation normally requires three months' notice.
9. The Foundation cannot support activities of more than three months' duration.
10. The Foundation does not provide capital grants.

Sending a completely inappropriate application is a waste of everyone's time. **Read the guidelines before applying!**

To find out about all of this, you will:

1. **Research** the donor you plan to approach, bringing together information from a variety of sources, and keep this information on record. A good starting point is their website (if they have one).
2. **Telephone** the donor organisation to find out the name and job title of the contact person, to check the address and to find out the application procedure.
3. **Suggest a meeting,** if this seems appropriate; or think of other ways in which you can bring your work to their attention. For large applications a meeting can be particularly important; this could either be at their offices or on your premises.
4. Invite the donor to **visit your project** to see the work you are doing.
5. **Find out** as much as you can about the decision-making process by asking the donor and by talking to others who have received support from them.
6. **Contact** any key advisers or trustees of the donor organisation to tell them about your proposal – if you can find out who they are and find a way of contacting them.
7. **Write a draft proposal,** personalised as much as possible to the needs of the donor organisation, seek comments on this and then write a final version.
8. Produce and send off your **final application,** together with (if necessary) any appended information providing extra detail.

You might want to ask (tactfully) when you talk to the donor whether they could suggest other bodies for you apply to. Care needs to be taken here, as this enquiry may present them with an easy way to say no.

8.3 Producing effective printed materials

Producing effective literature for fundraising and publicity is one of the fundraiser's most important tasks. Good fundraising ideas can be destroyed by poorly prepared or presented leaflets and reports. Good writing skills and an understanding of the design and production processes are vital.

The process of creating any printed material usually follows a similar path. The stages include:

1. **Conception or visualisation** (which may include producing a dummy or sample copy) – here you need to ensure that you are working to an economical format.
2. **Setting aside a budget**, and later on in the process getting estimates of costs (so that you keep within your financial constraints).
3. **Copywriting** and gathering together **photographs** and other visual material.
4. **Design.**
5. **Print and production.**
6. **Distribution.**

Many of these stages will be carried out by outsiders and each stage might be handled by someone different. This creates considerable opportunities for getting things wrong – deadlines can be missed as a result – and also for losing or watering down the original concept during the process. You need to decide who does what. There may be many people, within even a small organisation, who feel they can write effectively. Anyone, after all, can write a letter! You need specific writing skills to present a clear and logical case and to express your ideas forcefully. This may require bringing in an outside professional in advertising or marketing. Then you may be dealing with promotional consultants and designers. They may have the skills you need, but you have to brief them properly and be happy about their approach and their ability to produce what you need within your budget.

Two simple leaflets printed in one colour (black) only, explaining the work of the organisation. Note the use of photographs.

Principles of effective communication

You must have a clear idea of what you are trying to achieve. It is worth writing down the objectives of any particular piece of communication, and including this in the brief to the writer and designer (if you are not doing it all yourself). Is the purpose to generate awareness? To convey information? And if so, what information? To get a response of some sort? To raise money? This is especially important when it comes to annual reports which may have to serve a number of purposes. If the objective is to raise money, there must be a clear understanding as to how this is to be done. Is the brochure to be sent through the post and a postal response sought from the addressee? If so, will that response be a cash donation, a membership subscription, a legacy pledge, or what?

The next stage of the process must be to identify who you expect to read the material. If they are readers of a magazine or people on a particular mailing list, you will know something about them and their interests. Have they had any previous contact with you or do they have prior knowledge of your work? Your past donors might be expected to be fairly knowledgeable, and what you say to them will differ from what you say to those who know little or nothing about the organisation. Where your existing donors are concerned, you could try to get some picture of who they actually are. Some simple research (through a questionnaire, for example) will tell you something about their age, sex, interests and preferences, and also something about their degree of commitment to the organisation.

You will also need to bear in mind budget factors. You may have limited space (in an advertisement, for example) to get your message across. Or if you are sending out a mailing, the cost of printing all the material and the weight limits for postage will be factors. Printing in full colour will be more expensive than in one or two colours. And if you want to include photographs, have you got existing photos that you can use or will they need to be specially taken?

Ten suggestions for writers

1. Get to know your audience.
2. Use simple, direct and everyday language.
3. State your proposition boldly and clearly.
4. Feature real, identifiable cases and people.
5. Communicate the need.
6. State clearly what the reader's support will enable you to **achieve**.
7. Remember that cleverness rarely pays.
8. Avoid seeming too professional.
9. Remove any unnecessary detail.
10. Give a clear course of action.

Source: Ken Burnett, a communications consultant, gives this advice to his staff and clients.

The next stage is to set a clear deadline for when you need the materials. This is especially important if the material is going to be mailed, presented at an AGM, or distributed at a conference or reception. Give yourself a little extra time to allow for slippage, but make sure that everyone involved sticks to their agreed deadlines.

Conception

The concept stage (sometimes referred to as 'visualisation') of producing any fundraising material is important. This will generate a creative approach, a visual theme, a style and a headline or slogan.

Themes, headlines and ideas can be generated through brainstorming. This will involve putting a number of interested people together in a room; identifying the object of the exercise and the rules of the brainstorming process; then asking those present to contribute as many ideas as possible. Some may be zany, others may be done at speed, but all must be written up, so that new ideas build on old. There follows a process of refinement to select one of the suggestions or to develop an approach combining several of the ideas. From this your general approach will emerge, which can then be used to generate the actual copy.

Illustrations can enliven your publications. This is the front cover of the annual report of the Baroda Citizens Council.

You will now need a designer to produce roughs. This is an important stage, as it is the last major point at which you can turn back. If you don't like the rough design, you should ask for a new approach before too much time has been wasted. If you pass this stage and then decide a new approach is needed later on, this will cost money and you may miss your deadlines. The visualisation need be no more than the front cover for a leaflet with a sample page – enough to give you an idea of how it will feel and look.

Writing

Not everybody has the skills to write copy, though almost everybody needs at some time to communicate effectively in writing. A good copywriter can make your words come alive. However, small organisations do not always have the resources to pay copywriters, so fundraisers will often have to write their own copy.

A good copywriter requires a clear understanding of your cause and a proper briefing on what you are trying to say and to whom, together with the objectives of your communication. When hiring an outside consultant, always ask to look at their portfolio to see the work that they have done for similar organisations. Some will have an instinctive understanding of your work, alongside their flair with words, while others will be better at selling condensed milk. Though good copywriters are expensive, you may be able to find somebody prepared to volunteer.

If you are writing the copy yourself, there are a number of things to remember. The first is about structure. An acronym is useful here: AIDA. This describes the process of persuasion and communication.

- **Attention:** The reader's attention has to be attracted.
- **Interest:** If you don't identify a reason why the reader should be personally interested, you will lose their attention.
- **Desire:** The wish to support your cause is the next stage, and finally . . .
- **Action:** Headlines, pictures or strong ideas can all help attract the reader's attention in the first place . . . and this will lead to their taking action (by supporting you).

Their interest can be aroused by showing them why you exist and which needs you are serving. Don't imagine that your supporters will continue to assist you without regular reminders of the importance of what you are doing, or the human cost of ignoring the problem. Desire to support your cause is likely to be generated by an understanding that things can be changed if they give their support. Tigers can be saved, classrooms built and people in need helped, and your organisation has the wherewithal to do this. Action demands that you tell them what you want them to do and what sort and size of gift they are expected to make.

Keep everything simple and understandable. One problem is that organisations tend to develop shorthand ways of describing their work. These are useful when talking to colleagues, but can involve language that is quite meaningless to outsiders. Avoid using jargon at all costs.

Find someone to read your first draft who does not have anything to do with your organisation. Ask them to feed back what they have understood – and what they have not understood! A problem may arise when you have to agree the copy with others. Most people's reaction to checking someone else's text is to look for typographic errors and false statements, and then add their own thoughts. The result can often be an accurate but heavily qualified text that loses all its impact. Accept their comments, but remember that effective text cannot be written by a committee. They may have skills in providing the service or running the organisation, but you are the expert in fundraising and communication.

The KISS principle

An important principle is simplicity. **KISS** is the acronym often used to remind us of this:

K eep	And remember:
I t	■ Pythagoras's Theorem was written in 24 words.
	■ Archimedes Principle was written in 67 words.
S imple	■ The Ten Commandments were written in 179 words.
	■ The US Declaration of Independence was written in 300 words.
S tupid!	■ A recent European Commission directive on a minor food matter was written in 3,427 words!

Design

Design is what gives printed matter its character. A good designer can lift the central idea from the text and make it into something infinitely more compelling. You provide the designer with the written text, suggest the headlines to be used, and provide photographs and suggestions for illustrations. The designer creates the format and layout, decides the typefaces to be used for the text, the headlines and subheads (which act as signposts for the reader), and how and where illustrations are to be used. The designer also decides the number of colours to be used (usually one, two, or full colour), whether it is to be printed on white or tinted paper, and whether a block of colour with text reversed out or blocks of the page overlaid with a colour tint are to be used.

You may already have a house style. If you do, ensure that your designer is clearly briefed about it. Consistency is important, as it gives the reader a feeling of continuity and reassurance, and can also convey the spirit of your organisation.

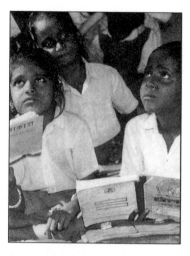

You can use pictures to illustrate your point. This one comes from an annual report of the Aga Khan Foundation, and is captioned 'Concern for the quality of education'.

Illustrations can help to bring a design to life. Photographs should be used only if they make or reinforce the point you want to put over – but they need to be of good enough quality. They should always be captioned, and the captions will be among the most-read part of your publication. The best photographs are those that show people doing things – not just pieces of equipment, buildings or groups of committee members posing for the camera. Illustrations, diagrams and plans can be used to illustrate things that cannot yet be photographed (such as the building you are planning to put up) or to make statistics come alive.

If you use an outside designer, ensure that you get a quote for the cost of the design work before agreeing to proceed. These days all but the most complicated design can be produced using a desktop publishing programme. The design for newsletters, handbills and leaflets which are published regularly can be created for you by a professional designer, and each edition then produced in-house to this pre-designed format.

Getting it into print

Getting your material printed is where you have to spend real money. You will normally seek quotations for doing the job from two or three printers in order to get the best price possible. It is surprising how much the prices vary, even on the most tightly defined jobs. This has a lot to do with how much the printer wants the job and whether what you are producing fits their capacity and their machine size. Do not be embarrassed about asking printers you are dealing with regularly to quote on new jobs. It does not demonstrate mistrust, but rather a keenness to get the best price. When asking for a quotation, you need clearly to understand the following:

For dealing with designers

- Date for the text and instructions to be given to the designer, and date by which the job must be completed.
- Visuals needed.
- Format, size and price guidelines for the job.
- Copywriting – who in your organisation does what and by when.
- Photographs and illustrations needed – what is required and by when.

For dealing with printers

- Date that the completed artwork will be sent to the printer and date required for receipt of completed job.
- Paper size (printers will use standard-sized sheets of paper; the less the wastage, the more economical the format).
- Print quantity (the unit costs of longer print runs are less than for shorter runs, but it is more expensive producing extra copies that you have no need for).
- Paper quality (it usually pays to print on stock paper supplied by the printer, which they buy in bulk) and colour of the paper (tinted paper is more expensive than white paper).
- Number of print colours (one, two or four).
- Illustrations (they can add to the cost, but increase the effectiveness of the communication).
- Folding (complicated folds will usually be more expensive than simple folding).
- Packing and delivery (the price quoted by a printer usually includes delivery to one address).

Every decision you make about the design and print quality of a book, leaflet or letter says something about your organisation and its ethos. A most obvious current issue is whether to print on recycled paper. It is hard for an organisation concerned with the environment not to be doing this, whatever the economics (and it is usually more expensive).

A similar problem surrounds the use of expensive-seeming paper. Donors expect NGOs not to waste money unnecessarily. But even though they say this, donors will always respond more positively if what you send them looks good and appears professional.

8.4 Appeal letters

Appeal letters are important as they will be sent to a large number of people, many of whom will not yet have heard about your work. Their aim is to get people to respond positively by sending you a donation; but they will create some kind of an impression whether the recipient responds or not. This awareness building is an important factor, particularly when 98 per cent or more of those who receive your letters will not respond.

There are several components of an appeal letter to consider: the envelope, the salutation, the entry, the appeal, the call to action, the postscript and the supporting literature. Though not all of these are actually contained in the letter itself, they all play their part in making your appeal effective.

The envelope

Research suggests that 70 per cent of recipients never get beyond opening the envelope. This is why you might want to include a slogan or a teaser line on the envelope, intriguing the recipient into opening it so as to find out what is inside. Alternatively, you may feel that since no personal mail ever has any advertising on the outside, using a plain envelope with a stamp may be more likely to encourage the recipient to open it, rather than immediately throwing it away as a piece of junk mail. A good knowledge of your audience and careful testing will determine the best approach.

The salutation

Once the recipient has opened the envelope, the more personal the letter inside seems, the more likely it is to capture their immediate attention. The first thing they will read is the salutation ('Dear so-and-so'). This should be as personal as you can make it. This is possible when writing personal letters, but only for small numbers of addresses (perhaps up to a hundred or so), where you can 'top and tail' all the letters personally with a salutation at the start and your signature at the end. For larger numbers, the salutation can be created from your mailing list using a laser printer, and for a few hundred letters you can then sign the letters personally. You will need to use a scanned version of your signature (if this is printed in blue, it can seem like a signature in ink). Most word processor systems have mail merge software that enables you to link a list of names and addresses with a given letter.

If none of these is possible, then fall back on a printed letter with the salutation 'Dear friend' or 'Dear supporter'. This will indicate to the recipient that a circular letter is being sent, and that you cannot do anything better than treat them as a statistic.

Grabbing attention

It took us 3,000 years to discover leprosy is curable. How long before we can eradicate it?

Source: The Foundation for Medical Research, Mumbai
Do you have a roof over your head? Do you eat at least one square meal every day? Do your children go to school? Do you have easy access to medical help? . . . For you the answer is 'yes'. For more than half of Mumbai the answer is 'no'.

Source: Nivara Hakk, Mumbai
Only one person can help this man . . . This man . . . Because we believe that people have the power to change their own lives.

Source: Concern India Foundation

The entry

You need to grab the reader's attention immediately. If this is not done, there is the danger that your letter will be thrown away before it has been read. The first paragraph you write might be the last paragraph that the recipient reads. An intensely emotional or powerful opening to the letter can make people read on. A message from a respected person or celebrity, or quoting an unexpected fact, might also do the trick.

The appeal message

Once you have gained the reader's attention, you must hold it as well as communicating all the important information needed. You will want to:

- State the **problem.**
- Show how you can **help resolve the problem.**
- Demonstrate your **credibility** by showing what you have achieved in the past and the others who have helped you.
- Indicate **how much you expect** the donor to give and what this will achieve.

The letter must be simply written and well laid out with short words, short sentences and a variety of paragraph sizes. Key ideas should be underlined, indented or highlighted.

The call to action

Join a Movement against Blindness by Filling up a Coupon
Source: Lok Kalyan Samiti, New Delhi

Unite to fight against Dowry . . . How you can help
Sakhya is a non-profit organisation largely dependent on volunteers. If you are convinced and motivated to fight against the dowry system, you could help us in various ways. We are always looking for artists, musicians, writers and others to help us spread our message. You can choose the type of work you wish to do and the number of hours you can devote. Sakhya welcomes donations too. You can contact us at the following addresses . . .

Source: Sakhya Anti-Dowry Guidance Cell, Mumbai

Your help is important
Nivara does not believe in charity. Rather it sees the development of a cleaner, safer environment in the city as a people's movement fuelled by people's participation. You can help us fight for a better city. Setting up medical services, balwadis and running legal aid for the poor is an expensive business. While we try and ensure that the poor themselves finance as much of these activities designed for their benefit, there is always a massive shortfall. To meet the ever-increasing demand for these services, it is crucial we form a large, functioning network of voluntary participants to meet the social challenges thrown up in the city. Do participate. And donate generously. Cheques can be mailed to . . .

Source: Nivara Hakk Welfare Centre, Mumbai

The call to action

The call to action is crucial, and this is the point at which many otherwise well-written appeal letters fail. Perhaps the reason is that many people are reluctant to ask directly for precisely what they want. Yet that is exactly what you need to do. Start flagging up the call to action earlier on in the letter. Repeat it to reinforce the message. And make it absolutely plain near the end what exactly you want the recipient to do. The call to action should state:

- **What you want** (money, time, goods?).
- **How much you want** them to give (perhaps quoting various sums of money and describing what can be done with each sum).

You will also need to provide the following information, perhaps on a separate reply coupon:

- **When.** How soon must it arrive (usually immediately, as you want to create a sense of urgency)?
- **How you want the amount to be paid** (usually in cash, by credit card or by standing order).
- **Who to send it to** (giving the name of a specific person to reply to will always be more effective than just requesting the payment be sent to some anonymous department).
- **Where.** Make sure that you provide a return address (this can sometimes be forgotten!).

The postscript

Save an important idea for the postscript (often referred to as a PS). This is one of the most-read parts of the letter. So use it to provide a final reason that will clinch their support or reinforce a point that you have already made. The PS can be produced in a printed typeface or in the same handwriting used for the signature.

Supporting literature

You will provide supporting information that will reinforce the message of your appeal. Don't be tempted to squeeze thousands of words of text into an accompanying leaflet that you couldn't find space for in your letter. Use all the ideas for effective communication. It is often a good idea to include photographs alongside the written text. And if you are producing a leaflet especially for the appeal, repeat your call to action.

Response mechanism

You will need to provide some way for donors to respond to you, hopefully with a donation or a pledge. The response mechanism could be a simple reply envelope with a donation coupon where they can fill in their personal details, the amount they are giving, and their credit card details – or they could enclose a cheque. Or you could provide them with your bank details so that they can pay the money directly into your bank account. Or you could provide a credit card hotline for them to telephone in their donations.

8.5 Annual reports

Every organisation will need to produce some sort of annual report. This can be an extremely useful aid for your fundraising. Your annual report is an opportunity for you to promote the strengths of your organisation, highlight the importance of the needs you are addressing, demonstrate your effectiveness, and celebrate your achievements.

Almost all your major funders will require a copy of your annual report and accounts each year as a condition of their grant. Legally too, you will be obliged to produce accounts annually. As a minimum, your report could be no more than a few paragraphs alongside your accounts. But most organisations will want to take the opportunity to do a lot more than this, and will see the annual report as an extremely useful promotional opportunity rather than just as something they have to do.

If you are to make the most of the opportunity, it is really important to identify what you are trying to achieve so that you can justify the time and expenditure involved. Here are a few important points:

- Don't use your annual report to complain. Use it to promote and celebrate.
- Use illustrations and photographs liberally. They can convey far more than the printed word.
- Don't start with long lists of supporters and committee members. You should be writing your annual report to create interest in your organisation . . . and eventually funds. It should be a promotional tool, and not just a document of record.
- But do list major donors. This recognition (you will be sending them a copy) will encourage them to think about giving again, and it will encourage others to give . . .
- Send copies of your report with a covering letter to potential supporters to remind them of the wonderful work that you are doing. This could help to generate interest as a prelude to asking for money.
- Think about to whom else you might send a copy, as a way of generating good PR for your organisation (this could include experts, opinion-formers and the media).
- Your annual reports could be a good vehicle for obtaining sponsorship. Not a large amount is needed to cover the costs of design, production and distribution. The sponsorship will be visible, as it will be seen by all your key supporters. And you could use the opportunity to mount a wider PR campaign using your report.
- If you want to use your report to raise money directly, enclose an appeal leaflet inside the report (which could be loose or stitched in).

Twelve criteria for the ideal annual report

1. A well-planned structure.
2. A clear statement of objectives.
3. A clear and understandable account of your financial situation.
4. Visible economy, which demonstrates sensible use of your resources.
5. Instant appeal.
6. Legibility.
7. Good design.

8. Well-written text.
9. Good use of photographs and illustrations.
10. Overall appropriateness of style, which provides a 'feel' of the organisation and its values.
11. Empathy with your principal audience.
12. A sense of excitement.

Based on Charity Annual Reports by Ken Burnett

8.6 Using the telephone

The telephone is an important and often under-used tool for the fundraiser. It can be used in a variety of different ways, either on its own or in conjunction with other media.

In thinking about the potential that the telephone offers, you need to make a distinction between incoming and outgoing telephone calls. Incoming calls may be requests for information or calls from people wanting to discuss making a gift. Outgoing telephoning can be used for a whole range of promotional and fundraising activities. This requires more skill (and sometimes courage), unless you have a naturally brilliant telephone manner.

Donation lines

With the increasing use of credit and debit cards to make donations, it may be sensible to have a phone line that donors can use to telephone in their donation. Some donors will want to speak to a real person, either to find out more about the organisation or to offer a large donation. Not many people would be prepared to donate $1,000 on an answering machine. You could have a dedicated telephone line with a person (possibly a trained volunteer) taking the calls. It is important to have an effective procedure in place for taking calls from potential supporters. But if you have to use a telephone answering machine, make sure that you have a good, clear message and enough capacity to record a number of calls, and that you tell donors exactly what information they need to leave. For very large appeals, you might consider using a call centre.

If you have a special number as a hotline for telephone donations, it is sensible to list your main telephone number in your appeal literature too, so that people can telephone in for advice and further information.

What can be achieved over the phone

Response rate and average pledge for donors phoned

- Donors who had already given between £20 and £34 – 61 per cent gave again, with an average of £54.42.
- Donors who had already given between £35 and £49 – 67 per cent gave again, with an average of £65.36.
- Donors who had already given more than £50 – 83 per cent gave again, with an average of £102.83.

These results were achieved by Friends of the Earth in a test which targeted groups of existing donors who had given in three different donation ranges. They tested 1,250 donors and raised £64,000 in pledges. There was an extremely high response rate for all previous donors, whatever their previous level of giving. But the bigger the donor, the higher the response rate and the larger the sum pledged.

Outgoing telephoning can be used for a range of different tasks:

- **Getting repeat donations.** Telephone solicitation can be an extremely effective way of getting repeat donations. Telephoning existing supporters is much more acceptable than unsolicited calls to potential new supporters, as you have a really good reason for ringing them (they have already given their support, and you want more of it). If you ring people out of the blue, you will find that you provoke many complaints, as people regard this as an intrusion into their busy lives. A further problem confronting telephone fundraisers is how to convert pledges into actual cash.
- **Soliciting gifts in kind.** If somebody has something you want or need, this provides a really good pretext for a call. You can make a specific request. Even if they turn you down, you could ask them for the name of somebody else to call or ask for a substantial discount.
- **Recruitment of people.** Teams of callers can be used for anything from selling books of raffle tickets to recruiting house-to-house collectors. You will be calling people who have supported you, and will be asking them to give time rather than money.
- **Membership and subscription renewals.** Where supporters have forgotten to renew, they may welcome the reminder. Additionally, this is an excellent way of finding out why members are not renewing.
- **Emergency appeals.** If there is a famine and people are dying, or if the medical costs for operating on a child need to be met immediately, that provides a sense of urgency and a reason for calling.

Phonathons

One important fundraising technique used extensively in the USA but less so elsewhere is the 'phonathon' or telephone fundraising campaign. This is different from a 'telethon', which is a television fundraising campaign, usually involving a TV programme broadcast over several hours or sometimes a whole day, where donors pledge their support by telephoning in. In a phonathon, you make a direct appeal to potential donors by telephone, by ringing up people and asking them to give. It is similar to direct mail fundraising, but with contact made by telephone rather than by letter.

There are two ways of organising a phonathon. One is to assemble a team of volunteers and get them busy telephoning supporters. The other is to use a promotions agency to organise the calling, where their employees might be selling air conditioning in the morning and fundraising for you in the afternoon.

Telephone fundraising will work best if the cause is really urgent (such as in the wake of a disaster), or if it can be made to seem so. Because the telephone is quite an expensive way of contacting people, the technique needs to be used with care. Response rates can be as high as 50 per cent when calling past donors, which is well in excess of normal mailing response rates. However, in situations where donors do not want to give by credit or debit cards and you have taken down payment details, you then need to turn the pledges into cash. To do this you will need to send a letter to people reminding them of their pledge and asking them to pay by cheque. With this and telephone follow-up, you might expect 60 per cent of pledged donations to be converted into actual support at the end of the day.

The essential tools for successful use of the telephone are the script and the list.

The script

Creating a good script for the telephonists to use is not easy, as the people being telephoned are likely to raise a huge range of issues. Unlike written communication, using the telephone gives the recipient an opportunity to interrupt or ask questions. But all the essential elements should be similar. A good script should contain:

- Information about **who you are** and about **the organisation** you represent.
- Whether it is a **good time to talk**. Anyone who has received calls at six in the evening just as the children are sitting down to a meal will vouch for the hostility this can generate. Callers should therefore attempt to ascertain whether now is a good moment to talk . . . or if not, when might be a good time. Failure to do this can seriously affect the outcome of the call.
- Reference to **previous support or past contact**. When calling people who have supported your organisation before, it is important right at the start to refer to their past help and thank them again for it. This can usefully lead into . . .
- **An introduction** to the organisation, its work and the current needs. This should help set the scene for your request for help.
- A **call to action**. Your call to action should be direct and clear. You need to state precisely what you want people to do. Getting a pledge or a verbal agreement for support is one outcome. If the people being telephoned are likely to have credit cards, getting a donation by taking their card details over the phone and completing the transaction there and then can be a better option. But you need to be registered as a merchant with the credit card company to enable this to happen.
- The **follow-up reminder**. If you have not completed the transaction on the first call, there needs to be a follow-up reminder, either by letter with a form to sign and return to you, or by giving bank details or PayPal instructions. This follow-up should be done immediately to achieve maximum response.

The list

Producing the list of people to telephone is not that easy, as most databases do not include phone numbers. If you plan to use the telephone, then include space on the reply coupons or membership forms in all your promotional literature for supporters to put their telephone numbers. If they fill in their number, this implies that they will not mind being called by you.

When telephoning individuals and companies out of the blue (known as 'cold calling'), the telephone directory is a good starting point. In many developing countries, having a telephone indicates at least potential wealth. The business *Yellow Pages*, where companies are classified by activity, can be a good hunting ground for soliciting gifts in kind.

8.7 Market research

Market research is important if an NGO is to maximise the donations it receives from the public. The more you can find out about your existing donors and those people you plan to approach, the more effectively you will be able to communicate with them and motivate them to give.

There are many different types of market research that you can carry out for a wide variety of purposes. Of particular importance are researching your own donor base, finding out what the public thinks of you, and using research to seek out new supporters. All research involves collecting data from small groups of people and extrapolating from that the attitudes of the wider public. There are three basic types of information that are used:

- **Demography**, which refers to the vital statistics of age, sex, and location of individuals in the general population.
- **Psychographics**, which denotes people's attitudes and preferences, as shown by newspaper readership, church going, voting patterns, and so on.
- **Opinion research**, which usually refers to the attitudes of the public to given issues. This might be put in a question such as 'Do you think stray dogs should be shot? Agree/disagree/don't know.'

Donor research

There will be a group of people upon whom the organisation's wellbeing depends. These may be volunteers, donors, sponsors or others. When an organisation is still very small, it is quite often just a few enthusiasts and well-wishers who are involved. At this stage, it is possible for the organisers to keep in touch with all their supporters personally. But as numbers grow, this becomes no longer possible.

It is at this point that the organisation will need to find out more about its supporters. You will want to know who they are, what they think of you, and why and how they became motivated to support you. This information will help you identify other sorts of people to try to recruit as new supporters – and it could indicate the sorts of people you have not yet been able to reach or influence. What your supporters think is important, as you are dependent on their time or money to carry out the organisation's work. If they are becoming disenchanted with what you are doing or you are no longer meeting their expectations, then you have a problem which needs addressing.

You can always chat informally to your supporters at events and open days, or on other occasions when you come into contact with them. You should be doing this anyway as a matter of course, to show that you are interested and to get their feedback on your work and the cause you are addressing. But you may want to do a more formal survey. A postal survey is the most usual way of doing this. Sending a questionnaire to your mailing list or enclosing it with a newsletter are both relatively easy and cheap methods.

There is an important issue affecting how you interpret the results of a survey: to what degree are the opinions of those people who responded representative of the whole (including those that didn't respond)? The responders are likely to be people who are more keenly interested than an average sample. If only a minority has responded, they have one thing in common – that they have responded. Do they also have other things in common? For example, if it was a long questionnaire, then only those people who had the time might have responded, and thus your results could be biased in favour of older people or those not going out to work. Poor survey techniques can lead to misleading results. To avoid this, you might want to seek professional help (*pro bono* or paid-for).

Surveying your own supporters is a great deal cheaper than sampling the views of the public at large. Your supporter survey can be relatively easy to carry out yourself, especially if you pay particular attention to the questions you ask and the methods you devise for getting the responses back to you with a minimum of effort (for example, by making the survey seem important and easy to respond to, by enclosing a reply-paid envelope, or by offering some incentive to those responding, such as a free entry into a prize draw and so on).

Not all research data is reliable. Proper samples are needed to give meaningful results. Samples can suffer from several forms of bias. One is associated with the nature of the sampling process. For example, does it cover all the areas of the country? Does it cover all age and income groups? And is the sample self-selecting, or have you only selected those who answered?

Equally important is sample size. For example, if you were to ask two people about their views in the hope that they were representative of a group of four people, you might be in for a shock. The question may be a simple yes/no attitude question, such as 'Do you agree with hanging as a punishment for murder?' Suppose that two people said yes, and two no. Researchers using a sample of two might get two yeses, or two noes, or one of each. All of these answers would have been completely wrong if the actual split for the population as a whole was 70:30. There are statistical formulae you can use to determine the sample size required to get the answer right 95 per cent of the time. If you can't afford to pay for professional expertise, you might be able to find a university lecturer or graduate to help you *pro bono* to design your sampling procedures.

Supporter surveys

Examples of questions you might want to ask, in addition to those seeking supporters' attitudes to your organisation and its work, might include:

- Age.
- Sex.
- Marital status.
- Number of children.
- Income band.
- Working status.
- Job.
- Newspaper readership.
- Voting habits.
- Religious membership.

- Trade union and other membership.
- Giving methods to the organisation.
- Frequency of giving.
- Preferred areas of support.
- Other good-cause organisations supported.
- Voluntary support (whether and how much time they give).
- Legacy support (whether they have written a will and included a charitable bequest).

With this information, you can also begin to build up a profile of a typical supporter, which will help you do two things:
- Communicate more effectively with them. If you have a picture in your mind of who they are, this becomes easier.
- Think about where else you might look to recruit people with a similar profile to your supporters.

Public opinion research

Finding out what the public at large feels is more difficult and expensive. But for some organisations it can be essential – for example, if you are trying to change the government's environmental policy, it will add weight to your argument if you can show that the public feels extremely concerned about the present state of affairs. There are a number of ways you can do this. Postal surveys are not usually effective, so are not often used.

Omnibus research is one useful technique: this is where a market research company puts together the questions from several organisations and sends interviewers out to ask all the questions in one survey. If you want to know just a few things, then this can be both quick and relatively cost-effective. If you want to know how the public are likely to react to a given appeal or style, then focus groups will be better *(see below)*; this is known as qualitative research, which is particularly useful for situations where simple yes/no answers will not do.

Interviews

These take time, require professional expertise and are expensive to organise. However, the findings can be invaluable. You can learn how your organisation is perceived, how it compares with others in the same field, what motivates people to support you, what sort of people they are, and what their attitudes are to the cause you are addressing. Professionals will construct the questionnaires to be used and conduct the interviews. You should get a well-balanced response and reliable results. One particularly important result will be the differences between the views of supporters and non-supporters. If you depend upon high levels of current public awareness of your cause for your success, this type of research will show you how well you are doing; prompted (in response to a direct question) and spontaneous awareness are two useful measures of how well your publicity is working.

Focus groups

These are useful when you want to explore some new idea prior to finalising it. You gather a number of people in one place for a period of discussion with an experienced facilitator who will help steer the conversation and record the results. A new name for your NGO, a new advertising strategy or house style, new fundraising materials, public attitudes to important issues – all these can be explored in depth this way. The groups are assembled in different locations and will include supporters and non-supporters. This will give a balance to the discussion and the attitudes of people towards the issue being explored. A report and a transcript will be provided to the client.

Research

Data on public attitudes is available from a number of sources. The National Archive or the public library system is a good starting point. Census data will contain demographic information at national and local levels. Market research companies may produce other information about people's behaviour and buying habits in published reports which may be available in business school libraries. Your local reference library or university social studies department should be able to tell you about any local research or relevant academic research that has been published. This information can be particularly important in assessing the importance to the public of specific issues and social problems.

8.8 Marketing

Effective fundraising requires a good understanding of the principles of marketing plus marketing skills. Marketing is often described in terms of the five Ps:

- Planning.
- Product.
- Price.
- Place.
- Promotion.

Although this may surprise you, the whole of this book is about marketing, which is an essential part of the fundraising process – you are marketing your cause to someone else and giving them the opportunity to contribute money and time to supporting it. This section shows the link between marketing theory and fundraising; most of the points covered are dealt with in more detail elsewhere in the book.

Planning your approach and understanding your market

A key part of the marketing process is the planning that precedes it. This should start with a clear understanding of the organisation and its work, the market in which it is operating, the other organisations doing similar things (your competitors in the non-profit, public and private sectors), and the attitudes of your potential supporters. Useful tools for developing this understanding include:

- SWOT analysis, which gives a picture of the Strengths, Weaknesses, Opportunities and Threats to your organisation.

- A **positioning map**, which plots where you are in relation to other organisations, and significant variables such as reliability, urgency, and so on – derived from how you perceive yourselves and from market research based on the public's perception of you.
- **Market share analysis**, which measures what proportion of a given sector of donated income you are currently receiving – for example, how much support in total is given by local companies, and how much of this your organisation is receiving.
- **Market research**, which identifies the attitudes of your potential or actual supporters to giving to the cause in general, and to your particular charity in particular.

The outcome of all this analysis should be a picture of those groups in the population which are the best for you to target in your fundraising – as the jargon puts it, these are your 'target audiences'.

Product: what you are offering donors

The service provided by your organisation is, in marketing terms, the product. It consists of the following ingredients:

- The actual, tangible product or service which your NGO exists to deliver.
- What the donor gets from the association with you – perhaps the satisfaction of knowing that one more child will walk, or of being publicly seen to be generous.
- The frills: the invitation to meet the child you have helped, attendance at a special function each year, meeting celebrities, and so on.

All these ingredients can be put together so that the package as a whole will appeal to your target audience. The point is that you are competing for a share of people's disposable income. You have to tempt them to support you rather than someone else. You need to make your product as attractive as you can to your target audience.

Each product you create will have a life cycle. According to marketing theory, from time to time you will need to re-promote your product to keep it attractive and in people's minds. Equally, theory teaches that every product will eventually run out of steam and have to be updated or replaced by another.

Just as each company will produce a range of products, so any NGO is likely to have a range of its own fundraising products. These might include a 'big gift' scheme which provides recognition for major donors, a membership scheme with member benefits for the mass support, a friends' group for committed supporters, and a schools fundraising scheme for young people. These can all happily co-exist, so long as they are not competing with one another.

Price: the amount you are asking people to give

Donors do not automatically know what is expected of them, nor if they want to support you, how much they are expected to give. Your role as fundraiser is to steer them towards what is likely to be achievable by you and affordable to them, and at the same time to ensure you are able to raise all the money you need.

The most obvious way of doing this is to ask for a precise amount: for example, 'We are asking each person to give £10.' However, this begs the question: 'Why £10?' The answer is to provide a specific example of what the money will achieve: '£10 can buy a new walking frame for a disabled child.' The donation may not actually be spent on that, so the appeal has to be carefully worded if you are not to create a binding obligation to spend the money in precisely the way you have indicated. To avoid any breach of trust, you should use the word 'can' rather than 'will'. Here are three ways of doing this:

1 **A shopping list** which illustrates a range of things (costing different amounts) on which the money might be spent. Donors will choose something that interests them at a price level that they are happy with.

2 **A range of levels of support** from which the donor can choose. Each will be labelled in such a way as to confer greater status on those who give more (for example, friend, good friend, best friend).

3 **A range of possible frequencies of giving** (annual, quarterly, monthly, or even weekly). You will find that smaller amounts given more frequently yield larger amounts to you. This is because people respond to the headlined figure more than to the actual cost to them.

Not only does the price you ask determine the type of supporter you get, it also determines the net amount after costs that you generate for your organisation. Costs include the amount you spend on raising the money plus the expenses of administering it. A £5 donation will cost as much to service as a £25 donation, so all of it might get immediately swallowed up by the fundraising and administration costs. Equally, a donation that continues over a long period will be more cost-effective than one-off support. There is often a tendency to ask for too little. Generally people are far more generous than you think. There is also the opportunity cost. For major potential donors, you will do yourself a disservice asking for only £50, not because this is expensive to administer, but because they might have given you £5,000!

Place: how people are being asked to give

The place of giving refers to the channel through which people give their support. This is always important. Whether it is providing pledge forms on each table at a fundraising dinner, a bucket at the door to collect money, a credit card hotline, or a well-placed advertisement in a brochure, the place of giving needs to be thought about when you are planning your promotion.

The place will also affect how people see the NGO. For example, an organisation that decides to raise money by running a series of balls or dinner dances will only interact with a certain range of people in a particular atmosphere. Equally, the same organisation could appeal to a wider audience by running a series of village fêtes. The two approaches might ultimately achieve the same result in terms of money raised. However, they are using completely different techniques, attracting quite different audiences, involving different resources and helpers, and in the process helping to create what are completely different organisations.

Promotion: how and where you are getting the message across

Promotion is about how you project yourself to the public. This includes not only the medium, but the message too. The message is conveyed by a whole range of things that are within your control. The name of your organisation and the title of your appeal send an important message, particularly if your name is well known. People recognise World Wide Fund for Nature (WWF) or Save the Children, and these names evoke images of what the NGO is doing (which may not in fact always be exactly what it *is* doing!).

How you present yourself can create an impression of credibility, urgency, dynamism, and so on. Most important is how you express your needs in your written and visual material. Are you making a rational or emotional appeal? Is it supported by human content that makes it personal? Good designers and copywriters can create the image and feel that you require for your organisation, but only if they are well briefed.

The medium of your promotion is another important ingredient. Are you going to rely on personal recommendation to get your message across? Or are you going to use other means of communication? Possibilities include TV, radio, newspaper advertising, public relations, direct-mail posters, house-to-house calling, exhibitions, company promotions, booklets, events, speaking at meetings, and many others.

The five Ps of the marketing mix are in fact interdependent: if one factor is changed, it will affect all the others.

8.9 Public relations

Good public relations (PR) will help create a positive climate of opinion and counter any negative feelings or images that people might have about your organisation, its work and the cause being addressed.

For a fundraiser the value of PR is twofold. First, it can draw the public's attention to a cause or a need, whether this is national or local. This attention will lead to a better understanding; and without this, the task of the fundraiser is much more difficult. If, for example, when you get to see the head of a local company, an article about your work has recently appeared in the local newspaper, you will now be treated much more seriously.

PR can also help position the organisation in relation to other organisations working in the same field. 'Why do we need so many NGOs all doing similar things? Shouldn't they all combine?' is a question that many people ask. Good PR can help the public recognise the special importance of your work and its particular ethos and contribution as against all the 'competing' organisations. This can help remove an important barrier to public generosity.

How public relations can help your fundraising

- PR can be used to highlight the importance of the need or the urgency of the problem.
- PR can be used to show that it is possible for something to be done.
- PR can be used to tell people of your achievements and successes – which will build the credibility of your organisation.
- PR can be used to show that ordinary people can help by making a financial contribution or by volunteering to do something, rather than just rich people or large businesses.

> - PR can be used to explain what you have been able to achieve with people's money, and how you have been able to change the lives of disadvantaged people for the better.
> - PR can be used to bring a sense of excitement to your fundraising work, which will motivate you to do better.

Damage limitation

The media relish a good story, and some stories can harm the reputation of your organisation. So you need to ensure that you are capable of countering any bad media coverage that you may occasionally receive.

For example, a newspaper might publish an article claiming that your organisation is being badly managed or that someone has run off with the money. The readership and reputation of the newspaper will be enough to do you a great deal of damage. If something like this appears, you will need to take quick action.

The first people to contact are your donors. They need to be reassured that what they have read is not true; and they need to be given all the facts. Next, you should reply to the offending article as quickly as possible. Though at this point the damage has already been done, it can be mitigated by an article or letter in reply. Then you should issue a statement to other papers and to your own staff and trustees setting out the real facts of the matter.

Sometimes you might get advance warning of negative coverage. In such cases you should: establish the exact facts; identify a spokesperson to put your case to the media; make sure that you keep the message consistent if several people are being approached for their opinion; invite the newspaper or TV station to withdraw the offending article or offer you a right of reply.

If there is some truth in the article, then your position is less defensible. In such circumstances, you should: accept responsibility for the situation; identify the immediate action that has been taken to remedy it; and invite the paper to do a follow-up, which should be in a more positive vein and which should help repair the damage.

Here are some useful guidelines for dealing with bad publicity:

- Ensure that the staff of your organisation **do not speak to the media unless they are specifically authorised to do so.** There is nothing so damaging as an inept comment from a well-meaning member of staff.
- Make sure that the accurate **facts are established** at an early stage. Then make these widely known.
- Make sure that your **internal communication systems** are working well, so that you can get any new twists to the story across to your colleagues as quickly as possible, and that trustees and supporters are kept informed.
- If you haven't already done this, draft **an emergency plan** which anticipates possible disasters and allocates responsibilities for dealing with them.

Fundraising and PR

For most NGOs, campaigning is not the primary part of their work. But many may need to campaign on a particular issue from time to time, or they may have successfully set themselves up as the 'expert' on a particular subject. This creates an interesting opportunity, since the media will naturally turn to these organisations when they have a story which needs informed comment.

You can also try to get the name of your organisation mentioned in the media as many times as possible. Hopefully this will usually be in a positive context. This can be done by:

- Issuing **press releases** whenever you think there is something newsworthy to report.
- Setting up **stunts** and other events (including fundraising events) which will naturally attract publicity.
- Holding **press conferences** whenever you think something is of sufficient media interest.
- **Writing letters** to the letters page of newspapers and magazines (see below).

Timing is all-important in media work. Not only because of the deadlines of the different media, but also because you will want to use the coverage to help your own fundraising. If media coverage is to any extent within your control, try and time it to happen just before you launch a major fundraising initiative, and target it at the people you are approaching for support.

Letters

One of the simplest and most helpful ways of creating a positive climate of opinion about your organisation and its work is to write letters to the newspapers. This can be done by staff, or better still by volunteers.

A local organisation or a local branch of a national organisation should target its local newspaper, local radio station and local TV channel (if one exists). This will enable you to get your work more widely known in your local area for little cost. The subject of your letter should be topical. If the letter is linked to a local event or signed by a well-known local personality, it is more likely to be published. But a letter that just alerts readers to new needs or new services you provide may also be published.

Answering letters from other people that have been published in the press provides another opportunity. You might also write a letter of thanks for all the help you received after a flag day or fun run, which could give you the opportunity to show how successful the event was, how efficiently the money was raised, and how well it is going to be spent.

You can also telephone in to a local radio phone-in programme – or get a volunteer to do so – in order to make a point, announce a new development, or even appeal for support in an emergency.

News releases and press conferences

When you have news to report, sending a press release to a selected list of newspapers, radio programmes and TV stations is one of the most effective ways of getting coverage for it. This could be in response to a recent development in your work, a major donation that you have received, a new publication that you have produced, research that you have completed, a celebrity becoming a supporter, or some form of stunt you are organising that is designed specifically to generate publicity for your work.

An effective press release answers these five questions: Who? What? When? Where? Why? To get your story covered at a local level, it should have a clear local angle. If you are a national organisation, there needs to be a link to a local person or a local event or a local issue. Ideally, you should write your press release in such a way that editors can use it verbatim if they wish. Some might be really interested in the story and want more background information, which you can include separately. Picture editors will appreciate a good photograph with a caption attached to the reverse.

If the event is of any importance, you might consider holding a press conference. You invite journalists and reporters to come in person to hear your story, and you can expect to be closely questioned on the project and on your organisation by those who turn up. The timing of your press conference is critical. Its proximity to other important news stories can make or break yours, though you may have relatively little control over this. For example, if there is a major political development or financial scandal, there will be little room in the newspaper for other news breaking at the same time. You also need to know the schedules and deadlines that the journalists are working to. If you are not sure, talk informally to a journalist or an editor before planning your PR initiative.

Location is important. An interesting venue can add to the feel of the story: for example, launching a campaign on climate change from the roof of the Meteorological Office. The venue also needs to be easily accessible to journalists, otherwise many won't bother to turn up. You could also think about holding a press conference at an event which is guaranteed to get good coverage itself – such as a national conference.

One way of making the press conference go with a swing is to announce that some well-known people will be present to add their views. These could be entertainment or sporting stars, or people known for their serious interest in the matter. If you are using a celebrity, having a senior person from your organisation chair the press conference will help control the questions and steer them away from the celebrity, who might not know the answer. To get your message across with no deviation or hesitation, there is nothing quite like a dry run first. If you can't manage this, you will have to give the spokesperson a full briefing.

For those who don't get to the conference, you should compile a briefing pack. It often transpires that some of the fullest coverage of a press conference comes from journalists who did not even attend. But you might never have got this coverage without having organised the conference in the first place!

Photo calls and events

The media are always attracted to the unusual, the famous and the picturesque. They will sometimes want to cover these with a photograph and a caption. You will need to find ways of publicising your work that will attract media interest, rather than expecting to arouse any interest in your fundraising itself. You need to be creative in planning your PR. And if you are to get photo coverage, there needs to be a strong visual angle that will attract editors. Once you have decided what you want to do, you can either invite photographers to come to a photo call, which is similar to a news conference; or you can send a captioned photo to newspapers with a short press release.

For example, if your main way of raising funds locally is to run coffee mornings, how might you use the media to help boost interest in these events and publicise the work of your organisation? Apart from a one-line mention in the listings section of the local paper, nobody in the media is going to be interested. You have to create that interest. One way is to use a celebrity. These do not need to be major national celebrities to be of interest to the local media (though it does help if they are). Find out which celebrities live in your area or who will be visiting the area at the time you plan to hold the press conference (the theatre, a concert or a sporting event often involve well-known people). If you can persuade them to pose for a picture, you could encourage interest in your story. Another idea is to invite photographers to come to a coffee tasting to select the best brand. Another could be to hold a coffee morning with supporters drinking from a huge coffee cup (it would be the extra dimension that makes the event newsworthy, and the visual aspect will attract the photographers).

A further idea is to organise a stunt of some sort. This need not involve a well-known person, but will use the unusual nature of the stunt to attract attention – and if it is really exciting, it could attract TV and radio as well as press coverage. A stunt built around your coffee morning campaign might involve a group of air cadets having a coffee morning in the back of an air-force transport plane in flight, or someone leaping off a bridge (with a bungee cord attached) nonchalantly sipping their coffee as if nothing were happening!

The challenge with stunts is not just having to organise them, but also selecting an activity that is relevant to your work so that the publicity reinforces the issues you are working on. Needless to say, dangerous stunts should not be encouraged, as there is the risk that if anything goes wrong your organisation will receive the blame, whether it was your fault or not.

Managing public relations

Ideally, your public relations and your fundraising should be working side by side. Some organisations see the two roles as being quite separate – with the result that the PR person does not do anything to maximise the fundraising potential of the organisation, nor does the fundraiser contribute to maximising its PR potential. Where there is someone who has a specific PR role, it is a good idea for them to discuss with the fundraiser how they can best support the fundraising process, while at the same time meeting the PR objectives of the organisation.

In small organisations, PR is unlikely be a separate function; if it is carried out at all, this will probably be by a senior member of staff or even a committee member. But however it is done, every organisation should recognise the importance of PR to the fundraising effort and to the ultimate success of the organisation.

One possible option is to appoint a PR agency to handle your public relations. You might be able to find one which works mainly with the non-profit sector; or you may be able to find a commercial agency interested in your cause and willing to take you on as a client at a reduced fee or even for free. Any agency needs to be briefed well, if it is to present your work as you would wish it to. You can monitor the results of your PR through the use of a press-cutting agency. This will show you whether you are getting media coverage in return for the money that you are spending.

However you handle PR, there should be proper coordination. Only designated people should handle links with the press, and they should preferably be channelled through one individual. The risks of any well-wisher discussing confidential issues, getting information wrong or just appearing ill informed are just too great to allow.

Contributed by Derek Humphries, updated by Michael Norton

Afterword

In this book, I have tried to describe the many sources of money that can be tapped for charitable support, some of the techniques that will help you in raising money, and some of the practical and personal skills you will need if you are to be successful.

There is a massive amount of information and advice in this book, which covers an extremely wide range of topics. All of this may seem overwhelming to an organisation just starting out in fundraising, or to somebody who has never raised any money before. I hope that you will have picked up some good ideas which will be useful to you, and that you will take heed of much of the advice, which is mostly just good common sense. But when it comes to getting started in fundraising or trying to identify new sources, new techniques or new approaches that you can use, then I have a few final words of advice:

1. **Select just one or two things** on which to concentrate that you believe can produce real returns for your organisation and in which you can be successful. Spreading yourself over too wide a range of activities will in the end probably mean that you will be able to do nothing well.

2. **Take time to think** clearly about what you are proposing, whether it is relevant, and how you might best approach the business of raising money. This thinking and planning time is important. But don't make it so long that you never get started!

3. **Find out as much as you can** from other people. Most people should be happy to share their fundraising experience with others – as you should be too. Other people's practical experience can give you a good idea of what you might expect. You can learn from it so as to do better. You can decide on the basis of what you have heard whether it is worth proceeding at all.

4. **Learn from your own experience**, and continue to learn. There is no magic answer to the problem of fundraising, no formula that will bring in the money with any certainty. What works best for you *is* best for you – and you have to discover what this is. It will be a mixture of your skills and personality, the type of organisation and cause you are raising money for, the culture and attitudes prevalent in your country and among potential donors, and the personal relations you can build with those you are intending to recruit as supporters. You can write the perfect application, taking a week to do it – and fail. You can dash off a note and make a phone call – and get the support you are asking for.

5. Remember too that there is a lot of luck involved. You are much more likely to succeed if you keep on trying. Indeed, if you give up, it is certain that you will fail. It also means that *you* should try to make your own luck. The successful fundraiser, as has been said again and again throughout this book, is someone who never gives up and someone who enjoys the business of raising money and of giving other people the opportunity to help create a better world.

My best wishes for success in your fundraising, and I hope that it will enable your organisation to thrive, and to continue to develop its important work.

Michael Norton
London, May 2009

Useful organisations

Capacity-building organisations

These organisations provide training and other support in a range of areas including general management, financial management and governance. Some work locally in a specific region or country.

Ashoka
Ashoka Headquarters Office
1700 North Moore Street, Suite 2000
Arlington, VA 22209
USA
Tel: +1 703 527 8300
Fax: +1 703 527 8383
http://www.ashoka.org

Association for Progressive Communications
Executive Director's Office
PO Box 29755
Melville 2109
South Africa
Tel: +27 (0)11 726 1692
Fax: +27 (0)11 726 1692
http://www.apc.org

AVINA Foundation
PO Box 1474
8640 Hurden
Switzerland
Tel: +41 (55) 415 1111
Fax: +41 (55) 415 1150
http://www.avina.net

Board Source
1828 L Street NW
Suite 900
Washington DC 20036–5114

United States
Tel: +1 202 452 6262
Fax: +1 202 452 6299
http://www.boardsource.org

Capacity.org
ECDPM
O.L.Vrouweplein 21
NL 6211 HE Maastricht
The Netherlands
Fax: +31 (0)43 3502 902
http://www.capacity.org

CEMEFI
Centro Mexicano para la Filantropía A.C.
Cda. de S. Alvarado #7
Col. Escandón
México D.F. 11800
Tel: (55) 5277–6111
Fax: (55) 5515–5448
http://www.cemefi.org/

The Civil Society Development Foundation (CSDF)
H-1117 Budapest
Mészöly u.4. III/3
Hungary
Tel: +36 1 385 2966
Fax: +36 1 381 0011
http://www.ctf.hungary.org

Global Legacy International
26 Trevor Place
London SW7 1LD
UK
Tel: +44 (0)779 695 1448
http://www.globalegacy.com

INTRAC
PO Box 563
Oxford OX2 6RZ
UK
Tel: +44 (0)1865 201851
Fax: +44 (0)1865 201852
http://www.intrac.org

Leadership for Environment and Development International (LEAD)
Sundial House
114 Kensington High Street
London W8 4NP
UK
Tel: +44 (0)870 220 2900
Fax: +44 (0)870 220 2910
http://www.lead.org

MANGO
Chester House
George Street
Oxford OX1 2AU
UK
Tel: +44 (0)1865 433342
Fax: +44 (0) 1865 204836
http://www.mango.org.uk

Mwengo
PO Box HG 817
Highlands
Harare
Zimbabwe
Tel: +263 4721 469
Fax: +263 4738 310
http://www.mwengo.org

The Non Profit Partnership
1st Floor Scat House
19 Loop Street
Cape Town 8000
South Africa
Tel: +27 (0)21 425 0386
Fax: +27 (0)21 425 0389
http://www.npp.org.za

Pact
1200 18th St NW
Suite 350
Washington DC 20036
United States
Tel: +1 202 466–5666
Fax: +1 202 466–5669
http://www.pactworld.org

Poverty Eradication Network Kenya
PO Box 4932 00200
Nairobi
Kenya
Tel: +254 (0) 20 445 0656
http://www.penkenya.org

The Resource Alliance
56–64 Leonard Street
London EC2A 4LT
UK
Tel: +44 (0) 20 7065 0810
http://www.resource-alliance.org

The South African Institute for Advancement
PO Box 818
Green Point
Cape Town 8051
South Africa
Tel: +27 (0)21 425 7929
Fax: +27 (0)21 425 7990
http://www.inyathelo.co.za

South Asia Fundraising Group
Surat Sandhu
D-7 / 7346, Vasant Kunj
New Delhi – 110 070
India
Tel No. 91–11–26132024/
26132086
Email: ceo@safrg.org
http://www.safrg.org

Synergos
51 Madison Avenue
21st Floor
New York NY 10010
USA
Tel: +1 (212) 447 8111
Fax: +1 (212) 447 8119
http://www.synergos.org

Ufadhili
PO Box 14041
00100, Nairobi
Kenya
Tel: +254 2 343061
http://www.ufadhilitrust.org

Union of International Associations
Rue Washingtonstraat 40
B-1050 Brussels
Ixelles / Elsene
Belgium
Tel: +32 (0)2 640 18 08
Fax: +32 (0)2 643 61 99
http://www.uia.org

Venture for Fund Raising
Unit 2801 Jollibee Plaza
Emerald Avenue
Ortigas Center
Pasig City
Metro Manila
Philippines 1605
Tel: +63 2 634 8889
Fax: +63 2 637 3545
http://venture-asia.org

YANAPAY Foundation
Av. de las Américas 4–43 y
Abraham Sarmiento
Cuenca-Ecuador
Tel: 5937 845097
http://yanapay.sphosting.com

Civil society networks

These organisations publish newsletters covering issues relevant to philanthropy and fundraising (for example, legal tax issues, impact and effectiveness), and hold workshops and conferences.

BOND
Regent's Wharf
8 All Saint's Street
London N1 9RL
UK
Tel: +44 (0)20 7837 8344
Fax: +44 (0)20 7837 4220
http://www.bond.org.uk

CEDES
Cedes
Sánchez de Bustamante 27
(C1173AAA) Buenos Aires
Argentina
Telefax: (54 11) 4865–1707/04/12
Email: cedes@cedes.org
http://www.cedes.org

CIVICUS
CIVICUS House
24 Pim Corner
Quinn Street
Newtown
2001 Johannesburg
South Africa
Tel: +27 (0)11 833 5959
Fax: +27 (0)11 833 7997
http://www.civicus.org

Fahamu
2nd Floor
51 Cornmarket Street
Oxford OX4 1BA
UK
Tel: +44 (0)845 456 2442
Fax: +44 (0)845 456 2443
Email: info@fahamu.org
http://www.fahamu.org

Idealist
Action Without Borders Inc
360 West 31st Street
New York NY 10001
USA
Tel: +1 212 843 3973
Fax: +1 212 564 3377
http://idealist.org

Institute for Global Communications
PO Box 29904
San Francisco
CA 94129–0904
USA
http://www.igc.org

Inter Action
1400 16th Street
N.W. Suite 210
Washington DC 20036
USA
Tel: +1 202 667 8227
http://www.interaction.org

The National Council for Voluntary Organisations/NCVO
Regent's Wharf
8 All Saints Street
London N1 9RL
UK
Tel: +44 (0)20 7713 6161
Fax: +44 (0)20 7713 6300
http://www.ncvo-vol.org.uk

NGONet
http://www.ngonet.org

Scottish Council for Voluntary Organisations
3rd Floor Centrum Building
38 Queen Street
Glasgow G1 3DX
UK
Tel: +44 (0)141 221 0030
Fax: +44 (0)141 248 8066
http://www.scvo.org

Southern African Non-Governmental Organisation Network (SANGONeT)
PO Box 31392
Braamfontrin 2017
South Africa
Tel: +27 (0)11 403 4935
Fax: +27 (0)11 403 0130
http://www.sn.apc.org

VANI
Voluntary Action Network India
BB-5 1st Floor
Greater Kailash Enclave-11
New Delhi 110048
India
Tel: (91) 11 642 8369
Fax: (91) 11 622 0674
http://www.vaniindia.org/

National fundraising associations

In an increasing number of countries local associations of fundraisers are forming. Local associations can be a very useful way to network with other fundraisers, and most organise networking events and conferences. There is also an informal summit of national associations which meets every eighteen months.

AEDROS
Asociación de Ejecutivos en Desarrollo
de Recursos para Organizaciones
Sociales
Scalabrini Ortiz 3562 7° C (1425)
Capital Federal
Argentina
Tel./fax: +54 (011) 4807 1697
http://www.aedros.org

Association Française des
Fundraisers
12 rue Guy de la Brosse
75005 Paris
Tel : + 33 (0) 1 43 73 34 65
Fax : + 33 (0) 1 43 49 68 77
http://www.fundraisers.fr/

Association of Fundraising
Professionals (AFP)
4300 Wilson Blvd
Suite 300
Arlington VA 22203
USA
Tel :+1 703 684 0410
Fax: +1 703 684 0540
http://www.afpnet.org

Association of Fundraisers (Singapore)
100 Clemenceau Avenue North #07–01
Singapore 229491
http://www.pc2006.org.sg

Association of Fundraisers'
Organisations
Keizersgracht 317
1016 EE Amsterdam

Netherlands
Tel: +31 20 422 9977
www.vfi.nl

Association for Healthcare Philanthropy
313 Park Ave
Suite 400
Falls Church VA 22046
USA
http://www.ahp.org

Association of Italian Fundraisers
Studio Lentati
Via Macedonio Melloni 34
Milan
Italy
Tel: +39 (0)276 00 3304
http://www.assif.it

Brazilian Association of Fundraisers
(ABCR)
Brazilian Fundraisers' Association
(ABCR)
Av. Prof. Almeida Prado 532, prédio 56
térreo (IPT)
São Paulo SP 05508–901
Brazil
Email: elarroude@terra.com.br

Council for Advancement and Support
of Education (CASE)
1307 New York Avenue NW
Suite 1000
Washington DC 20005–4701
USA
Tel: +1 202 328 2273
http://www.case.org

Dutch Association of Fundraising
Organisations and the Dutch
Fundraisers Association
Keizersgracht 317
1016 EE Amsterdam
The Netherlands
Tel: +31 20 422 9977
http://www.vfi.nl

Danish Fundraising Association
I.S.O.B.R.O.
Kloverprisvej . 10B
2650 Hvidovre
Denmark
Tel: +45 3635 9622
http://www.isobro.dk

Dutch Fundraising Association
PO Box 2047
4200 BA
Gorinchem
Netherlands
Tel: +31 183 64 1015
www.ngf.nu

European Fundraising Association
Royal Oak House
78 Back Hill
Ely
Cambs CB7 4BZ
UK
http://www.efa-net.org

Fundraising Institute of Australia
Mail Suite 504
71–73 Archer Street
PO Box 642
Chatswood NSW
2057 Australia
Tel. +61 2 9411 6644
http://www.fia.org.au

Fundraising Institute of
Austria
FMA – Verband der
Fundraising
ManagerInnen Austria
1090 Wien
Liechtensteinstraße 12/9
Austria
Tel: +43 1 315 14110
http://www.fundraising.at

Fundraising Institute of New
Zealand
Level 2 Willbank House
57 Willis Street
Wellington 6001
New Zealand
Tel: +64 (0)4499 6223
Fax: +64 (0)4499 6224
http://www.fundraising.org.nz

German Fundraisers Association
(Deutscher Fundraising Verband
e.V.)
Emil-von-Behring-Str. 3
D-60439 Frankfurt
Germany
Tel: +49 69 95733070
Fax: +49 60 95733071
Email: info@fundraisingverband.de
http://fundraisingverband.de

Institute of Fundraising
Park Place
12 Lawn Lane
London SW8 1UD
UK
Tel: +44 (0)20 7840 1000
Fax: +44 (0)20 7627 3508
http://www.institute-of-
fundraising.org.uk

Institute of Fundraising for NIS
Countries
c/o Center for Philanthropy
36-e Yaroslaviv Val of. 33
Kyiv 01034
Ukraine
Fax: +38 44 212 3150
Email: bulletin@philanthropy.org.ua
http://www.philanthropy.org.ua

Norwegian Fundraisers Association
(FFIO)
P.B 1172 Sentrum
Oslo 0107
Norway
Tel: + 47 2231 8127

Southern Africa Institute of Fundraising
(SAIF)
PO Box 2913
North Riding 2162
South Africa
Tel: +27 (0)11 794 5224
Fax: +27 (0)11 794 8054
http://www.saifundraising.org.za

Spanish Fundraising Association
Calle Ribes 9
entresuelo 2a
08013 Barcelona
Spain
Tel: +34 932 651 374
Fax: +34 932 457 150
http://www.profesionalesfundraising.org

Swedish Fundraising Council (FRII)
PO Box 2054
S-103 12 Stockholm
Sweden
Tel: +46 8677 3090
Fax: +46 8677 3091

Swiss Association for Fundraising
Professionals
Sozialmarketing
CH 1005 Lausanne
Chemin Du Levant 83
Switzerland
Tel: +41 (0)21 721 1414
http://www.swissfundraising.org

Organisations promoting philanthropy

These organisations can be a useful source of information about trends within the donor community – especially foundations and wealthy families. Some organise conferences.

Asia Pacific Philanthropic Consortium
(APPC)
RM 207–208
CSPPA Building
Ateneo de Manila University
Loyola Heights
1108 Quezon City
Philippines
http://www.asianphilanthropy.org

Association of Charitable Foundations
(ACF)
Central House
14 Upper Woburn Place
London WC1H 0AE
UK
Tel: +44 (0)20 7255 4499
http://www.acf.org.uk

Canadian Association of Gift Planners
National Office
10665 – 109 Street
Edmonton AB T5H 3B5
Canada
Tel: +1 888 430 9494
Fax: +1 780 438 4837
http://www.cagp-acpdp.org

Canada Grants Service
100–2 Bloor Street W.
Toronto ON M4W 3E2
Canada
Tel: +1 800 464 2048
http://www.interlog.com

Charities Aid Foundation
25 Kings Hill Avenue
West Malling
Kent ME19 4TA
UK
Tel: 01732 520 000
http://www.cafonline.org/

ePhilanthropyFoundation.org
1101 15th Street, NW
Suite 200
Washington DC 20005
USA
Tel: +1 877 536 1245
Fax: +1 202 478 0910
http://www.ephilanthropy.org

European Association for Planned Giving
c/o Brakeley Ltd
Paramount House
162–170 Wardour Street
London W1V 4AB
UK
Tel: +44 (0)20 7734 0777
Fax: +44 (0)16 2285 0771
http://www.plannedgiving.co.uk

The European Foundation Centre
51 rue de la Concorde
Brussels
Belgium
Tel.: +32 2.512 8938
Fax: +32 2.512 3265
http://www.efc.be

The Foundation Centre
79 Fifth Avenue
New York
NY 10003
USA
Tel: +1 212 620 4230
Fax: +1 212 691 1828
http://fdncenter.org

International Network on Strategic Philanthropy
Bertelsmann Foundation
Carl-Bertelsmann-Str. 256
33311 Guetersloh
Germany
Tel: +49 5241 81 81 391
Fax: +49 5241 81 81 958
http://www.insp.efc.be

Institute of Philanthropy
2 Temple Place
London WC2R 3BD
UK
Tel: +44 (0)20 7240 0262
Fax: +44 (0)20 7240 8022
http://www.instituteforphilanthropy.org.uk

The South African Institute for Advancement
PO Box 818
Green Point
Cape Town 8051
South Africa
Tel: +27 (0)21 425 7929
Fax: +27 (0)21 425 7990
http://www.inyathelo.co.za/

Worldwide Initiatives for Grantmaker
Support (WINGS)
Room 202, CSPPA Building
Ateneo de Manila Univerisity
Katipunan Avenue
Loyola Heights
Quezon City 1108
Philippines
Tel: +63 2926 9446
Fax: +63 2512 3265
http://www.wingsweb.org

ZEWO
Lagernstrasse 27
8037 Zurich
Switzerland
Tel: +44 366 9955
Fax: +44 366 9950
www.zewo.ch

Governmental and public sector organisations

Bilateral and multilateral agencies can be sources of funding to civil society organisations.
Usually grant-making is decentralised, so it is best to make contact with the local mission.
Please check the interests and requirements of funders carefully before submitting
proposals.

British Council
10 Spring Gardens
London SW1A 2BN
UK
Tel: +44 (0)161 957 7755
Fax: +44 (0)161 957 7762
http://www.britcoun.org

Charity Commission
Harmsworth House
13–15 Bouverie Street
London EC4Y 8DP
UK
Tel: +44 (0)870 333 0123
Fax: +44 (0)20 7674 2300
http://www.charity-commission.gov.uk

The Commonwealth Secretariat
Marlborough House
Pall Mall
London SW1Y 5HX
UK
Tel: +44 (0)20 7747 6500
Fax: +44 (0)20 7930 0827
http://www.thecommonwealth.org

Department for International
Development
1 Palace Street
London SW1E 5HE
UK
Tel: +44 (0)20 7023 0000
Fax: +44 (0)20 7023 0019
http://www.dfid.gov.uk

European Union
http://europa.eu
International Labour Organisation
4 route des Morillons
CH-1211 Genève 22
Switzerland
Tel: +41 (0) 22 799 6111
Fax: +41 (0) 22 798 8685
Email: ilo@ilo.org
http://www.ilo.org

Organisation for Economic Cooperation
and Development
Co-operation and Development (OECD)
2 rue André Pascal
F-75775 Paris

Cedex 16
France
Tel: +33 1 45 24 82 00
http://www.oecd.org

SIDA
Valhallavagen 199
105 25 Stockholm
Sweden
Tel: +46 (0)8 698 50 00
Fax: +46 (0)8 20 88 64
http://www.sida.org

**United Nations Development
Programme (UNDP)**
One United Nations Plaza
New York NY 10017
USA
Fax: +1 212 906 5364
http://www.undp.org

**United Nations Environment
Programme**
United Nations Avenue
Gigiri
PO Box 30552
Nairobi
Kenya
Tel: +254 2 621234

Fax: +254 2 624489
http://www.unep.org

United Nations Population Fund
UNFPA
220 East 42nd St
New York NY 10017
USA
Tel: +1 212–297–5000
http://www.unfpa.org

US Aid
US Agency for International
Development Information Center
Ronald Reagan Building
Washington DC 20523–100
USA
Tel: +1 202 712 4810
Fax: +1 202 216 3524
http://www.usaid.gov

World Bank Development Gateway
1889 F Street, NW, Second Floor
Washington DC 20006
USA
Tel: +1.202.572.9200
Fax: +1 202 572 9290
info@dgfoundation.org
http://www.developmentgateway.org

Educational organisations

A number of universities and business schools run programmes in philanthropy, social
enterprise and corporate social responsibility. Some offer scholarship programmes.

Cass Business School
106 Bunhill Row
London EC1Y 8TZ
UK
www.cass.city.ac.uk

**Indiana University Center on
Philanthropy**
550 W. North St. #301

Indianapolis IN 46202–3272
USA
Tel: +1 317 274 4200
Fax: +1 317 684 8900
http://www.philanthropy.iupui.edu

Institute of Development Studies
Brighton BN1 9RE
UK

Tel: +44 (0)12 73 606261
Fax: +44 (0)12 73 621202
http://www.ids.ac.uk/ids

The Johns Hopkins University
School of Advanced International
Studies
1740 Massachusetts Avenue NW
Washington DC 20036–1983
USA
Tel: +1 202 663 5600
http://www.jhu.edu

London School of Economics (LSE)
Houghton Street
London WC2A 2AE
UK
Tel: +44 (0)20 7405 7686
http://www.lse.ac.uk

**New York University School of
Continuing and Professional Studies**
Room 201
145 4th Avenue
New York NY 10003
USA
www.scps.nyu.edu

The Social Enterprise Academy
Thorn House
5 Rose Street
Edinburgh EH2 2PR
UK
Tel: +44 (0) 131 243 2670
www.theacademy-ssea.org

**The Hauser Center for Nonprofit
Organizations at Harvard University**
John F. Kennedy School of
Government
Harvard University
79 John F. Kennedy Street Box #143
Cambridge MA 02138
USA

Tel: (617) 496–5675
Fax: (617) 495–0996
http://www.hks.harvard.edu/hauser

Skoll Centre for Social Entrepreneurship
Saïd Business School
University of Oxford
1 Park End Street
Oxford OX1 1HP
UK
Tel: +44 (0)1865 288838
http://www.sbs.ox.ac.uk

Saint Mary's University of Minnesota
700 Terrace Heights
Winona MN 55987–1399
USA
www.smumn.edu

University of Cambridge
Madingly Hall
Madingly
Cambridge CB23 8AQ
UK
www.cont-ed.cam.ac.uk

The University of Hull
Scarborough Campus
Filey Road
Scarborough YO11 3AZ
UK
Tel: +44 (0) 1723 362392
www.hull.ac.uk

The Westminster Schools
1424 West Paces
Atlanta
Georgia 30327
USA
Tel: + 404 355 8673
www.westminster.net/about_us/
education.asp

Research- and publication-based organisations

The following organisations publish research relevant to fundraising and philanthropy. Some can be of an academic nature, but some of it is aimed at practitioners.

ALliance Publishing Trust APT
24 Weydown Hill Road
Farnham
Surrey GU9 8NX
UK
Tel: +44 (0) 1252 737504
Fax: +44 (0)20 7833 8347
http://www.alliancemagazine.org/en/
content/alliance-publishing-trust

Association for Research on Nonprofit Organisations and Voluntary Action (ARNOVA)
550 West North St.
Suite 301
Indianapolis IN 46202–3272
USA
Tel: +1 317–684–2120
Fax: +1 317–684–2128
http://www.arnova.org

Centre for Effective Philanthropy
675 Massachusetts Avenue
7th Floor
Cambridge MA 02139
USA
Tel: +1 617 492 0800
Fax: +1 617 492 0888
http://www.effectivephilanthropy.org

Council of Foundations
1828 L Street NW
Suite 300
Washington DC 20036
USA
Tel: +1 202 466 6512
Fax: +1 202 785 3926
http://www.cof.org

Development Research Capacity in the UK and Ireland
http://www.devstud.org.uk/research
guide

Directory of Social Change
24 Stephenson Way
London NW1 2DP
UK
Tel: 020 7391 4800
Fax: 020 7391 4808
http://www.dsc.org.uk

Guidestar
4801 Courthouse Street
Suite 220
Williamsburg VA 23188
USA
Tel: +1 757 229 4631
http/www.guidestar.org

Innovation and Development Centre
Desiatynna Str. 4/6
Box 228 2nd floor
252025 Kyiv-25
Ukraine
Tel: +380 44 229 1748
Fax: +380 44 220 6063
http://www.voiceinternational.org/idc/

International Society for Third-Sector Research ISTR
559 Wyman Park Building
3400 N. Charles Street
Baltimore
Maryland 21218–2688
USA
Tel: +410 516 4678
Fax: +410 516 4870

http://www.istr.org

**International Centre for
Non-for-Profit Law**
1126 16th Street NW
Suite 400
Washington DC 2005
USA
Tel: +1 202 452 8600
Fax: +1 202 452 8555
http://www.icnl.org

Internet Nonprofit Centre
The Evergreen State Society
PO Box 20682
Seattle WA 98102–0682
USA
http://www.nonprofits.org

NGO Voice
43 avenue Louise
B-1050 Brussels
Belgium
Tel: +32 2 5411 360
Fax: +32 2 5349 953
http://www.ngovoice.org

**OneWorld International
Foundation**
2nd Floor River House
143/145 Farringdon Road
London EC1R 3AB
UK
Tel: +44 (0) 20 7239 1400
Fax: +44 (0) 20 7833 8345
http://www.oneworld.net

**OSSREA
Organization for Social Science
Research in Eastern and Southern
Africa**
PO Box 31971
Addis Ababa
Ethiopia
Tel: +251 1 55 11 63
Fax: +251 1 55 13 99
http://www.ossrea.net

Participatory Research in Asia (PRIA)
42 Tughlakabad
Institutional Area
New Delhi 110062
India
Tel: +91 11 2995 8599
Fax: +91 11 2995 5819
http://www.pria.org

Professional Fundraising
41 North Road
London N7 9DP
UK
http://www.professionalfundraising.co.uk

SOFII
http://www.sofii.org
TGCI – The Grantmanship Center
5th Floor
1125 W 6th Street
Los Angeles CA 90017
USA
Tel: +1 213 482 9860
Fax: +1 213 482 9863
http://www.tgci.com

Social enterprise

The term 'social enterprise' usually denotes an organisation serving a social purpose which generates all or most of its revenues through fees for goods and services. Some people see this as an alternative model to traditional philanthropy. The organisations listed promote and support social enterprises.

Blendedvalue.org
http://www.blendedvalue.org

Community Action Network
The CAN Centre
Mezzanine Floor
Elizabeth House
39 York Road
London SE1 7NQ
UK
Tel: 0845 456 2537
Fax: 0845 456 2538
http://www.can-online.org.uk

Global Links Initiative
2 Ballinger Grange
Ballinger
Great Missenden
Buckinghamshire HP16 9LQ
UK
Tel : +44 (0)1494 864687
http://www.glinet.org/splash.asp

INAISE
rue de la Science 10
B-1000 Brussels
Belgium
Tel: + 32 2 230 16 07
Fax: + 32 2 230 49 65
http://www.inaise.org

Impetus Trust
Office 1607
16–19 Southampton Place
London WC1A 2AJ
UK
Tel: +44 (0)20 7745 7203
http://www.impetus.org.uk

NESsT International
4401 Tahama Lane
Turlock
CA 95382
USA
Tel: +(1 209) 988–9604
Fax: +(1 815) 846–1775
http://www.nesst.org

Omidyar Network
1991 Broadway
Suite 200
Redwood City
CA 94063–1958
USA
http://www.omidyar.net

Prince of Wales's International Business Leaders Forum
15–16 Cornwall Terrace
Regent's Park
London NW1 4QP
UK
Tel: +44 (0)20 7467 3600
www.iblf.org

Skoll Foundation
250 University Avenue Suite 200
Palo Alto
CA 94301
USA
Tel: 650.331.1031
Fax: 650.331.1033
http://www.skollfoundation.org

Social Enterprise Alliance
43 South Cassady Avenue
Columbus

OH 43209
USA
Tel: (614) 235–0230
http://www.se-alliance.org

Social Venture Network
PO Box 29221
San Francisco
CA 94129–0221
USA
Tel: +1 415–561–6501
Fax: +1 415–561–6435
Email: svn@svn.org
http://www.svn.org

Social Venture Network Europe
Kalkovenweg 30
2401 LK Alphen a/d Rijn
Tel: 172 – 423 845
Tel (SVN Europe): 31 172 – 423 845
Fax: (for both) 31 172 – 423 841
Email: info@svneurope.com
http://www.svneurope.com

**Social Venture Network – Asia
(Thailand)**
333 Soi Rungsang
Bangna-Trad Road
Bangna
Bangkok 10260
Thailand
Tel: 662 361 3311
Fax: 662 399 4874
Email: prida@pranda.co.th
http://www.geocities.com/svnasia

World Resources Institute
10 G Street, NE (Suite 800)
Washington
DC 20002
USA
Tel: 1+202/729–7600
Fax:1+202/729–7610
http://www.wri.org/

Online giving

In the past few years a number of websites have been launched that enable donors to give directly to specific NGOs or projects. The process for getting a project accepted varies from one site to the next. Some charge a fee and/or deduct a percentage of any funds donated to cover overheads. Please check the criteria for each site carefully.

Give 2 Asia
465 California Street
9th Floor
San Francisco
California 94104–1832
USA
Tel: +1 415 743 3336
Fax: +1 415 392 8863
http://www.give2asia.org

Give to Brazil
http://www.givetobrazil.com

Give to Colombia
Cra 9A No. 99–02, Of. 802
Bogota
Colombia
Tel: +57 618 3146
Fax: +57 618 3003
http://www.givetocolombia.org

GiveIndia
3rd Floor
West Khetwadi Municipal School
Khetwadi Lane No 5
Mumbai – 400 004

Maharashtra
India
Tel: +91 022 2389 4944
http://www.giveindia.org

Global Giving
The Global Giving Foundation
1816 12th Street NW
Washington DC 20009
USA
Tel: +1 202 232 5784
Fax: +1 202 232 0534
http://www.globalgiving.com

HelpArgentina
Luis Saenz Peña 310,
piso 3
C1110AAD -
Ciudad Autónoma de
Buenos Aires
Tel: (54–11) 4381–5444
http://www.helpargentina.org

Kiva
http://www.kiva.org/

MyC4
MyC3 A/S
Frederiksholms Kanal 4,4.
DK-1220 Copenhagen K
Denmark
Tel: +45 7026 2015
Fax: +45 4926 2015
http://www.myc4.com

Reconnect
35th flr. GT Tower
Ayala Avenue Cor
HV. Dela Costa
Makati City
Philippines 1227
Tel: +63 02 814–6245
Fax: +63 02 814–6171
http://www.reconnect.org.ph

The Big Give
info@theBigGive.org.uk
http://www.thebiggive.org.uk
Turkish Philanthropic Fund
http://www.tpfund.org

Wild Life Direct
African Conservation Fund
PO Box 24926
Karen 00502
Nairobi
Kenya
Tel: +254 (0)20 386 5120
http://wildlifedirect.org/

Useful publications

The following is a selection of publications available from the Directory of Social Change (DSC). For more details of prices and other titles visit our online shop at our website below. Please note also that new editions of DSC directories are usually published every two years. For up-to-date information and advice, please contact:

Directory of Social Change, 24 Stephenson Way, London NW1 2DP
Website: www.dsc.org.uk
DSC Books tel: 020 7209 5151; fax: 020 7391 4804;
Email: publications@dsc.org.uk

Fundraising directories and subscription websites

The following directories give detailed information, including independent commentary, on the largest UK's grant-making trusts:

- *A Guide to the Major Trusts* Volume 1
- *A Guide to the Major Trusts* Volume 2

Or you can find less detailed information, but on a greater number of trusts, in:

- *The Directory of Grant Making Trusts*

The most comprehensive coverage of all is provided by subscribing to the online trust database www.trustfunding.org.uk

If you are trying to raise money or other support from the UK corporate sector, you can refer to either a directory:

- *The Guide to UK Company Giving*

or the online database

- www.companygiving.org.uk

Other funding guides

- *Government Funding Guide*, DSC 2009

or the online database:

- www.governmentfunding.org.uk

- *Directory of American Grantmakers*, 4th edition, Chapel & York 2008
- *Directory of Asia Pacific Grantmakers*, 1st edition, Chapel & York 2007

- *A Guide to European Union Funding for NGOs* Volumes 1-2, ECAS 2009 (published annually)

Fundraising and other handbooks

- *The Complete Fundraising Handbook*, 5th edition, Nina Botting Herbst & Michael Norton, DSC 2007

A bestselling title for nearly 19 years.

- *Effective Fundraising*, 1st edition, Luke Fitzherbert, DSC 2004

By one of the great names in fundraising and based upon his highly popular courses that ran for more than 15 years.

- *Getting Started in Fundraising*, 1st edition, Michael Norton and Murray Culshaw, Sage Publications (India) 2000

A starter guide written specifically for voluntary organisations in India and other Southern countries.

- *The Porcupine Principle and other Fundraising Secrets*, 1st edition, Jonathan Farnhill, DSC 2007

Brings meaning and a sense of perspective to the art of fundraising through 33 pin-sharp and humorous vignettes. Down to earth and thought-provoking at the same time.

- *Writing Better Fundraising Applications*, 4th edition, Michael Norton & Mike Eastwood, DSC due 2010

Practical workbook that will help you produce punchy, effective applications that will get results.

Other handbooks include:

- *The Charity Trustee's Handbook*, 1st edition, Mike Eastwood, DSC 2001

A starter guide to the responsibilities of management committees, providing straightforward advice on planning the work of the organisation.

- *The Complete Guide to Business and Strategic Planning*, 3rd edition, Alan Lawrie, DSC 2007
- *Complete Guide to Creating and Managing New Projects*, 3rd edition, Alan Lawrie, DSC 2009

Two practical handbooks with examples and exercise to help you in your organisation and project planning.

- *DIY Guide to Public Relations*, 2nd edition, Moi Ali, DSC 1999

Everything you need to know about PR for charities.

- *Keeping Volunteers*, 1st edition, Steve McCurley & Rick Lynch, DSC 2007
- *Recruiting Volunteers*, 1st edition, Fraser Dyer & Ursula Jost, DSC 2002 (updated 2006)

Two books that will help your volunteer management.

■ *Managing without Profit*, 3rd edition, Mike Hudson, DSC 2009
Essential guide to leading, managing and governing third-sector organisations.

■ *Promoting Your Cause*, 1st edition, Karen Gilchrist, DSC 2002
Full of ideas about how to raise the profile of your organisation, establish a positive reputation, increase awareness of your cause and communicate effectively with your target audience.

■ *Relationship Fundraising*, 2nd edition, Ken Burnett, Jossey-Bass 2002
An accessible resource that identifies successful techniques for marketing to donors and emphasises the need to build mutually rewarding long-term relationships.

Contains more than 100 good ideas for raising money in your local community, plus practical and legal advice to help you run fundraising events for maximum success.

Index of organisations

Index of topics

CORE STATUTES ON CONTRACT, TORT & RESTITUTION 2020–21

Graham Stephenson

The *Macmillan Core Statutes* series

Core Documents on European and International Human Rights — Rhona Smith

Core Documents on International Law — Karen Hulme

Core EU Legislation — Paul Drury

Core Statutes on Commercial & Consumer Law — Graham Stephenson

Core Statutes on Company Law — Cowan Ervine

Core Statutes on Conflict of Laws — Emmanuel Maganaris

Core Statutes on Contract, Tort & Restitution — Graham Stephenson

Core Statutes on Criminal Justice & Sentencing — Martin Wasik

Core Statutes on Criminal Law — Mark James

Core Statutes on Employment Law — Rachel Horton

Core Statutes on Evidence — Jonathan McGahan

Core Statutes on Family Law — Frances Burton

Core Statutes on Intellectual Property — Margaret Dowie-Whybrow

Core Statutes on Property Law — Peter Luther & Alan Moran

Core Statutes on Public Law & Civil Liberties — Rhona Smith, Eimear Spain & Richard Glancey